THE WORLD
ENCYCLOPEDIA
—— OF ——
BEER

THE WORLD ENCYCLOPEDIA

OF

BEER

BRIAN GLOVER

HERMES HOUSE

This edition published by Hermes House
27 West 20th Street, New York, NY 10011

HERMES HOUSE books are available for bulk purchase for sales promotion
and for premium use. For details, write or call the sales director,
Hermes House, 27 West 20th Street, New York, NY 10011;
(800) 354-9657

Hermes House is an imprint of
Anness Publishing Inc.

ISBN 1-84038-403-4

Publisher: Joanna Lorenz
Project Editor: Jo Wells
Researchers: Alison Heatherington, Daniel King
Designer: Siân Keogh, Axis Design
Photographer: David Jordan Photography

Printed and bound in Hong Kong

Acknowledgements

The publishers would like to thank the following for additional images reproduced in this book: Axiom Photographic Agency: pp24tl, 24tr, 29bl, 51t, 207br; The Beer Cellar and Co. Ltd.: pp132b; Bruce Coleman Picture Library: pp57bl, 160tr; Edifice: pp17br, 18t, 38b, 208b, 219t; ET Archive: pp10b, 11tr, 12br, 40b, 181b; Greg Evans Photo Library: pp30b, 52t, 172, 251b; Mary Evans Picture Library: pp13tr, 16b, 29t, 37t, 41b; Fine Art Photographic Library: pp8, 15t, 21b; John Freeman: pp39t, 101b; Guinness Archives: pp78tr, 79tr; Jayawardene Travel Photography Library: pp168t, 199, 218b; The Kobal Collection: pp18b, 23b; Peter Newark's American Pictures: pp22tc, 23t; Peter Newark's Historical Pictures: pp79tl, 79tc, 103t, 104bl, 105br, 153tr; Peter Newark's Military Pictures: pp56; Peter Newark's Western Americana: pp239b, 245br; Ann Ronan: pp10tl, 17t, 18tr, 20t, 43b, 52b; Trip Photographic Library: pp36t (photo C. Treppe), 115br (photo R. Powers), 170, 171, 173t (photos T. Noorits), 173b (photo I. Burgandinov), 203 (photo D. Saunders), 249b (photo R. Belbin); Zefa Pictures: pp28, 31t, 31b, 38tl, 41t, 42, 47t, 51b, 55t, 153tl, 153b. The publishers would also like to thank Brian Glover for images from his archive.

CONTENTS

The Hoppy Drop   **6**

History   *8*

Ingredients   *28*

Brewing   *44*

Beer Drinking   *56*

A World Tour   **70**

A Globe Trotter's Beer Guide   *72*

Ireland   *74*

Wales   *80*

England   *86*

Scotland   *106*

Denmark   *112*

Norway   *116*

Sweden   *118*

Finland   *120*

Iceland   *123*

Belgium   *124*

The Netherlands   *138*

Luxembourg   *144*

Germany   *146*

Austria   *162*

Poland   *166*

Eastern Europe   *169*

The Czech Republic and Slovakia   *174*

Italy   *180*

Greece and Turkey   *183*

France   *184*

Switzerland   *190*

Spain   *193*

Portugal   *196*

Africa   *197*

China   *204*

Japan   *206*

The Rest of Asia   *210*

Australia   *212*

New Zealand   *220*

Canada   *224*

The United States of America   *230*

Latin America   *246*

The Caribbean   *250*

Index   **252**

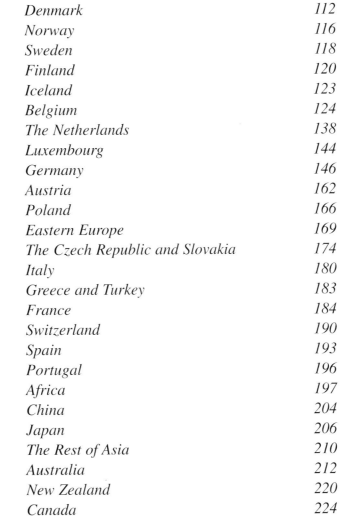

THE HOPPY DROP

Explore the mysteries that lie behind a glass of beer. In History, *we trace beer's origins and the development of brewing through to the present day.* Ingredients *explains all the different elements that go into a brew, then* Brewing *reveals the complex series of processes that combine the raw materials to make a satisfying drink. Finally,* Beer Drinking *outlines the many different types and tastes of beer that are on offer.*

HISTORY

Beer has always been the drink of the people. Malt and hops may not have inspired as many precious pens as the noble grape, but they have always provided good company. Beer is much more sociable. It is the best long drink in the world.

THERE ARE NO BARRIERS around a shared jug. "Beer cheers and heartens. It is the accompaniment of simple friendliness," said a churchman during the dark days of the Second World War. "In times such as these, people need some liquid sunshine." Beer is a most ancient drink that has had a chequered and varied history. It has been used by preachers as a religious symbol, by doctors as a medicinal treatment and by workers as a means of relaxation after a hard day's toil. Throughout the ages, in different countries beer has been both promoted as a health drink and reviled as the draught of the devil.

The brewing industry has changed fundamentally since the early medieval ale wives brewed from their kitchens, and it has been affected profoundly by the advances in technology sparked by the Industrial Revolution of the 19th century and continuing innovation of the 20th century. It has developed into one of the largest and most modern multinational industries. Beer is shipped all around the globe and large companies produce their brews thousands of miles from home. But there is still room for the small-scale producer in today's richly varied marketplace.

The huge range of beers that is drunk all over the world is dazzling, as is the variety of customs associated with it. A glass of beer does not just mean a sparkling golden lager, familiar in every land. It could be a stout or strong ale, a white beer, a wheat beer, a porter or a double bock. All are waiting to be enjoyed. This book will show you some of the glasses to raise on your journey around the global bar.

Above: "Beer is Best". An advertisement from 1933 emphasizes beer's nourishing qualities.

Opposite: "A Warming Brew", from the painting by Edwin Thomas Roberts, 1840-1917.

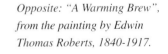

Left: In the 19th century large breweries were appearing all around Europe. This print shows the original Salzburg premises of Josef Sigl, an Austrian brewery that is still going strong.

CLOUDED IN MYSTERY

The origins of beer are lost somewhere in the mists of time but, as one of the world's most ancient and satisfying drinks, it has played an important part in many of the major cultures of the past.

Above: A statue of an Egyptian brewer pressing out fermented bread in a basket. The "beer" drains into the jar beneath.

Below: The King of Ur and his nobles raise their glasses at a banquet – c. 2,500 BC.

MANY BELIEVE that the Middle East and Egypt were the birthplace of beer. In the mid-19th century, archaeologists excavating tombs of the Pharaoh's came across whole baskets full of grain, preserved for centuries amongst the gold and other treasures. It is no surprise that an Egyptian king should carry cereal grains into his grave. He would need bread in the next world. However, the barley grains may well have been for brewing rather than baking. Many tombs since have yielded remains of beer and preserved loaves of bread as well as barley and wheat grain. Stories abound of ancient grains being sprouted thousands of years after their entombment, but unfortunately scientific analysis has shown that, although very well preserved, the grain found in the ancient tombs is no longer fertile.

THE FIRST BREWERS

Although the great early Middle Eastern civilizations did develop brewing to a fine art, they were not the first. Though no one understood how the process of fermentation worked, it was not a difficult art to carry out, and many other brewers were making grain-based alcohol long before the pharaohs. In fact, brewing alcoholic drinks developed independently more or less the world over – the end product depending on what local crops and fruits were available.

The Africans were making their own intoxicating drinks using sorghum and millet, and the Chinese were brewing beer at the same time as the Egyptians, using more advanced techniques, though they were reliant chiefly on millet and rice. In Latin America, the Aztecs in Mexico boasted their own beer gods, and Brazilian Indians produced dark, smoky-tasting brews from manioc roots and grain roasted over hardwood fires. South American Indian women brewed chicha by chewing maize kernels, spitting them into pots, mixing the mush with water and leaving it to ferment. This ancient beer is still made in some areas today.

In 1938 a cave-dwelling near Dryden, in West Texas, yielded up the remains of an early brewery and proved that the North Americans too were brewing in their prehistory.

One belief that many of these very early brewers shared was that the beer they brewed was a gift from the gods.

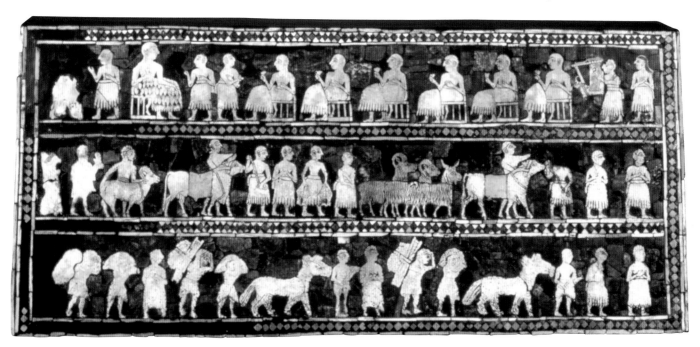

A civilizing influence

Some historians even argue that beer was such an important source of nourishment, and played such an important cultural role, that when people first switched from a nomadic existence as hunter-gatherers and settled down to till the land, the bulk of the grain crop was cultivated not for food, but to brew beer. The need for intoxicating liquor may have been one of the very first civilizing influences on mankind. Beer certainly played a crucial role in ancient diet as an important source of essential amino acids and vitamins, as well as providing a social drink.

The brewing civilizations of the Middle East, however, were certainly the first to record their craft and the essential role that it played in their culture.

THE SUMERIANS AND BABYLONIANS

The first detailed mention of beer was made more than 5,000 years ago by the Sumerians, who lived in the fertile land between the Tigris and the Euphrates in the area now known as Iraq. They invented writing, and among their surviving records on clay tablets more than 20 varieties of beer are mentioned and detailed recipes that include beer as an ingredient are documented.

One type of beer called *sikaru* played a central role in the Sumerian culture. It was used to honour their gods, pay their workers and feed the sick. They believed that its heady effects were a spiritual experience.

Documented brewing methods

Sikaru was liquid bread. The Sumerians moistened and germinated cereal seeds (including emmer wheat and barley), then coarsely ground them into flour before part-baking them into small cakes. The cakes were then soaked and crumbled into large earthenware pots of water and allowed to ferment for several days. The ancient brewers used dates and honey to flavour the thick, but nourishing, drink that resulted.

The final concoction was drunk in a social

Above: A 17th-century French engraving showing Brazilian Indian women making beer by chewing grain and spitting it into a vat for fermentation.

BABYLONIAN JUSTICE

In an attempt to regulate the quality of the beer produced by the larger-scale commercial brewers, the Babylonians ruled that any brewer producing unfit beer would be drowned in their own drink.

TOP BREWING NATIONS

1	US	5,220	12	France	458
2	China	2,695	13	Netherlands	449
3	Germany	2,539	14	Australia	398
4	Japan	1,518	15	Czech Republic	392
5	Brazil	1,254	16	Venezuela	354
6	UK	1,247	17	Korea	337
7	Mexico	900	18	Belgium	323
8	Russia	539	19	Colombia	319
9	Spain	535	20	Ukraine	308
10	South Africa	497			
11	Canada	486			

(Figures for 1993 given in millions of imperial gallons.
1 million imperial gallons is equivalent to 45,460 hectolitres)

TASTES OF THE PAST

In 1989, Fritz Maytag, owner of the Anchor Brewery in the United States, decided to recreate the flavour of the early Sumerian beer from 50 centuries before. He commissioned a bakery to produce 5,000 small loaves from raw barley flour with a little roasted barley and malt. These were soaked in water at his San Francisco brewery, to make a mash. Honey and syrup of dates were added for flavouring.

"We started cooking it and it was a very eerie feeling, as though we were rubbing the magic lamp," Maytag said later. The resulting cloudy, orange-red brew, named "Ninkasi", after the Sumerian goddess of brewing, was served at a brewers' conference. Guests drank the beer from huge jugs through tubes, just as the Sumerians had done.

"It wasn't wonderful beer," admitted Mr Maytag afterwards. "But it was interesting."

In 1986, Scottish home-brew shop owner, Bruce Williams, revived the ancient art of brewing *fraoch* or heather ale. First using the small West Highland Brewery in Argyll in Scotland, and then the larger Maclay's Brewery in Alloa, Williams tested different varieties of the wild heathers that colour the highland glens purple in late summer. He now produces batches of *fraoch* each flowering season. The heather flowers and the leaves of the wild myrtle, gathered at the same time, give an acidic, peaty brew with a powerful floral bouquet.

Scottish and Newcastle Breweries in Britain produced Tutankhamun Ale at their pilot plant in Edinburgh in 1996. They used the findings of Dr Delwen Samuel, of Cambridge University's archaeology department. Her research on 3,000-year-old dried remains of beer from Tell el-Amarna and Deir el-Medina, helped them to brew a beer made from malted emmer wheat, and flavoured with coriander and juniper. The husky emmer, which had not been cultivated in Egypt for over 2,000 years, had to be grown specially in England. Only 1,000 bottles of the beer were produced. They were sold at the London department store, Harrods, for £50 a bottle, the proceeds going towards further research into ancient Egyptian beer making.

Left: Tutankhamun Ale produced in 1996 was described by tasters as fruity and spicy.

way sitting round a jar. It was sucked up through reeds to avoid the husks and other debris floating at the neck. Rich Sumerians would carry their own beer-drinking reeds, decorated in gold, for drinking from the communal pot.

This early brewing required no major buildings or equipment. A maltings, bakery and brewhouse combined, consisted of a mud or reed hut with a hole in the floor for an oven, a mat and a few earthen vessels. Two flat stones served as a mill. Making beer was a domestic operation, just like preparing food.

Later, as the civilizations of the Middle East grew more sophisticated, larger brewing operations met the needs of the army, the temples and the palaces. Excavations at Ur (now located in modern Iraq, but once part of Sumerian and later Babylonian territory) uncovered a major civic brewery, dating from sometime between 2,000 and 539 BC, during the Babylonian era.

THE BREWERS OF ANCIENT EGYPT

The Egyptians were brewing a strong beer flavoured with juniper, ginger, saffron and herbs, called *heget* and also known by the Greek name *zythum,* from as early as 3,000 BC. An ancient papyrus gives instructions for brewing *zythum,* a stronger beer called *dizythum,* and a weak family beer called *Busa.*

In order to supply the grand courts of the pharaohs and to provide the armies of pyramid workers and the bulging population with their daily rations of alcoholic relaxation, the Egyptians also perfected the art of brewing on a large scale.

As with the Sumerians and Babylonians, beer was very important culturally. It was a most important offering to the gods, and accompanied the dead on their journey to the afterlife. It was frequently mentioned on offering lists and

Right: A tavern scene on a 2nd-century Roman relief.

other documents, and the Egyptian Book of the Dead contains a reference to an offering of zythum at the altar. One of the Egyptians' most important gods, Osiris, was believed to be the protector of brewers.

Doctor's orders

In addition, the zythum helped the Egyptians to remain healthy. Ebers Papyrus is one of the most important surviving works on ancient medicine. It was compiled sometime between 1,550–1,070 BC from now-lost documents and word-of-mouth remedies from as far back as 4,000 BC. It contains more than 600 prescriptions and remedies, many of which rely on a beer mixture to provide cures for a variety of ailments.

The end of a tradition

The Egyptians also developed the malting process, the practice of part-baking the cereal grains, discovered earlier in Mesopotamia.

In 1990, a massive kitchen complex in Queen Nefertiti's Sun Temple was discovered at Tell el-Amarna, the birthplace of Tutankhamun. Researchers examining the remains of brewing there found that the beer had been made from an ancient strain of wheat called emmer, as well as with barley.

By the 8th century AD, however, Egypt had been invaded by Muslims. The Koran, which is the Muslim holy book, bans the drinking of alcohol, and the Egyptian brewing industry went into a decline from which it has never recovered. The knowledge of beer had already been spread far and wide. The historian Herodotus, for example, from the hot Mediterranean wine-drinking land of Greece, had travelled through Egypt in 430 BC and wrote that, "The Egyptians drink a wine which they get from barley, as they have no vines in their country."

As agricultural production of grains became more common around the world, there were plenty of other countries where grains were being grown and used for beer production.

THE NORTH-SOUTH DIVIDE

Beer brewing travelled to Europe, following the cultivation of grain. In cooler climates grapes for wine production were difficult to grow, but wheat and barley flourished. This variation in climate created something of a north-south divide in alcohol consumption.

In the 1st century AD, the Roman historian

Tacitus stated that beer was the usual drink of the Germans and the Gauls, while Pliny the Elder in his *Naturalis Historia* of 77 AD, remarked that the tribes of Western Europe made "an intoxicating drink from corn steeped in water". In contrast, in the Mediterranean areas of Europe the vine reigned supreme.

The Norsemen of the far north had a culture swimming in beer. They had a tradition of feasts of celebration, where the party was kept going with copious quantities of beer drunk from ale horns, traditionally decorated with runes to ward off poisons. Ale was regarded so highly that according to Norse mythology, the warrior's resting place, Valhalla, was where Vikings slain in battle passed their days happily drinking beer.

Beer was not confined to the marauding warriors. When a young woman was buried in Jutland 3,300 years ago, she was laid to rest with a small pail at her feet containing beer. The brew, which was to sustain her in her life after death, was brewed from wheat and flavoured with bilberries, cranberries and myrtle.

Above: 19th-century archaeologists discovered baskets of grain in tombs in the Valley of the Kings in Luxor, which are believed to have been for brewing beer in the after-life.

Below: The Sumerians drank beer through straws to avoid the debris floating inside.

A MEDIEVAL TALE

By the medieval period the practice of growing grain to make beer had spread into Europe, bringing a competitor for wine – the alcoholic drink that had previously reigned supreme in some societies.

Below and right: The names of Ridleys Bishops Ale and Marston's Merrie Monk reflect the early church connection with brewing and beer.

Below: Leffe Abbey, by the River Meuse in Belgium, had a brewery from the 13th century until Napoleonic times. Today beers under its name are produced by a commercial brewery.

IN MEDIEVAL TIMES, beer was more than a warming and intoxicating refreshment – it also provided a safe drink in an age when the purity of water and milk was uncertain, and drinks like tea and coffee were unknown. The process of boiling, followed by the production of alcohol, removed the main dangers of infection. The reasons were not understood, but the effects were widely welcomed.

Outside the warmer wine regions, the everyday drink was weak table beer. Stronger brews were used to celebrate the main events of the social and religious calendar. Brewers used many cereals, including wheat, rye and oats to make beer, but increasingly barley was preferred, because it was easier to malt, and produced more sugar, which then turned to alcohol. Also, in times of famine, the authorities often insisted that all the available wheat crop was used to make bread.

THE HOLY ALLIANCE

The monks across Europe helped to nurture the art of brewing during this period and their malt was especially valued. Large-scale breweries could be found in the monastic settlements that sprang up across Europe from the 5th century onwards. The monasteries supplied not only their own needs, but also those of thirsty travellers and pilgrims. Many secured their financial stability through the sale of ale outside the walls. In the 9th century, the abbey of St Gallen in Switzerland, for example, boasted its own maltings, a mill and three brewhouses, each containing a large copper cauldron heated by an open fire, a cooler and fermenting tun. Each brewhouse may have been used to brew a different quality ale – *prima melior* for the fathers and distinguished guests; *secunda* for lay brothers and other workers; and *tertia* for passing travellers and local visitors.

Though its use in the communion was later forbidden, the early church looked kindly on

ale, regarding it as a blessing from God. An early name for yeast was "God is good", and its action was regarded as a minor miracle. Many saints, such as St Florian in Bavaria, were credited with looking after brewers.

The monks' legacy

Monasteries were so central to the development of brewing in England that the industry adopted the monks' method of marking the strength of beer – with crosses on the barrels.

Monasteries in Belgium, the Netherlands and Germany still brew beer. Some, such as the Abbaye de Notre-Dame de Scourmont in Belgium, which sells its famous Chimay ales all over the world, brew on a surprisingly large commercial scale.

Holy communities in central Europe are also credited as having been the first to brew with hops. Hops were introduced not so much for their flavour – many drinkers did not welcome the bitter taste – but for their preservative value. There are references to abbey hop gardens in the Hallertau district of Germany as early as 736 AD. The records of the Bishopric of Freising in Bavaria mention the cultivation of hops in the 9th century. In 1079, a leading herbalist, Abbess Hildegard of St Ruprechtsberg, near Bingen, wrote that the climbing plant "when put in ale, stops putrefaction and lends longer durability".

Before the hop gained ascendancy, a mixture known as gruit was added to the brew. This typically consisted of herbs, such as bog-myrtle, rosemary and yarrow. More expensive spices were used to flavour stronger ales: cinnamon, cloves, ginger, or even garlic and pepper. The heavier spices also helped to mask off-flavours and the taste of sour ale.

Lager arrives

The monks of Bavaria were responsible for an innovation that was to change the face of beer brewing – bottom-fermentation.

During the hot months of summer, fermentation was likely to run out of control and bacteria could spoil the drink. The problem was so great that in Germany in 1533, Prince Maximilian I ordained that anyone wishing to brew between April 23 and September 29 had to obtain special permission.

The Bavarian monasteries first attempted to store beer for long periods in cool cellars. This storage method caused some yeasts to change their character. At the lower temperatures,

instead of frothing to the top of the fermentation vessel, the yeasts sank to the bottom and fermented much more slowly. This bottom-fermented beer could be stored for much longer periods – a process known as lagering, from the German word for storage.

EARLY HOME BREWS

Apart from the larger-scale brewing of the church, most beer drunk was brewed in the home. Brewing was a domestic chore, along with cooking and cleaning, and was dominated by women. In medieval Britain, most ale was produced at home by women known as "ale wives". In parts of northern Germany, brewing utensils were a vital part of a young woman's dowry until the 16th century.

The more successful home-brewers attracted people to their houses. As a natural consequence, their dwellings became the social centres (public houses) of their community.

As villages grew into towns, some families concentrated on brewing, and sold ale to the public and to other pubs and taverns.

Above: A monastic master brewer takes a well earned rest in "The Brewmaster's Break" by Eduard Grutzer, 1846–1925.

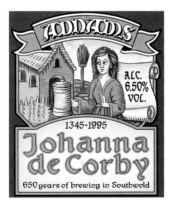

Above: Adnams brewery celebrates a notorious early English ale wife with a special beer. Apparently she was often in trouble for selling poor beer.

THE ROLLING BARREL

As the Industrial Revolution swept Europe, the brewing industry rose to meet the thirsts of the new industrial workers, harnessing the new innovations and discoveries to large-scale production.

Below: In medieval times barrels of beer would be carried short distances by hand, slung on poles.

Below: Barrels of beer being delivered by horse and cart for the 1906 Munich Oktoberfest.

B Y THE 16TH CENTURY, brewing was a well-established local craft, and most beer was still brewed at home, either for domestic consumption or for sale to neighbours. Breweries that rolled out barrels for sale chiefly supplied their own beerhouse and the local outlets they could reach easily; few went much further afield. In an age when even the best roads were rutted and pot-holed, and the only real means of transport on land was the horse and cart, there was little purpose in transporting heavy casks of beer.

Beer is a bulky, product of relatively low value; brewers found that it was much easier and more cost efficient simply to brew it on the spot where it was to be consumed. Only in major cities, where there was a large market close at hand, could brewing plants grow to any reasonable size.

Beer's raw ingredients, however, were lighter and easier to handle before the water was added. As a consequence, hops, barley and malt were traded over long distances and malting (roasting part-germinated barley and other grains) rather than brewing became a major industry first. Malt was of high enough value and light enough to mean that it could be transported economically over relatively long distances. The fact that taxes were generally levied on malt rather than beer indicates the malting industry's dominant position. The prosperous maltsters tended to look down on the humble small-scale brewers that they supplied.

THE INDUSTRIAL REVOLUTION

Brewing on a large scale can only flourish where there is easy access to transport. Many breweries were established alongside rivers. This was not for water supply, but to allow boats to collect the beer for transporting further afield. Many of the large London breweries, for example, supplied a thirsty market in the Netherlands and northern Germany during the 16th century. However, it was not until the development of canal transport in the 18th century, then the spread of the railways across the world in the mid-19th century, that large casks could be moved more easily than had previously been possible, and brewing, at last, was able to develop into a global business.

The power of steam

Brewing had changed little over the centuries. An ale wife from the year 1400 would have had little difficulty in recognizing the basic equipment and techniques used in 1750. Perhaps the dominance of the hop as an ingredient and the scale of the operation would have seemed surprising, but little else. All the power came from men's arms. The only steam rose from the boiling wort.

Above: Bass celebrates the arrival of steam power in the brewing industry.

However, in 1774 Scotsman James Watt patented a steam engine, and the leading brewing companies in London soon embraced this new mechanical age. Whitbread installed a Boulton and Watt steam engine in its Chiswell Street brewery in London in 1785, to grind malt and pump water. The engine made 24 horses redundant, and it was considered such a wonder that King George III visited to see the steaming mechanical marvel for himself.

The large breweries were also quick to pioneer other scientific innovations such as thermometers, hydrometers, attemperators and mechanical mashing rakes. Many of the leading names of the British and Irish industries date from the second half of the 18th century, among them William Younger of Edinburgh (1749), Arthur Guinness of Dublin (1759) and William Bass of Burton (1777).

In 1796, the Whitbread brewery in London became the first in the world to produce 200,000 barrels in a year.

The combined power of the new technology and the steam locomotive railways ushered in the era of the international brewing companies. The Industrial Revolution had transformed brewing from a predominantly local trade into a major industry.

Above: Fäffer beer from the Lederer Brewery, Nuremberg. This beer mat shows beer barrels being carried to the waiting train.

Below: A barge on the Polntcysllte Aquaduct, Wales. The growing canal network enabled brewers to market their beer more widely.

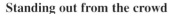

GOLDEN TRANSFORMATION

The 19th century was a period of spectacular change in the brewing industry. One innovation – a mere change in colour – was eventually to alter the way the world thinks of beer.

IN EUROPE the monks' great innovation of bottom-fermented beers had caught on. However, the 19th-century brewer still worked hard to control the beer's strength and temperature during brewing.

In 1836 Gabriel Sedlmayr took over the running of the Spaten Brewery in Munich and developed the art of producing more stable, bottom-fermented beers through cold storage (the German name for which is lagering).

Despite their novel brewing method, however, these new lagered beers remained a fairly conventional dark brown or amber-red colour, like other types of beer, until 1842. It was another part of the Austro-Hungarian Empire that made the clear, golden breakthrough.

SPARKLING ACCIDENT

After yet another disastrous brew was poured down the drain in 1838, the inhabitants of the Bohemian town of Plzen (later part of the Czech Republic) decided enough was enough and built a new brewery. They then employed a Bavarian brewer named Josef Groll to brew their beer using the more reliable bottom-fermentation method.

On October 5 1842 Josef Groll mashed his first batch of beer in Plzen and the world's first ever golden-coloured lager was born.

The pale colour was probably nothing more than an accident. The barley that was grown locally happened to be low in protein, which would have helped clarity. In addition, the water in the Bubenc district of Plzen where the brewery was sited was also very soft – it contained little limestone, which tends to draw colour from the malt into the beer, so the colour remained in the malt and the beer remained pale and clear.

Above: Lager was not always a pale golden hue. For many years it was dark brown or amber-red, like most other beers.

Standing out from the crowd

In another age, in another place, perhaps no one would have noticed the sparkling, golden colour of Josef Groll's brew. But Bohemia was also famous for another industry at that time – glass making. Previously beer had been served in tankards made from wood, pottery, stoneware, various metals, and even leather. The clarity and colour of the beer didn't really matter, as long as the aroma and taste were good. But as mass-produced glass started to appear, so Plzen's sparkling golden lager stood out and began to gain popularity.

Popular pils

At the time the town of Plzen was better known by its German name of Pilsen. Soon, what came to be known as the Pilsner style began to be copied across Germany, Europe, and around the world, where they were often called pils, after their town of origin. Although some excellent Pilsners are brewed in other countries, most lagers have simply used this style as the basis for a much blander approximation of the style. Countries that had little or no brewing tradition of their own have since adopted this universally popular golden brew and Pilsner-inspired lagers have become the most widely brewed international beer.

KEEPING IT COOL

Good transport and a source of cheap mechanical power took a lot of the hard work out of the brewing process; however, these did not prove a solution to the brewers' age-old battle with the temperature. The more reliable technique of bottom-fermentation went some way towards reducing the problem of brews souring and yeast multiplication running out of control.

But the temperature of beer was becoming increasingly important, both in the bar and at the brewery. Brewers wanted to be able to brew all year round without warmer weather spoiling the brew, and beer drinkers increasingly demanded an ice-cold, thirst-quenching draught.

Above: Before refrigeration, ice was collected in winter and stored in underground chambers in ice houses, where it would last all summer.

A chilling breakthrough

One writer has described the 19th century as the "Century of Refrigeration". Initially, improved transport allowed greater use of ice from the lakes and mountains. Huge blocks, used on a prodigious scale, helped to keep beer cool during the summer. In the brewing city of Strasbourg, France, in 1867, there were 46 large cold stores. In the US in 1875, breweries used an estimated 30 million tons of ice.

But the technological breakthrough that freed brewers to produce their beer any time and anywhere was the advent of mechanical refrigeration. Not surprisingly, one of its pioneers came from the hot climate of Australia. James Harrison of Geelong, Victoria, developed a compression machine in the 1850s, which was used for storing many perishable products.

A problem solved

The large brewers were quick to take advantage of this breakthough. In 1870, Guinness of Dublin installed four refrigerating sets in its St James's brewery. In 1873 the Spaten brewery in Munich introduced a refrigeration plant.

Below: The advent of the refrigerated rail car allowed the transport of many perishable goods, such as meat and beer.

Refrigeration took over the industry. In the late 1870s, Anheuser-Busch in North America launched the first fleet of refrigerated railway freight wagons for transporting its goods from coast to coast, and by 1908, the Linde refrigeration company had supplied 2,600 machines, more than half to brewing companies. The concept of ice-cold, pale lager had arrived.

Below: The idea of a cold, golden lager, born in the 19th century, has persisted into the 20th. In the film "Ice Cold in Alex", the cold beer at the end of their desert trek keeps the heroes struggling ever onwards.

THE BROKEN BARREL

Prohibition spelled the end of beer's rising fortunes around the developed world, as a sweep of puritanical fervour knocked the stuffing out of the prospering brewing industry.

Right: Tea drinking spread from Asia – where the samovar was a convivial focus – into Europe, where it provided a safe and sober alternative to beer.

Below: When he was Chancellor of the Exchequer, David Lloyd George introduced draconian restrictions against drink in 1915.

THE GROWING RANKS of industrial workers who, despite appalling conditions in the factories, were still more affluent than their country cousins, found comfort in cheap and powerful beer.

Public bars sprang up in the cities and drunkenness spread, as people rolled and stumbled down the streets. But by the start of the 19th century, there was, at last, a safe, alternative drink to beer. Tea and coffee were proving popular in continental Europe and North America. For the first time, beer was no longer a vital part of the everyday diet.

THE DEMON DRINK

Religious leaders were appalled by the social evil of drunkenness. Temperance preachers, raging against the evils of drink, found a swelling audience. Across Europe, campaigners against alcohol held rallies, addressed meetings and argued strongly for restrictive legislation. The gospel and the glass no longer went hand in hand.

The church was particularly keen to outlaw drinking on the Lord's Day. Calvinist Scotland – despite boasting a thriving brewing industry in Edinburgh, Glasgow and Alloa – forced through the Forbes-Mackenzie Act in 1853, introducing Sunday closing of pubs. In 1878 the Irish followed, and in 1881 Wales obtained its own Sunday Closing Act. Brewers were furious, not so much because of the trade they lost on one day a week, but because of the implied threat to their whole industry. They feared the advent of full-scale Prohibition.

The enemy within

During the First World War, the Defence of the Realm Act of 1915 slashed the number of hours that British pubs could open. The State took over breweries in sensitive areas, such as the munitions manufacturing town of Carlisle, and it closed some down altogether. Only the fear of a workers' revolt prevented the wartime government from banning the sale and consumption of alcohol outright.

When he became British Prime Minister in 1916, David Lloyd George went as far as to claim that, "Drink is doing us more damage in the war than all of the German submarines put together."

A worldwide trend

Some countries did not shrink from the drastic step of a total ban. In Canada, for example, the province of New Brunswick had prohibited the sale of intoxicants as early as 1855, and later, local option laws allowed many communities to go dry. By 1898, 603 out of 933 municipalities in Quebec operated a ban on drink. Canada introduced national Prohibition in 1918. New Zealand and Australia also teetered on the brink, as did the Scandinavian countries of Denmark, Norway and Sweden. Finland had applied Prohibition from the start of the war, even though its law did not come into effect until 1919. Iceland too froze the liquor trade in 1915. Many nations, while not banning alcohol entirely, restricted the sale of spirits, including beer-loving Belgium.

PROHIBITION IN THE UNITED STATES

The seeds of a future conflict over the issue of alcohol were sown in the very first colonies in America, among settlers arriving on the eastern seaboard of New England.

When the British sailed into North America, they brought a love of beer with them. Two years after establishing a settlement at Jamestown in Virginia in 1607, the settlers advertised in England for brewers to join them and quench the population's thirst.

At the same time, many of the new arrivals also brought a strong streak of Puritanism. The Pilgrim Fathers arrived in Massachusetts 13 years later, to escape persecution in Europe, and founded communities based on strict moral principles. For some, this religious code meant no alcohol.

The golden age of US brewing

At first this tension was hidden beneath the respectable head on the new nation's beer. President George Washington insisted that beer was provided for his troops during the War of Independence and Thomas Jefferson brewed on his Virginia estate. James Madison was eager to encourage American brewing and so in 1789 he introduced a Bill in Congress to tax imported beers.

In the New York area, British, Irish and Dutch immigrants brewed beer as they had in Europe. This practice was reinforced from the 1840s onwards by the arrival of waves of German immigrants who introduced their own styles of beer, and founded most of the US's leading commercial breweries – from New York to Milwaukee and St Louis.

During the second half of the 19th century thousands of breweries produced a wide spectrum of beers, from Pilsners to porters. In 1890, Philadelphia alone boasted 94 breweries.

Forces against drunkenness

However, the flood of immigrants from many nations, many extremely poor, also brought widespread social problems. Some drowned their sorrows when dreams of good fortune failed in the "Promised Land". Drunkenness became a major problem, and temperance campaigners began to find converts.

Reverend Lyman Beecher, a Presbyterian minister, founded the American Temperance Union in 1826, which initially objected only to strong spirits, but ten years later opposed all intoxicants. It set up organizations in every state to fight for laws banning the production and sale of alcohol.

Local law

In 1833, the Supreme Court ruled that states were free to regulate the liquor trade within their borders. In 1851 Maine passed the first Prohibition law. "The glorious Maine law was a square and grand blow right between the horns of the devil," exulted Lyman Beecher. Inspired by Maine's example, 13 more states introduced Prohibition before the Civil War bloodily intervened.

The Temperance Union, founded in 1874, was highly vocal and influential. Between 1912 and 1919, 27 states had adopted local Prohibition. One prominent member, Mrs Rutherford B. Hayes, the wife of the 19th US President, banned drink at the White House and was christened "Lemonade Lucy" by her husband's political opponents.

Above: Temperance campaigners sought to provide more wholesome alternatives to the demon drink.

Below: Drunkenness was a social problem in many countries at the beginning of the 19th century. Irish shebeens were notorious drinking dens.

Right: People came up with ingenious methods of hiding bottles in an attempt to avoid the Prohibition laws.

National Prohibition

The 65th US Congress of 1917 was dedicated to putting the nation on a war footing against Germany. Prohibitionists took advantage of a proposal to control food production to insert a clause outlawing the manufacture of alcohol in order to conserve grain. Soon, additional wartime rulings temporarily banned the sale of all alcohol. The wet cause was not helped by rumours that the country's brewers, who were mainly of German descent, were trying to undermine the American war effort through strong beer.

The 18th Amendment shot rapidly through the House of Representatives. The end of the war brought no respite. On January 16 1919, national Prohibition of the sale and manufacture of alcohol was adopted. To enforce the amendment, Representative Andrew Volstead of Minnesota introduced the National Prohibition Act.

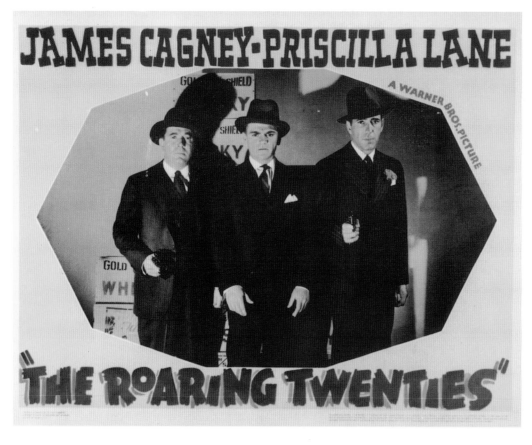

Shops, bars, hotels and restaurants that were found selling intoxicating liquors were to be shut down and the manufacture of all liquors (anything containing more than 0.5% alcohol) was banned. The Volstead Act passed both houses in record time and came into effect on January 17 1920.

The Roaring Twenties

The history of much of the 20th century rests on the belief that what the United States does today, the rest of the world does tomorrow. Many expected Prohibition to blaze a trail across the globe. Drink seemed to be in retreat everywhere.

There was just one problem. The laws were widely evaded. What was worse, Prohibition in the United States encouraged a whole new criminal culture built around smuggling and selling hard liquor and beer, and tacitly supported by a large section of the population. Illicit manufacture of alcoholic drinks was rife. New York, which had 15,000 bars before Prohibition, soon concealed an estimated 32,000 undercover drinking dens known as speakeasies. The United States appeared to be a country ruled by gangsters and guns. The most famous American was the ruthless bootlegger Al Capone, while the St Valentine's Day Massacre in Chicago in 1929 became one of the most notorious events of the decade. The bloody massacre, when one gang of bootleggers machine-gunned another, triggered the beginning of the end for the dry era.

Pressure to repeal

Prohibition was causing a complete breakdown in law and order, and public opinion turned against it. Franklin D. Roosevelt pledged to repeal the 18th Amendment in 1932 and was duly elected President.

The 21st Amendment, ratified on December 5 1933, allowed states to make their own liquor laws. Beer could

Below: Prohibition was a popular theme for movies. This poster advertises a Warner Brothers gangster movie of 1939, starring James Cagney.

Left: Herbert Chase was the first drunk to be arrested in New York City after the repeal of Prohibition.

WORLD WAR TWO

During the First World War, the British authorities had regarded alcohol as the enemy behind the lines. But during the Second World War, beer was seen as vital for maintaining morale, both at home and among the soldiers abroad. Its value was appreciated right at the top.

"Make sure that the beer – four pints a week – goes to the troops under fire before any of the parties in the rear get a drop," thundered Prime Minister Winston Churchill in a note to his Secretary of State for War in 1944, following thirsty complaints from his army in Italy. The Royal Navy even installed a brewing plant on one of its amenity ships, *HMS Menestheus*, serving the Allied forces in the Far East. This Davy Jones Brewery – "the world's only floating brewery" – produced English mild ale from distilled sea water, hop concentrate and malt extract.

On the other side of the European firing line, as the war turned against them, the Germans were forced to abandon their beer purity law, the Reinheitsgebot, and throw a variety of substances into the mash tun. One of the stranger brews was whey beer, which was made from the milky liquid left behind from making butter and cheese. Boiled up with a few hops and then fermented, it was said to produce a palatable, if ghostly, pale beer.

The conflict took its toll on breweries everywhere. A number were bombed out of business, and most in Europe were left exhausted and in need of substantial repair. The end of the war brought little relief. In the austere late 1940s, rationing of materials and restrictions on investment grew worse rather than better.

Still the battered brewers could afford to smile, for the war had completed the rout of one foe – Prohibition. The comfort of a glass of beer had sustained many through the dark days.

Above and below: "Beer away!" The RAF developed a new way of transporting casks of beer to troops at the front.

flow freely again – but not in the same heady market where it had once flourished.

CONCENTRATED INDUSTRY

Once beer was big business, companies realized that the quickest way to grow was to buy their smaller rivals. Some companies even rolled across borders to form huge international combines.

Above: After the end of Prohibition a few big names, Budweiser among them, came to dominate the US marketplace.

Below: Guinness headquarters in Ghana – this old name is one of the new international giants, now brewing all over the world.

IN THE TEN YEARS following the repeal of Prohibition, a small basketful of brands and a handful of giant companies came to dominate the revived American brewing industry.

In countries where Prohibition had not laid its withering dry hand on the brewing business, the same process of concentration was taking place too, but at a slower pace. It rolled on remorselessly around the globe. France, for example, could boast 3,543 breweries in 1905; 90 years later fewer than 20 remained.

In Britain, strict opening hours for pubs that had been imposed during the First World War and the crushing taxes levied on beer also took a heavy toll, closing many breweries. In 1900, there were 6,477 breweries, from small pub plants to large concerns. By 1939, the number was down to less than 600. At the same time, convictions for drunkenness in England and Wales fell sharply by three-quarters, from 188,877 in 1914 to 46,757 in 1937.

THE RUSH TO GROW

The larger breweries in Britain aimed to increase sales by buying up the tied estates of smaller breweries. A new generation of entrepreneurs believed that the time was right to create international brands. The Canadian Eddie Taylor successfully introduced the lager Carling's Black Label into Britain by buying 12 breweries in ten months to form Northern United Breweries. Smaller companies rushed to grow too big to swallow, and leading breweries combined to form larger firms.

Some companies went to extreme lengths to keep their pending merger deals a close secret. Representatives of three leading regional breweries in Britain – Tetley-Walker of Leeds, Ind Coope of Burton-on-Trent and Ansells of Birmingham – met high on the moors in the Peak District of Derbyshire on a freezing February day in 1961. Over a perishing cold picnic, sheltered by a stone wall, they agreed to combine. Allied Breweries was born. After a frenzy of takeovers in the 1960s, six large groups controlled the bulk of the beer trade in Britain. By 1997 only three remained.

Above: German beers are served to Japanese holiday-makers on the Ishigaki Island resort.

Above: The vast array of beer brands from overseas, as shown in this Cambodian market stall, disguises the shrinking number of producers.

Just over 50 surviving regional breweries were left with little more than 15% of the market.

Concentration worldwide

The concentration of the beer industry is an international phenomenon. For example, two giant brewing groups, led by BSN (Kronenbourg) and Heineken, now control three-quarters of the French beer market. And in Denmark, Carlsberg accounts for that amount by itself.

Outside Europe, the picture is more extreme. In Australia, two giants – Foster's and Lion Nathan – account for 90% of the trade. In Canada, Molson and Labatt control 92% of the market.

Not all countries have rushed headlong down this rapidly narrowing path, however. In Germany, for example, a large number of small breweries have managed to survive, helped by the fact that the conservative German drinker remains firmly loyal to his local brew.

National brands have struggled to find favour in this complex, patchwork market, which maintains a rich diversity of beer styles, often helped by regional regulations. Thus Cologne is known for its golden Kölsch beer, which can only be brewed in the immediate

Above: Carlsberg's name is well known in its home town of Copenhagen and the world over.

area, while the nearby city of Düsseldorf remains true to its copper-coloured alt style.

Germany, and Belgium to an extent, are exceptions. In most countries brewing has become heavily concentrated. Even in Germany, falling demand has meant that the smaller firms are beginning to disappear. In 1996, the brewers' organization, Deutscher Brauer-Bund, warned that intensified competition would inevitably lead to concentration. One industry expert has predicted that half of Germany's breweries will have vanished by the year 2010.

An international industry

Brewing is no longer a national, but an international, industry. Some breweries have sold beer beyond their borders for decades, even centuries – the Dublin-based giant Guinness, and German breweries; Beck's, St Pauli Girl of Bremen and Löwenbräu of Munich, for example. Others have established licensing agreements to have their beers brewed abroad by local breweries, sometimes setting up breweries overseas, often in partnership with local firms.

Leading beer brands are now well known across the globe.

Collecting breweriana

The marketing paraphernalia used by brewers to promote their beers has spawned a whole new international hobby – the collecting of "breweriana". Many beer magazines have regular articles on the subject, and the range of collectibles – from antique beer mats and postcards to foam skimmers and wrist watches – is vast. Collectors correspond and swap their finds over great distances – from the Czech Republic to Australia.

CONSUMER REVOLUTION

*One group had not been consulted about the new mass market – the consumers.
A revolution, sparked in Britain, spread around the world. The demand for "real"
beer has stimulated the mushrooming of new breweries.*

THE INTERNATIONAL companies that now dominate the world beer market inevitably wanted brands that they could sell across a wide area – brews that would appeal to everyone and offend no one. Light, mildly hoppy Pilsners, such as Carlsberg and Heineken, were often the result. The emphasis was on wide acceptability, perhaps to the detriment of individuality. Distinctive local tastes were out.

Above: The trend for "light" beer with little flavour was taken to an extreme in the 1970s with the launch of Miller Lite in the US.

A UNIVERSAL PRODUCT

By the 1960s the leading brands in the United States, such as Budweiser, Miller High Life and Pabst Blue Ribbon, were already low in malt and hop character and flavour, while high in carbonation. As far as some consumers were concerned, the beer had almost vanished. Packaging and mass marketing were all that remained.

In Britain, for example, the big six national brewers wanted draught ales that they could promote from the north of Scotland to the southern tip of England.

From the 1960s on, the giant breweries embraced pasteurization, to ensure a standard taste and a long shelf life. Traditional handpumps, and local cask beers that matured in the cellar, disappeared from bars. They were replaced by bright plastic fonts serving the new processed and pressurized keg beers. These were sweetish and gassy, pale shadows of the distinctive bitters that they replaced.

THE CONSUMER STRIKES BACK

After muttering into their glasses that draught beer was not what it used to be, a handful of British drinkers, led by journalists Michael Hardman and Graham Lees, formed the Campaign for Real Ale (CAMRA) in 1971.

Real, living, ale that continues to ferment and develop its full flavour in the cask, was what the campaign was determined to revive. Its first annual meeting in 1972 was widely reported. Today the campaign boasts over 50,000 members and tries to promote the interests of all beer drinkers – striving to maintain a wide choice of tasty beers and good pubs. It also produces a newsletter, organizes festivals and campaigns for the consumer on relevant issues – from full measure pints to sensible opening hours.

Those regional breweries who had remained true to traditional beer welcomed the new strident voice of the consumer, and others

Above: CAMRA commissioned a special birthday brew from Ridleys brewery to celebrate its 10th anniversary.

began to put handpumps back on the bar to serve cask beer. Even the national brewers began to brew real ale again.

The CAMRA revolution

The CAMRA campaign was more successful than its founders could have hoped, although even they did not expect one development – the appearance of a host of new small breweries producing real ale. In Britain CAMRA's *1997 Good Beer Guide* recorded that 68 new breweries had appeared in just 12 months.

European initiative

The consumer revolution has taken off in Europe too. The European Beer Consumers Union (EBCU) is a blanket organization coordinating the activities of consumer pressure groups. Its members and associate members currently include the Estonian Union of Beer Clubs, the Swiss Association des Buveurs d'Orges, in Finland the FINNLIBS association, Norway's NORØL, Sweden's SÖ, OBP in Belgium, Les Amis de la Bière in France, PINT in Holland and CAMRA in the UK.

The EBCU sets out its aim as trying to help preserve European beer culture. In particular it has pledged its support for breweries that still produce high-quality traditional brews, using traditional methods.

The EBCU also campaigns against activities that are likely to lead to further concentration of control in the European brewing industry. The momentum generated by such consumer pressure shows no sign of slowing down. New breweries have appeared in almost every country – from Hungary and Romania, to Italy, France, Scandinavia and the Netherlands. Even in Germany, where many small breweries have survived, interest is stirring.

International revival

Interest in real, traditional beers has caught on throughout the world – from Canada and the West Indies to New Zealand. Experienced brewers have acted as consultants to the new breweries. British brewers, spreading the word of real ale, have even helped to start up community breweries as far afield as China.

In Australia, a former employee of the Swan Brewery in Perth, Philip Sexton, first flew the small brewery flag in 1983 at the Sail and Anchor pub in Fremantle, which developed into the larger Matilda Bay Brewing Company.

In the US, where consumer muscle has obvious weight, the revival of small breweries and a diverse range of styles have perhaps been the most extreme. In the 1970s there were only about 40 breweries in the whole vast country, but the total number of new breweries in the US is today pushing 1,000. Good beer has taken a well-deserved place in American foodie culture.

Left: Traditional bottle-conditioned ales have gained in popularity in the UK since CAMRA's activities reminded the public of their tasty qualities.

Below: Consumers have banded together all over Europe to protect their favourite tipples.

TOP BEER-DRINKING NATIONS

1	Czech Republic	155.3	11	Finland	86.1
2	Germany	138.0	12	US	85.5
3	Denmark	126.4	13	Netherlands	85.2
4	Ireland	123.0	14	Hungary	77.0
5	Austria	116.7	14	Venezuela	77.0
6	Belgium	108.1	16	Canada	68.3
7	New Zealand	102.5	17	Spain	67.0
8	UK	101.0	18	Switzerland	65.5
9	Slovenia	100.3	19	Portugal	64.1
10	Australia	97.5	20	Sweden	63.7

(1993 annual consumption in litres per head of population.
1 litre equals 1.7598 imperial pints)

INGREDIENTS

Beer, like many things we take for granted, is little understood. It is a much more complex drink than many realize. Beer is the juice of the good earth. Its colours, from deep copper and ruby black to pale-yellow, reflect the passing of the seasons – from bare soil through to the golden harvests of barley and wheat.

THE FOAMING HEAD on a glass hides many mysteries, not least of which are beer's basic ingredients. Malt and hops feature regularly on beer labels and in promotional photographs, but how many drinkers would recognize the aromatic hop cone, one of the most unusual species in the plant kingdom? Apart from a few Belgian gourmets, nobody eats them today. Besides, how many know what malt really is? It may begin life as a waving field of cereal, but the grain has to undergo a complex series of changes – germination, roasting, and mashing – between its initial harvest and reaching the drinker's glass. There are many different types of malt. Each varies in colour, flavour and sugar content, depending upon the precise methods used to produce it. Each beer has its own "signature" combination of different malt types.

Yeast is the crucial, "magical" ingredient and its role in the transformation of the sugar in a brew to intoxicating alcohol remained a mystery for centuries. Again, there are many varieties to choose from, each with its own characteristics – its speed of action, flavour and the amount of alcohol and carbon-dioxide that it produces.

Hops are a relatively recent addition to the list of essential ingredients. The natural oils that are contained within the hop cones impart the bitterness that many drinkers demand, and help to preserve the brew. There is a mind-boggling range to choose from.

In addition to the basic ingredients, brewers sometimes add more unexpected ingredients to the recipe, such as cherries or ginger, to impart an individual flavour to their particular beer. The result of the vast number of permutations of ingredients available to the beer brewer is a mouth-watering world of choice in the global bar for the lucky beer drinker.

Above: A photograph dated 1910 shows hops being delivered to an oast-house in Kent, England.

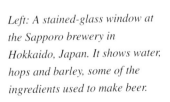

Above left: Drip mats and labels commonly use the ingredients of beer as a motif.

Left: A stained-glass window at the Sapporo brewery in Hokkaido, Japan. It shows water, hops and barley, some of the ingredients used to make beer.

Opposite: A golden field of barley ripening in the summer. Barley is the traditional cereal used in beer making.

WATER

Ask any group of drinkers what beer contains, and they may mention malt and hops. They rarely remember the greatest ingredient of all – water. Yet without a good supply, brewing good beer is impossible.

BEER IS MADE UP mainly of water, and its quality and mineral content directly affect the character of the brew. Brewers have even given water their own name – liquor.

Water contains six main component salts: bicarbonate, sodium, chloride, calcium, magnesium and sulphate. The proportions of these in the liquor used will greatly affect the flavour and sometimes the colour of the finished product. High levels of bicarbonate, for example, can produce a highly acidic mash, which will give a poor rate of sugar extraction from the malt. Too much sulphate will produce a sharp, bitterness in the brew and magnesium is an essential nutrient for the yeast.

Many brewers like to boast about the refreshing source of the water they use to brew their beers. Hürlimann of Switzerland, for example, sells the liquor used at its Zurich brewery as a bottled mineral water under the tradename "Aqui".

In the United States, Coors of Colorado built its sales and reputation by proclaiming that its water poured from the snow-capped Rocky Mountains. To reinforce the point, a waterfall plunges from its cans and bottle labels. And in parched Australia, Tasmanian Breweries make a similar appeal with their Cascade Lager.

Some breweries have unusual water sources. Rodenbach in Belgium, famous for its sour red ales, uses underground springs to feed an ornamental lake which then supplies the West Flanders brewery, and on the parched, rocky island of Malta in the Mediterranean, where every drop of water is precious, one brewery has a rooftop reservoir in order to catch and store each brief shower of rain.

JEALOUSLY COVETED LIQUOR

A good water source was a particularly key requirement for the earliest breweries. Many of the great brewing towns sprang up around a good liquor supply. The town of Plzen in the Czech Republic, for example, had very soft water, perfect for brewing the

Above: The label for Cascade Lager from Tasmania uses an image of a local waterfall to emphasize the pure source of the water contained in the brew.

Below: The unique taste of Guinness was often mistakenly attributed to the River Liffey, in the heart of Dublin. In fact Guinness is brewed with water from the Grand Canal.

Pilsner-style lagers, and the water in Burton-on-Trent in England had exactly the right mineral content for brewing the pale ales which made the town so famous.

In England, London brewers were so jealous of the water in the small Staffordshire town of Burton that they built their own breweries there, and a Lancashire brewer miles away transported Burton water to his brewery by rail.

This fine liquid was drawn from wells sunk deep into the layer of gypsum beneath the town. Purified by slow, natural filtration, it contains high levels of trace elements of gypsum (calcium sulphate) which make for clear, bright bitters, because the calcium increases malt extraction during the mashing process. Today, breweries all over the world that want to produce pale ales usually "Burtonize" their water first by artificially adding gypsum salts.

Burton's leading independent brewer Marston's, founded in 1834, still draws more than four and a half million litres (a million gallons) each week from 14 wells, the shaft of the deepest descending nearly 300 m (1,000 ft). The family firm analyses its water daily in their laboratories, and its composition has not varied in any significant way since the company records began.

KEEP OFF OUR LIQUOR!

Good water can take on mythical properties. Many Irish beer drinkers, for example, swear that the Guinness brewed in Dublin is far superior to that produced at its sister stout plant in London. They attribute the difference to the River Liffey which runs through the Irish capital. In fact, since 1868 the Guinness Brewery at St James's Gate in Dublin has taken its water from the Grand Canal which flows from St James's Well in County Kildare.

The supply of liquor to the world-famous brewery was threatened with being cut off by the Dublin Corporation in 1775. When Arthur Guinness saw that he was in danger of losing his liquor supply and potentially his livelihood, he seized a pickaxe from a workman and dared the Corporation to continue over his dead body – they backed away.

Good water is so essential for brewers that it has to be protected at all costs. So in 1994, when a concrete company planned to fill in a nearby quarry with rubbish, the Burton brewers, who feared that the scheme, would pollute their pure supply, banded together to oppose it.

MORE RELIABLE SUPPLIES

Many breweries today have abandoned traditional wells and springs because of the threat of contamination, particularly by farmers' fertilizers. Instead, they use treated town water from the mains supply and can add the minerals that they require. It is not as romantic as a well, but it is more reliable. Breweries need vast amounts of water on tap. For every litre of beer produced, at least five more are required for cleaning and cooling.

Above: A water treatment plant may not be romantic, but it is a reliable source of good water.

Below and left: Fresh, fast flowing water straight from the Rocky Mountains of Colorado is illustrated on the Coors label.

MALT

Malt is the body and soul of a brew. It is this partially germinated, roasted grain that provides not only the alcohol, but also much of the flavour and nearly all of the colour in a glass of beer.

Mᴀʟᴛ ɪs ᴍᴜᴄʜ ᴍᴏʀᴇ than the harvested grain. Raw ears of barley, for example, will barely ferment, and are of little use to the brewer. First they need to pass through the hands of the maltster, and in ten days a grain of barley can be turned into a grain of malt, ready to make beer. It is possible to malt other cereals besides barley: wheat, oats and rye may also be used. In fact some beer styles, such as German wheat beers, demand a wheat malt. Oats were widely used for brewing during the Second World War when barley was scarce. Barley, however, provides the best extraction rate of sugars and is therefore by far the most favoured by brewers the world over.

Barley itself comes in many forms, not all of them suitable for malting. Maltster Robert Free observed in 1888, "The art of making good malt from bad barley has not yet been found."

To produce good malt the barley must have plump, sound grains and must germinate at an even rate. It should also be low in nitrogen, as nitrogen can affect fermentation.

THE MALTSTER'S MAGIC

When batches of barley first arrive with the maltster from the field, they are screened and sieved to remove straw and dirt. Next, the barley is dried in order to reduce the moisture that it has retained, so that the harvested grain can be stored for use throughout the year. If the grain is too damp, it may go mouldy or start to germinate prematurely. Maltsters prefer to keep the barley dormant for at least a month, because this improves later germination.

Soaking the grain

In traditional floor malting, the grain is soaked in large water cisterns containing up to six tons (6.1 tonnes) of barley and 1,500 gallons (6,800 litres) of water. This steeping process takes two to three days. The barley is not kept under water the whole time. It is soaked for half a day, then the tank is drained so that the grain can breathe for between six to 12 hours before it is immersed in water again.

Germination

Next, the damp grain is emptied on to huge germinating floors, and evenly spread to a depth of 6–9 in (15–20 cm). Here it stays

Above: Barley is the grain most commonly used for malting.

Right: Oakhill's Mendip Gold label reminds us of the grain at the heart of the brew.

Below: Part-germinated grains are baked in a kiln for two days to produce the malt.

for five days to allow the seeds to begin to sprout and grow. This is the all-important process of germination, which turns inaccessible starches in the seeds into sugar.

The germinating grain is turned and raked regularly to ensure adequate aeration and an even growth, and to prevent the seed roots from becoming tangled together. If the workers at the maltings didn't turn the grain three times a day, you could roll it up like a coconut mat. In former times, this back-breaking work would have been done with a shovel, but today, electrically powered tools or turning machines are usually used.

Baking the green malt

After five days, when the sprouting shoots reach three-quarters the length of the grain, germination is brought to a sharp halt. The maltster does not wish to lose the newly created sugars, which the brewer will later turn to alcohol. This "green malt" is then sent to the kiln where it is baked for two days at high temperatures; the exact temperature determines the type of malt that results. Some Bavarian maltings still use wood-fired kilns, giving the malt a smoky flavour.

Nothing is wasted and the malt is screened after baking to remove the rootlets – known as "malt culms", which are sold as animal feed.

Final transformation

Once the roots are removed, the malt looks little different from the original grain. However, one bite will reveal the miraculous transformation in its flavour. The baked grains are no longer hard but good to eat, with a crunchy, nutty texture.

This delicious final product is used not only to brew beer, but also to make malted drinks, biscuits and breakfast cereals, and as an essential ingredient in malt whisky.

THE MODERN INDUSTRY EMERGES

Traditional floor malting was the system used in most countries until well into the 20th century. The buildings can be seen in many grain-growing areas, usually alongside watercourses or railway lines. Some maltings are substantial – long and heavily built with thick walls and narrow windows, and layer upon layer of germinating floors. Some breweries once had their own maltings, larger than the brewhouse itself, but nearly all have now been converted to other uses such as a bottling hall or warehouse. Others have been demolished, turned into industrial units or converted into shopping malls.

In general, traditional floor malting, which was highly labour-intensive and seasonal, has been abandoned. As mechanization spread

Left: Wheat, oats and rye can all be used to produce brewing malt, as well as barley. Oat Malt Stout is a traditional brew from Alloa, Scotland.

Below: A combine harvester cutting a field of barley. Malting barley is subject to rigorous quality controls to ensure that it is low in nitrogen.

Above: The Estonian Saku brewery celebrates the grain harvest on this bottle label.

Right: The Efes brewery of Turkey gets its barley from the plains of Central Anatolia and processes over 100,000 tons a year at its malting plants. Their malt is exported to breweries in South America and Africa.

Below: There are several types of malt, differing in flavour and appearance according to the precise way that the barley has been kilned.

throughout industry in the 19th century, some maltsters began to look for new methods.

A Belgian maltster named Galland developed drum malting in the 1870s. This system transferred the grain from steeping tanks into huge, airtight metal cylinders that slowly revolved to turn the grain.

About the same time, a Frenchman called Saladin introduced the efficient drying method – the "Saladin Box" system that forced air through the perforated floor of a box containing grain to the depth of 2 to 3 ft (60 cm – 1 m). This technique was later further developed in Germany into the Wanderhaufen or "moving piece" process, in which the grain slowly flows through the box.

The new systems saved space and labour, and could operate throughout the year. However, they caught on quite slowly, partly due to mechanical problems, and also because of the expense of buying new equipment. Many brewers believed that floor malting was best and indeed some still insist on traditionally made malt.

The global market
It wasn't until after the Second World War that mechanical malting methods were widely adopted, bringing in their wake even larger-scale malting plants and concentration in the industry. By the 1970s in Britain, for example, two huge companies – Associated British Maltsters (ABM) and Pauls &

Sandars – had come to dominate the malting trade, accounting for more than half of all sales. Some companies operated maltings in several countries and exported far and wide.

In fact only a third of beer-making countries produce significant amounts of malt, and only eight countries supply three-quarters of the world's needs (see table). Malting depends on a reliable supply of barley. There is a huge international market – a grain-growing country such as Australia supplies its neighbours, including the Philippines. Some major brewing nations, such as Japan, have no large malting industry and the brewers there import the bulk of their requirements.

The brewers' search for a particular quality of barley resulted in an international grain market. In the 19th century, Denmark and France were regarded as excellent grain-growing countries, and barley from there was highly coveted. An area of central Europe covering Moravia, Silesia and Bohemia also developed an excellent reputation. Grain from here was known as Saale barley, and sold well, mainly through the Hamburg market. By the 1930s, brewers were competing with each other all around the globe to purchase sun-ripened crops from California, Chile and Australia.

Barley varieties
Surprisingly, much of this worldwide market was in barley that came from a few original varieties. In the 1820s, the Reverend J.B. Chevallier spotted a barley growing in an English labourer's cottage garden in Debenham, Suffolk. He was struck with the barley's extraordinary quality, and saved the

Pale malt

Crystal malt

seed. From that the Chevallier barley strain was developed. Archer was another popular English variety.

The barley plant produces kernels of grain which grow in either two or six rows. Chevallier and Archer are both two-rowed barleys. In the United States, six-rowed barley is preferred.

After the Second World War, Archer and its hybrids Spratt-Archer and Plumage-Archer gave way to Proctor, which was better suited to mechanized farming. Modern varieties include Triumph, Kym, Klages, Halcyon and Pipkin.

Some more traditional brewers have remained true to lower-yielding (for the farmer) but more characterful and reliable grains (for the brewer), for example Maris Otter and Golden Promise.

GLOBAL MALT PRODUCTION

US	2.85
Germany	2.16
Britain	1.67
France	1.18
China	1.08
Canada	0.76
Belgium	0.76
Australia	0.64
Others	4.62
Total	15.72

(All figures in millions of tons. 1 ton = 1.016 tonnes)

TYPES OF MALT

Malt comes in a variety of styles, depending on how it is kilned. The higher the temperature, the darker the colour and more profound the flavour. The brewer skilfully blends different malts to produce different beers.

Pale malt

This is the standard malt in most beers. The barley is baked in the kiln over 48 hours with a slowly rising temperature. Pale malt is ideal for both light-coloured ales and golden Pilsners. Some specific Pilsner types are known as lager malts. Other varieties tend to be used in small amounts in conjunction with pale malt.

Amber and brown malts

This barley is heated to higher temperatures than pale malt to give more coppery colours to the brew. Amber and brown malts are rarely used today. In Continental Europe, Vienna malt provides a reddish tinge to the beer.

Crystal malt

An exceptionally rapidly rising temperature in the kiln dries out the barley husk, leaving behind a hard, sugary, crystalline core. Crystal malt adds a fuller, sweeter flavour to beer. Dark varieties are called caramel malts; lighter ones, carapils malts.

Chocolate malt

The barley is steadily heated to about 200°C (400°F). This deep chocolate malt generates a complex mix of roasted flavours as well as a dark colour.

Black malt

Black malt is chocolate malt that has been taken almost to the burning point. Because of its powerful bitter taste, it is used sparingly, even in stouts and porters.

Above: Autumn Frenzy's label evokes the harvest season.

Chocolate malt

HOPS

The cones of the hop plant were originally added to beer as a preservative. They prevent the brew from going sour, but also bring a characteristic bitter flavour and aroma to the drink.

IF MALT PROVIDES BEER with its body and colour, hops add immeasurably to its flavour by countering the cereal's sweetness with a sharp, bitter tang. The hop also gives beer its heady aroma. It is the seasoning and spice in the barley meal.

Medieval holy communities in central Europe are credited as having been the first to brew with hops. But while the monastic brewers may have welcomed the hop plant, which preserved the life of their beer, various vested interests strongly resisted its development. The powerful Archbishop of Cologne, for example, enjoyed a monopoly on the herbs used for flavouring beer and so tried to suppress the use of hops. Only in 1500 did he agree to take a rent in lieu of his rights.

In the Netherlands in the 14th century, many drinkers were developing a taste for hopped Hamburg beer from over the border in Germany, in preference to their locally brewed gruit ales. The Dutch nobility, who had vested interests in the sale of herbs, tried to exclude foreign beers or impose high import duties. But the barrel barrier failed and soon many Dutch brewers were brewing hopped beer to compete with Hamburg. In response, the Emperor Charles IV granted the nobles a tax on hops.

The hop spread from the Low Countries into England. Hopped beer was imported into Winchelsea in Sussex by 1400, and before long brewers from Flanders followed, setting up their own beer breweries, much to the disgust of the English ale makers.

Above: The type of hop used affects the flavour of the resulting beer. The Hogs Back Brewery is proud of the Goldings variety that it uses in its Traditional English Ale.

Below: Hops may be added either slightly crushed (as shown), or as condensed pellets.

Above: In the days before mechanical harvesting stilts were necessary in order to reach the cones of the tall, spindly hop vine.

Their concern was understandable, for hopped beer kept much better than the sweeter ale, especially in summer. For a while they had the backing of the authorities – Henry VIII banned the royal brewer from using hops in 1530. Nevertheless, by 1600, the use of the hop was widespread. True unhopped ale was in decline. James Howell, a Royalist imprisoned during the Civil War, wrote in 1634, "In this island, the old drink was ale, noble ale, but since beer hath hopped in amongst us, ale is thought to be much adulterated."

CULTIVATING THE HOP

The hop plant (*Humulus lupulus*) is a tall, climbing vine that is a member of the hemp family. It is distantly related to both cannabis and the nettle.

A single plant carries either male or female flowers. Only the female flowers form the vital cones required by the brewer.

The female cone is made up of a number of petal-like structures called bracts. As the cones ripen, the bases of these bracts bear glands

Left: Tallying up the day's work – from a 1910 postcard. The hop harvest in Kent, England was the traditional holiday for gypsies and workers from the East End of London.

that are filled with a yellow resinous substance known as lupulin. It is this complex oil, found nowhere else in the plant kingdom, that contains the alpha acids which give the hop its characteristic bitterness.

The hop plant needs deep soil to grow, as its roots can go down for over 6 ft (2 m). It can thrive in any temperate climate, as long as there is sufficient heavy rainfall during the growing period, and plenty of sun to help the flowers ripen.

Growing at breakneck speed

Each year the plant is cut back to the rootstock, then in the spring shoots covered with hooked hairs called bines surge upwards. The hop farmer provides a support network of poles and wires for the hairy shoots to wind around and form the characteristic tall, leggy plants. Shoots can grow as much as 1 ft (35 cm) in a single day, and eventually reach 15–18 ft (5–6 m) in height.

The flowers appear in summer and are followed by the cones which are harvested in early autumn. Traditionally this was done on stilts, but today mechanization has made the task much easier.

AN ANCIENT PROFESSION

At one time, hordes of hop-pickers came from the cities to carry out the work by hand, living in tents or wooden huts on the land. For many poor families from the industrial towns, this was their annual holiday – a breath of fresh country air away from the grime and smoke. Nowadays, the labourers have been replaced by machines.

Once harvested, the hops are dried gently in kilns, then pressed into tall sacks or pockets (bales), as long as 6 ft (2 m), ready for the brewery, or for further processing. These pockets usually carry the emblem of the growing area.

HOP BY-PRODUCTS

Many traditional brewers still prefer to use whole hop cones in their recipe, but processed derivatives are commonly used today. About two-thirds of the world's hop crop is treated in some way before it is used by a brewer.

Below: Modern harvesting methods and short-growing varieties have revolutionized the previously labour-intensive business of hop picking.

Above: The hop, Humulus lupulus, *is the raw ingredient which provides beer's bitter flavour.*

Below: The distinctive witch's-hat-shaped cowls, wind vanes and hot air outlets of traditional oast-houses became a characteristic feature of the landscape in hop-growing regions.

The simplest by-product is made by grinding the cones into powder, which is then pressed into pellets that are easy to transport and work well with modern equipment. However, pellets do not provide the filter bed of hops required by some older breweries.

Hop extract is another alternative. This treacle-like substance is sold in a can. It is very stable and highly efficient, but can give the beer a more cloying flavour than whole or pelleted hops.

TYPES OF HOP

Traditional aroma hop varieties give beer a subtle, fine flavour and an enticing nose. In recent decades, the emphasis has been on extracting more bitterness by developing "high-alpha" varieties.

Because many hop farms have been badly hit by fungal infections, notably Verticillium Wilt, creating disease-resistant varieties is now a research priority in many countries.

Bramling Cross

A 1920s cross between an English Golding and a Canadian wild hop. It was unpopular in the past because of its "blackcurrant" nose, but its character is more appreciated today.

Cascade

A fruity American aromatic hop first introduced in 1972.

Above: Brewers throughout the world feature hops on the labels of their beer.

Crystal

A mildly aromatic American hop.

Fuggles

Propagated by Richard Fuggle in Kent in 1875. It is also grown in Oregon, US, and Slovenia. In Slovenia it has adapted to local conditions and is known as "Styrian Goldings".

Goldings

Originated in East Kent in the 18th century. It has a flowery bouquet and is used for dry-hopping traditional English ales in the cask.

Left: At the Hop Exchange in London, England hops of many different varieties were traded from all over the world.

High-alpha hop varieties

Admiral (England)
Brewers' Gold (England, Belgium and Germany)
Centennial (US)
Challenger (England, Belgium and France)
Chinook (US)
Cluster (US)
Eroica (US)
Galena (US)
Magnum (Germany)
Northdown (England)
Northern Brewer (Germany, England)
Nugget (US, Germany)
Orion (Germany)
Phoenix (England)
Pride of Ringwood (Australia)
Super Styrians (Slovenia)
Target (England, Germany and Belgium)
Yeoman (England)

Hallertauer Mittelfrüh
A traditional aroma hop from the Hallertau district in Bavaria, the world's largest hop-growing area (responsible for a fifth of global production). This hop has been almost wiped out by disease.

Hersbrucker
A traditional variety from the Hersbruck hills, this has now replaced Hallertauer as the most popular German aroma hop in the brewing industry. It is grown throughout the Hallertau region in Bavaria.

Huller
Huller is a new German aromatic variety, which was developed at the Hull Research Institute in Hallertau.

Mount Hood
Based on the German Hallertauer, this American aroma hop was introduced in 1989.

Perle
Perle is a newer German aroma hop. It is also grown in America.

Progress
This Wilt-resistant hop was introduced in the 1950s in England as an alternative to Fuggle.

Quingdao da Hua
Derived from Styrian Goldings, this is the predominant Chinese hop.

Saaz
The classic aroma hop from Zatec in the Czech Republic provides just the right flowery bouquet for Bohemian Pilsners.

Select
The Hull Research Centre in Hallertau developed this new German aromatic variety.

Spalter
A traditional German variety mainly grown in the Spalt region near Nuremberg.

Styrian Goldings
Slovenia's main aromatic hop.

Tettnanger
This is a delicately aromatic German hop, mainly grown in the Tettnang region by Lake Constance on the Swiss border.

Tradition
Despite its name, Tradition is a new German hop variety.

WGV
Whitbread Goldings Variety was widely planted in the 1950s in England, as it can survive Wilt attacks.

Willamette
An American variety related to the English Fuggle, introduced in 1976.

YEAST

Without yeast, malt, hops and water will never make beer. It is the catalyst that transforms the hopped cereal solution into a potent drink, hiding its magic beneath a living cloak of froth and foam.

YEASTS ARE LIVING ORGANISMS, members of the fungus family. Their scientific name is *Saccharomyces Cerevisiae*. Each yeast plant consists of a tiny, single cell, invisible to the naked eye. It is only when many millions are massed together that they become visible – as when they multiply to make beer.

The spherical yeast cells reproduce by budding. A bud forms on the parent, then, when it has grown to the same size, it separates to form another cell. Multiplying in this way, under good conditions (such as in a nutritious sugar solution) the cells can reproduce every two hours.

THE BREWER'S FRIEND
During the fermentation process, the yeast cells clump together (flocculate). In top-fermenting beers such as stout, the yeast cells rise to the surface of the liquid in the fermenting vessel.

By contrast, in bottom-fermenting beers such as lagers, they sink.

The yeast gets the energy for its growth during brewing by consuming the sugar solution in the mash provided by the malt. Alcohol and carbon dioxide are the waste products of its reproduction cycle. In fact, the yeast growth and the fermentation of the brew slow down, and

eventually stop, once the solution contains too much alcohol.

Many brewers use the same yeast, jealously guarded, for years. Each different strain has its own characteristics. Some work especially quickly, while others ferment to a greater degree. Each gives its own unique flavour, and particular types produce specific types of beer.

Some brewers even leave the yeast in the beer to give extra flavour; the cloudy Hefe wheat beers of Germany are classic examples of this technique.

At the end of each brew the brewer skims off some of the yeast, ready for use in the next batch. But the vast bulk is pressed, dried, and sold as nutritious yeast extract.

UNRULY ORGANISM
When yeast is working it can quickly run riot. This unpredictable organism often surprises even modern laboratories, and causes deep despair for brewers as they search for consistency.

Yeast may be a plant, but it can be a beast to control, and anyone who has seen a vigorously fermenting vat of beer, popping and heaving, will understand this fear. Yeast has a life of its own. Some brewers talk about yeast as though it were a difficult friend, and most agree that it can be awkward. Yeast can be greedy and troublesome and liable to let the brewer know if it is not being treated correctly.

SECRET LIFE
Scientists have spent many years peering through microscopes in order to uncover the workings of this secret beer agent. A Dutch-man named Leeuwenhoek first described the appearance of yeast in 1685; however, it was not until Frenchman Louis Pasteur's work in the 19th century that its true role in fermentation was understood.

Below: Louis Pasteur, from the portrait by Albert Edelfelt, 1885. Pasteur, who gave his name to pasteurization, was the French scientist who discovered that yeast was a living organism.

Above: Gazing down a powerful microscope the tiny, single, living cells of the yeast fungus become clearly visible.

LOUIS PASTEUR

French scientist Louis Pasteur is the father of modern brewing. His work on yeast allowed brewers to understand for the first time exactly what happened during fermentation. Previously, it had been almost as big a mystery at the start of the 19th century as it had been in medieval times or even in ancient Egypt. Beer frequently went off and became undrinkable, and the brewers had no idea why. Most companies expected losses of 20% or more through waste, and regularly had to destroy whole batches of sour beer.

Beer of national revenge

Pasteur was already a world-famous scientist when he started to study beer in 1871. His work was motivated by national pride in the aftermath of France's humiliating defeat by German forces in the Franco-Prussian war. He started his researches "with the determination of perfecting them and thereby benefiting a branch of industry wherein we are undoubtedly surpassed by Germany," he wrote in the preface to his ground-breaking work *Etudes sur la Bière*, published in 1876. He called his resulting brew, which he went on to patent, "Bière de la Revanche Nationale" (Beer of National Revenge).

By examining yeast through a microscope, Pasteur demonstrated that yeast was a living organism, and he was able to identify and isolate the contaminants that had been causing brewers so many problems.

His work prompted J.C. Jacobsen to build a magnificent laboratory at the Carlsberg Brewery in Copenhagen in the late 1870s, where another great scientist, Emil Hansen, was able to break yeasts down to single strains.

Left: Top-fermenting yeast boils and heaves itself to the top of the fermenting vessel.

Above: Dormant dried yeast.

Hansen also showed that by isolating and using the right strain of yeast, brewers could produce dependable beers. The art of brewing was never the same again.

The main bottom-fermenting yeast, *Saccharomyces Carlsbergensis*, is named after the Danish brewery in honour of the innovative work that Hansen carried out there.

MULTIPLE STRAINS

Although pure, single yeast strains are more predictable to brew with, many brewers still prefer to use multiple yeast strains. Each reacts with the others to produce the final beer. Bass of England, for example, uses two strains, while Palm of Belgium juggles with four.

Belgian brewers of lambic beers still use wild yeasts. They rely on the natural spores of yeast carried in the air spontaneously to ferment their beer – as their ancestors did centuries before.

Above: Ten minutes later, after water and sugar are added, the yeast is frothing and bubbling.

Handle with care

Yeast must always be handled with care. It is all too easy to break the delicate balance of multiple strains through chance infection by other microbes – or even by the introduction of new equipment. Cleanliness is vital. Even the introduction of new equipment or a change in the shape of the fermentation vessel can alter the characteristics of the yeast, and therefore the taste of the beer.

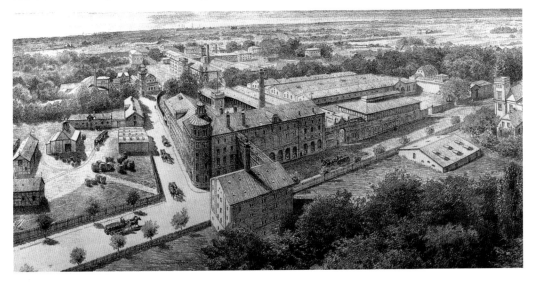

Left: The Carlsberg brewery, where Emil Hansen carried out his ground-breaking research on brewing yeasts.

OTHER INGREDIENTS

Although the basic four ingredients – water, malt, hops and yeast – are all that you need to brew beer, many brewers add other substances to their recipe, perhaps to produce a distinctive flavour and aroma, or simply to save money.

A BREWER IS NOT RESTRICTED to the four main ingredients. There are as many recipes and potential ingredients as there are brews. As well as the great variety to be found within malt, hops and different water compositions, there are also many extra ingredients that can be added to the brew to produce a highly individual recipe. As a result, flavours can vary enormously even within one beer type. As well as flavour variations, however, there are other reasons for including additional ingredients in the brew – to reduce costs or to improve the colour, for example.

Below and right: Kriek is a traditional Belgian recipe that includes cherries in the brew to produce a tart, fruit-flavoured, red beer.

ADJUNCTS

Some brewers add other substances to the mash besides malt. These "adjuncts" are added to the grist, when the malt is cracked in the mill. Adjuncts can be used to provide a cheaper substitute for part of the malt, or when malt is in short supply. Sometimes, however, the extra ingredients can simply be added to enhance the flavour of the beer. Light beers in particular tend to use additional unconventional grains in their mash. Brewers who spurn the temptation of using adjuncts boast that they produce "all-malt" beers.

Sugar

The most common adjunct is sugar, in blocks or as syrup. It ferments easily and quickly to give more alcohol, but leaves little in the way of body. Heated sugars or caramels are sometimes used instead of coloured malts to darken beers. Belgian brewers often use a less-refined candy sugar. This adjunct is particularly favoured in Africa, where barley is scarce. For example, sucrose is one of the main ingredients in Castle Lager from South African Breweries.

Flaked maize

Maize (corn), usually processed into flakes, is widely used. In some American breweries it accounts for as much as half the mash, giving a very dry, light-coloured beer.

Rice

Rice, like maize, can be a partial alternative to malt. The world's best-selling beer, Budweiser, from Anheuser-Busch of the US, uses rice to give a clean, crisp finish.

Torrefied wheat

This heated cereal, or popcorn, is added to help head retention.

Malt extracts

Malt syrups are sometimes used to make a larger brew than the capacity of the mash tun allows. They are also popular in home-brew kits, since using extract allows the home brewer to miss out the process of mashing altogether.

Roasted barley

Unmalted roasted barley is sometimes used to blacken brews. It gives a harsh, dry flavour. The classic Irish stout Guinness uses a small amount of roasted barley in the mash to give the beer its distinctive bitter flavour.

FLAVOUR ENHANCERS

Adding extra flavourings in beer is an old tradition. In the days before the hop, brewers made their own flavouring called gruit. The recipe for each brewer's mix was a secret but it would often contain herbs, spices or fruit, such as juniper or bog-myrtle. In some countries the tradition of adding extra ingredients for flavour died out, but some brewers clung on to their tradition and the Belgian brewers, for example, never gave up their age-old fruit beers. With the revival of small-scale breweries, unusual flavourings are also making a comeback.

Spices

Ginger beer is a familiar non-alcoholic relic from prohibition. However, ginger is also used to flavour alcoholic beer.

Herbs

Adding herbs such as coriander to flavour the brew is an ancient tradition that has been revived by Hoegaarden.

Fruit

Orange and lemon peel, apples, raspberries, cherries and bananas have all been added to beer with various degrees of success. Some of the newer fruit-flavoured brews were conceived by modern marketing departments and often use fruit juice or extract simply as a flavouring. However, some traditional recipes use the fruit to spark a natural secondary fermentation as well as to add flavour. Two ancient Belgian recipes, Kriek and Frambozen, use cherries and raspberries.

Below: Hoegaarden is spiced with coriander seeds and curaçao orange peel.

Honey

Honey is one of the oldest flavour enhancers known to man, and it has been used in cooking and in drink making for centuries.

Chilli

Beers with whole chillies in the bottle are a relatively new innovation, presumably a follow-on from the craze for Mexican lagers in the 1980s. It is an unusual taste sensation.

ADULTERANTS

Unscrupulous brewers seeking to maximize their profits by using inferior ingredients in the brew have long been a problem that the authorities have tried to legislate against for centuries. One common illegal additive in the 19th century was salt, which was used to "bob" the beer – to make two or three casks from one good one. It is shown here in the *Illustrated London News* in 1850, being added to the brew in blocks. Other common substances used to make the beer go further were treacle and water.

BREWING

Brewing is easy – until something goes wrong. In days gone by, the brewer's success depended on luck to a great extent since the chemical processes underlying it were little understood.

For CENTURIES brewing was the preserve of women – part of their traditional role of nourishing the family. In the German province of Mecklenburg as late as the 19th century, a newly married woman would pray,

> "Our Lord
> When I brew, help the beer
> When I knead, help the bread."

Divine intervention, or the luck of the devil were often hoped for by early brewers. If an ancient brew were to fail, the brewer had little choice but to frown, pour away the sour beer, scrub and clean the vessels, and try again, having checked the supplies of malt, hops, yeast and water.

The industry underwent great changes during the 19th century – benefiting from scientific breakthroughs (such as Louis Pasteur's discovery that yeast was a living organism) and technological innovation (such as the invention of steam power).

During the 20th century brewing grew into a worldwide industry and became dominated by huge multinational companies. Even in these days of careful regulation and scientific precision, things can go wrong. Whole vats can be affected, and a great deal of money lost. Rather than relying on prayer, a team of analysts, technicians and experts try to sort out any problems.

Recently brewing is enjoying a renaissance, as small localized breweries, making traditional beers, spring up all over the world.

Above: An external view of a 16th-century German brewery. Mules deliver malt and hops, and barrels of the finished product are carried to the taverns by horse and cart.

Opposite: A brewer pours hops into the copper.

Left: Vats at a modern Sheffield brewery.

THE BASIC PROCESS

The basics of brewing are little changed since the time when it was a domestic chore like baking. The vessels may be larger and more complicated, but the principles remain the same.

ONCE THE MALTED CEREAL has been delivered by the maltster and the hops have arrived, either in pellets or as whole dried cones, the brewer is ready to begin one of the oldest crafts in the world. It doesn't matter whether brewing is carried out in an enormous city plant or in a tiny back room behind a tavern or bar, the basic processes that are involved remain the same.

EXTRACTING THE SUGARS

The first step in making beer is to extract the sugars that are stored up in the malt, no matter whether it is malted barley, wheat or any other grain. The malted grain is ground in a mill. The crushed malt is known as grist. The grist is then mixed with hot liquor (the brewer's term

for water) to produce a sweet-smelling mash that looks rather like porridge and is left to settle in a vessel known as a mash tun. There are two methods of extracting the sugars from the malt: infusion and decoction.

Infusion

The hot liquor is left to dissolve the sugars in the crushed malt until, after a couple of hours, the mash tun contains a warm, thick, sweet liquid called sweet wort and the remaining soaked cereal. The sweet wort is then drained away through slotted plates in the base of the mash tun. The soaked cereal that is left behind is sprayed (sparged) with more hot liquor to wring out any final sugars lingering in the malted grain. The spent grain by-product is then sold as cattle feed.

This relatively simple system is most commonly used in ale brewing.

Decoction

In the more complex decoction system that is usually used for bottom-fermenting beers, such as Pilsner beers, the mash is drawn off (decocted) from the tun little by little at different stages. Each part is passed to a cooking vessel called a mash cooker, where it is slowly brought to the boil, in some cases through precisely controlled temperature steps.

After a few minutes at boiling point the wort is then returned to the mash tun. The aim of the decoction process is to extract as much sugar from the malt as possible by mashing in various temperature steps. This is particularly important in lager brewing because lighter malts, which contain less sugar, are used. Brewers seek to maximize the rate of sugar extraction from the malt by drawing off twice (double decoction) or even three times (triple decoction) over a period of a few hours.

The decoction method is usually used in conjunction with another filter vessel, the lauter tun. The lauter tun contains rotating knives or blades that keep the bottom of the mash open, and so allows the sweet wort to drain away more easily.

Below: An African woman sits outside her home in Zambia brewing beer for her family.

BREWING UP

Some of the names given to the utensils used in brewing still have a reassuring kitchen ring about them – a throwback to the days when brewing was a domestic chore. The brew-kettle for example – the vessel that the sweet wort is run into once it has been extracted from the malt – was once just that. Its other name, "the copper", is another relic from the past, because it would traditionally have been made of shining copper. Today in the large breweries the brew-kettles are usually closed and heated by internal steam coils. This is where the actual process of "brewing" takes place, as the

liquid is boiled up with the hops for an hour or more. Some hops are added at the start of the boil to help clarify the wort and impart bitterness.

Late copper hops are sometimes added nearer the end, and boiled just long enough to release their oils, to provide the final aroma.

TURNING SUGAR TO ALCOHOL

After the boiling is complete, the hopped wort passes through a filtering device known as a hopback, to remove the spent hops. It may also be passed through a whirlpool or centrifuge to remove unwanted proteins, before being cooled in preparation for fermentation.

Originally, the brew would have been cooled in large, open trays, but in modern breweries heat exchangers (paraflows) or chilling devices are usually used to speed up the process.

Fermenting

Once in the fermentation vessels, the yeast is pitched in. The millions of tiny fungus cells begin to feast on the sugar-rich wort for four to eight days, turning the sugars to alcohol and producing carbon-dioxide gas as part of their natural life cycle.

In top-fermenting ales the yeast rises to the surface, creating a heaving rocky head that

Left: A lauter tun is a filter vessel used in the decoction process when making bottom-fermented beers.

Above: In bottom-fermenting lagers, the yeast sinks to the base of the fermentation vessel.

Below: Huge, shiny coppers in the Saku Brewery, Estonia.

may need skimming to prevent it overflowing. In bottom-fermenting beers, the yeast eventually sinks to the bottom of the fermenting vessel.

Fermentation vessels range in size and shape from small, wooden rounds to vast stainless steel tanks. In the simplest and oldest systems large barrels are used for fermentation and the yeast bubbles up through the bung hole in the top. Modern breweries tend to prefer huge enclosed conical fermenters, stacked like upright rockets alongside the brewhouse.

When fermentation is complete, the yeast is then drained from the bottom of the fermentation vessels.

MATURING AND CONDITIONING

After the initial, vigorous fermentation, the liquid, which is known as "green beer" is run into conditioning tanks where it is left to settle and mature.

The length, nature and location of this final process differs from beer to beer. For some ales, such as mild, this settling period is quite short. For bottom-fermenting beers the maturing process takes place at temperatures close to freezing and can last for many weeks, even months, purging and cleaning the brew and slowly completing the fermentation.

Conditioning builds up the beer's carbon dioxide, and it is this gas that will give the beer its head in the glass when poured.

Some brewers add a portion of young, vigorously fermenting wort to the green beer in order to stimulate a final fermentation. This is

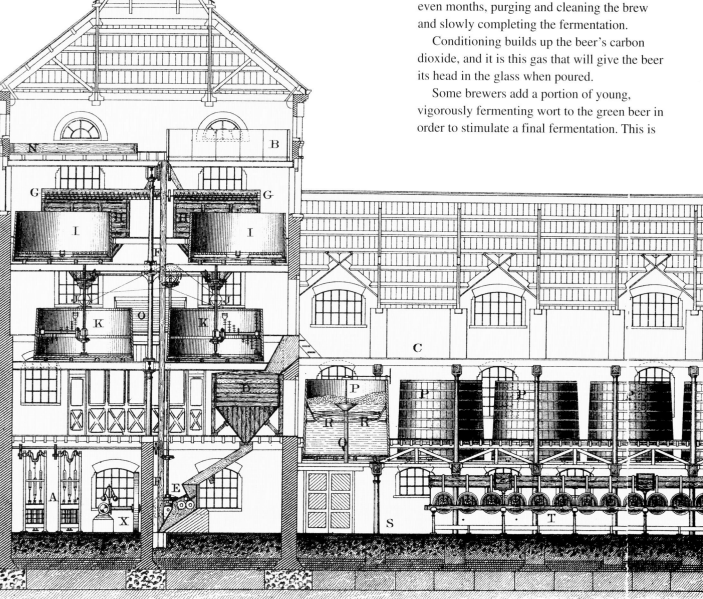

known as krausening. The modern, industrial alternative is to pump in extra carbon dioxide.

Most beers are filtered between conditioning and packaging at the brewery. Some breweries use a natural mineral known as kieselguhr on fine mesh screens; others use fine sheet filters.

Some traditional beers are racked directly into wooden or metal casks or bottles ready to go to the customer without filtration or any other processing. These beers are known as cask or bottle-conditioned brews.

Finings (a glutinous substance made from fish swim bladders) are also added to the cask to clear the beer.

The brew may also be primed with sugar in the bottle or cask, in order to encourage further fermentation. Dry hops may also be added in the cask to give the beer extra aroma. Some brewers even add extra yeast at this stage.

Cask-conditioned or bottle-conditioned brews continue to mature right until they are served, developing complex fruity flavours.

Left: Fermenting vats in Truman's brewery in the East End of London early in the 19th century.

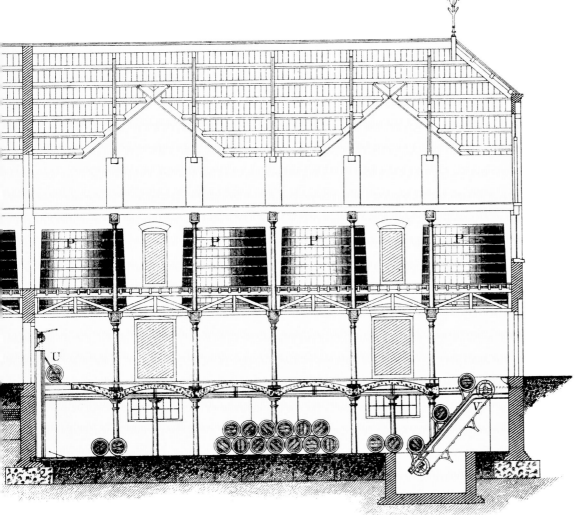

Left: A cross-section of a 19th-century brewery highlights the complex journey that the ingredients make during brewing. Modern breweries look quite different, but many of the items shown – mash tuns for example – can still be found.

A Pumps
B Cold liquor tank
C Malt store
D Malt hopper
E Malt rolls
F Elevator
G Malt screws
H Grist cases
I Hot liquor backs
J Mashing machines
K Mash tuns
N Cooler
O Refrigerator
P Fermenting tuns
Q Skimming apparatus
R Attemperator
S Tun room
T Cleaning casks
U Cask-lowering machine
V Cask-raising machine
X Steam engine

HI-TECH BREWING

Although the principles of brewing remain the same, there have been a number of attempted improvements in efficiency in the second half of the 20th century.

Above: Dominion Breweries of New Zealand pioneered the continuous brewing system.

Below: The brew is monitored at each stage to ensure a consistent end product.

THE DRIVING FORCE in the brewing industry, as in all large industries, has been to improve efficiency and reduce overheads. There has certainly been a great deal of success in increasing the amount of control the brewers have over the brewing process. The chemistry and biological action involved in making a brew are now clearly understood, and major brewers leave as little as possible to chance, using science to carefully monitor and regulate the progress and content of each brew. Huge plants are run by banks of computers and the increasing scale that it is now possible to brew beer on has reduced the cost to the producer of each final pint. However, few of the technological advances that have been made seem to have provided a major step forward in beer quality.

INCREASING THE THROUGHPUT

Normally, brewing is done by the batch method. Individual brews are put through the process, from the raw ingredients to the finished product, one after another.

This system means that for some period, the equipment used at each stage is being unused while it waits for the next batch to arrive. It is also necessary to clean and prepare the vessels for the next batch.

Of course, in a large-scale operation this period of waiting time is minimized because the batches are sent quickly through one after another. However, some companies felt that they could make enormous cost savings if they could introduce continuous brewing, with wort and fermenting beer continually flowing through the plant.

This method was pioneered by Morton Coutts of Dominion Breweries of New Zealand in the 1950s, then Watney's developed a system in England in the 1970s. However, it did not provide the expected savings and the resulting flavour of the beer was disappointing.

Above: Computers now manage the complicated modern brewing process in many breweries.

High-gravity brewing

Another method of increasing the output of breweries that has been more widely adopted in the industry is high-gravity brewing. In this system the beer is first produced at higher strength than is intended for the finished product. The brew is then diluted at the end with water to bring it down to the required gravity – a technique rather like making orange squash.

High-gravity brewing allows the brewer to produce more beer than was previously possible in the same plant.

Some companies are now investigating taking this concept even further and brewing just one high-gravity bland brew that can then be diluted to produce different strength beers and, through the addition of different flavourings, colourings and extracts, used to produce a range of different products.

BIO-SCIENCE AT WORK

Advances in bio-technology and genetics mean that it is now possible to manipulate and control the process of fermentation by changing the nature of the yeast. Enzymes have even been used by some brewers, notably in America, to speed up the brewing process.

Biological science has also been employed

in the brewer's fight against contamination, in the form of techniques for disinfecting and cleaning the equipment in the brewery.

Pasteurization

It is now common practice for manufacturers to attempt to prolong the shelf-life and stability of their products through pasteurization. Virtually all canned and many bottled beers are pasteurized, as are pressurized keg beers for serving at the bar.

During pasteurization the beer is heated in order to kill off any rogue bacteria that may have entered it during the brewing process, and that may turn it sour. One method of pasteurizing is to spray the bottles or cans with hot water for about an hour; another method is to spray extremely hot water or steam over the can or bottle for a minute or so.

Pasteurization not only eradicates any unwanted organisms in the beer, but it also completely kills the yeast in the beer and inevitably the flavour and character of the beer are affected. Pasteurized beers are usually artificially carbonated in order to give them a semblance of life when served and to ensure a satisfactory head on the glass.

Indeed, Louis Pasteur, who developed the process for wine, not beer, noted in a footnote

to the English edition of *Etudes sur la Bière*, "This process is less successful in the case of beer than in that of wine, for the delicacy of flavour which distinguishes beer is affected by the heat."

Some leading lager brewers, such as Grolsch, have demonstrated that it is possible even for widely distributed beers to remain unpasteurized.

Above: The modern Sapporo brewery in Hokkaido, Japan, where beer brewing is a science.

Below: Huge lager tanks outside a German brewery highlight the sheer scale of today's breweries.

FROM BREWERY TO GLASS

The advent of metal casks and cans has led to a revolution in the way that beer is packaged and sold. Consistency and reliability have improved, but often at the expense of quality and character.

Above: Once the beer is brewed the next problem for the brewer is getting it into the glass.

Below: A cooper and his apprentice hard at work in their brewery workshop.

U NTIL WELL INTO THE 20TH CENTURY, most beer was served at the bar or tavern directly from wooden casks. The casks rested on a stillage (a wooden framework) in order to allow them to be tilted as they were emptied. If the casks were kept in a cellar, a pump would be used to raise the beer to the bar at the point of sale. The wooden casks that held the beer were usually made and maintained by each brewery in its own cooperage. Huge pyramids of wooden casks were one of the wonders of brewery yards.

CASK'S PROGRESS

Coopering – the art of building and repairing the wooden casks – was vital. It played a major part in the brewing business because without the casks the beer in the brewhouse would never reach the thirsty customers waiting at the bars. The casks had to be soundly constructed. They had to be able to withstand the heavy handling involved in

Above: Even today some brewers maintain the tradition of beer from the wood, keeping the coopers' ancient craft alive.

transporting them about the countryside. They also had to resist the pressure of the live beer inside without leaking. The most suitable wood for this purpose was the strong, but flexible, Memel oak from the Baltic, which was exported around the world.

Coopering was a highly skilled craft and the apprentices underwent as much as five years training. Some large breweries boasted extensive cooperages employing hundreds of coopers. In the 1880s Bass, in Burton-on-Trent, England, had a stave store for storing loose wood that covered 25 acres.

A revolution

In the 1930s an innovation almost wiped out the coopers' trade: metal casks made from stainless steel or aluminium were introduced. These containers were lighter, cheaper and required less maintenance than wood. Within 40 years the metal newcomers had largely replaced handsome, handmade wooden casks.

Above: Large, high-speed bottling and canning plants were made possible as technology improved.

Above: The old and the new, as a dray team gets loaded up with modern metal kegs.

However, some breweries have hung on to the traditional oak barrels, partly because of the flavour and colour that the wood adds to the beer as it sits inside, and partly because during hot weather a wooden cask offers the beer better insulation from ruinous high temperatures.

BOTTLING UP

The brewing industry has long sought to provide more convenient containers to enable its customers to carry their beer home in small quantities. Bottled beer is much older than many imagine.

Earthenware vessels date back many centuries, and hand-manufactured glass bottles, which first appeared in the 17th century, were especially favoured for exporting beers.

Bottled beer came into more widespread use once steam-powered glass-bottle-making machines were introduced in the mid-19th century. Mechanization allowed bottles to be produced and filled with drink much more quickly and cheaply than before, and enabled the brewers to develop their own mass-produced, distinctively shaped bottles.

The sealing problem

Most early beer bottles were coloured brown or green in order to prevent the light penetrating and spoiling the contents.

The bottles were originally corked like wine bottles, but then Englishman Henry Barrett patented the internal screw stopper in 1872, which enabled the bottle to be re-sealed.

The metal crown cap, which was patented by an American, William Painter, followed the screw stopper 20 years later. It may not offer the advantage of being able to reseal the bottle, but it is cheap and lends itself to mass-production techniques. It is still the most common method used for sealing bottles.

Moving back to tradition

The bottled beer trade really took off after 1900. The emphasis was on bright, sparkling beer that looked good through the glass. The content of the bottles was increasingly chilled, filtered, carbonated and pasteurized.

In recent years, more flavoursome bottle-conditioned beers with a sediment, which continue to mature after they have been packaged, have made a comeback. In Belgium many bottled beers, such as the famous Trappist ale Orval, continue to mature in the bottle and contain a heavy sediment. In France, bière de garde is traditionally bottle-conditioned and improves with age like a good wine. It is often produced in wine-shaped bottles and sealed with a wine cork.

Below: Bottles of French bière de garde from farmhouses in northern France are traditionally corked.

DAWN OF THE SIX-PACK

The tin can – perhaps the ultimate convenience package for beer – appeared in the 1930s. Solid foods and soups had been sold in cans since early in the 19th century, but tinned beer presented greater difficulties. A beer-filled can would have to withstand extremely high pressures from within or it would burst along the seam. Another problem was that the tin tainted the taste of whatever was kept inside. In addition, tin cans at that time were more expensive than glass bottles. Breweries simply were not interested.

Breaking into the market

After the end of Prohibition in the United States, beer sales shot up and American can manufacturers were eager to break into the glass-dominated beer market. One firm, CanCo, eventually managed to develop a tin can with an internal lining, capable of resisting the pressures placed upon it by beer. In 1933 the pioneering company persuaded a hard-

Above: An early can of Coronation Brew with a coned top.

pressed brewery, Kreuger of Newark, New Jersey, to test out the tinny brew. The trial was a success and in January 1935 the company launched two canned beer brands – Kreuger's Finest Beer and Cream Ale.

A good response

The shiny novelty went down well with the public. The compact cans were lighter to carry home than a bottle, and fitted more easily into the refrigerators that were now appearing in every kitchen. Other companies were quick to seize on the new marketing opportunity and by the end of the year, 37 breweries, including the giants Pabst and Schlitz, were rattling out tinned supplies. The six-pack era had arrived in America.

Gradually the trend for canned beer spread and as cans were being churned off the production lines in the US, the first Europeans took their tentative steps forwards in the packaging revolution. The first brewery to can

Above: Despite initial reluctance, brewers the world over have now adopted cans as a convenient packaging medium.

Right: Beer's image improved so much after the end of Prohibition that by the 1950s the new refrigerators appearing in most American homes were stocked with cans of beer alongside other everyday groceries.

Left: Perhaps the ultimate in convenience packaging is the cardboard carton, seen in use here in Malawi.

beer in Europe was the Felinfoel Brewery of Llanelli in Wales. In a bid to boost the declining local tinplate industry of South Wales, it launched its pale ale in a can in December 1935.

Reluctant market

The brewing industry was pressed into the move to canned beers to some extent by the can manufacturers. The brewers' initial reluctance to make this innovation was understandable. The can has never really proved an ideal container for quality beer. At best, it provides a convenient, throwaway package, but the flavour and aroma of the processed contents often leave much to be desired. But as cheaper aluminium cans were introduced, the economic argument for canning beer was hard to resist.

Perhaps it is significant that relatively few wines have appeared in cans, and that in some major beer-drinking countries like the Czech Republic and Germany, the consumers have been reluctant to accept their favourite beers in what they see as an inferior container.

In Britain, where beer consumers have a long tradition of drinking draught beer, the breweries have ploughed a lot of money and effort into trying to make their take-home products as similar as possible in taste and "feel" to their cousins served in the pub. In the early 1990s beer manufacturers trumpeted a breakthrough in this area with the introduction of the "widget" in the can.

This small plastic device sits in the bottom of a can and when the ring pull is removed, the release of pressure triggers an injection of nitrogen into the beer, to provide it with a creamy, thick head. Although the feel of the beer is certainly improved, it is doubtful that this ingenious device has actually improved the taste of the beer.

Below: Cans are cleaned, filled and sealed on a prodigious scale and with hair-raising speed on modern canning production lines.

BEER DRINKING

Asking for "a beer" is a vague statement of intent. Many take beer for granted, assuming that a glass has little to offer beyond quenching a thirst and providing intoxication. But beer is much more than a chilled Pilsner on a hot day. You should never rush a good beer.

THE ANTICIPATION is part of the enjoyment. Take the trouble to pour the beer carefully into a clean glass, ensuring a reasonable head. First drink with your eyes and appreciate the colours in your beer – even a dark stout conceals a ruby in its depths. Don't necessarily worry if the beer is not sparkling and bright. Some brews, yeasty wheat beers from Germany for example, are meant to be cloudy. Then savour the aroma. Some have a subtle scent, others can be almost overpowering, but all should be enticing. At last, let the beer flow right over your tongue to pick up all the different taste sensations. Then swallow, and wait. Savour the flavours left behind. A good beer should linger long on the palate. The taste should not be strangled in your throat.

Generally, the best beer of most styles is on draught, and the closer the pub or bar to the brewery, the better the beer. It is at the heart of the community in many countries – in a cosy English pub, a huge German beer cellar, a packed Czech bar or a roadside bar in Africa. Tasting local beer is often a good way to meet the locals, who will probably know where to find the best brews.

There is a beer for almost every occasion – ice-cold lager is perfect for the beach and a pink framboise makes an excellent aperitif.

Above: Saison-style beers from Belgium should be sipped from goblet-shaped glasses.

Above: German beer gardens are perfect for enjoying good beer.

Opposite: 17th-century Cavaliers drank beer for breakfast with beef.

Above: A group of Zambian men take a seat, enjoy a well-deserved after-work drink of home-brewed beer and share a joke, in the relaxed surroundings of a roadside bar.

STYLES OF BEER

The title "beer" runs the gamut from dark, hearty ales to tangy, spritzy gueuzes. The myriad different tastes, colours, flavours and aromas can, to some extent, be squeezed into groupings with similar characteristics and methods of production.

Above: The names of abbey beers may be misleading since most are now brewed under licence by commercial breweries.

Below: Ale is a convenient, catch-all term that is generally used to mean beer made using top-fermenting yeast.

NEWSPAPERS AND MAGAZINES have had tasteful columns about the mysteries of wine for many years, but it is only recently that writers have begun to discuss beer in the same way. Beer is much more complex than wine. Wine is based on a single ingredient – grapes. Beer is a fine balance between two – malt and hops. The variety of hops is as great as the variety of grapes and there are many different styles of malt and different cereals. In addition, there is an exotic store of extra spices for the more adventurous brewer. Today, interest in local styles and different qualities has never been greater. Drinkers increasingly appreciate that there is a rich variety of beer tastes to explore around the world.

ABBEY BEERS
Strong fruity ales, abbey beers are brewed in Belgium by commercial companies, sometimes under licence from religious communities. They copy the style of the surviving beers produced in monasteries, or name their brews after a church or saint. Examples include Leffe from Interbrew, Grimbergen from the Union Brewery and Maredsous from Moortgat. (See Trappist.)

ALE
Nowadays this is a vague term meaning any top-fermented beer. It is one of the two main branches of the beer family, the other being lager. Of the two, ale is the older, dating back thousands of years. England is the country where ales are now most commonly brewed.

ALT
Alt is the German word meaning "traditional" or "old", and in the context of Altbier it indicates a

bitter-tasting brew produced by the ancient style of brewing using top-fermentation. Alt is a copper-coloured aromatic ale, made in the city of Düsseldorf and a few other cities in northern Germany. It is a firm-bodied but quite bitter beer that contains just over 4.5% alcohol. Major, well-known brands include Diebels, Schlosser and Uerige.

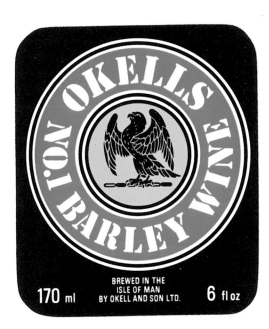

dry and hoppy with an alcohol content of 3–5%. Traditionally reddish amber in colour, paler varieties are now proving popular in England. Stronger versions used to be called Best or Special.

BLACK BEER

In Germany, Schwarzbier is a strong-tasting, bitter-chocolate lager. It is not a stout but a very dark lager and is a speciality of eastern Germany, particularly around Bernau. The town of Kostritz in the former East Germany is noted for its black lager, and Kulmbach and Erlangen are also known for their deep brown beers. This style is also made in Japan.

In England, especially Yorkshire, black beers are strong, pitch-black, treacly malt extracts, usually bottled for mixing with lemonade to make distinctive shandies.

BOCK

A strong malty, warming German beer of about 6.5% alcohol, bock was originally brewed for the colder months. Traditionally dark in colour, today it is more likely to be golden-bronze. This powerful smooth brew originated in Einbeck in Lower Saxony, but is now more associated with Bavaria. Bock is also produced in Austria, the Netherlands and other countries surrounding Germany. The word bock means "billy goat", and a goat's head often features on the label. The brew is sometimes linked with seasonal festivals, such as Maibock which celebrates the arrival of spring. Extra-potent versions are called doppelbocks (and are chiefly associated with Bavaria), with more than 7% alcohol, such as Paulaner Salvator. Eisbocks, in which frozen water is removed from the beer, are even more powerful. This brew (10%) is the speciality of Reichelbrau of Kulmbach.

BROWN ALE

A sweetish, bottled mild ale, dark in colour and low in alcohol, from England, brown ale was once a popular workers' drink, although sales have declined heavily in recent years. The north-east of the country produces stronger,

Above: Bitter is not bitter in taste as its name might suggest. It usually has a floral, fruity flavour.

BARLEY WINE

Barley wine is the English name for a powerful, almost syrupy, strong ale, that is usually sold in small nip-size bottles. These well-matured brews can be golden or dark in colour. The darker versions of barley wine were once called Stingo.

BERLINER WEISSE

A light, sharply acidic German wheat beer made predominantly in Berlin, this refreshing brew is relatively low in alcohol and is often laced with a dash of green woodruff or raspberry juice to add colour to its cloudy white (weisse) appearance.

BIÈRE DE GARDE

A top-fermenting "beer for keeping" from north-west France, this was originally made in farmhouses, but is now produced by commercial breweries. This style produces medium to strong, spicy ales; some are bottle-conditioned, and many are sealed with champagne-style wired corks.

BITTER

The distinctive style of draught ale in England and Wales is generally served in pubs. It is usually

Above: Bocks were originally drunk by fasting monks because they were considered nutritious.

Above: Brown ale was one of the traditional drinks of the working classes in England. Nowadays sales have declined.

drier versions like the well-known Newcastle Brown Ale.

Belgium boasts its own sweet-and-sour brown ales from East Flanders. The main producer is Liefmans of Oudenaarde. The sour taste comes from a slow simmering rather than a boil, and from the addition of a lactic yeast. Other producers include Cnudde, also of Oudenaarde, the nearby Roman Brewery and Vanden Stock.

CHILLI BEER

Produced by only a handful of American breweries this is an odd, slow-burning speciality. The Pike Place Brewery of Seattle produces an occasional Cerveza Rosanna Red Chilli Ale, while the hotter Crazy Ed's Cave Creek Chilli Beer of Phoenix, Arizona, has a whole chilli pod in each bottle. It reputedly goes well with Mexican food.

CREAM ALE

A sweetish, smooth, golden ale from the United States, cream ale was originally introduced by ale brewers trying to copy the Pilsner style. Some cream ales are made by blending ales with bottom-fermenting beers.

DIÄT PILS

Nothing to do with dieting, diät pils is lager which undergoes a thorough fermentation which removes nearly all the sugars from the bottom-fermented, Pilsner-derived brew. This leaves a strong, dry-tasting beer, which is still packed with calories in the alcohol. It was originally brewed as a beer suitable for diabetics, rather than slimmers. Because it misled many, the word "diät" has now been removed.

DOPPELBOCK

An extra-strong bock beer; doppelbock is not double in strength, but usually around 7.5% alcohol. It is rich and warming. The names of the leading Bavarian brands usually end in "ator", Salvator from Paulaner of Munich, for example.

DORTMUNDER

Dortmunder is a strong, full-bodied export style of lager from Dortmund in Germany, the biggest brewing city in Europe. It was originally brewed for export and was once sold under this name across the globe, but is now declining in popularity. Malty, dry and full-bodied, these brews usually have an alcohol strength of around 5.5%, being firmer and less aromatic than a Pilsner. The leading examples include DAB, Kronen and DUB.

DRY BEER

First produced in Japan by the Asahi Brewery in 1987, this is a super diät pils with a parching effect, which was widely adopted in North America. The beer taste is so clean it has been swept away almost entirely through further fermentation.

Dry beer, in which more of the sugars are turned to alcohol leaving little taste, was developed in Japan and launched in America in 1988. After an initial surge in sales when Anheuser-Busch introduced Bud Dry, the market has faded almost completely away.

DUNKEL

German lagers were traditionally dark, and these soft, malty brown beers are associated with Munich, often being known as Münchner. Like the paler hell, they contain around 4.5% alcohol. Most of the major Munich breweries produce a dunkel.

DUPPEL/DOUBLE
This is a term used to describe dark, medium-strength Trappist and abbey beers in Belgium.

EISBOCK
An extra-potent bock, eisbock is produced by freezing the brew and removing some of the frozen water to leave behind more concentrated alcohol. The most notable producer is Kulmbacher Reichelbrau in Northern Bavaria. Eisbock is the original ice beer.

EXPORT
This term was originally used to denote a better-quality beer, worth selling abroad. The Dortmunder style is also known as Dortmunder Export, since it became popular around the world. In Scotland, the term export is widely adopted for premium ales.

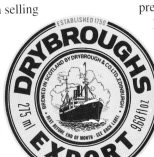

FARO
Once the most common manifestation of Belgian lambic beer, faro is a weak lambic sweetened with sugar. Now this style has largely disappeared.

FRAMBOISE/FRAMBOZEN
These are Flemish and French names for a Belgium fruit beer made by adding raspberries to a lambic. Framboise has a sparkling, pink champagne character and the raspberries impart a light, fruity flavour. Because the whole fruit is too soft, producers usually add raspberry syrup. In recent years a whole variety of other fruit juices have been tried, from peaches to bananas, with varying degrees of success.

GINGER BEER
Despite its name, this is a refreshing, low or no-alcohol soft drink flavoured with root ginger. However, long before the hop appeared, ginger was used in beer and some pioneering micro-brewers are trying it again: Salopian in England adds ginger to its dark wheat beer, Gingersnap.

GREEN BEER
Any young beer which has not had time to mature is known as a green beer. The term is also used to denote a beer made with organic malt and hops. Organic green beer is known as biologique in France (where Castelain makes an organic beer called Jade) and biologisch in Germany. In Scotland, the Caledonian Brewery of Edinburgh has pioneered organic ale with Golden Promise.

GUEUZE
This is a ripe blend of old and new Belgian lambics. By blending young and old lambics, a secondary fermentation is triggered. The resulting distinctive, sparkling beer, often sold in corked bottles like champagne to withstand the pressure, packs a fruity, sour, dry taste. Blending is such an art that some producers do not brew, but buy in their wort. Often this beer is matured for many more months in the bottle. In some cases the secondary fermentation is triggered by the addition of various fruits. Traditionally gueuze should not be filtered, pasteurized or sweetened, though some more commercial brands do all three.

Above: Several breweries have sprung up producing "green" beer using only organic ingredients.

HEAVY
Scottish brewers use this term to describe a standard strength ale, between a Light and an Export. A "wee heavy" is a bottled strong ale, the wee referring to the small nip-size of the bottle.

HEFE
The German word for yeast is used to describe a beer that is unfiltered, with a sediment in the bottle. Draught beers "mit Hefe" are usually cloudy.

HELL
This word means pale or light in German and indicates a mild, malty golden lager, often from Munich. Notable examples include Hacker-Pschorr and Augustiner.

Below: The word "Hefe" on a label indicates that the beer still contains yeast.

HONEY BEER
The Celts and other ancient peoples used to make mead from fermented honey. They also produced a beer,

Right: The attractively named Waggle Dance honey beer brewed by Ward's of Sheffield is a revival of an old traditional drink of the Celtic people.

Far right: A selection of IPAs.

Below: US brewers have followed the Canadian innovation of ice beers.

bragot, to which honey was often added as a soft sweetener. A hazy honey brew called Golden Mead Ale was produced in England by Hope & Anchor Breweries of Sheffield, and was widely exported until the early 1960s. Today, a few breweries have revived the style, notably Ward's of Sheffield with Waggle Dance and Enville Ales of Staffordshire. Some new American brewers also use honey, as do the innovative Belgian De Dolle Brouwers in their Boskeun beer.

ICE BEER

A chilling innovation of the early 1990s; the brew is frozen during maturation to produce a purified beer, with the ice crystals removed to increase the strength.

Many ice beers were originally developed in Canada by Labatt and contain around 5.5% alcohol. Canadian brewers Labatt and Molson introduced the new beer style in 1993 in which the beer is frozen after fermentation, giving a cleaner, almost smoothed away flavour. Sometimes the ice crystals are removed, concentrating the beer. Most major US brewers have launched their own brands such as Bud Ice and Miller's Icehouse, but ice beer still accounts for less than 4% of the beer market.

In 1996, Tennent's of Scotland produced a Super Ice with a strength of 8.6%.

IMPERIAL STOUT

See Stout.

IPA

The words behind the initials betray IPAs imperial origins – India Pale Ale. This strong, heavily hopped beer was brewed in Britain, notably in Burton-on-Trent by companies like Allsopp and Bass. The recipe was designed to withstand the long sea voyages to distant parts of the British Empire like India. According to legend, a cargo of 300 casks of Bass's East India Pale Ale was wrecked off the port of Liverpool in 1827. Some of the rescued beer was sold locally and won instant fame among English drinkers. Specialist American brewers like Bert Grant's Yakima Brewing Company now probably produce the most authentic versions.

IRISH ALE

A soft, slightly sweet reddish ale from the "Emerald Isle". Top and bottom-fermenting versions are brewed commercially. This ale followed many of the Irish in migrating to other lands. George Killian Letts, a member of the Letts family who brewed Ruby Ale in County Wexford until 1956, licensed the French brewery Pelforth to produce George Killian's Bière Rousse and the American brewers Coors to produce Killian's Irish Red. Smithwick's of Kilkenny (owned by Guinness) is the best-known ale in Ireland today.

KÖLSCH

The refreshing golden beer of Cologne may look like a Pilsner (though it may sometimes be cloudy), but its light, subtle fruity taste reveals it to be a top-fermenting ale. Its fleeting aromatic nature masks an alcohol content of 4–5%.

Kölsch is produced only by some 20 breweries in and around the busy cathedral city of Cologne and it is usually served in small glasses. The leading producers include Kuppers and Fruh.

KRIEK

In this Belgian lambic beer, secondary fermentation is stimulated by adding cherries to give a dry, fruity flavour and deep colour. This is not a novelty drink, but draws on a long tradition of using local fruit to flavour an already complex brew, balancing the lambic sourness and providing an almond character from the cherry stones. The kriek is a small dark cherry grown near Brussels.

KRISTALL

This term, taken from the German word for a crystal-clear beer, usually indicates a filtered wheat beer or Weizenbier.

LAGER

Lager is one of the two main branches of the beer family. The word lager is derived from the German word "to store". In Britain it refers to any golden, bottom-fermented beer, but elsewhere it has little meaning, apart from a general word for beer.

LAMBIC

The wild beers of Belgium have their roots deep in history. One of the most primitive beers brewed on earth, these spontaneously fermenting beers are unique to Belgium, or to be more exact, to an area to the west of Brussels in the Senne Valley.

Lambic brewers use at least 30% unmalted wheat in order to produce a milky wort from the mash. Old hops are used, as they are only required for their preservative value, not for their flavour or aroma.

Unlike most other beer styles, in which a carefully cultivated yeast is used to ferment the wort, the wheat brew used to produce lambic beer is left exposed to the air to allow spontaneous fermentation to happen from wild yeasts in the atmosphere. As in previous

centuries, this beer is only brewed in the cooler months of the year, as the wild yeasts would be too unpredictable in summer. The fermenting wort is then run into large wooden casks and left to age in dark, dusty galleries from three months to many years.

The result is a unique, tart, sour beer, probably similar to the ales made in ancient times. The taste is almost like a flat, acidic cider, which attacks the tongue and sucks in the cheeks. It has an alcohol content of around 5%. This can be drunk young on its own, often on draught in cafés in the Brussels area, but it is usually blended with older lambics to produce gueuze. Sometimes fruit is added to create framboise (raspberry) or kriek (cherry) beers. The lambic range of beers is mainly produced by small, speciality brewers, like Boon, Cantillon, De Troch, Girardin and Timmermans. But there are a few more commercial brands, notably Belle-Vue (part of Interbrew) and St Louis.

LIGHT ALE

In England, this term indicates a bottled low-gravity bitter. In Scotland, it means the weakest brew, a beer light in strength although it may well be dark in colour.

Far left: Apart from in Britain, the term lager is used generally for beer.

Below: The term lambic indicates a Belgian wheat beer that is spontaneously fermented by wild, airborne yeast.

Above: In Miller Lite more of the sugar is turned to alcohol in the brewing process to produce a lower-calorie beer.

Below: Relatively low alcohol, mild is usually a dark brown ale which was originally brewed for English workers.

LITE

In North America, this term is used to describe a thin, low-calorie beer, the best-known being Miller Lite. In some countries, Australia for instance, lite can mean low in alcohol.

LOW ALCOHOL

Since the late 1980s, many breweries throughout the world have added low- or no-alcohol brews to their beer range, usually in response to increasingly strict drink-driving laws. Low alcohol (or LA) can contain as much as 2.5% alcohol. Alcohol-free brews should contain no more than 0.05%. Some of these near beers are produced using yeasts which create little alcohol, or the fermentation is cut short.

In others the alcohol is removed from a normal beer by distillation or reverse osmosis. It has proved difficult to provide an acceptable beer taste. Some of the more successful brews, Clausthaler from Frankfurt in Germany and Birell from Hürlimann of Zurich in Switzerland, now sell or licence their low- or no-alcohol beers across many countries.

MALT LIQUOR

In the United States, this term indicates a strong lager, often made with a high amount of sugar to produce a thin but potent brew. These beers are designed to deliver a strong alcoholic punch (around 6–8%) but little else. They are light beers with a kick, often cheaply made with a high proportion of sugar and using enzymes to create more alcohol. Sales of malt liquor account for about 4% of the total American beer market.

MÄRZEN

A full-bodied copper-coloured lager, this beer style originated in Vienna, but developed in Munich as a stronger Märzen (March) brew (6% alcohol), which was laid down in March, to allow it to mature over the summer for drinking at the Oktoberfest after the harvest. It has largely been replaced in Germany by more golden "Festbiere". Smooth and malty, most are now stronger versions of the golden hell, containing more than 5.5% alcohol. Notable examples include Spaten Ur-Märzen and Hofbrauhaus Oktoberfest.

MILD

Mild was the dominant ale in England and Wales until the 1960s, and later in some regions. It is a relatively low-gravity malty beer, usually lightly hopped, and can be dark or pale in colour. Mild was traditionally the workers' drink and would be sold on draught in the pub or club. Today, the style has vanished from many areas; it survives mainly in the industrial West Midlands and the north-west of England.

MILK STOUT

See Stout.

MÜNCHNER

The German name for a beer from Munich traditionally refers to the city's brown, malty lager style.

OATMEAL STOUT

See Stout.

OLD ALE

This strong, well-matured, rich, dark ale is usually sold as a seasonal beer in England as a winter warmer. Sometimes such ales are used as stock beers for blending with fresher brews.

OUD BRUIN

Old Browns in the Netherlands are weak, sweetish lagers.

OYSTER STOUT

See Stout.

PALE ALE

An English bottled beer, pale ale is stronger than light ale and is usually based on the brewery's best bitter. See IPA.

PILSNER

Strictly speaking, Pilsner is a golden, hoppy, aromatic lager from the Bohemian Czech town of Plzen (Pilsen in German), where this classic style was first produced in 1842. The original Pilsner Urquell (original source) is still brewed there. Czech Pilsner has a complex character with a flowery hop aroma and a dry finish.

This golden classic has spawned a thousand imitators, some excellent, others pale, lacklustre imitations of the original. Variations on the style now dominate the world beer market.

Pilsner is now the predominant lager beer of Germany. German Pilsners are dry and hoppy with a light, golden colour. They contain around 5% alcohol and often lack the smooth maltiness of the original Czech version.

Leading German brands include Warsteiner, Bitburger and Herforder.

Left: The original Pilsner comes from Plzen in the Czech Republic, but it has spawned many imitators.

PORTER

The origins of porter are shrouded in myths and legends. It was said to have been invented in London in 1722 by Ralph Harwood when he grew tired of making Three Threads, a popular drink of the day, by mixing strong, brown and old ales. He decided to brew one beer – or entire butt – combining the characteristics of all three.

In fact, porter was the product of the world's first major breweries, which were rising in London at this time. By brewing on a large scale with huge vessels, they were able to concoct a beer that was much more stable with far better keeping qualities than previous ales – porter.

The first porter was a traditional London brown mild ale which was much more heavily hopped than usual in order to improve its keeping qualities. The beer was then matured for months in vast vats, to increase its alcoholic strength. Older brews were then blended with fresher ones to produce an "entire" beer.

Only major brewers, such as Barclay, Truman and Whitbread, could afford to build the expensive plants that were necessary to produce beer on this scale and to tie up so much capital in maturing beer. In return for their investment, they captured the English capital's beer market, as porter was much more reliable than previous ales. The economies of scale in its production also made it cheaper.

Porter proved so successful that it was widely distributed and exported.

Enterprising brewers elsewhere, like Guinness in Dublin, followed this example and began to brew their own porter. Sales gradually declined in the 19th century as it was replaced in popularity by paler ales and only the stronger or "stouter" porters survived. The name is still used around the world today to indicate a brown beer.

In the Baltic countries, strong porters are still made, based on the original export brews. Some new micro-brewers have also tried to revive the dark, dry style in England and North America.

Porter, however, was never a craft beer. It flowed from the Industrial Revolution. It was the first mass-produced beer.

RAUCHBIER

The intense smoky flavour of these German smoked beers from the region of Franconia comes from malt that has been dried over moist beechwood fires. There are nine breweries in the town of Bamburg that produce this dark, bottom-fermented speciality. Leading examples include Schlenkerla and Spezial.

Below: Dark porters have diminished in popularity relative to when they were first introduced.

Above: The Campaign for Real Ale celebrated its tenth anniversary with a traditional brewed beer.

REAL ALE

The British drinkers' consumer organization, CAMRA, the Campaign for Real Ale, devised this name for traditional cask-conditioned beer which continues to mature in the pub cellar. Real ale is not filtered or pasteurized.

RED BEER

The reddish sour beers of West Flanders in Belgium are sometimes dubbed the Burgundies of Belgium. The colour comes from using Vienna malt. The prime producer is Rodenbach of Roeselare, who matures its beers in a remarkable forest of huge oak vats.

Younger brews are blended with old to create the distinctive Rodenbach brand. Some of the more mature beer is bottled on its own as the classic Grand Cru. Other brands include Petrus from Bavik and Duchesse de Bourgogne from Verhaeghe of Vichte.

ROGGEN

Only a few breweries make this German or Austrian rye beer. Some English and American breweries have started to use rye to add flavour to barley malt, and one American brewer produces its own Roggen Rye.

ROOT BEER

An American temperance soft drink, not a beer, it was originally flavoured with sassafras root bark. Root beer is boiled but not fermented.

RUSSIAN STOUT

See Stout.

SAISON/SEZUEN

This Belgian speciality beer is now hard to find. A refreshing, slightly sour summer style, saison (which means "season" in French) is mainly made in rural breweries in the French-speaking Wallonia region, some of which have closed in recent years.

The orange, highly hopped, top-fermenting ales are brewed in winter and then laid down to condition in sturdy wine bottles for drinking in the hot summer months. They are sold in corked bottles after ageing. Some also contain added spices like ginger.

Small producers include Silly, Dupont and Vapeur. The larger Du Bocq brewery makes Saison Régal, while in Flanders Martens of Bocholt produces Sezuens.

Above: The De Dolle brewery in Silly, Belgium, produces a strong, dark, Scotch-style ale.

SCHWARZBIER

See Black Beer.

SCOTCH ALE

Scotland's ales, brewed many miles from the nearest hop field, tend to be more malty in character than English beers. Bitters are called Light, Heavy, Special or Export in Scotland, depending on their strength, or are sometimes rated 60/-, 70/- or 80/- shillings according to an old pricing system.

Bottled Scotch Ale in Belgium is the name given to a powerful, rich ale, which is often brewed in Belgium itself.

STEAM BEER

An American cross between a bottom-fermented beer and an ale, steam beer was originally made in the Gold Rush days in California. It was brewed with lager yeasts at warm ale temperatures, using wide, shallow pans. Casks of this lively brew were said to hiss like steam when tapped. Now it is brewed only by the Anchor Steam Brewery of San Francisco.

STEINBIER

German "stone beer" is brewed using a primitive method of heating, in which red-hot rocks are lowered into the brew to bring it to the boil. The sizzling stones become covered in burnt sugars and are then added back to the beer at the maturation stage to spark a second fermentation. This smoky, full-bodied brew is made only by Rauchenfels at Altenmünster near Augsburg.

STOUT

One of the classic styles of ale, originally a stout porter, stout has survived and prospered thanks to its sharp contrast in taste and colour to the popular Pilsner – and also to the determined marketing and enterprise of one brewer, Guinness of Ireland.

This dry black brew is made with a proportion of dark roasted barley in the mash and is heavily hopped to give its distinctive taste. Draught stout tends to be much creamier and smoother than the more distinctive bottled beer, because it uses nitrogen gas in its dispenser. Guinness also produce a much heavier Foreign Extra Stout for export. Some other countries also produce dry stout, notably Australia, with fine examples from Cooper's of Adelaide and Tooth's of Sydney.

Besides dry or bitter stout, there are a number of variations of this dark style:

Milk or Sweet Stout

This is a much weaker and smoother bottled English stout, originally called Milk Stout because of the use of lactose (milk sugar). The name was banned in Britain in 1946 because of the implication that milk is added to the brew, though it is still used in some countries such as South Africa and Malta. The leading brand, Whitbread's Mackeson, still maintains a creamy connection through the sketch of a milk churn on the label. The Boston Beer Company in America produces a Samuel Adams Cream Stout. In addition, there are stronger tropical sweet stouts, notably Dragon brewed in Jamaica and Lion which comes from Sri Lanka.

Oatmeal Stout

Many sweet stouts were sold as nourishing, restorative drinks for invalids. Some were further strengthened by the addition of oats. Once a popular bottled brew, most oatmeal stouts have vanished, but a few have been revived, including Sam Smith's Oatmeal Stout from Yorkshire in England and Maclay's Oat Malt Stout from Scotland. The latter claims to be the only beer in the world to be brewed using malted oats, rather than oatmeal added to the mash.

Above: The characteristic dark, heavy, opaque hue of stout is unmistakable in the glass.

Below: Stout is a derivative of porter. There are many varieties within the general category.

Oyster Stout

Stout has always been seen as an ideal accompaniment to a dish of oysters. Some brewers went further and added oysters to their beer. Famous examples from the past include Castletown on the Isle of Man and Young's of Portsmouth in England, who boasted that their oyster stout contained the "equivalent to one oyster in every bottle". The seaport brewers used concentrated oyster extract from New Zealand. Some American and English brewers have occasionally revived the style, but the main bottled oyster stout today from Marston's of Burton-on-Trent contains no oysters.

Russian or Imperial Stout

Originally brewed in London in the 18th century as an extra-strong, export porter for the Baltic, this rich, intense brew with a fruit-cake character was reputed to be a favourite of the Russian Empress Catherine the Great, hence the Russian Imperial title. Many Baltic breweries took up the style, including Koff in Finland, Pripps of Sweden (whose porter was sold under the Carnegie brand name) and Tartu in Estonia.

In England, Courage still produces an occasional Imperial Russian Stout, which is matured for more than a year in the brewery. The nip-size bottles are year-dated, like vintage wines.

TARWEBIER

This is the Flemish word for the Belgian style of wheat beer. See Witbier.

TRAPPIST

Trappist is a strict designation referring only to beers from the five Trappist monastery breweries of Belgium and one in the Netherlands. These silent orders produce a range of strong, rich, top-fermenting ales. The Chimay, Orval, Rochefort, Westmalle and Westvleteren breweries are in Belgium, while Koningshoeven (La Trappe) is Dutch. All the complex, spicy brews are bottle-conditioned. Some number their beers in strength, terming them dubbel or tripel.

Commercial breweries producing ales in the same style, or under licence from the religious communities, have to call their brews abbey beers.

TRIPLE/TRIPEL

These are Flemish or Dutch terms, usually indicating the strongest brew in a range of beers, especially in Trappist or abbey beers. They are hoppy, golden brews, stronger than the darker doubles or dubbels.

Below: The term Trappist is an "appellation". By law only beers produced by the Trappist monasteries can carry this mark.

URQUELL

Urquell is the German word meaning "original source". The term should be used to show that the beer is the first or original in its style, such as Pilsner Urquell from the Czech Republic. Often only Ur is used, as in Einbecker Mai-Ur-Bock.

VIENNA

The term Vienna indicates the amber-red lagers developed by the Austrian brewing pioneer Anton Dreher, but these beers now have little association with the city. The style is best found today in the Märzen beers of Germany.

WEISSE OR WEIZEN

This wheat beer style has grown from almost nothing to a quarter of Bavaria's beer market in 20 years since the early 1970s. The white or wheat beers of Bavaria are made with 50–60% malted wheat. These ghostly pale, often cloudy brews have become a popular summer refresher in Germany. They have the quenching qualities of a lager but, as they are top-fermented, all the flavour of an ale.

This is particularly true in the more popular unfiltered cloudy version containing yeast in suspension, Hefeweizen. Filtered wheat beers are Kristall. Stronger brews are called

Weizenbock; dark ones Dunkelweizen. Notable Bavarian wheat beer brewers include Schneider and Erdinger. There is also a stronger Weizenbock at around 6.5% alcohol compared to Weissbier's usual 5%. In north-eastern Germany, a weaker, sourer style made with about half the wheat is Berliner Weisse. Fruit syrups are often added to Berliner Weisse by drinkers to provide a sweet and sour summer refresher. The leading brewers are Kindl and Schultheiss.

WITBIER

The white wheat beers of Belgium are also known as "Bières Blanches" in French. These are brewed using around 50% wheat, but then a variety of spices are added, notably orange peel and coriander. This style is also known as tarwebier.

The witbier or bière blanche style has risen like a pale ghost from the dead to haunt every corner of the market, and the best-known example is the pioneering Hoegaarden. When Pieter Celis revived the art of brewing this spiced wheat beer in the small town of Hoegaarden in 1966, he could not have imagined how it would grow. Now many breweries in Belgium and other countries have copied the style.

Hoegaarden is brewed from roughly equal parts of raw wheat and malted barley. The cloudy top-fermented brew differs from German wheat beers through the use of coriander and curaçao (orange peel) to give a spicy, fruity flavour and enticing aroma. Other leading brands include Brugs Tarwebier (Blanche de Bruges) from the Gouden Boom brewery, Dentergems Witbier from Riva, and Du Bocq's Blanche de Namur.

Left: Triple beers are a sub-category of the abbey style.

Above: Hoegaarden is one of the best-known examples of Witbier or bière blanche.

A WORLD TOUR

A globe-trotting journey around the world of beer, giving a glimpse into the thousands of beers brewed worldwide today. The world of beer is a complex one, so for ease we have chosen the main brews of note in each country or region. Large international brewers and brands can be found in their country of origin and in each country the main emphasis is on the native beers and brewers.

A GLOBE TROTTER'S BEER GUIDE

We begin our journey in Ireland, the home of perhaps the most stout in the world – Guinness – then stroll through the ale-drinking countries – Wales, England and Scotland. Then it is a small hop across the North Sea into Scandinavia, taking in Iceland on the way. From the frozen north the tour heads south through Europe.

From there we head further south still, into the vast continent of Africa, to discover native beers and dip into modern lagers. Turning east, we sample the beers of the brewing giants, China and Japan , and see the influence of overseas brewing traditions on the rest of Asia. Leaving Asia behind we head for Australia, the home of Fosters, then New Zealand provides the jumping-off point to head out across the vast Pacific Ocean to the Americas.

We travel down through the Canada to the USA and south into Latin America. From there we finish in relaxed Caribbean sunshine to find the journey has come full circle and ends with strong black stouts.

For each nation or region, there is an overall view of the drinking and brewing habits, followed by an A-Z guide to the most important and interesting brews to be found there, and a summary of the major brewers.

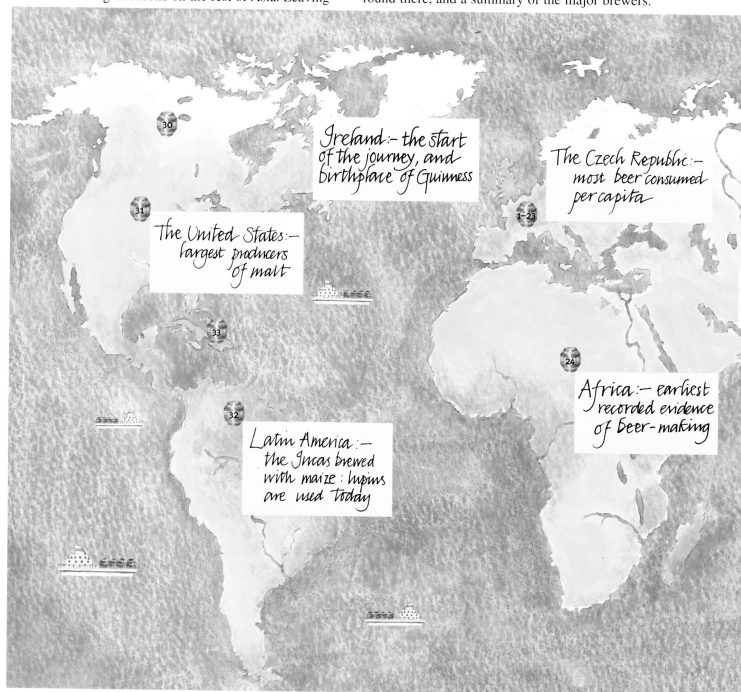

Ireland :- the start of the journey, and birthplace of Guinness

The Czech Republic :- most beer consumed per capita

The United States :- largest producers of malt

Africa :- earliest recorded evidence of beer-making

Latin America :- the Incas brewed with maize : lupins are used today

Although some companies own breweries in several countries, the major international names appear only in their "home" country. For example, although Heineken, is a major producer in Asia, its beers and information about the company will only appear in The Netherlands.

In all countries the alcohol measurements are given as alcohol by volume (abv), except for the United States of America where the measure is more usually alcohol by weight (abw). This may make American beers seem weaker than those from Europe – a beer which is 5% abv, for example, is 4% abw.

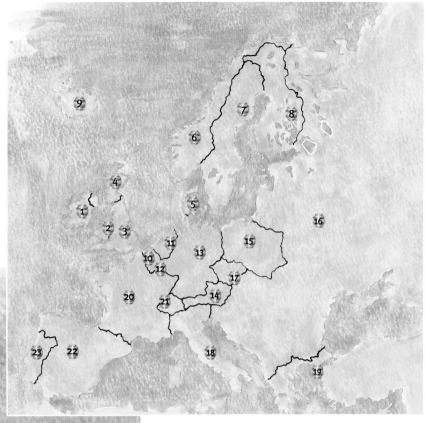

:- the future
r-making

KEY

		18	Italy
		19	Greece and Turkey
		20	France
		21	Switzerland
		22	Spain
		23	Portugal
1	Ireland	24	Africa
2	Wales	25	China
3	England	26	Japan
4	Scotland	27	The Rest of Asia
5	Denmark		
6	Norway	28	Australia
7	Sweden	29	New Zealand
8	Finland	30	Canada
9	Iceland	31	The United States of America
10	Belgium		
11	The Netherlands		
12	Luxembourg	32	Latin America
13	Germany	33	The Caribbean
14	Austria		
15	Poland		
16	Eastern Europe		
17	The Czech Republic and Slovakia		

IRELAND

When people think of Irish beer, they picture a dark glass of stout. Ireland is the only country in the world where this creamy brew is the most popular drink, consumed in great quantities in the famous Irish pubs.

THE IRISH HAVE PROBABLY BEEN BREWING since the Bronze Age. Although spirits have always been popular, beer is very much a traditional tipple and brewing is a major industry, with the majority of the malting barley crop going directly into whisky and beer production. One particular type of beer – stout – still accounts for around half of all beer sold in Ireland, the vast bulk of it Guinness. The only serious competition comes from Cork where Beamish and Murphy's, both now owned by foreign companies, brew rivals. But even in Cork, Guinness control half the market.

Dry, bitter stout is the quintessential Irish drink and some obliging barmen will even sketch a shamrock leaf in the foam, to prove it. But Irish stout is actually based on a dark English beer, porter, imported into Ireland in the 18th century.

Irish brewers copied the increasingly popular style, then in the early 19th century Guinness introduced its own, bigger-bodied, drier version – Extra Stout Porter – which eventually became known simply as stout.

In Ireland drinking is a highly sociable tradition. The nation is full of bars and pubs, famous the world over for their good music and convivial atmosphere. It is here that beer is generally consumed, rather than at home, and as a result most beer (more than 80%) is still served on draught. Up until the 1950s, stout was served through a two-cask system. One wooden cask contained fresh, still-fermenting stout, while another contained more mature stout. The glass was filled with the fresh brew, and then, when the foam had settled, was topped up with the older, flatter stout. This system was replaced in the 1960s by pressurized containers which used nitrogen to give a smoother, creamier texture.

Above: Drinking in Ireland generally means a pint of stout in the pub. But brewers have tried to bottle the experience to be enjoyed at home.

The beer was served from one keg and was filtered and pasteurized. At the same time weaker porter was phased out and the strength of stout was lowered from around 5% alcohol by volume to 4%. Today, there is an increasing tendency to chill it, thereby reducing its flavour and aroma.

THE BEERS

Beamish Red Ale
This recent addition to the Beamish range is a smooth, traditional Irish-style red ale (4.5%). It has a rich, red colour, created by the black and crystal malts that are used in the brew. It has a full, sweet flavour.

Beamish Stout
The chocolatey Beamish Stout (4.2%) is the only stout brewed nowhere but Ireland. In fact it is not even brewed outside the town of Cork. Its distinctive flavour is partly due to the use of malted wheat, as well as barley, in the mash. Beamish is exported to Britain, Europe and North America.

Black Biddy Stout
A rare, cask-conditioned stout (4.4%) brewed at the Biddy Early pub, County Clare.

Caffrey's Irish Ale
This strong, creamy, traditional, Irish ale (4.8%) is brewed at the Ulster brewery in County Antrim. It is named after Thomas R. Caffrey, who founded the brewery in 1891. Caffrey's pours like an old-fashioned stout and takes about three minutes to settle from a creamy liquid to a rich auburn colour, topped with a creamy head. The beer is served chilled like a lager, but has the flavour of an ale. It was launched in the UK on St Patrick's Day 1994.

Great Northern Porter
This rare cask Irish porter (4%) is a black, traditional seasonal brew with a rich, sweetish, burnt flavour, from the Hilden brewery.

Guinness Draught
Draught Guinness (4.1%) is a smooth and creamy stout (partly due to the nitrogen- dispensing system) with a refreshing, roasted flavour and a rich black hue. It is filtered and pasteurized. In 1989, canned "draught" Guinness was launched, after five years' research, so that dedicated Guinness drinkers could enjoy the smooth brew in the comfort of their homes.

Guinness Extra Stout
This quality bottled stout (4.3%) uses unmalted, roasted barley and is heavily hopped to give a ruby-black colour and a complex, bitter flavour. It is still unpasteurized in Ireland. One of the world's classic beers.

Guinness Foreign Extra Stout
A strong export stout with a richly astringent taste (7.5%), it is a partly blended brew, using specially matured stout.

Guinness Special Export
This delicious, strong, mellow export stout (8%) is produced exclusively for the Belgian market.

Harp Export
This is a stronger (4.5%) version of Harp Lager and is produced at Guinness's Great Northern Brewery in Dundalk.

Harp Lager
This pioneering golden lager (3.6%) was developed by Guinness in 1959, to mark the bicentenary of the firm. Harp was launched in 1960 and was named after the company's famous Irish harp logo. It is brewed at the Great Northern Brewery in Dundalk.

The Crack
Irish pubs are famous the world over for their great beer and convivial atmosphere. The pub, as much as the church, is the traditional meeting place for the local community and is a place for good talk, good music and good drink. "The Crack" as it is known is one of the country's best known exports as "Irish pubs" spring up as far afield as Milan and Sydney.

Hilden Ale

This hoppy, cask bitter (4%), produced by the Hilden Brewery, is a hoppy, light-amber brew, which is mainly exported to Britain.

Hilden Special Reserve

A dark, amber mild (4.6%), brewed using dark malts, by the Hilden brewery.

Hoffmans Lager

This lager (3.3%) is produced in Waterford for south-east Ireland.

Irish Festival Ale

This amber-coloured, fruity bitter (5%) was originally brewed for important calendar events and beer festivals, but it is now a regular offering from the Hilden brewery.

Kaliber

This is a non-alcoholic lager brewed by Guinness.

Kilkenny Irish Beer

This red ale (4.3%) is a creamy, premium ale, initially produced for export in 1987 by Smithwick's. It was launched in Ireland in 1995. A stronger version (5%) is exported to the United States.

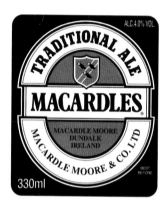

Macardles Ale

This Irish ale (4%) is produced at the small traditional Macardle Moore brewery in Dundalk.

Murphy's Irish Stout

This is a relatively light, smooth stout (4%). It should be served cooled to lager temperature, with a head about 1½ cm (½ in) deep.

Murphy's Red Beer

This pressurized red ale (5%) was launched by Murphy's in 1995. Its distinctive red hue is entirely natural.

Oyster Stout

This classic Irish beer (4.8%) includes real oysters in the boil. It is produced by the Porter House brewpub in Dublin. In its first year this stout won two awards.

Phoenix

This traditional Irish ale (4%) is produced at Macardle Moore of Dundalk.

Plain Porter

This classic, light stout (4.3%) has a dry, roast flavour and an uncompromising black colour. Yet another quality brew from the Porter House brewing company, Parliament Street, Dublin.

Porter House Red

A traditional Irish red ale (4.4%) with a hoppy, caramel flavour. Produced by the Porter House brewery.

Smithwick's Barley Wine

Despite its name, this barley wine (5.5%) is actually brewed at Macardle's brewery in Dundalk.

Smithwick's Export

This auburn Irish ale (5%) is brewed in Ireland for the Canadian market.

Whitewater Mountain Ale

This cask-conditioned Irish ale (4.2%) is produced by the Whitewater brewery, a new brewery founded in 1996 in Kilkeel, County Down.

Wrasslers XXXX Stout

This fine stout (5%) is made to a recipe using four different types of malt, originally brewed by Deasy's of West Cork in the 1900s. The Hilden brewing company bills it as "a stout like your grandfather used to drink".

THE BREWERS

Beamish and Crawford

The Cork-based brewers first produced porter in 1792 and early in the 19th century they were the largest brewers in the land, bigger than Guinness. However, by the mid-20th century the brewery was run down and since 1962 it has been owned by a succession of foreign breweries. A modern brewhouse now stands alongside the half-timbered city centre offices. As well as Beamish Stout, it also produces a Beamish Red Ale.

Guinness

This international giant is, perhaps, one of the most renowned brewers in the world. The name has become almost synonymous with Irish stout (see next page).

Hilden Brewery

This small brewery located alongside a Georgian country house in Lisburn, County Antrim, was set up in 1981. It is the oldest surviving independent brewery in Northern Ireland.

Lett's

The Ghost Brewer of Ireland, Lett's, ceased brewing at Enniscorthy in County Wexford in 1956, but an enterprising member of the family – George Killian Lett – licensed two major foreign brewers to produce their Ruby Ale. Pelforth of France produce George Killian's Bière Rousse, while Coors of the United States brew a lighter Killian's Irish Red. English brewers Greene King have since also rolled out Wexford Irish Cream Ale brewed to a Letts recipe.

Murphy's

Murphy's was established in 1856 by the Murphy brothers, on the Lady's Well site in Cork. Following a disastrous trading agreement with English brewers Watney's in the 1960s to sell keg Red Barrel in Ireland, the Lady's Well brewery had to be rescued by the Irish Government and a consortium of publicans before being bought by Dutch giants Heineken in 1983. Today Murphy's Stout (4%) is exported to more than 50 countries.

Above: A village pub advertises its wares – beer, food and music – in Killarney, County Kerry.

Porter House

A brewpub brewing classic Irish beers. Porter House opened in 1996 in the heart of Dublin in Parliament Street. Its brews include Porter House Plain Porter (4.3%), Porter House Red (4.4%), 4X Stout (5%) and an Oyster Stout (4.8%).

Smithwick's

Ireland's oldest brewery, built around the impressive ruins of Kilkenny's St Francis Abbey, dates from 1710. It is now owned by Guinness. The soft, red Smithwick's (3.5%) is Ireland's best-selling draught ale. It also produces Kilkenny Irish Beer (4.3%), mainly for export.

THE GUINNESS STORY

Arthur Guinness began brewing in Dublin in 1759.

For many, Guinness is the first, last and only word on Irish beer. Initially Arthur Guinness produced ale, but seeing the success of imported porter from England, he completely switched to brewing the dark drop by 1799. He reversed the beer trade, sending exports to England. By 1815, Guinness was so well known that wounded officers at the Battle of Waterloo were calling for the beer by name.

In the 1820s, the second Arthur Guinness (1768–1855) perfected an extra stout porter which eventually became known simply as stout. He made Guinness the largest brewer in Ireland. His son Benjamin (1798–1868) turned St James's Gate into the largest brewery in the world. Its stout sold around the globe.

A franchise was granted to McMullen of New York in 1858; Speakman Brothers of Melbourne started distribution in Australia in 1869. The familiar buff label with its harp trademark first appeared in 1862, and in 1878 a completely new brewhouse was built under Edward Guinness (1847–1927).

By 1910, the ever-expanding plant was producing two million hogsheads (54-gallon/245-litre casks) of stout a year. A quarter of a million wooden barrels were stacked in mountains on the 64-acre (26-hectare) site.

In 1936 a second brewery was opened at Park Royal in London to meet demand in England. Since 1962, Guinness has built breweries around the world: in Nigeria, Malaysia, Cameroon, Ghana and Jamaica. In addition, the stout is brewed under licence from North America to Australia.

In the 1950s, Guinness re-entered the ale trade through Irish Ale Breweries, with a beer called Phoenix from Waterford. The firm celebrated its bicentenary in 1959 by planning its own Harp lager. The black stuff, however, remains at the heart of the business.

Guinness stout varies in strength and character, depending on the market that it is being sold in. Stronger stouts are brewed for export, partly blended using specially matured stout. St James's Gate also exports concentrated versions of mature stout to blend into Guinness brewed abroad to provide the characteristic flavour and

Above: By the 19th century the St James's Gate brewery had become a city within a city, complete with its own power station and internal railway system, and employing an army of men.

colour. Sweeter and stronger Guinness is especially popular in Africa and the Caribbean.

Besides its Dublin brewery, Guinness in Ireland also owns ale and lager breweries at Kilkenny, Dundalk and Waterford.

Since it merged with United Distillers in 1986 and Grand Metropolitan in 1997 it has become one of the world's top drinks companies.

Below: Altogether, Guinness is brewed in 50 countries and is on sale in a further 100.

NUTRITIOUS AND DELICIOUS

Dublin's famous stout brewer Guinness was one of the first brewers to achieve international recognition. It had little choice, since it had already saturated its home market. By 1959, when the Irish brewer celebrated its bicentenary, 60% of production at its huge Dublin plant was for export.

Despite its huge success Guinness never ceased its search for new sales, and as a result its distinctive advertising campaigns have become well known the world over.

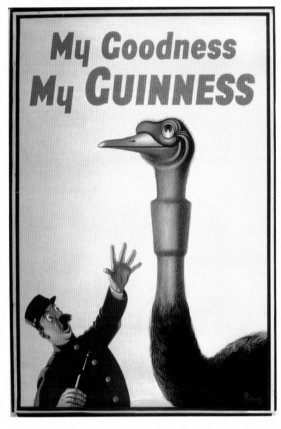

Above: The Guinness toucan. *Above: A drink to come home to.* *Above: A cartoon by H. Bateman and J. Gilroy.*

Above: Guinness has used several effective slogans but this one probably made the most lasting impact.

WALES

As you step from the train in the Welsh capital of Cardiff, you cannot miss the heady aroma of malt and hops drifting across the platform from Hancock's brewery behind the station and Brains old brewery in the city centre.

THE WELSH have a long brewing tradition. However, a chilling draught of takeovers and closures swept through the industry in the 1960s. Today, two English companies, Bass and Whitbread, dominate South Wales, alongside the family brewery, Brains of Cardiff. Further west, in Llanelli, another two breweries – Felinfoel and Crown Buckley – still operate, though in 1997 Brains took over Crown Buckley.

The Welsh beer trade was built in the 19th century on the raging thirst of miners and steelworkers who worked in the heavy industries of the valleys. At the same time, however, there was a strong temperance movement led by the powerful Methodist chapels of the area. Demon drink was top of the sin list during the religious revivals of the 19th century. At a temperance meeting in Tredegar in 1859, 7,000 signed the teetotal pledge. That summer the receipts of the local Rhymney brewery plunged by £500 a month.

The twin influences of heavy industry and temperance ensured that the typical Welsh ale was a low-gravity brew, relative to English beers. It was brewed for drinking in quantity. The two leading brands today, Allbright from Welsh Brewers (Bass) and Welsh Bitter from Whitbread, reflect this weak tradition: both are light-processed beers.

However, some tastier traditional brews still survive, notably Brains Dark and Worthington Dark.

When Welsh brewing recovered somewhat in the early 1980s, 20 new breweries frothed up to meet the demand for traditional cask ale. Most, however, found it difficult to establish a reliable trade and went rapidly to the brewhouse wall. The only survivors from this period are the Bullmastiff brewery in Cardiff and Plassey near Wrexham.

In the mid-1990s, a second wave of new ventures appeared, led by Dyffryn Clwyd of Denbigh, Cambrian of Dolgellau and Tomos Watkin of Llandeilo.

Above right: Roberts of Aberystwyth is one of the many breweries which have vanished.

Above: The Brains brewery of Cardiff has long kept the flag of cask-conditioned ales flying. It has only recently released its premium brew S-A in bottles.

THE BEERS

Allbright
This is the most popular beer in Wales. It is a standard, pale-amber keg bitter (3.2%), produced by Bass-owned Welsh Brewers in Cardiff.

Archdruid
This flavoursome ale (3.9%) is one of a range of beers from the small Dyffryn Clwyd brewery, located in the old, stone butter market in the centre of Denbigh.

Brains Bitter
This hoppy, golden-amber cask bitter (3.7%), is Brains' best-selling brew.

Brains Dark
This lightly hopped, dark mild (3.5%) is traditionally served with a creamy head. Brains Dark is a smooth brew that is less sweet than most beers of the dark mild type, a stronger (4%) processed version is sold as Dark Smooth.

Brenin
Crown Buckley's low-gravity keg bitter (3.4%) takes its name from the Welsh word for "king".

Brindle
A strong, tasty ale (5%), produced by the small Bullmastiff brewery.

Buckley's Best Bitter
This well-balanced bitter (3.7%) has a pleasing, hoppy character. It has been famous for generations in west Wales and is still Crown Buckley's best-selling brew. Buckley's Best Bitter is available in cask, keg and cans.

Bullmastiff Best Bitter
A malty, fruity beer (4%) brewed by Bullmastiff of Cardiff.

Cambrian Original
Hoppy, session bitter from the Cambrian brewery of Dolgellau. They also brew a malty Best Bitter (4.2%) and full-bodied Premium (4.8%).

CPA
Crown Pale Ale is the light-amber, refreshing bitter (3.4%) that was once known as "the champagne of the valleys", when it slaked the thirsts of the miners. It is brewed by Crown Buckley.

Cwrw Castell
The name of this beer (4.2%) means "Castle Bitter" in Welsh. It is produced by Dyffryn Clwyd.

Cwrw Tudno
This is Plassey's malty premium bitter (5%). "Tudno" is the patron saint of the seaside resort of Llandudno.

Dr Johnson's Draught
This traditional draught beer (3.6%) is one of the range from Dyffryn Clwyd.

Double Dragon
Felinfoel's famous full-bodied premium bitter (4.2%) won the Challenge cup for cask beer at the Brewers' Exhibition in London in 1976. A stronger version of the dark-amber, moderately malty, delicately hopped brew is bottled for export, mainly to the US.

Dragon's Breath
This is Plassey's fiery, spicy-flavoured, dark-amber winter warmer (6%).

Ebony Dark
This distinctive, rare cask ale (3.8%) comes from Bullmastiff in Cardiff.

Felinfoel Bitter
An amber, lightly hopped session bitter (3.2%) brewed using pale pipkin malt in the mash by the Felinfoel brewery.

Felinfoel Dark
This deep, dark beer (3.2%) is brewed using extra caramel to produce a slightly sweeter brew than the standard.

Gold Brew
This amber-coloured, tasty, cask ale (3.8%) is produced by the Bullmastiff brewery in Cardiff.

Hancock's HB
Hancock's HB is a malty, cask bitter (3.6%) from the Bass-owned Hancock's brewery in Cardiff.

Jolly Jack Tar Porter
This is Dyffryn Clwyd's dark, dry traditional porter (4.5%).

Main Street Bitter
This is the Pembroke brewery's fine, cask-conditioned bitter (4.1%).

Off the Rails
This strong beer (5.1%) is produced at the Pembroke brewery, for the free trade. It is available at the Station Inn at Pembroke Docks.

Old Nobbie Stout
A dark beer from the Pembroke brewery (4.8%). It is available for the free trade and at the Station Inn.

Pedwar Bawd
This strong ale (4.8%) comes from Dyffryn Clwyd of Denbigh. The name means "four thumbs". In 1994, it won the CAMRA accolade of "Welsh Beer of the Year".

Plassey Bitter
A straw-coloured beer (4%) with a fruity flavour from Plassey brewery.

Reverend James

Buckley's full-bodied, warming, spicy, fruity premium ale (4.5%) is named in honour of the Reverend James Buckley. A Methodist minister, Buckley combined saving souls with satisfying thirsts when he inherited the brewery in Llanelli from his father-in-law in the 1820s.

BRAGOT

Centuries ago, Welsh ale was a highly prized commodity throughout Britain. For example, when King Ine of Wessex in southern England drew up a law concerned with payments in kind received in return for land, some time between 690 and 693 AD, he decreed that for every ten hides of land, the food rent paid should include 12 ambers (an ancient liquid measurement) of Welsh ale.

Records of the Saxon period divide ale into three types – clear, mild and Welsh. Welsh ale, which was known as Bragawd or Bragot, was more highly valued than either clear or mild ale. It was recognized as a separate style, and did not necessarily have to be brewed in Wales. The savoury brew, which was flavoured with expensive spices and honey, was driven west by the invading Saxons, but then welcomed back into England by the new masters who greatly appreciated its heady flavour. In ancient Britain, Welsh ale was second only to mead, that other honey brew.

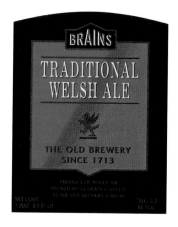

S-A

Brains' best-known beer is a dark-amber, malty, fruity premium bitter (4.2%) that is affectionately known as "Skull Attack" by Welsh drinkers. However, its name actually comes from the initials of the brewery's founder, Samuel Arthur Brain. S-A is exported to the United States under the name Traditional Welsh Ale.

SBB

Special Best Bitter (3.7%) is brewed by Crown Buckley in Llanelli. This rounded, mature, cask-conditioned bitter is particularly popular with beer drinkers in the Cynon valley.

Son of a Bitch

This full-bodied and dangerously drinkable ale is the strongest, regularly brewed, cask beer in Wales (6%). It comes from Bullmastiff of Cardiff.

Watkin BB

A malty bitter (4%) from Tomos Watkin of Llandeilo.

Watkin OSB

A slightly stronger old style bitter (4.5%) from Watkin.

Welsh Bitter

Whitbread's well-known weak keg bitter (3.2%) from its vast plant at Magor.

Worthington Dark

Welsh Brewers' dark-ruby, creamy mild (3%), named after the famous Burton brewers. It is popular in the Swansea area.

Worthington Draught

A smooth, creamy bitter (3.6%) from Welsh Brewers with subtle bitterness and pear-and-peach aroma.

THE BREWERS

Brains

This traditional family brewery has been operating in Cardiff since 1882. The brewery is famous for its slogan "It's Brains you want". It produces three cask ales for its 189 pubs.

Bullmastiff

Bob Jenkins founded this colourful brewery in 1987, and named it in honour of his pet dogs. Now located in Cardiff, this small brewery produces distinctive but hard-to-find cask beers, including Gold Brew and Ebony Dark, Best Bitter, Brindle and the infamous Son of a Bitch.

Above: The Williams brothers toast the success of their fledgling Cambrian brewery.

Cambrian

Brothers Kevin and Keith Williams set up the only brewery in north-west Wales in 1996, to serve the mountainous Snowdonia National Park. Based in Dolgellau, the small brewery produces Cambrian Original, Best Bitter, Premium and Mountain Ale, as well as various seasonal brews.

Crown Buckley

Buckley's brewery in Llanelli claims to be the oldest in Wales, dating back to 1767. Crown brewery, which was previously D.T. Jenkins of Pontyclun, has been rolling out barrels as Crown since 1919. D.T. Jenkins became Crown when the local clubs banded together to buy their own brewery in an attempt to overcome shortages of beer caused by rationing. In 1989 Crown and Buckley merged, and the

brewing was then concentrated at the former Buckley site in Llanelli. The old Crown site is used for bottling and kegging. In 1997 the company was taken over by Brains of Cardiff and is now known as Brain Crown Buckley.

Above: Vans load up with barrels of Brains for the pubs (c. 1930).

Dyffryn Clwyd

A small brewery located in the old, stone butter market in the centre of Denbigh.

Felinfoel

This village brewery, situated just outside Llanelli, is one of only two surviving breweries in west Wales. In 1935, it became the first brewery to can beer in Europe, in an effort to help the local tinplate industry during the Depression. Felinfoel is best known for its robust and patriotically named Double Dragon ale (a red dragon is the symbol of Wales). It also brews a fine bitter and a tasty dark (both 3.2%) for its 85 pubs.

Hancock's

William Hancock took over North and Low's Bute Dock brewery in Cardiff in 1883. From there the company expanded by taking over several other breweries around South Wales, until eventually it could easily claim to be the largest brewer in Wales. When this regional force was taken over by the English giant Bass in 1968, Welsh Brewers was born through a merger of Hancock's with Webb's of Aberbeg and Fernvale of the Rhondda. Today only Hancock's Brewery in Cardiff remains.

Pembroke

David Lightley set up this small brewery in 1994, in converted stables behind his 18th-century guest house. Pembroke mainly supplies his pub, the Station Inn, on the railway platform at Pembroke Docks. Beers produced include a rare cask-conditioned lager (4.1%).

Plassey

This small brewery was set up in a caravan site at Eyton in 1985. Plassey produces a hoppy Plassey bitter (4%), a dry stout (4.6%) and two stronger ales for the three bars on the caravan site, as well as for the local free trade.

Watkin

Tomos Watkin and Sons is named after a former Llandovery brewery. It was established in 1995 in Llandeilo in south-west Wales by Simon Buckley, a member of the famous Buckley brewing family. The plant produces two cask beers: Watkin's Brewery Bitter and Watkin's Old Style Bitter. Watkin has ambitious plans to expand to larger premises and to build up a pub estate.

Welsh Brewers

Bass's South Wales subsidiary is based in Cardiff.

Whitbread

This famous company is England's third largest brewing group. It has a weighty presence in Wales through its huge plant at Magor. As well as the best-selling Welsh Bitter, it also brews many foreign beers at the plant for the Welsh market.

Below: Tin plating was a traditional industry of West Wales. Its decline prompted Felinfoel to adopt beer in cans more readily than most in a bid to boost the tin industry and the pockets of its local drinkers.

HOME-BREW PUBS

Wales has four pubs that brew their own beers:

• The Joiners Arms, Bishopston. The Swansea Brewing Co. was set up behind this pub in 1996. The main beer is Bishopswood Bitter.

• The Nag's Head, Abercych, near Newcastle Emlyn, is a restored old smithy producing Old Emrys (4.1%).

• The Red Lion, Llanidloes, Powys, brews Blind Cobbler's Thumb (4.2%), Witches' Brew (7.5%) and, at Christmas, the powerful barley wine Blind Cobbler's Last (10.5%).

• The Tynllidiart Arms, Capel Bangor, near Aberystwyth, is a cottage brewpub that produces Rheidol Reserve (4.5%).

WREXHAM LAGER

Wrexham was once the centre of beer making in Wales, as its springs provided ideal water for brewing. The town boasted 19 breweries, and its beers were famous across Britain. The last of the Wrexham ale breweries, Border, closed in 1984 – but one unique concern remains.

German and Czech immigrants established the Wrexham Lager Beer Company in 1882. When it first began brewing, it claimed to be the first lager brewery in Britain. Much of its early production was shipped abroad, particularly by the army.

Burton brewer Ind Coope took over Wrexham in 1949, and it switched to producing foreign lagers under licence. It was the first brewery in Britain to brew American Budweiser. It still brews a light Wrexham lager for the local trade and occasional export.

Below and above: The Wrexham brewery struggled to convert Britain's ale drinkers with its lager beer.

ENGLAND

In the first half of the 20th century, the main beer in England was mild, the worker's drink. Since the Second World War mild has been replaced by another top-fermenting ale, the stronger, more heavily hopped bitter.

DESPITE THE FACT that the golden tide of lager has washed over the shores of England, in the shape of imitations of the Pilsner style from overseas, ales are still very popular and account for around half the market.

No country in the world drinks more. Ale, which varies in colour from pale gold through to dark ruby, is a social drink, usually of modest strength, from 3.5 to 4.5% alcohol by volume. It is brewed for drinking in quantity (usually in pints or halves) in company.

To find the native beers of England, walk into an English pub (public house) where the bulk of beer is still enjoyed on draught, served over the bar usually from a tall handpump, rather than being bought in a bottle or a can in a shop or supermarket and drunk at home. Traditional English beer is cask-conditioned – it is a living beer which continues to ferment and mature in the cask in the pub cellar after leaving the brewery. This allows the beer's flavour to develop fully.

English beer has a reputation for being "warm", but though it should not be heavily chilled, like lagers, it should always be served cellar cool.

In the 1960s the major breweries in England tried to replace cask beer with easier-to-handle keg beer, which was filtered and pasteurized at the brewery (to make it easier to store), then served chilled and carbonated at the bar. But the beer drinkers of England rose in revolt. Many objected to losing their traditional local tastes. They wanted cask beer's fuller flavour. A campaign was launched in the early 1970s called CAMRA – the Campaign for Real Ale. It sparked a major revival of cask beer. As a result around 55 traditional local and regional breweries have survived, and some of the national companies have relaunched their own cask beers. CAMRA began a brewing revolution, and following that hundreds of new breweries have been set up since the 1970s, some reviving old styles of ale such as porter.

Above: English beer is brewed to be drunk in quantity. Stronger ales such as Fuller's 1845 are for special occasions.

THE BEERS

Abbot Ale

This robust, bright-amber, fruity premium bitter (5%) from Greene King is named after the last abbot of Bury St Edmunds in East Anglia – the brewer's home town.

Adnams Bitter

Adnams bitter is a dark-gold classic of its type (3.7%), with a hoppy, orangey flavour. Adnams also brews a smooth, malty, dark mild (3.2%), Regatta Ale (4.3%), a light summer ale, and its Extra, a pleasant best bitter with a dry, hoppy flavour, was voted Champion Beer of Britain in 1993.

AK

This long-established and popular ale (3.7%), produced by McMullens of Hertford, is a refreshingly light bitter.

Amazon Bitter

Additive-free beer (4%) from the Masons Arms brewpub, Cartmel Fell, Cumbria.

Ansells Mild

A liquorice-tasting, dark mild (3.4%) brewed by Ind Coope at Burton-on-Trent.

A Pint-a Bitter

A tasty, cask-conditioned bitter (3.5%) from the Hogs Back brewery in Surrey. Also known as APB.

Archers Best

A malty, fruity bitter from Archers of Swindon.

Arthur Pendragon

A full-bodied, fruity, premium ale (4.8%) from the Hampshire brewery in Andover, Hampshire.

Arundel Best Bitter

This gold-coloured, additive-free bitter (4%) is produced by Arundel of Sussex.

Badger

The popular name for a range of beers by the historic Hall and Woodhouse brewery in Blandford Forum, Dorset.

Ballard's Best

Copper-coloured malty ale from the Sussex country brewery, Ballard's of Nyewood.

Banks's Ale

A reddish-amber mild (3.5%), made with Maris Otter malt, Fuggles and Golding hops and caramel.

Banks's Bitter

A bittersweet, crisp bitter (3.8%) from Banks's brewery in Wolverhampton.

Banner Bitter

A flavoursome, light-brown bitter (4%) from the Butterknowle brewery in Bishop Auckland.

Barn Owl Bitter

A darkish-brown, fruity, rich bitter (4.5%) from the Cotleigh brewery, Somerset.

Batham's Best

Sweetish, golden bitter (4.3%) from the famous Black Country brewery, Batham's, of Brierley Hill.

Battleaxe

A smooth, slightly sweet cask beer (4.2%) from the Rudgate brewery, near York.

Beacon Bitter

A refreshing bitter (3.8%) brewed by Everard in Narborough, near Leicester.

Beast

A potent winter brew (6.6%) from the Exmoor brewery in Wiveliscombe, Somerset.

Beaumanor Bitter

This light-brown, strong-tasting bitter (3.7%) is brewed by the Hoskins brewery in Leicester.

Beechwood

A full-bodied draught beer (4.3%) with a nutty character from the Chiltern brewery.

Benchmark

A pleasantly bitter, malty ale (3.5%) produced by Bunces brewery, Wiltshire.

Bishops Ale

A potent, full-flavoured, warming barley wine (8%) from Ridleys brewery near Chelmsford.

Bishops Finger

A ruby-red ale (5.4%) with a fruity flavour and a malty aftertaste from the Shepherd Neame brewery in Kent.

Black Diamond

A dark-ruby-coloured, rich, malty bitter (4.8%) from the Butterknowle brewery in Bishop Auckland.

Black Jack Porter

A rich, black, winter beer (4.6%) with a fruity, sweetish flavour, from Archers in Swindon, Wiltshire.

Black Magic

Bitter stout (4.5%) from Oakhill brewery of Somerset.

Black Rock

A strong ale (5.5%) from the Brewery-on-Sea, Lancing, Sussex.

Black Sheep Best

A hoppy bitter (3.8%) fermented in traditional Yorkshire stone squares at the Black Sheep brewery, Masham, North Yorkshire.

Bishop's Tipple, The

A strong, rich, deep-amber barley wine (6.5%) with a sweet and smokey, complex flavour brewed within view of the city's towering cathedral spire by Gibbs Mew of Salisbury.

Black Adder

This dark stout (5.3%) with a roast-malt character, from the Mauldon brewery, was voted Champion Beer of Britain in 1991.

Black Cat Mild

A dark, full-tasting cask bitter (3.2%) from the Moorhouse brewery, Lancashire.

Black Sheep Special

A full, amber ale (4.4%) brewed in traditional stone squares. It is sold bottled as Black Sheep Ale.

Blunderbus

An intense porter (5.5%) from the Coach House brewery in Warrington.

Boddingtons

A straw-coloured brew (3.8%) from this famous Manchester brewery. It was once worshipped for its parch-dry bitterness, but it now has a smoother flavour.

Bodgers

A bottle-conditioned barley wine (8%) from the Chiltern brewery, near Aylesbury.

Bombardier

A mild, smoky, malty cask beer (4.3%) from the Charles Wells brewery in Bedford.

Boro Best

A full-bodied cask beer (4%) from the North Yorkshire brewery in Middlesborough.

Bosun Bitter

This smooth, amber, cask beer (4.6%) has a strong malt flavour. Brewed by the Poole brewery, Dorset.

Bosun's Bitter

A refreshing, amber cask bitter (3.1%) with a bitter, hops taste from the St Austell brewery, Cornwall.

Brakspear Bitter

A well-hopped, aromatic light bitter (3.4%) produced by this Oxfordshire brewery.

Brakspear Special

A golden-brown, malty, dry bitter (4.3%).

Brand Oak Bitter

This well-balanced cask beer (4%) has a dry finish and a citrus, sweet flavour. It is brewed by the Wickwar brewery in Gloucestershire.

Branoc

An amber bitter (3.8%) brewed by Branscombe Vale in Devon using the local spring water.

Brew XI

A sweetish, malty cask bitter (3.8%) from the Mitchells & Butlers brewery in Birmingham.

Brew 97

A full-bodied, malty cask beer (5%) with a good hops taste, from the Moles brewery, Wiltshire.

Brewer's Droop
A strong ale (5%) available on draught and in bottles from the Marston Moor brewery, North Yorkshire.

Brewer's Pride
An amber, light, refreshing, fruity cask bitter (4.2%) from the Marston Moor brewery, North Yorkshire.

Bridge Bitter
A fruity, hoppy bitter (4.2%), brewed by Burton Bridge in Burton-on-Trent.

Bristol Stout
A tasty, seasonal stout (4.7%) from the Smiles brewery, Bristol. It has a red-brown hue and a pleasant roast malt taste.

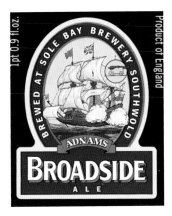

Broadside Ale
Adnams' strong garnet-coloured, bitter, hoppy ale (4.7%) was brewed to mark the 300th anniversary of the battle of Sole Bay in 1672. The ale in its bottle version (6.3%) packs more cannon fire than the draught beer.

Buccaneer
A light, pale gold bitter with a sweet malty taste (5.2%) brewed by Burtonwood.

Bullion
Fruity dark ale (4.7%) from the Old Mill brewery, Snaith, Yorkshire.

Bulldog Pale Ale
A strong, yellow-coloured, hoppy, bottled pale ale (6.3%), produced by Courage in Bristol.

Bunce's Best Bitter
This aromatic, fresh and fruity bitter (4.1%) is brewed in a watermill in Netheravon, Wiltshire.

Burton Porter
This tawny-brown, dry porter (4.5%) has a light, malty taste. It is also available as a bottle-conditioned beer. Brewed by the Burton Bridge brewery in Burton-on-Trent.

Burtonwood Bitter
A smooth, smoky-tasting bitter (3.7%), brewed near Warrington at the Burtonwood brewery.

Butcombe Bitter
A dry, hoppy bitter (4%) brewed near Bristol in the Mendip Hills.

Buzz
A cask beer primed with honey (4.5%) produced by the Brewery-on-Sea, Lancing, Sussex.

Cains Bitter
A dry, spicy, amber bitter (4%) from this popular Merseyside brewery in Liverpool.

Cambridge Bitter
A traditionally brewed, amber, hoppy bitter (3.8%) from the Elgood brewery in the Fens at Wisbech.

Camerons Bitter
An orange-coloured, light, malty bitter (3.6%) from the Hartlepool brewer, which is very popular with the local workers.

Carling Black Label
This smooth, sweet lager (4.1%) is Britain's best-selling beer. It was introduced to England from Canada in 1953 and was adopted by Bass as its leading lager brand.

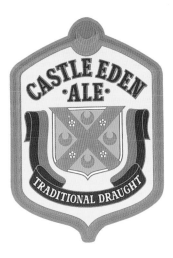

Castle Eden Ale
An amber-coloured, sweet, malty ale (3.8%) from the Durham-based brewery owned by Whitbread.

Castle Special Pale Ale
One of a range of bottled beers (5%) from the McMullen brewery in Hertford.

Challenger
A premium bitter (4.1%), which despite carrying the name of a hop, has a fruity, malty flavour. It is brewed by the Ash Vine brewery, Trudoxhill, Somerset.

Chiltern Ale
A tangy, light draught beer (3.7%) from the Chiltern brewery of Terrick.

Chiswick Bitter
This refreshing bitter (3.5%) with a subtle, floral, smoky flavour, from Fullers of London, is much acclaimed.

Coachman's Best
A medium-coloured full-bodied bitter (3.7%) with a hoppy, fruity flavour, from the Coach House brewery in Warrington.

Cocker Hoop
A golden, refreshing bitter (4.8%) with a hoppy, fruity flavour, from the independent Jennings brewery in the Lake District.

College Ale
A strong seasonal, winter cask ale (7.4%) from the Morrells brewery, Oxford.

Conciliation
This dark, tawny-brown bitter (4.3%) has a good, hoppy taste. It is the flagship brew of the Butterknowle brewery in Bishop Auckland, County Durham.

Coopers WPA
A popular, refreshing, yellow-gold cask beer (3.5%) with a hoppy, citrus tang, which comes from the Wickwar brewery in Gloucestershire.

Country Best Bitter
A full and fruity, clean-tasting bitter (4.3%) from the McMullen brewery in Hertford.

Country Stile
A mid-brown draught beer (4.1%), produced by Daleside brewery in Harrogate, Yorkshire.

Courage Best
A traditional golden-brown, malty, dry cask bitter (4%) brewed in Bristol by Courage.

Craftsman
A hoppy, gold, premium ale (4.2%) from Thwaites brewery in Blackburn, Lancashire.

Cromwell Bitter
A gold, fruity cask bitter (3.6%) from the Marston Moor brewery, North Yorkshire.

Cumberland Ale
A gold-coloured bitter (4%) with a delicate flavour, from the Jennings brewery in Cockermouth in the Lake District.

Daredevil Winter Warmer
A smooth, fruity brew (7.1%) with a strong, mature flavour, produced by Everards in Narborough, near Leicester.

Deacon
A pale-gold, orangey, dry bitter (5%) from the Gibbs Mews brewery in Salisbury, Wiltshire.

Deep Shaft Stout
This black stout (6.2%) produced by the Freeminer brewery, Gloucestershire, has a roast-malt flavour.

Devon Gold
A straw-coloured, fruity, summer brew (4.1%) from Blackawton in South Devon.

Director's
A traditional dark, rich, cask bitter (4.8%) brewed in Bristol by Courage.

Dolphin Best
This dry, amber, cask bitter (3.8%) is brewed by the Poole brewery, Dorset.

Dorset Best
Also known as Badger Best Bitter (4.1%). This Hall and Woodhouse cask ale has a bitter hop and fruit flavour.

Double Chance
A malty bitter (3.8%) from the Malton brewery of North Yorkshire.

Double Diamond
Ind Coope's famous dark-amber bottled pale ale from Burton-on-Trent, which after a period of promotion as a weak keg beer, has seen its reputation restored as a bottled ale (4%), particularly in the stronger export version (5.2%). Also occasionally available as a cask beer.

Double Maxim
A classic, strong, amber-coloured brown ale (4.7%) with a smooth, fruity taste from the giant Vaux brewery.

Double Stout
An old-fashioned stout (4.8%), revived in 1996 after 79 years by the Hook Norton brewery in Banbury.

Dragonslayer
A yellowish real ale (4.5%) with a dry malt and hops flavour, from B&T, Bedfordshire.

Draught Bass
A superb bitter (4.4%) with a malty flavour and light hop bitterness. This is the biggest-selling premium ale in the country.

Draught Burton Ale
A full-bodied ale (4.8%) from the Carlsberg-Tetley brewery in Burton-on-Trent.

Drawwell Bitter
A cask beer (3.9%) from the Hanby brewery in Shropshire.

Eagle IPA
A sweet, malty, amber-coloured cask beer (3.6%) from the Charles Wells brewery in Bedford.

Eden Bitter
A smooth, sweet bitter (3.6%) from the Castle Eden brewery in County Durham.

Edmund II Ironside
A tasty, cask-conditioned bitter (4.2%) from the Hampshire brewery in Andover.

Elizabethan
A golden, barley wine (8.1%) originally brewed to mark the Queen's coronation in 1953 by Harveys brewery.

Enville Ale
One of a range of honey beers produced by the Enville Farm brewery in Staffordshire. The pale-gold ale (4.5%) is primed with honey after a rapid initial fermentation and then lagered. The brewery uses its own honey and barley.

Enville White
A golden wheat beer (4%) with a clean, sweet flavour from Enville Farm brewery.

ESB
The revered Extra Special Bitter (5.5%) from Fuller's of London is much stronger than most bitters. It has great character with a complex malt, fruit and hops flavour and has won the Champion Beer of Britain title an unprecedented three times.

ESX Best
A fruity cask bitter (4.3%) produced by Ridleys brewery, near Chelmsford, Essex.

Everard Mild
A dark mild (3.3%) which forms an unusually large head when it is poured. It is brewed in Narborough, near Leicester by Everard.

Exmoor Ale
This pale-brown, malty bitter (3.8%), from the Exmoor brewery in Wiveliscombe, Somerset, won the best bitter award at the Great British Beer Festival in 1980.

Exmoor Gold
An amber bitter (4.5%) from the Exmoor brewery.

Fargo
A rich, amber-coloured cask ale (5%) with a soft hop and roast-malt taste, from the Wells brewery in Bedford.

Farmer's Glory
A dark, fruity premium bitter (4.5%) from Wadworth's of Devizes, Wiltshire.

Fed Special
This bright, pale-amber, filtered bitter (4%) is brewed for the working men's clubs by the Federation Brewery in the north-east of England.

Festive
A fruity premium ale (5%) from the King & Barnes brewery, Horsham, Sussex.

Flowers IPA
A coppery-coloured, creamy pale ale (3.6%) produced by Whitbread in Cheltenham.

Flowers Original
A tasty bitter (4.5%) with a good malt and hop balance, produced by Whitbread in Cheltenham, Gloucestershire.

Flying Herbert
This red, refreshing, malty cask bitter is from the North Yorkshire brewery.

Formidable Ale
Strong golden-coloured ale (5%) with a full taste from Cains brewery, Liverpool.

Fortyniner
A well-balanced, fruity bitter (4.8%) from the Ringwood brewery, Hampshire.

Founders
A pale-brown bitter (4.5%) with a slight citrus and sweet-malt taste, from the Ushers brewery in Wiltshire.

Franklin's Bitter
A distinctive floral, aromatic, hoppy bitter (3.8%) brewed in Harrogate, Yorkshire.

Freedom Pilsener
This fresh, slightly fruity Pilsner (5.4%) is brewed by the Freedom brewery in Fulham, London.

Freeminer Bitter
A pale, hoppy bitter (4%) from the Forest of Dean, Gloucestershire.

Fuggles Imperial
A pale, strong, premium bitter (5.5%) from Whitbread's Castle Eden brewery, County Durham.

Gargoyle
A tasty cask bitter (5%) from the Lichfield brewery in the Midlands.

GB Mild
A smooth, malty, fruity brew (3.5%) brewed by the Lees family brewery in north Manchester.

Georges Bitter Ale
A light, refreshing bitter (3.3%) from the Courage brewery which was formerly Georges, in Bristol.

Gingersnap
A dark, orangey-coloured wheat beer (4.7%), brewed with fresh root ginger from the Salopian brewery, Shrewsbury.

Ginger Tom
A ginger-flavoured ale (5.2%) from the Hoskins & Oldfield brewery, Leicester.

Gladstone
A refreshing, smooth bitter (4.3%) from the McMullen brewery, Hertford.

Golden Best
A fine mild (3.5%) from the Timothy Taylor brewery, Keighley, Yorkshire.

Golden Bitter
A fruity bitter (4.7%) from Archers in Swindon.

Golden Brew
A golden, aromatic, bitter (3.8%) from the Smiles brewery, Bristol.

Gold Label
England's best-known bottled barley wine. This spicy, warming brew (10.9%) is produced by Whitbread.

Gothic Ale
A dark ale (5.2%) from the Enville Farm brewery, Staffordshire.

Governor
An amber bitter (4.4%) from the Hull brewery.

Graduate
A roasted-malt-flavoured premium bitter (5.2%) from the Morrells brewery, Oxford.

Granary Bitter
An amber-coloured brew with a bitter, fruity character (3.8%), from the Reepham brewery near Norwich.

GSB
A dry, fruity bitter (5.2%) from the Elgood brewery near Wisbech.

Gunpowder
A liquorice-black mild (3.8%) from the Coach House brewery, Warrington.

Hammerhead
A robust, strong, rich, malty ale (5.6%) brewed by Clark's of Wakefield, West Yorkshire.

Harrier S.P.A
A light-brown bitter (3.6%) with a light, hoppy taste, from the Cotleigh brewery, Somerset.

Harvest Ale
A staggeringly strong bottled ale (11.5%) that is produced each year from the new season's malt and hops by the Lees brewery in Manchester. This vintage brew can be laid down to mature in the cellar for several years.

Harveys Christmas Ale
A strong warming ale produced annually by the Harveys brewery, Lewes, Sussex.

Harveys Firecracker
This brew was bottled in honour of the emergency services who fought a disastrous fire at the Harveys brewery in 1996. It is a strong, dark pale ale with a smoky flavour (5.8%).

Harveys Sussex Best Bitter
A golden, hoppy bitter (4%) from Harveys of Lewes.

Harveys Sussex Pale Ale
A light, hoppy ale (3.5%) from the Harveys brewery.

Harveys Tom Paine
A strong pale ale (5.5%), from Harveys brewery.

Hatters
A fine, light mild (3.3%) from the Robinson's brewery, Stockport.

Headstrong
A fruity bitter (5.2%) from the Blackawton brewery in Devon.

Heritage
A full-bodied beer (5.2%) with a roast-malt, fruity flavour from the Smiles brewery, Bristol.

Hersbrucker Weizenbier
A light wheat beer (3.6%) from the Springhead brewery, Nottinghamshire.

Hick's Special Draught
Also known as HSD, this full-bodied, fruity cask bitter (5%) is produced by the St Austell brewery, Cornwall.

High Force
A complex, smooth beer (6.2%) with a sweet, malt flavour, from the Butterknowle brewery in Bishop Auckland.

Highgate Dark Mild
A dark-brown, smooth mild (3.2%) produced in this Victorian tower brewery in Walsall, West Midlands. It is fermented using a vigorous four-strain yeast to give a complex flavour.

Highgate Old Ale
A dark, red-brown, fruity ale (5.6%) with a complex flavour, brewed in winter by this Walsall brewery.

High Level
This sweet and fruity, bright, filtered brown ale (4.7%) is brewed for the working men's clubs by the Federation Brewery in the north-east of England. It is named after the bridge in Newcastle which crosses the River Tyne.

Hobgoblin
A robust, red ale (5.5%) sold in the cask and bottle in Britain and also in Europe and North America. It is produced by the Wychwood brewery, Oxfordshire.

Holden's Black Country Special Bitter
A sweetish, full-bodied bitter (5.1%) from Holden's brewery in Woodsetton in the West Midlands.

Holt's Bitter
This uncompromising dry bitter (4%) is sold at a relatively low price and still supplied in huge hogsheads (54-gallon casks) by Holt's brewery of Manchester.

Hook Norton Best Bitter
A dry, hoppy, cask-conditioned beer (3.4%) from this old Oxfordshire village brewery.

Hop and Glory
Complex bottle-conditioned beer (5%) from Ash Vine brewery, Somerset.

HSB
Famous, full-bodied bitter (4.8%) from Gale's of Horndean, Hampshire.

Imperial Russian Stout
A classic beer from Scottish Courage, the dark-brown, smooth brew (10%) has a rich malty flavour.

Indiana's Bones
A rich, dark, cask ale (5.6%) which is sold both as a cask beer and a bottled brew, from the Summerskills brewery, South Devon.

Innkeeper's Special
This smooth, malty brew (4.5%) has a rich, ruby-port hue and a crisp, hop taste. It is produced by the Coach House brewery in Warrington.

Inspired
A dark, malty cask bitter (4%) from the small Lichfield brewery.

Ironbridge Stout
A dark, rich stout (5%) from the Salopian brewery, Shrewsbury.

Jennings Bitter
A light, dry malty bitter (3.5%) from Jennings brewery in Cumbria.

John Smith's Bitter
A dark-amber, sweet, malty cask bitter (3.8%) with a creamy texture, from Yorkshire. One of the most popular beers in England.

Kimberley Classic
A light-coloured premium bitter (4.8%) with a dry, hoppy taste, from Hardys & Hansons brewery, Nottinghamshire.

King Alfred's
A hoppy cask beer (3.8%) from the Hampshire brewery.

Kingsdown Ale
This powerful, fruity, draught beer (5%) is produced by the Arkell's Kingsdown brewery, Swindon.

Lancaster Bomber
A straw-coloured cask ale (4.4%) from the Mitchell brewery in Lancaster.

Landlord
A classic, amber-coloured, premium bitter (4.3%) with a buttery flavour, from Timothy Taylor's brewery in Keighley, Yorkshire. It won the Champion Beer of Britain award in 1994.

Larkins Best Bitter
A full-bodied, fruity bitter (4.4%) from this Kent brewery.

London Pride
Fuller's fine, deep-red best bitter (4.1%) has a rich, dry, malty, hoppy taste.

Lynesack Porter
This is very dark, even for a porter (5%) with a sweet, malty finish. It is produced by the Butterknowle brewery in Bishop Auckland.

Mackeson's Stout
England's best-known bottled sweet stout (3%) from Whitbread is a blackish colour with a sugary, fruity taste. It was originally brewed by the firm of Mackeson in Hythe, Kent, in 1907. At that time it was claimed to be a tonic for invalids because it contained milk sugar or lactose. The sugar does not ferment, so the beer is low in alcohol.

Mackeson's was called milk stout until the British Government banned the term in 1946. However, Whitbread continues the connection through a milk churn on the label. It is still the leading brand in a declining sweet stout market and was once exported to 60 countries, and brewed under licence in Belgium, Jamaica, New Zealand and Singapore.

Above: A 1950s advertisement for Mackeson's before the British Government banned the term "milk stout" as misleading.

Magnet

A nutty-tasting premium bitter from the John Smith's brewery, Tadcaster, North Yorkshire.

Malt and Hops

A lively, seasonal ale (4.5%) made by Wadworth's, in Devizes, Wiltshire. It is one of a range of seasonal brews made using the new season's unkilned fresh hops.

M&B Mild

A reddish, full-bodied cask mild (3.2%) from Mitchells & Butlers brewery in Birmingham.

Mann's Original

England's best-known bottled, sweet brown ale (2.8%) has a sticky, sugary texture and a fruity taste, and is now brewed by Ushers in Wiltshire.

Mansfield Bitter

This refreshing, sweetish bitter (3.9%) is brewed using traditional Yorkshire squares by the Mansfield brewery, Nottinghamshire.

Marston's Bitter

A light-brown, hoppy cask bitter (3.8%) from Marston's brewery, Burton-on-Trent.

Mauldon Special

A very hoppy cask beer (4.2%) from the Mauldon brewery in Suffolk.

Millennium Gold

This fruity, amber, cask beer (4.2%) is produced by Crouch Vale brewery, Essex.

Ministerley Ale

A complex, pale, cask bitter (4.5%) from the Salopian brewery, Shrewsbury.

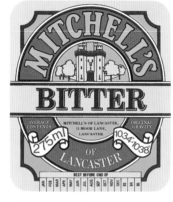

Mitchell's Bitter

An amber-coloured, mild-tasting, hoppy bitter (3.8%) from Mitchell's of Lancaster.

Moles Best

A fruity cask bitter (4%), the leading beer from the Moles brewery, Wiltshire.

Monkey Wrench

A smooth, dark, sweetish, potent beer (5.3%) which is produced by Daleside brewery in the spa town of Harrogate, Yorkshire.

COMMEMORATIVE BEERS

Brewers often make one-off brews to commemorate special occasions. Harveys of Lewes in Sussex, for example, bottled a special strong pale ale, called Firecracker, in honour of the emergency services who fought to save it from disaster when a fire broke out in the brewery in 1996. Many brewers bottled ales to keep for the Queen's Coronation in 1953 and later royal marriages.

Moonraker

A rich, strong, orangey ale (7.5%) from the J.W. Lees brewery, Manchester.

Morocco Ale

This dark, rich, spicy bottled ale (5.5%) is said to be based on a 300-year-old recipe. It is produced by the Daleside brewery, Harrogate, Yorkshire.

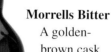

Morrells Bitter

A golden-brown cask bitter (3.7%) from the Morrells brewery in the university town of Oxford.

Mutiny

A reddish, full-bodied cask ale (4.5%) from the Rebellion brewery, Buckinghamshire.

Natterjack

An aromatic, golden ale (4.8%), named after the natterjack toad, produced by the Frog Island brewery, Northampton.

Newcastle Amber

This less-well-known cousin of Newcastle Brown was introduced in 1951 as a lighter version. It has a malty, sugary taste.

Newcastle Brown

This pioneering northern brown ale (4.7%) has a nutty, caramel taste. It was first produced by Newcastle Breweries in 1927. Newcastle Brown is strong, dry and light in colour. Drinkers usually expect a small glass so they can keep topping up. This best-selling bottled beer is exported to more than 40 countries. It is now brewed by Scottish Courage on Tyneside.

Nightmare Porter

A smooth, dry porter (5%) with a roast-malt and liquorice taste from the Hambleton brewery near Thirsk, North Yorkshire.

Noel Ale

A Christmas ale (5.5%) from the Arkell's Kingsdown Brewery, Swindon.

Norfolk Nog

The 1992 Champion Beer of Britain. This tasty old ale (4.6%) is produced by Woodforde's of Norfolk.

Norman's Conquest

A dark, strong ale (7%) from the Cottage brewery in West Lydford, Somerset. It won the Champion Beer of Britain title at the Great British Beer Festival in 1993.

North Brink Porter

A special, reddish-black winter beer (5%) from the Elgood brewery in Wisbech.

Nut Brown

A nut-brown ale with a nutty, sweet flavour (4.5%) from the Whitby brewery, North Yorkshire.

OBJ

An intense, fruity, winter ale (5%) produced by the Brakspear brewery.

Old Baily

A copper-coloured, fruity, malty bitter (4.8%) from the Mansfield brewery in Nottinghamshire.

Old Bircham

An amber, sweet, malty winter beer (4.6%) from the Reepham brewery, near Norwich.

Old Bob

A dark-amber strong bottled pale ale (5.1%) from Ridleys brewery.

Old Brewery Bitter

A malty, nutty cask bitter (4%) from Samuel Smith's who also brew a distinctive orangey-coloured bottled pale ale (5%).

Old Buzzard

This winter beer (4.8%) is almost black. It has a smooth, rich flavour and is produced by the Cotleigh brewery, Somerset.

Old Ebenezer

A dark, tawny-coloured, rich ale (8%) from Butterknowle brewery in Bishop Auckland, County Durham.

Old Expensive

A strong, fruity winter barley wine (6.7%) brewed by Burton Bridge in Burton-on-Trent.

Old Growler

A complex porter (5.5%) with a sweet fruit and malt taste and chocolatey character, which comes from the Nethergate brewery, Suffolk.

Old Hooky

A strong, reddish-brown beer (4.6%) with a honey, orange and malt flavour. This cask brew is produced by the Hook Norton brewery in Oxfordshire.

Old Knucker

An additive-free rich, dark old ale (5.5%) from the Arundel brewery, Sussex.

Old Masters

A dry, tawny bitter (4.6%), brewed by Morland's of Abingdon.

Old Mill Mild

A dark-red, malty mild (3.5%) from the Old Mill brewery, Snaith, Yorkshire.

Old Nick

A devil of a bottled barley wine (6.9%) with a dark-reddish-brown hue and a pungent, but mellow, fruity flavour from Young's.

Old Original

A premium bitter (5.2%) with a strong, rich, malty character from Everard.

Old Peculier

Theakston's famous, rich, dark old ale (5.7%) with a roast-malt flavour, comes from Masham, North Yorkshire.

The odd name refers to the Peculier of Masham, the town's ancient ecclesiastical court.

Old Smokey

A warming, malty dark ale (5%) with a slightly bitter, liquorice taste, brewed by Bunces brewery, Wiltshire.

Old Speckled Hen

A deep-gold, premium pale ale (5.2%) with a good malt, hop balance from Morland's of Abingdon, Oxfordshire. It is named not after a farmyard fowl, but an old MG car made in the town which was speckled black and gold.

Old Spot Prize Ale

A reddish, fruity cask ale (5%) from the Uley brewery in Gloucestershire. The spent grains from brewing go to a local pig herd, and the ales have retained the porky connection. Others include Hogshead, Pig's Ear and Severn Boar.

Old Stockport Bitter

A malty, fruity cask bitter (3.5%) from Robinson's brewery, Stockport.

Old Thumper

A pale-coloured, strong ale (5.8%) with a rounded grain and hops flavour, from Ringwood, Hampshire.

Old Tom

Robinson's rich, fruity, barley wine (8.5%) from Stockport, Cheshire, was originally named after the brewery cat. It was first brewed in 1899.

Olde Merryford Ale

A light-brown, full-bodied, sweet bitter (4.8%), with a good malt and hop balance, from the Wickwar brewery in Gloucestershire.

Olde Stoker

A dark-brown, smooth winter bitter (5.4%) from the Branscombe Vale brewery, Devon.

Original Porter

A ruby-brown porter with a roast-malt and liquorice flavour from the liquorice used in the recipe (5.2%). Produced by the Shepherd Neame brewery, Kent.

Owd Rodger

A rich, strong, creamy winter ale (7.6%) from Marston's brewery, Burton-on-Trent.

Oyster Stout

A creamy, bottle-conditioned stout which, despite its name, doesn't contain oysters, by Marston's, Burton-on-Trent.

Pedigree

A classic, coppery-coloured pale ale (4.5%) with a dry hop and malt taste and woody, spicy overtones, from Marston's of Burton-on-Trent. It is brewed using the traditional Burton Union system.

Pendle Witches Brew

A tasty, full-bodied ale (5.1%) which comes from the Moorhouse brewery in Burnley, Lancashire.

Penn's Bitter

A reddish, sweet bitter (4.6%) from the Hoskins brewery in Leicester.

Peter's Porter

A seasonal porter (4.8%) brewed in autumn and winter by the Arkell's Kingsdown brewery, Swindon.

Phoenix Best Bitter

A light-tawny, hoppy cask bitter (3.9%) from the Phoenix brewery, near Manchester.

Prize Old Ale

This remarkable bottle-conditioned ale (9%) from Gales of Horndean, Hampshire, is intensely warming with a hop and fruit-cake flavour. It is matured for six to twelve months before being put into corked bottles, where it continues to mature for several years.

Progress

A malty ale (4%) from the Pilgrim brewery, Reigate, Surrey.

Rain Dance

A golden, fruity wheat

beer (4.4%) from the Brewery-on-Sea, Lancing, Sussex.

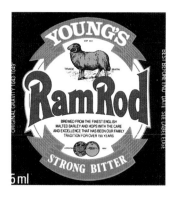

Ram Rod

A full-bodied ale (5%) with a bitter hops and malt flavour, produced by Young's brewery in Wandsworth, London.

Ramsbottom Strong

A tawny-brown, rich and complex bitter (4.5%), brewed using local spring water by the Dent brewery in the Yorkshire Dales.

Rapier Pale Ale

An amber, malty, fruity cask ale (4.2%) from the Reepham brewery, near Norwich.

Rebellion IPA

This refreshing, sweet, malty pale ale (3.7%) comes from the Rebellion brewery in Marlow, Buckinghamshire.

Ridley Champion Mild

A dark cask mild (3.5%) with a fruity, malt flavour and a dry, hops finish, brewed by Ridleys, near Chelmsford, Essex.

Riggwelter

A complex, dark ale (5.9%) with a roasted flavour. It is fermented in traditional Yorkshire stone squares by the Black Sheep brewery, North Yorkshire.

Roaring Meg

A malty, light-brown cask bitter (5.5%) from the Springhead brewery, Nottinghamshire.

Robinson's Best Bitter

A hoppy, amber, malty, fairly bitter beer (4.2%) from this Stockport brewery.

Rooster's Special

A challenging, amber-coloured, malty, hoppy ale (3.9%) from this Harrogate brewery, Yorkshire.

Royal Oak

A red-brown, fruity, sweet ale (5.0%) produced by Thomas Hardy of Dorset.

Ruddles Best Bitter

A characterful cask bitter (3.7%) from this famous Rutland brewery in Langham.

Ruddles County

A full-bodied, malty, strong cask bitter (4.9%) from Ruddles.

Rumpus

A ruby-coloured nutty ale (4.5%) with a fruit and malt flavour, from the Ridleys brewery, near Chelmsford.

Ryburn Best Bitter

A fine, hoppy cask bitter (3.8%) from the Ryburn brewery, Sowerby Bridge, West Yorkshire.

Rydale

A brown, malty cask bitter (4.2%) from the Ryburn brewery.

Salem Porter

A deep, dark porter with a nutty, dry taste (4.7%) from the Bateman family brewery in Wainfleet, Lincolnshire.

Salisbury Best

A sweetish bitter (3.8%) from the Gibbs Mews brewery in the cathedral town of Salisbury, Wiltshire.

Salopian Bitter

A fruity, hoppy cask bitter (3.5%) from the Salopian brewery, Shrewsbury.

Samuel Smith's Imperial Stout

A rich, heavy, bottled stout (7%) from this famous North Yorkshire brewery in Tadcaster, which is best served and enjoyed as a liqueur.

Samuel Smith's Oatmeal Stout

A distinctive stout (5%) with a thick, dark texture and chocolatey, fruity flavour.

SAS

Strong Anglian Special is a dry, well-balanced cask bitter (5%) produced by the Crouch Vale brewery, Essex.

SBA

A malty bitter from the Donnington brewery, Stow-on-the-Wold.

Shakemantle Ginger

A cloudy, ginger wheat beer (5%) produced by the Freeminer brewery, Gloucestershire.

Shefford Bitter

A good, well-balanced, real ale (3.8%) from B&T, Bedfordshire.

Shropshire Lad

A flavoursome bitter (4.5%) produced by the Wood Brewery, next to the Plough Inn, Wistanstow.

Shropshire Stout

A deep-red, rich, dry cask beer (4.4%) from the Hanby brewery, Shropshire.

Single Malt

A powerful, seasonal ale (7.2%), which uses whisky malt in the brewing process, from Mitchell's brewery in Lancaster.

Slaughter Porter

A dark, roasted, malty porter (5%) produced by the Freeminer brewery, Gloucestershire.

Smiles Best Bitter

A rich, brown-coloured, clean-tasting, sweetish bitter (4.1%) with a dry, bitter finish from this Bristol brewery.

Smuggler

A bitter-sweet, hoppy, fruity beer (4.1%) from the Rebellion brewery, Buckinghamshire.

Sneck Lifter

A rich, dark malty premium bitter (5.1%) from the Jennings brewery in the Lake District. Also available in a bottle.

SOS

Shefford Old Strong is a malty, fruity real ale (5%) from B&T, Bedfordshire.

Spinnaker Bitter

This smooth, hoppy ale (3.5%) is one of the Brewery-on-Sea's range of cask beers. Brewed at Lancing, Sussex.

Spitfire

An amber-coloured, mild, smoky malt ale (4.7%) from the Shepherd Neame brewery, Kent.

Stabber's

A brown, strong bitter (5.2%) with a rich, malty flavour from the Ryburn brewery, West Yorkshire.

Stag

A light-brown, malty, sweet bitter (5.2%) from the Exmoor brewery in Wiveliscombe, Somerset.

Steeplejack

A light-brown cask bitter (4.5%) with a fresh, hoppy taste, from the Lichfield brewery in the Midlands.

Stig Swig

A golden, seasonal ale (5%) brewed by Bunces brewery, Wiltshire, using the herb Sweet Gale (bog-myrtle), an old Viking ingredient.

Stones Bitter

This famous straw-coloured bitter (3.9%) with a sweet, malt and hops flavour was introduced by the Cannon Sheffield brewery in the 1940s.

Strongarm

Camerons premium ruby bitter (4%) with a smooth, creamy head from Hartlepool was originally brewed for the steelworkers of Teesside.

Stronghart

A rich, dark, strong beer (7%) produced by the McMullen brewery in Hertford.

Strong Suffolk

An intriguing, unique, complex bottled ale (6%) which comes from Greene King of East Anglia. It is produced by blending an old ale that has been matured in oak vats for at least two years with a fresh brew of dark beer.

Summer Lightning

A striking, strong pale bitter (5%) which comes from the Hop Back brewery, near Salisbury, Wiltshire.

Summerskills Best Bitter

A good, brown-coloured, malt and hops bitter (4.3%) from this South Devon brewery.

Sussex Bitter

A light-coloured, tasty bitter (3.5%) from the King & Barnes brewery in Horsham, Sussex.

Sussex Mild

A dark-brown, malty mild (3%) from Harveys brewery, Lewes, Sussex.

Taddy Porter

A distinctive dark-brown, rich, dry, bottled porter (5%) from Samuel Smith's, Yorkshire.

Tally Ho

A rich, warming barley wine (7%) brewed by Adnams at Christmas. Palmer's of Dorset also brew a dark nutty ale (4.7%) which is sold under the same name.

Tanglefoot

A toe-tingling strong, sweet, amber bitter (5.1%) brewed at the Badger brewery, Blandford St Mary, Dorset, by Hall & Woodhouse.

Tetley Bitter

This pale-amber, hoppy, fruity bitter (3.7%) is traditionally served through a tight tap to give a creamy head. Brewed by Tetley in Leeds, Yorkshire.

Tetley Mild

This amber, hoppy mild (3.3%) with a malt finish, is produced by Tetley, Leeds.

Theakston Best Bitter

A bright-gold, soft bitter (3.8%) with a nutty flavour, which originally came from the North Yorkshire Theakston brewery in Masham. It is now also brewed by Scottish Courage in Newcastle.

Thomas Hardy's Ale

This bottle-conditioned ale (12%) was introduced by Eldridge Pope of Dorset in 1968 to celebrate that summer's Thomas Hardy festival in Dorchester, marking the 40th anniversary of the novelist's death. It was brewed the previous autumn "about as strong as it is

possible to brew" by head brewer Denis Holliday to match Hardy's description of Dorchester strong ale in his novel *The Trumpet Major*: "It was of the most beautiful colour that the eye of an artist in beer could desire; full in body yet brisk as a volcano; piquant, yet without a twang; luminous as an autumn sunset; free from streakiness of taste; but, finally, rather heady." After maturing in casks for six months, the highly hopped ale was filled into bottles, corked, sealed with wax and displayed with velvet ribbons. The brewery said it would continue to mature for up to 25 years. It was only expected to be a one-off special brew, but such was interest and demand that it was repeated, and now drinkers compare different vintages. Each bottle is year-dated and gradually changes from a rich, fruity brew when young to a deeper, mellower flavour, like a spicy Madeira wine.

Three Sieges
A winter ale (6%) flavoured with liquorice, from the Tomlinson brewery in the Yorkshire town of Pontefract.

Thwaites Best Mild
This smooth, dark mild (3.3%) is the best-known brew from Thwaites brewery in Blackburn, Lancashire, which still uses shire horses for local deliveries.

Tiger Best Bitter
A good malt-and-hops-flavoured bitter (4.2%) brewed by the Everard brewery in Narborough, near Leicester.

Tinners Ale
A good, light, hoppy cask ale (3.7%) from the St Austell brewery, Cornwall.

Toby
A light mild (3.2%) brewed by the giant Bass group.

Tolly's Strong Ale
This reddish-coloured, mild, creamy bottle-conditioned ale (4.6%) has a slightly sweet taste. Brewed by the Tolly Cobbold brewery, Suffolk.

Tom Hoskins Porter
A traditional porter (4.8%), brewed using honey and oats by the Hoskins and Oldfield Leicester brewery.

Top Dog Stout
A dark, strongly roasted winter brew (5%) from the Burton Bridge brewery, Burton-on-Trent.

Top Hat
A malty, nutty bitter (4.8%) brewed by Burtonwood near Warrington.

Topsy-Turvy
A dangerously drinkable strong ale (6%) from the small Berrow brewery at Burnham-on-Sea, Somerset.

T'owd Tup
A dark-coloured, strong old ale (6%) from the Dent brewery in the Yorkshire Dales.

Traditional Ale
This light-brown ale (3.4%) is one of a range of cask beers from the Larkins brewery in Kent.

Traditional Bitter
A smooth, hoppy, copper-coloured bitter (3.8%) with a strong malt character and a dry after-taste, produced by Clark brewery in Wakefield, West Yorkshire.

Traditional English Ale
A light-brown, malty, fruity ale (4.2%) from the Hogs Back brewery in Tongham, Surrey. It is commonly known as TEA.

Trelawny's Pride
A light, mild-flavoured cask bitter (4.4%) from the St Austell brewery, Cornwall.

Umbel Ale
A coriander-spiced brew (3.8%) from the Nethergate brewery in Clare, Suffolk. There is also a stronger version, Umbel Magna (5.5%).

Ushers Best Bitter
A golden-brown, hoppy bitter (3.8%) from this Wiltshire brewery.

Valiant
A golden, slightly fruity bitter (4.2%) with a bitter hops flavour, from the Bateman brewery in Lincolnshire.

Varsity
A cask beer with a good balance of sweet and bitter tastes, from the Morrells brewery, Oxford.

Vice Beer
A wheat beer (3.8%) brewed by Bunces brewery, Wiltshire.

Victory Ale
A full, fruity pale ale (6%) first brewed in 1987 to celebrate the Bateman brewery's narrow escape from closure after a family split.

Viking
A hoppy, malty, cask beer (3.8%) with a fruity finish, from the Rudgate brewery, near York.

Village Bitter
A light, hoppy bitter (3.5%) brewed by Archers of Swindon.

Waggle Dance
A golden honey beer (5%) brewed by Ward's of Sheffield for Vaux.

Wallop
A fresh, fruity, light bitter (3.5%) with a hoppy finish, from the Whitby brewery, North Yorkshire.

Ward's Mild
A malty cask ale (3.4%) brewed by Ward's, a traditional Sheffield brewery.

Wassail
A full-bodied draught and bottled beer (6%) from Ballard's, Sussex.

Wherry Best Bitter
The 1996 Champion Beer of Britain. This amber-coloured, hoppy cask bitter (3.8%) is produced by Woodforde's of Norfolk.

Whistle Belly Vengeance
A malty reddish ale (4.7%) from Summerskills of South Devon.

White Dolphin
A fruity wheat beer (4%) from the Hoskins & Oldfield brewery in Leicester.

Willie Warmer
A fruity cask beer (6.4%) produced by Crouch Vale brewery, Essex.

Wilmot's Premium
A strong ale (4.8%) brewed by the Butcombe brewery near Bristol.

Wiltshire Traditional Bitter
This dry, malty, hoppy bitter (3.6%) is produced by the Gibbs Mews brewery in Salisbury, Wiltshire.

Winter Royal
Wethered's famous rich, fruity brew (5%) now brewed by Whitbread at Castle Eden, County Durham.

Winter Warmer
A red-brown seasonal ale (5%) with a rich fruit and malt flavour and a sweetish aftertaste, produced by Young's in London.

Wobbly Bob
A robust cask beer (6%) from the Phoenix brewery, Heywood, near Manchester.

Worthington White Shield
This bottle-conditioned, pale ale (5.6%) has a delicate, yeasty, hoppy, malt flavour. It is now brewed at Mitchells and Butlers in Birmingham. For years White Shield was the only widely available bottled pale ale which retained a sediment of yeast. This meant it was a living beer – a brewery in a bottle. It developed a complex character and required careful handling. Bar staff had to pour the ale steadily into the glass without disturbing the sediment – but some drinkers preferred their glass cloudy and added the yeast anyway. It was not just a beer but a ritual.

Wye Valley Bitter
A bitter, hoppy cask bitter (3.5%) from the Wye Valley brewery in Hereford.

XL Old Ale
A bottled Christmas beer (6.9%) from Holden's brewery in Woodsetton, West Midlands.

XXX
A rare, dark, sweet, mild (3.6%) with a fruity finish, from the Donnington brewery near Stow-on-the-Wold, Gloucestershire.

XXXB Ale
A complex-tasting premium bitter (4.8%) from the Bateman brewery in Lincolnshire.

XXXX Mild
A dark, malty beer (3.6%) from the St Austell brewery, Cornwall.

THE BURTON UNION SYSTEM

In the Burton Union brewing system the beer is fermented in several linked oak casks – in union – with the fermenting beer rising through a swan-neck pipe connecting each cask to a top trough which runs the length of the whole system.

From the trough, the beer then runs back down into the casks, leaving any excess yeast behind in the trough. This constant circulation while the beer is fermenting ensures a vigorous fermentation and fully aerates the beer, giving the yeast enough oxygen to work properly.

The Burton-on-Trent giants Bass dropped the Burton Union system in 1982, claiming that it had become too expensive to maintain. In contrast, however, the traditional Marston's brewery has heavily invested in new unions and still uses the Burton Union system to brew its Owd Rodger and some of its Pedigree. The system is also used to provide the yeast for some of Marston's more conventionally fermented beers.

Yates Bitter
A fruity, straw-coloured bitter (3.7%) from this Cumbrian brewery.

Young's Ordinary
A classic bitter (3.7%) from this traditional London brewery.

2XS
An aptly named strong real ale (6%) from B&T, Bedfordshire.

3B
A draught beer (4%) from Arkell's Kingsdown brewery, Swindon.

4X
A winter warmer (6.8%) from Hydes in Manchester.

6X
Wadworth's premium fruity bitter (4.3%) from Devizes in Wiltshire, which has become well known way beyond the south-west of England. It is also sold in bottles in a stronger export version which clocks in at (5%).

1066
A strong pale ale (6%) which is available in bottle from the Hampshire brewery in Andover, Hampshire.

THE BREWERS

Adnams

This seaside family firm from Southwold, dating from 1872, sprang to fame outside Suffolk in the real ale revival of the 1970s. Adnams is now one of the top quality brewers of Britain. Most production is devoted to its traditional draught beers.

Ansells

This Birmingham brewery, known for its Aston ales, closed in 1981. However its liquorice-tasting dark mild lives on, brewed by Carlsberg-Tetley at Burton-on-Trent.

Archers

Enterprising brewery set up in the old Great Western Railway workshops in Swindon, Wiltshire, in 1979.

Arkell

In 1843 after John Arkell returned from Canada, where his family had founded the village of Arkell near Toronto, he established the Arkell company. Its Kingsdown brewery in Stratton St Margaret, Swindon, is a classic Victorian brewhouse still with its steam engine.

Badger

Hall & Woodhouse's historic Dorset brewery in Blandford Forum, established in 1777, now goes by the popular name of "Badger", after its traditional "Badger" beers.

Ballards

This Sussex country brewery, founded in 1980, is famous for producing an annual bottled beer with a staggering strength to match the date. In 1997 the brewery at Nyewood produced Old Pecker (9.7%). Each new year's beer, with its cartoon label, is launched at a charity walk on the first Sunday of December.

Bass

England's best-known brewery was founded by William Bass in 1777 in Burton-on-Trent. The firm's flagship ale in England, Draught Bass, lost a little of its reputation when the Burton Union system of brewing was abandoned in 1982. Bass's Burton home also houses England's leading brewing museum, which includes a pilot brewing plant used to produce special ales.

Bass is Britain's largest brewing group and if the proposed merger with Carlsberg-Tetley in 1997 is allowed by the Office of Fair Trading, Bass would control 40% of Britain's beer business. Besides Burton, it also owns notable breweries in Birmingham (Mitchells & Butlers), and Sheffield (Stones). Outside England it controls Tennents in Scotland, Hancock's in Wales and the Ulster Brewery in Ireland. In addition to exporting to 70 countries, in the 1990s Bass took over brewing groups in the Czech Republic, notably Staropramen in Prague and launched a joint venture with Ginsberg Brewery in China.

Bateman

This Lincolnshire brewery was founded in Wainfleet in 1874 and narrowly survived a family split in the mid-1980s thanks to the determination of Chairman George Bateman to keep brewing his "Good Honest Ales".

Batham

A traditional Black Country family brewery which was founded at Brierley Hill, near Dudley, in 1877.

Black Sheep

When Paul Theakston of North Yorkshire's famous brewing family lost control of Theakston's Masham brewery, he was determined to start brewing again. The Black Sheep brewery, founded in an old maltings at Wellgarth, Masham, in 1992, is the result. Built on a much larger scale than most new breweries, it installed equipment taken from the former Hartley's brewery in Cumbria. Black Sheep brewery ferments its beer in traditional Yorkshire stone squares and boasts its own visitor centre, making Masham a place of pilgrimage for serious beer drinkers.

Boddingtons

This Manchester brewery, founded in 1778, was once worshipped for the parch-dry bitterness of its straw-coloured bitter. It was taken over by Whitbread in 1989.

Brakspear

A traditional brewery dating back to the 17th century in Henley-on-Thames, Oxfordshire. Its pubs pack the streets of the small town that is famous for its rowing regatta. It is one of the least spoilt breweries in Britain.

Burtonwood

A north-west regional brewery dating from 1867. It built a new brewhouse in Burtonwood, near Warrington, in 1990.

Butcombe

One of the most successful new breweries, set up in the Mendips near Bristol in 1978.

Above: A beautifully decorated English pub with the handpumps for serving traditional draught beer visible on the curving bar.

Cains

This Liverpool brewery has enjoyed a history as elaborate as its towering Victorian brewhouse. After many years as Merseyside's most popular brewery, Higson's, the site is now owned by a Danish brewing group, who restored it to its original title of Robert Cain.

Camerons

The north-east's major brewer of real ales was bought by the Wolverhampton & Dudley Breweries in 1992 as part of their expansion programme. The Hartlepool brewery is best known for its ruby-red ale Strongarm, which once sustained the many steelworkers in the area.

Below: Draught Strongarm from Camerons brewery.

Castle Eden

Whitbread's specialist ale brewery in County Durham produces a wide range of limited-edition brews, often using imaginative flavourings and spices. Formerly Nimmo's Brewery, this County Durham plant also brews beers from breweries closed by Whitbread like Wethered's, Fremlin's and Higson's.

Courage

Originally Courage was a London brewer, founded in 1787. It developed into a national combine before being taken over by a series of multinational companies starting with Imperial Tobacco in 1972 and ending up with the Australian brewers, Foster's. Control of Courage was brought back to Britain in 1995 when Scottish and Newcastle Breweries bought the company from Foster's to form Britain's second largest brewing group, which is now known as Scottish Courage. Courage's traditional cask bitters are today brewed in Bristol.

Donnington

Described as the most picturesque brewery in Britain, time seems to have stood still since the Cotswold stone buildings were first built as a medieval cloth mill near Stow-on-the-Wold, Gloucestershire. Trout rise in the mill pond and ducks nest in the reeds. The brewery was added in 1865 by Richard Arkell. The plant is powered by a waterwheel.

Elgood

This classic Georgian riverside brewery in the Fens at Wisbech has been run by the Elgood family since 1878. It uses open trays for cooling the beers, and also has its own small pilot plant for brewing special beers.

Everard

A family brewery established in 1849 which originally brewed in both Leicester and Burton-on-Trent. Everard opened a new plant in Narborough in 1991 and since then has concentrated its brewing there.

Exmoor

A venture set up in the old Hancock's brewery in Wiveliscombe, Somerset, in 1980, which won the best bitter award at the Great British Beer Festival in its first year.

Federation

The only surviving clubs brewery in England was set up in 1919 in Newcastle by working men's clubs because of a postwar beer shortage. The co-operative opened a brewery at Dunston on the south side of the Tyne in 1980. It brews mainly bright, filtered beers for the clubs.

Flowers

The former Stratford-upon-Avon brewer was taken over and closed by Whitbread. The name is now used for the group's Cheltenham brewery.

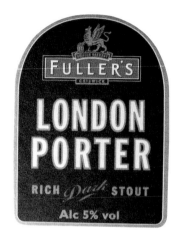

Fuller's

This famous family brewer has been in Chiswick, London, since 1845. Fuller's had to boost its brewing capacity in the 1990s to keep up with demand for its traditional ales. The three main brews – Chiswick Bitter, London Pride and ESB – have won more awards at the Great British Beer Festival than the beers of any other brewer.

Gales

Hampshire family brewery at Horndean with an impressive tower brewery built in 1869.

Greene King

The East Anglian regional giant based at Bury St Edmunds, Suffolk, was founded in 1799. In 1995 it added a range of seasonal cask ales to its well-known IPA and Abbot Ale.

Hardys & Hansons

Two Nottinghamshire breweries started in the 19th century in Kimberley, that merged in 1930. The firm is still family controlled.

Harveys
Founded in 1790, this quality family brewer still brews at its attractive riverside site in Lewes, Sussex, despite a damaging fire in 1996.

Highgate
A West Midlands Victorian tower brewery in Walsall, famous for its Dark Mild. Since being bought out by the management from Bass in 1995, Highgate has added a Saddlers Best Bitter to its range of beers.

Holden
Black Country family brewery in Woodsetton in the West Midlands which goes back four generations.

Holt
This Manchester family brewery since 1849 is famous for the uncompromisingly dry bitterness of its bitter. Holt is also known for its low prices. One of the few breweries to still use hogsheads (huge 54-gallon casks) in its pubs.

Hook Norton
This dramatic Victorian tower brewery in a small Oxfordshire village near Banbury still retains much of its original equipment.

Hydes
A traditional family brewer in Manchester since 1863, turning out ales under the Anvil trademark. Unusually, Hydes still brews two milds, light and dark.

Ind Coope
This historic brewing group was originally based in Romford, Essex. It became part of Allied Breweries in 1961, and merged with Carlsberg in 1993 becoming

Above: A 1952 advertisement for Ind Coope's Arctic Ale, a famous rich, strong ale which is no longer brewed.

Carlsberg-Tetley. The proposed merger with near-neighbours Bass is currently awaiting approval from the Office of Fair Trading. It brews a range of specialist beers under the Allsopp name.

Jennings
The only surviving long-standing brewer in Cumbria, dating back to 1828.

J.W. Lees
A well-established north Manchester family brewery since 1828, still committed to delivering its beers in oak casks.

King & Barnes
A Sussex family firm in Horsham, dating back to 1800, which has extensively modernized its brewery.

McMullen
A Hertford family brewer since 1827, located in a fine Victorian brewhouse.

Mann's
This famous east London brewer's Albion brewery was taken over by Watneys in 1958 and closed in 1979. But the name lives on in England's best-known bottled, sweet brown ale, Mann's Original, which is now brewed by Usher's in Wiltshire.

Mansfield
A regional brewery in Nottinghamshire, founded in 1855, which has expanded considerably since opening its new brewhouse in 1984. It still uses traditional Yorkshire squares to ferment its ales.

Marston Thompson & Evershed
This is the last brewery in Britain that still uses the Burton Union system and the last major independent company brewing in Burton-on-Trent. Besides its famous Pedigree, it now brews a range of special cask beers under the Head Brewer's Choice label.

Mauldon
This Suffolk brewing family from Sudbury started brewing in 1795. The brewery closed in 1960 but restarted brewing in 1982.

Melbourn
This brewery in Stamford, Lincolnshire closed in 1974 and became a museum under Samuel Smith. Since 1993 Melbourn have brewed fruit ales in the old brewery, using wild yeasts from Belgium.

Mitchell's
Traditional family brewer in Lancaster since 1880.

Mitchells & Butlers
Often just known as M&B, Mitchells and Butlers are the dominant Birmingham brewers and merged with Bass in 1961. Their Cape Hill brewery in Smethwick, near Birmingham has been heavily modernized.

Morland

The second-oldest English brewery founded in 1711. The Abingdon firm sprang to fame outside Oxfordshire in the 1990s with the success of its strong pale ale, Old Speckled Hen.

Morrells

The only brewery left in the university town of Oxford which has been run by the Morrell family since 1782.

Oakhill

A historic stout brewery founded in 1767 at Oakhill, near Bath, which was badly damaged by fire in 1924, and then closed. In 1984 the brewery was restarted and moved to the Old Maltings, a larger site in 1993.

Palmer

England's only thatched brewery which was founded at Bridport, Dorset in 1794.

Ridleys

This family brewery was established in 1842 by Thomas Ridley at Hartford End, near Chelmsford, Essex.

Ringwood

Set up by Peter Austin in 1978 in the Hampshire town. In 1995 Ringwood moved beyond the micro-brewery stage with the opening of a 125-barrel modern brewhouse.

Robinson's

A major regional family firm from Stockport, near Manchester, founded in 1838.

Ruddles

One of the most famous names in English brewing, Ruddles lost its independence in 1986 when Watneys bought up the Rutland brewery in Langham. Since 1992, it has been owned by the Dutch brewers, Grolsch.

St Austell

Cornwall's only remaining long-established independent family brewery, founded in 1851. The solid Victorian brewery dominates the town.

Shepherd Neame

England's oldest brewery dates back to 1698. It is fittingly to be found in the

Above: A game of cards is a traditional accompaniment to a pint.

hop garden of Kent, at Faversham. Shepherd Neame still uses steam engines and two teak mash tuns from 1910. It produces a range of cask and bottled beers.

Smith, John

A magnificent Victorian building in Tadcaster, North Yorkshire, built in 1884, houses the John Smith's brewery. The company is now owned by Scottish Courage. Today the towering stone buildings house a modern brewhouse.

Smith, Samuel

Samuel Smith was the first of the two Smith brewers of Tadcaster and the firm is still brewing in the Old Brewery which dates back to 1758. The family firm has remained fiercely independent. The beer is still fermented in Yorkshire stone squares and racked into wooden casks.

Stones

The Stones brewery has quenched the fire of the steel city of Sheffield in Yorkshire since 1865. It was taken over by Bass in 1968.

Taylor

One of the top quality brewers of England. Timothy Taylor began brewing in Brontë country at Keighley, Yorkshire, in 1858.

Tetley

England's leading brewer of bitter was founded in Leeds, Yorkshire, in 1822. A modern brewhouse was built in the 1980s and more Yorkshire squares for fermenting the beer were added in 1996. It became known as Carlsberg-Tetley in 1993 following the merger with Carlsberg.

Theakston

This North Yorkshire brewer has been at Masham since 1827. Theakston is famous for rich, dark Old Peculier. The family lost control in the late 1970s, and after a succession of takeovers the country brewery is now owned by Scottish Courage. Most Theakston beers are brewed at its Tyne brewery in Newcastle, as well as at the original Masham brewery.

Thomas Hardy

Formerly Eldridge Pope of Dorchester, this grand brewery, founded in 1837, was renamed after their most famous customer, the novelist Thomas Hardy.

Thwaites

A major Lancashire regional brewer founded in Blackburn in 1807 that still uses shire horses for local deliveries.

Tolly Cobbold

A Suffolk brewer since 1746 in a fine Victorian brewhouse in Ipswich which was closed in 1989 – but was then saved by a management buyout. The popular name comes from the merging of Cobbold with another well-known Ipswich brewery, Tollemache, in 1957. The grand Cobbold brewery in Ipswich was built on Cliff Quay on the banks of the River Orwell in 1894–6. It is a classic example of a tower brewery, and still retains many fine old brewing vessels. Following the management buyout in 1990, the brewery has become one of the main tourist attractions in the town, with guided tours. The offices alongside have been turned into the Brewery Tap pub.

Ushers

This Wiltshire brewery was founded in Trowbridge in 1824. After being taken over by Watneys of London in 1960 it lost its local identity. A management buyout in 1991 restored its independence.

Vaux

The giant northern brewery which is based in the town of Sunderland on the River Wear. Vaux also owns Ward's of Sheffield.

Wadworth

A traditional family brewery whose towering brewhouse has dominated the Wiltshire market town of Devizes since 1885. The brewery includes a rare open copper.

Ward's

A traditional Sheffield brewery which was founded in 1840, 15 years before the better-known Stones brewery in the steel city.

Watneys

This once-famous London brewery ruined its reputation by leading the movement to processed keg beers. It is now part of Scottish Courage. Its Mortlake brewery is used by Anheuser-Busch to brew Budweiser. Most remaining Watneys beers are brewed abroad for foreign markets.

Wells

Enterprising Bedford family brewers since 1876 who rebuilt their brewery in 1976. Wells brews various foreign lagers under licence, including Kirin from Japan and Red Stripe from Jamaica.

Whitbread

This famous London brewer since 1742 closed his brewery in the capital city in 1976. Originally Whitbread was known for its porter. It is England's third largest brewing group, brewing foreign lagers under licence, notably a weak version of Heineken and Stella Artois. It also produces a wide range of cask beers under local names such as Wethered, Fremlins and Higsons, now produced at Flowers brewery in Cheltenham, Gloucestershire, and at Castle Eden, County Durham. Whitbread also owns Boddingtons in Manchester.

Wolverhampton & Dudley

Wolverhampton is the home of this brewery, famed for its reddish-amber Banks's mild, a favourite in the industrial West Midlands. It trades as Banks's and Hanson's in the Black Country. It is the largest regional brewing group in Britain, with around 1,100 pubs and in 1992 bought Camerons brewery in the north-east.

Wood

A small brewery behind the Plough Inn in Wistanstow, Shropshire.

Woodforde's

Quality Norfolk brewery since 1980 which has the rare distinction of having twice won the Champion Beer of Britain title.

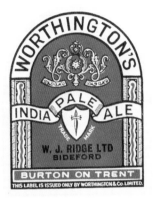

Worthington

This famous Burton brewing name merged with Bass in 1927. The brewery has since been demolished, but the name lives on in a national bitter brand and more notably in the bottle-conditioned pale ale Worthington White Shield, now brewed at Mitchells & Butlers brewery in Birmingham.

Young's

A firmly traditional London family brewery situated at the Ram brewery in Wandsworth since 1831. Young's is noted for cask beers. Deliveries are still made by horse-drawn drays, a wonderful sight in south London, although these are now under threat from the increased traffic in the area. The Victorian brewery also houses geese, peacocks and a ram (the company mascot). In recent years Young's has added seasonal ales including a summer wheat beer. Its bottled ales are also sold abroad.

Below: Cheers!

SCOTLAND

Once Scotland was famous for its beer, and during the 19th century the capital Edinburgh ranked alongside Burton-on-Trent in England, Munich in Germany and Plzen in the Czech Republic as a notable brewing centre.

AT THE START OF THE 20TH CENTURY Edinburgh boasted 28 breweries, most packed into an area with an excellent water supply known as the "Charmed Circle". Alloa, just across the River Forth, was also a famous beer town.

In 1960, Edinburgh still had 18 breweries and Scottish brewers were vigorous exporters, but as the overseas trade dried up many companies fell into financial difficulties and were taken over and closed down like Robert Younger. Two giants – Scottish & Newcastle and Tennent's – came to dominate the market. This hastened the disappearance of traditional cask beer. Eventually only two breweries were left in Edinburgh. Overall, just three independent breweries survived in the whole of Scotland. A once-thriving industry had almost vanished. Since 1980 there has been a small revival, with the appearance of a number of new breweries bringing back welcome variety to the bar. Scottish beers are darker, more full-bodied, and sweeter than English ales. Perhaps because hops are not grown in the country, there is less emphasis on bitterness. Perhaps the malty warmth helps to keep out the northern cold. Local specialities include strong barley wines known as "wee heavys", as well as "oatmeal stout", made using a local cereal. The English terms of mild and bitter are not generally used north of the border. Instead, beers are traditionally rated in strength according to the invoice price charged per barrel in the 19th century. Under the "shilling system" the weakest beer is 60/-, an average-strength beer 70/-, and a premium brew 80/-. Strong ales are 90/-. These designations usually refer to cask beers. Keg beers are more popularly known as light (this refers to the light alcoholic content, not the colour, which may well be dark); special or heavy indicate mid-strength brews; and export is the name given to premium ales. Scotland also has its own individual dispensing system, which uses tall air-pressure fonts, rather than handpumps, to serve traditional ales.

Above: Traditional ales are still brewed in Scotland, despite its radically reduced brewing industry and the increasing popularity of lager.

THE BEERS

Ale of Atholl
A rich, malty beer (4.5%) from the Moulin brewery, near Pitlochry.

Arrol's 80/-
A fruity, cask-conditioned Scottish heavy (4.4%) with a hoppy aftertaste, brewed by the Alloa brewery.

Auld Alliance
Tart, hoppy refreshing bitter (4%) from the Fife brewery, Kirkaldy.

Bear Ale
This cask ale (5%) is fermented in oak vessels at the historic Traquair House manor brewery.

Black Douglas
This distinctive, dark, winter ale (5.2%) comes from the Broughton brewery.

Borve Extra Strong
A powerful, extra-strong ale (10%), which is matured in oak whisky casks at the Borve home-brew pub.

Broadsword
This golden cask ale (3.8%) with a fruity, malty flavour and bitter finish is brewed at Alloa by Maclay.

Buchan Bronco
This cask beer (4.6%) is produced by the Aberdeenshire brewery in Keith, fermented using Yorkshire squares. The brewery also produces the lighter Buchan Gold (4%).

Calder's
This is the brand name for keg beers made by the Alloa brewery, including Cream Ale (4.5%) and 80/-.

Caledonian
A range of beers from the Caledonian brewery. The weakest is a flavoursome, dark, malty 60/- beer (3.2%) with a refreshing hint of roast barley. Caledonian 70/- (3.5%) is a more tawny coloured, creamy brew and Caledonian 80/- (4.1%) has a complex malt and hops flavour.

Cuillin
Red Cuillin (4.2%) and Black Cuillin (4.5%) are two cask beers produced by the Isle of Skye brewery at Uig on Skye.

Dark Island
A rich, wine-coloured, refreshing beer (4.6%) with a fruity aroma, from the Orkney brewery.

Deuchars IPA
This very pale "pale ale" (4.4%) is late-hopped to produce a refreshing brew. Brewed by Caledonian.

Douglas
See Gordon's.

Dragonhead Stout
This smooth, classic stout (4%) is produced by the Orkney brewery.

Edinburgh Strong Ale
A strong, premium ale (6.4%) with a complexity of malt and hop flavours, but without the usual sweetness of strong beers. It is brewed by Caledonian.

Fraoch
Bruce Williams has been brewing Fraoch (the Gaelic word for heather) at Maclay's Alloa brewery every flowering season since 1993. Instead of adding hops – which are not grown in Scotland – to the boiling wort, he follows the example of the ancient Picts and uses native heather tips and

myrtle leaves. The hot liquid is also infused in a vat of fresh heather flowers before fermentation. The spicy, floral brew that results comes in two strengths – Heather Ale (4.1%) and Pictish Ale (5.4%).

Gillespie's
First introduced in 1993, Gillespie's keg and canned creamy, sweet-malt stout (4%) is named after a closed Dumbarton brewery. It is produced by Scottish Courage in Edinburgh.

Golden Pale
A pale-amber-coloured, aromatically hoppy, organic beer (4%), from the Caledonian brewery.

Golden Promise
The first organic beer from Caledonian, Golden Promise is slightly stronger (5%) than Golden Pale. A quality brew, it is named after Scotland's traditional variety of barley.

Gordon's
This warming range of bottled, strong ales is brewed in Edinburgh by Scottish Courage, mainly for the Belgian market. It includes Gordon's Scotch Ale (8.6%), Christmas Ale (8.8%) and Gold Blond (10%). It is sold in France under the Douglas name.

Greenmantle

This distinctive, smoky, fruity ale (3.9%) is available in bottles and cask. It is produced by the Broughton brewery.

Grozet

First produced in 1996 by Bruce Williams at the Maclay brewery in Alloa, this hazy beer (5%) is a wheat ale to which whole gooseberries are added after fermentation.

Highland Hammer

This powerful, full-flavoured strong ale (7.3%) is a seasonal speciality of the Tomintoul brewery.

Jacobite Ale

This strong brew (8%) is fermented in oak and flavoured with coriander. It comes from the Traquair House brewery.

Kane's Amber Ale

This amber cask beer (4%) with a good malt and fruit flavour is produced in the brewing town of Alloa by the Maclay brewery.

Laird's Ale

The weakest cask ale (3.8%) from Tomintoul is a traditional, dark-mahogany 70/- ale, with a malty flavour and fine hop balance.

McEwan's Export

A sweet and malty Scottish ale (4.5%) produced by McEwan's in Edinburgh.

MacAndrew's

A strong, amber-coloured ale (6.5%) brewed for sale in the US by Caledonian.

Maclay

Maclay brewery's cask beers include a full-flavoured, malty, fruity 70/- ale (3.6%) with a sweet, fresh flavour. The flagship 80/- Export (4%) is a creamy, malty beer with a dry finish. There is also an oat malt stout (4.5%).

Malcolm's

A range of beers, named after King Malcolm III who slew Macbeth, including Malcolm's Ceilidh (3.7%), Folly (4%), and Premier (4.3%), from the Backdykes farm brewery in Fife.

Merlin's

This distinctive, hoppy, golden ale (4.2%) is one of a range of beers produced at the Broughton brewery.

Merman

A mellow, reddish-bronze, malty, fruity, bottled pale ale (4.8%) from Caledonian, based on an 1890 recipe.

Montrose

A tasty, tawny cask beer (4.2%) from the Harviestoun brewery.

Murray's Heavy

An amber-coloured, traditional Scottish heavy beer (4.3%), produced by Caledonian.

Old Jock

A distinctive dark-ruby, sweetish, fruity, bottled strong ale (6.7%). It is produced by the Broughton brewery in the borders.

Old Manor

This old ale (8%) is brewed each winter by the Harviestoun brewery. Molasses gives the beer a good ruby colour and a rich fruitiness. This is one of a range of seasonal brews.

Ptarmigan

An outstanding pale-golden, fruity, premium beer (4.5%) from the Harviestoun brewery. It has a light, refreshing flavour and is brewed using Saaz hops.

Raven Ale

An amber-red, nutty, dry ale (3.8%) from the Orkney brewery.

Red MacGregor

A full-bodied, smooth, red-brown beer(4.1%)from the Orkney brewery,

St Andrew's

A rich, brown, malty cask beer (4.9%) with a fruity butterscotch flavour, brewed by Belhaven.

Sandy Hunter's

A bitter-sweet, roasted-malt, hoppy cask beer (3.6%) from the Belhaven brewery. It was named after a former head brewer.

Schiehallion Lager

A cask-conditioned, Bohemian-style lager (4.8%), brewed using German Hersbrucker hops, from the Harviestoun brewery. It won a Gold Medal at the Great British Beer Festival in 1996. Schiehallion, a local mountain, was once climbed as part of an experiment by Astronomer Royal Neville Maskelyn.

THE OUTWARD-LOOKING SCOTS

Scottish brewers have always been enthusiastic exporters of their wares, partly because of the relatively small size of the home market. The strong, rich, dark brews have been widely drunk throughout Britain for centuries, and in the heyday of the British Empire they also reached the former colonies scattered across the world, from the US to Australia and India. The ales were dispatched overseas in great quantities to quench the thirsts of Scots who had emigrated. The "export" brews became well known and well regarded. They were so popular in parts of Europe that Belgian brewers began to produce their own "Scotch" ales – a style that persists today.

Left: At the beginning of the 20th century, many brewers produced beers for the export market but declining sales spelled the end for most of them.

Skull Splitter
An powerful, strong, dark-amber barley wine (8.5%), from the Orkney brewery.

Stag
A dark, malty ale (4.1%) from the Tomintoul brewery in the Highlands which is sold in cask and bottle.

Stillman's 80/-
This mid-gold, mild beer (4.2%) with a complex flavour is produced by the Tomintoul brewery. Its name reflects the local whisky distilling industry in the Spey valley.

Sweetheart Stout
This very weak (2%), sweet and fruity brew is produced by Tennent's, but bears little resemblance to a real stout.

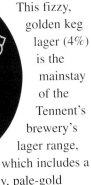

Tennent's Lager
This fizzy, golden keg lager (4%) is the mainstay of the Tennent's brewery's lager range, which includes a grainy, pale-gold Pilsner (3.4%), a stronger Extra (4.8%), Gold (5%) and a weighty, amber-coloured, sweetish, strong Super (9%). Tennent's are Scotland's dominant lager brewers.

The Ghillie
This distinctive bottled ale (4.5%) is produced by the Broughton brewery.

Traquair House Ale
A dark, strong classic oak-fermented ale (7.2%) from the Traquair House brewery. It has a fruity, malt flavour and a slight dryness. This distinctive ale is exported to the US.

Triple Diamond
This is the special, extra-strong, export ale brand (8.5%) produced by the Alloa brewery.

Wallace IPA
A hoppy, fruity pale ale (4.5%) with a bitter finish, produced by Maclay.

Waverley 70/-
A chestnut-coloured, hoppy, cask beer (3.7%), from the Harviestoun brewery.

Wild Cat
A deep-amber ale (5.1%) with a complex flavour from the Tomintoul brewery.

Young Pretender
A golden, dry ale (4%) from the Isle of Skye brewery named after Bonnie Prince Charlie. It was first produced in 1995 to mark the 250th anniversary of the Jacobite rebellion.

Younger's Tartan
A dark-amber Scottish keg ale (3.7%) with a sweet and fruity flavour from William Younger of Edinburgh.

THE BREWERS

Alloa

Founded in 1810, the Alloa brewery became known in the 1930s for its lager, Graham's, then Skol (3.6%) after becoming part of Allied Breweries. It also produces keg ales under the Calder's name and special export brands such as Triple Diamond. Since 1982 it has brewed cask beer, notably Arrols 80/-.

Belhaven

Scotland's oldest brewery, Belhaven dates back to at least 1719. Built on former monastery land on the coast at Dunbar, its ales were sold way beyond Scotland and found their way to the Imperial Court of Austria, where the Emperor declared them "The Burgundy of Scotland". This claim is still carried by its robust 80/- ale (4.2%). Other malty cask beers include 60/- (2.9%), 70/- (3.5%), St Andrew's and Sandy Hunter's besides a rich, warming 90/- (8%).

Above: The Caledonian brewery in Edinburgh was restored after a fire in 1994. It produces a wide range of cask and bottled beers. Caledonian 80/- was the Champion Beer of Scotland in 1996.

Borve

Originally set up on the Isle of Lewis in 1983, this home-brew pub is now on the mainland at Ruthven.

Broughton

David Younger, a descendant of the George Younger brewing family of Alloa, set up the brewery in 1980 in the Borders region at Broughton. In 1995 it relaunched its distinctive cask and bottled ales as "Beers with Character".

Caledonian

Caledonian is the sole survivor from an era when Edinburgh boasted 30 independent breweries. The Victorian brewhouse still uses direct-fired open coppers, one dating back to 1869 when the firm was founded as Lorimer and Clark. Its wide range of quality cask and bottled beers includes 60/- (3.2%), 70/- (3.5%), 80/- (4.1%), Deuchars IPA, Murray's Heavy, Double Amber, Merman, Edinburgh Strong Ale (6.4%) and two organic beers. The Caledonian 80/- was the first champion Beer of Scotland in 1996.

Harviestoun

A village brewery in an old stone dairy at Dollar, near Stirling, since 1985, Harviestoun produces a prize-winning range of cask beers including Waverley 70/-, Original 80/- (4.1%), Montrose, Ptarmigan and Old Manor.

McEwan's

A famous firm since 1856 which merged with Younger's in 1931 and is now part of Scottish Courage. McEwan's still brews at its Fountain brewery in Edinburgh which has recently been completely rebuilt. Though McEwan's is best known for its keg and canned beers (McEwan's Export is the best-selling canned beer in Britain), it also produces some cask-conditioned beers in the old classic Scottish shilling ratings – 70/- and 80/-.

ALLOA

The town of Alloa at the head of the Firth of Forth has long been a brewing centre, using water from the Ochil hills, local barley and coal from nearby mines. Early in the 20th century it boasted nine breweries, the most famous being George Younger's which closed in 1963. By 1996 only two were left, Alloa (now part of Bass) and the independent Maclays.

HOME-BREW PUBS

Scotland boasts a handful of home-brew houses, most established in the mid-1990s:

- Aldchlappie Hotel, Kirkmichael, Perthshire.
- Harbour Bar, Kirkcaldy, Fife.
- Lugton Inn, Lugton, Ayrshire.
- Mansfield Arms, Sauchie, Alloa.
- Moulin Hotel, Moulin, Pitlochry.
- Rose Street, Edinburgh.

Above: Stirring the brew in modern shiny coppers.

Maclay's

The last independent family-owned brewery left in Alloa was founded in 1830. The traditional tower brewhouse was built in 1869. Maclay's still uses bore-hole water drawn from 300ft (100m) below ground for its brewing. Cask beers include 70/- (3.6%), the flagship 80/- Export (4%), Maclay's Oat Malt Stout (4.5%), Wallace IPA and also a strong, golden Scotch Ale (5%).

Orkney

Britain's most northerly brewery is located on the Orkney's main island off the north coast of Scotland. It was set up at Quoyloo in 1988 by Roger White. Its cask and bottled beers are Raven Ale, Dragonhead Stout, Red MacGregor, Dark Island and the powerful Skull Splitter.

Scottish Courage

This is Britain's second-largest brewing group. It is based in Edinburgh and was formed in 1995 when Scottish & Newcastle Breweries bought the Courage brewing group of England. It has only one brewery in Scotland, located in Edinburgh. Its beers are still marketed under the McEwan's and William Younger names.

Tennent's

Founded in Glasgow around 1776, the Wellpark Brewery became famous as Scotland's first lager brewers in 1885. Today, the brewery produces a range of lagers for the British and overseas markets. It also brews keg ales and bottled stout.

Tomintoul

This brewery in the heart of the Highlands malt whisky country, just a couple of miles from the Glenlivet distillery, claims to be the highest brewery in Britain. It was set up in 1993 in an old watermill by Andrew Neame, a member of the brewing family in Kent, England. Its cask beers include Laird's Ale (3.8%), Stag (4.1%), Stillman's 80/- (4.2%), Wild Cat (5.1%) and Highland Hammer (7.3%).

Traquair House

A rare survivor from an age when all great manor houses had their own breweries. Traquair House at Innerleithen, near Peebles, dates from the 12th century and is said to be the oldest

inhabited building in Scotland. Its beer was first recorded in an account of a visit to the house by Mary Queen of Scots in 1566. The present brewery, dating back to the 1730s, was revived in 1965 by the Laird, Peter Maxwell Stuart. A second brewhouse has since been added to keep up with demand. All the beer is fermented in oak vessels.

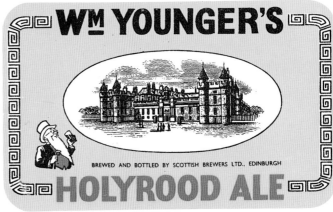

Younger's

William Younger founded his brewery in 1749. It is now part of Scottish Courage. The Holyrood brewery closed in 1986, and production moved to McEwan's Fountain brewery. Younger's is best known for its Tartan ale. Its cask ales, Younger's Scotch and Younger's IPA, are the same as McEwan's. Younger's No. 3 is McEwan's 80/- with added caramel.

DENMARK

Perhaps because it is further south and much more firmly attached to mainland Europe than its northern neighbours in Scandinavia, Denmark has always enjoyed a relatively relaxed attitude to beer and to its brewing industry.

WHEN DRINKERS THINK of Denmark, one name stands a thick foaming head above all others – the famous Carlsberg. Besides having a worldwide reputation, the Carlsberg group controls the domestic market. It absorbed its main rival Tuborg in 1970, and it also holds stakes in the other leading brewing groups. This domination by one brewery has restricted choice. Drinkers in Copenhagen have to look hard in their bars to find anything apart from Carlsberg and Tuborg. The variety of beer styles is also on a tight rein with Pilsners reigning supreme.

Denmark has played a major role in spreading the popularity of bottom-fermenting lagers and a malty, mild style of Pilsner is by far the most widely available beer today. Before this most brewers once produced top-fermenting wheat beers. Carlsberg, more than any other brewery, has popularized the golden lager style, devised in central Europe, around the world. In 1993 its worldwide sales were more than five times larger than its home sales. So profound has this company's contribution been to the development of lager, that the classic bottom-fermenting yeast used by brewers, *Saccharomyces Carlsbergensis*, has been named after the Copenhagen brewery.

As well as golden lagers, however, there are some seasonal brews and darker beers to be found in Denmark. You may even come across the occasional porter – a reminder of the days when English ale was sold in the Baltic. There is also a tradition of brewing an extremely weak, dark, top-fermented table beer called hvidtol, which is so low in alcohol that it escapes the tax levied on other beers. Despite the lack of variety and relatively high taxes on alcohol, the Danes certainly enjoy their beer – drinking more per head of population than any other nation, apart from the Czech Republic and Germany.

Above: There are occasional unusual brews to be found in Denmark, such as this red beer from Ceres. However it is Carlsberg's world-famous golden lager, that is associated with Danish beer, and lagers that dominate brewing and drinking.

THE BEERS

Albani Porter
A strong, smooth all-malt porter (7.8%) from the Albani brewery in Odense.

Bering
Bering is an unusual cross between a strong spicy stout and a lager blended with lemon and rum (6.3%), brewed by Ceres.

Bjørne Bryg
A bright-gold, strong lager (8.3%) with a bitter hops after-taste from Harboe. The name means "Bear Beer".

Buur
A deep-gold, strong, sweet, hoppy, Dortmunder-style beer (7.6%) from Thor, part of the Ceres brewing group.

Carlsberg Let
A light, golden, weak table-beer (2.7%) with a malty and bitter hoppy taste, from Carlsberg.

Carlsberg Master Brew
A highly alcoholic, strong, beer (10.5%) created for the firm's 150th anniversary.

Carlsberg Pilsner
Also known as Carlsberg Lager Beer (or sometimes as Hof after the royal court), this lager (4.6%) with the green label has a clean, soft flavour.

Ceres Royal Export
This strong golden lager (5.8%) produced by Ceres, has a ripe, malty flavour with a hoppy finish.

Dansk Dortmunder
A strong, malty, golden lager (7.7%) brewed by Ceres that is widely exported under the name Ceres Strong Ale.

Dansk LA
This low-alcohol beer is probably the best-known beer made by Wiibroe, a Carlsberg subsidiary at Elsinore, founded in 1840, which mainly produces lower-priced products.

Elephant
A rich golden lager (7.5%) in the German bock style, from Carlsberg. It is named after the brewery's elephant gates.

Faxe Premium
A malty lager with a soft, malt finish (5%) from the Faxe brewery.

Gamle Special Dark
This dark lager (4.2%) from Carlsberg recalls the brewery's original malty, Munich-style lager.

Gammel Porter or Imperial Stout
This strong, Baltic-style stout from Carlsberg (7.5%) is bottom-fermenting, and has a rich, roasted flavour. "Gammel" means old.

Giraf
A pale, strong lager (6.8%) with a long-neck label, produced by Albani of Odense. It was first brewed to help sponsor the purchase of giraffes for the local zoo.

Grøn
Tuborg's main brand is known as Grøn after the green colour of the label, with a premium Guld (gold) and a dark lager Rod (red).

Hof
See Carlsberg Pilsner.

The dominant bottle

One peculiarity of the beer market in Denmark is that the vast bulk is sold in returnable bottles and relatively little is available on draught. The litter-conscious Danes are vehemently opposed to the can, and they have banned its use for the sale of drinks on environmental grounds. This has brought the country into conflict with the European Union's free-market directives.

Kongens Bryg
This low-alcohol golden lager (1.7%) is produced by Tuborg.

Red Erik
This lager from Ceres is named in honour of the Viking who discovered Greenland and began brewing there.

Silver Pilsner
This tasty Pilsner is the selling beer from the Harboe brewery.

Sort Guld
Sort Guld or "Black Gold" is a malty, dark beer (5.8%) produced by Carlsberg.

THE BREWERS

Albani

One of the larger independent breweries in Denmark was founded in Odense in 1859. It is best known for its tall-necked pale, strong lager Giraf, and it also brews a porter, Albani Porter (7.8%), an Easter brew, Albani Påske Bryg, Albani Christmas Jule, as well as a range of Pilsners.

Apollo

A home-brew pub in Copenhagen near the famous Tivoli Gardens. This establishment first appeared in 1990 at the Hereford Beefstouw restaurant in co-operation with the Wiibroe brewery of Elsinore. It produces a range of unfiltered lagers.

Carlsberg

See panel opposite.

Ceres

After a merger with the Thor and Faxe breweries, Ceres of Aarhus in Jutland is now part of the second-largest brewing group in Denmark. The brewery was founded in 1856, and is named after the goddess of grain. Besides a range of Pilsners, it brews a strong, dark Ceres Stout (stout, 7.7%) and a range of stronger golden lagers that are widely exported.

Faxe

This brewery at Fakse gained cult status in the 1970s with its Faxe Fad beer. "Fad" means draught, and the bottled brew was unpasteurized. The brewery has linked up with Ceres to form Brewery Group Denmark, the second largest combine in the country.

Harboe

The independent family-owned brewery was founded in Skaelskor on Zealand in 1883. It initially brewed the non-alcoholic hvidtol before starting to brew lager in 1890. Its modern brewery, built in 1960, is best known abroad for its powerful Bjørne Bryg ("Bear Beer") but its best-selling brew is its Silver Pilsner. It also brews a premium Harboe Guld (5.9%) and a range of seasonal beers. Harboe is the sole Danish producer of malt extract and still produces low-alcohol malt brews.

Danish dynasty

Some have said that the Carlsberg story is like a dynastic blockbuster. Danish television agreed and in 1996 made its most expensive production, a 12-part series based on the remarkable life of J. C. Jacobsen. It is simply called *The Brewer*.

Tuborg

Although Tuborg is less well known on the international market than its sister brewery Carlsberg, this Copenhagen brewery outsells Carlsberg in the home market and in the other Nordic countries. Tuborg was founded in Tuborg, to the north of Copenhagen, in 1873 by a group of bankers.

At first it sold the same dark Munich-style lagers that had been introduced by Carlsberg, but in 1880 the Tuborg brewer Hans Bekkevold launched Denmark's first Pilsner. The Tuborg brewery was also one of the first in Denmark to bottle its beers and the green-labelled Pilsner proved a major success with consumers – so much of a success in fact that in 1903, a new seven-storey brewhouse was built to keep up with demand. A clock looked down on the new shiny coppers, with the financiers' favourite words below the dial, warning slack workers, "Time is Money".

One of the odder features of the Tuborg brewery in Copenhagen which, like Carlsberg, has a large visitor centre, is a massive 26-metre (85-foot)-high beer bottle. This city landmark was originally built for the Great Nordic Industrial Fair in Tivoli Park in 1888, and was fitted with Denmark's first ever hydraulic lift. At its centenary in 1988, the towering bottle was shipped back to the town centre to stand alongside the city hall.

Throughout the 20th century Tuborg and Carlsberg co-operated closely, and finally in 1970 the two major brewers merged, and the combined company now accounts for about 80% of domestic beer sales. Each still retains its own independent management and takes control of its own marketing. Tuborg has also maintained production at its own brewery in Copenhagen. The company has made its mark on the international scene, being sold and brewed in more than 130 countries.

The Tuborg range of beers is similar to Carlsberg's, although its Pilsners tend to be a little lighter and hoppier. The main Tuborg brand is known as Grøn after the green colour of the label. There is also a premium Guld and a dark lager, Rod. Like Carlsberg, Tuborg also produces some seasonal brews and a dark, rich, creamy porter.

THE CARLSBERG STORY

Since 1901, four stone elephants have stood guard at the gates of the Carlsberg brewery in Copenhagen. They symbolize the enduring power of one of the most famous names in brewing and signify that this is no ordinary company. The story of Carlsberg is an epic tale.

The Carlsberg brewery was founded in 1847 by Jacob Christian Jacobsen on a hill at Valby just outside Copenhagen. He named it after his five-year-old son Carl and the Danish word for a hill – "berg". At the time, many small Danish breweries (including one run by his father) were producing top-fermented wheat beers, but Jacobsen was determined to brew on a grand scale – and to brew the new bottom-fermented lagers, which were then being pioneered in Bavaria.

Jacobsen travelled to Munich to study under the famous Gabriel Sedlmayr of the Spaten brewery and, according to legend, returned from one trip in 1845 with 2 litres (3½ pints) of the vital bottom-fermenting yeast, which he kept cool throughout the long stagecoach journey by frequently dousing it with cold water and covering the

containers with his stovepipe hat. After successful experiments to produce the dark, Munich-style lager, using the cellars under the city ramparts while his new brewery was being built, he began to brew the first batch at his plant at Valby on November 10 1847.

Jacobsen became one of the leaders of the new science of brewing and built a famous set of laboratories. It was here in 1883 that Emil Hansen isolated the first single-cell yeast culture *Saccharomyces Carlsbergensis*. This major development allowed brewers to control the quality of their beers by eliminating bad yeast strains. Jacobsen also established the Carlsberg Foundation in 1876, to promote scientific research. After his death in 1887, this foundation became the owner of the brewery.

Jacobsen's son Carl, often in dispute with his father, set up his own brewery on an adjoining site to brew Pilsners. His interest lay in

the arts, and in 1901 he designed a new brewhouse on an elaborate scale, complete with Florentine flourishes and elephant gates. The Carlsberg Foundation took over this cathedral of beer in 1902. Today the company is uniquely run as a charity for the benefit of the sciences and, following Carl's intervention, for the arts. Its huge trust fund donates vast amounts of money. Carl Jacobsen helped develop Copenhagen as a city of soaring spires. In 1913, he donated the Little Mermaid statue, which has become the symbol of the city. Carlsberg first became known outside Denmark when its beer was shipped to Scotland in 1868. The other Scandinavian countries

and the West Indies soon followed. Carlsberg is a particularly big brand in the Far East. The first brewery outside Denmark was built in Malawi in Africa in 1968. In 1970, Carlsberg merged with Tuborg to form United Breweries, which in 1987 became Carlsberg.

Today, Carlsberg has about 100 subsidiary and associated companies, mostly abroad. More than 80% of its sales are outside Denmark. Its beer is sold in 150 countries and brewed in 40. In Denmark, where it serves four out of every five glasses of beer, it also owns Wiibroe of Elsinore, and in 1979 opened a new brewery at Fredericia to serve western Denmark.

Above: The imposing Carlsberg brewery in Copenhagen

NORWAY

The frozen lands of northern Europe might conjure up images of hard-drinking, ale-quaffing Vikings, but the truth is that few regions have done more to try to curb alcoholic drinks.

FEW COUNTRIES SQUEEZE THEIR DRINK into a tighter strait-jacket. Norway levies the highest and most punitive rate of duty on beer in the world. One result of this is that home-brewing is a potent tradition in Norway, with some rural recipes still incorporating home-grown juniper berries. The styles and strengths of commercial beers are strictly regulated by the State. The positive side of this strict regulation has meant the introduction of a beer purity law along German lines, which gives the all-malt Norwegian beers a smooth, clean taste.

Since 1995 there have been seven tax bands in operation, known by letters of the alphabet. The biggest leap is between the third level (for beers with an alcohol content of 2.75–3.75%) to the fourth level, (3.75–4.75%). Despite this price hike, the fourth level, (band D), is by far the most popular, accounting for more than three-quarters of all sales. Virtually all of this is Pilsner-style beer. A dark variety of Pilsner is also brewed, called baierol or bayer. The three stronger bands, up to a maximum 7%, include export-style lagers or gullol (gold beer) and some darker, seasonal brews, such as bokkol or juleol, at Christmas. Lower-alcohol beers are called brigg or lettol. All are bottom-fermented. There are few nationally sold brands. Instead, regional beers tend to dominate in their local areas. Dahls Pils rules Trondelag for instance; Tou Pils is pre-eminent in Stavanger; and Arendal Pils reigns supreme in the Sorlandet region. In the mid-1980s there were around 15 independent breweries. Since then the largest company, Ringnes, has been taking over its rivals and now controls all the dominant brands mentioned. This concentration in the industry has inevitably led to the closure of some plants.

Above: Norway taxes its beer heavily, and the variety of brews available is limited. The most popular beers tend to be light lagers, and the main brewery is Ringnes, founded in 1877.

THE BEERS

Aass Bock

A creamy, copper-coloured, malty bock beer (6.1%), from the Aass brewery.

Aass Classic Special Brygg

An aromatic, dark-gold lager (4.5%) with a crisp, clean hop taste from the Aass brewery in Drammen.

Akershus Irish Stout

This uncompromisingly black stout (4.6%) from Akershus has a smooth, rich chocolatey flavour.

Akershus Pale Ale

A copper-coloured, hoppy pale ale (4.6%) from the Akershus brewery.

Akershus Weissbier

This filtered, German-style wheat beer (4.6%) is brewed using wheat and barley by the Akershus brewery.

Arctic Pils

This golden, hoppy Pilsner (4.5%) is brewed by Mack.

Christmas Juleol

A seasonal celebration brew from Aass, Drammen. It has a deep-caramel colour and a toasted-malt flavour.

Frydenlund Pilsener

A well-hopped, traditional Pilsner now brewed by Ringnes following the closure of the Frydenlund brewery in Oslo in 1995.

Hansa Bayer

A tasty, dark, Bavarian-style brew (4.5%) from Hansa.

Hansa Eksportol

A tawny-gold lager (4.5%) with a salty, malt flavour. It is brewed for export.

Hansa Premium

A light-tasting wheat beer (4.5%), brewed by Hansa in Bergen, which is very popular in western Norway.

Lauritz

This Dortmunder-style beer is named after the founder of the Aass brewery Lauritz Aass.

Ludwig Pils

A golden, hoppy Pilsner from the Hansa brewery.

Lysholmer

Ringnes-owned Dahl's brewery in Trondheim produces this range of nationally popular brews which includes the golden special and an ice beer.

Mack Bayer

A Bavarian-style, dark chocolatey brew from the Mack brewery.

Mack Polar Bear

A hazy, amber lager with a malty taste, from Mack.

Pilsener Mack-Ol

This malty, golden Pilsner from the Mack brewery in the far north of the country is reputedly the best brew with which to wash down a local delicacy – seagulls' eggs.

Ringnes Pils

A golden Pilsner-style lager with a fresh, mild hop and malt flavour. This is the flagship brand for Ringnes.

THE BREWERS

Aass

Norway's oldest brewery was founded in Drammen in 1834. A medium-size independent company, it generates tremendous loyalty among local drinkers with its own beer club boasting more than 8,000 members. It also offers one of the widest range of beers, with more than ten different brews.

Akershus

This firm was founded in the Oslo suburb of Enebakk in 1992. It brews a variety of top-fermenting styles.

Hansa

The large Bergen brewery was founded in 1891 and is best-known for its Ludwig Pils, but it brews a large range of beers. It also runs a traditional farmhouse brewery for tourists and makes a juniper beer. The firm regained its independence in 1996, following the merger of Ringnes and Pripps.

Mack

The world's most northerly brewery at Tromsø, inside the Arctic Circle, was founded in 1877. As well as its flagship Pils, Mack also brews hoppier Mack Norges and Arctic Pils, besides other beers which have a more Bavarian accent.

Mikro

Norway's first home-brew pub, the aptly named Mikro Bryggeri, in Oslo, has brewed top-fermented English-style draught bitters and stout since 1990.

Ringnes

Norway's major brewery, founded in Oslo in 1877, also owns many other brands and breweries. Its main national beers are Ringnes Pils and Lysholmer Ice from Dahl's brewery in Trondheim. In 1995 it merged with Pripps of Sweden to form Pripps Ringnes.

SWEDEN

Brewers in Sweden have long struggled to keep their heads above water due to the strict laws that govern alcohol consumption. However, in recent years the rules have been relaxed and there has been a revival of small-scale brewing.

Above: Swedish brewers have long struggled against a strong temperance movement. Spendrup's is one of the few hardy survivors.

L IKE ITS NEIGHBOURS, Sweden has had to contend with a powerful temperance movement. Both politicians and church leaders regularly hold up alcohol as the source of the nation's moral ills. The production and sale of beer is tightly controlled, including strict demarcation according to strength. Beers are sold in three different strengths (Class I to 1.8%; Class II to 3.5%; Class III to 5.6%) – often with the same label. Only Class I and Class II beers can be sold in bars or food stores. Laws were introduced that severely restricted the sale of stronger, Class III beers. Under the legislation, stronger beers could only be bought in restaurants or from State shops (which are closed in the evenings and at weekends) and large taxes were levied on their consumption.

In 1960 there were 85 breweries in the country, but this strait-jacket on sales proved to be the final straw for many struggling companies, who went out of business in the years that followed. Many of the other brewers switched to producing medium-strength beers. At one stage, the State owned some breweries, including the leading brewer Pripps.

However, since Sweden's entry into the European Union in 1995, some of the State monopolies and restrictions have had to be relaxed, to conform with rules on free trade within the union. A ban on beer stronger than 5.6% was dropped, and the country is now adopting a uniform rate of duty on alcohol instead of the three-class system, which heavily favoured the brewing and sale of weaker brews.

A licence has been granted for a brewpub in Stockholm, and a growing number of new, small, local breweries has begun to spring up, mainly devoted to brewing the stronger Class III beers.

THE BEERS

Dart
This English-style copper-coloured, hoppy bitter is brewed by Pripps.

Falcon Export
This gold Pilsner has a bitter, hop taste and a light-malt finish. It is produced by Falcon, Falkenberg.

Gorilla
This new extra-strong beer (7.6%) is one of the potent brews that have arrived on the Swedish market since the relaxing of the beer laws. It is produced by the speciality Abro brewery, Vimmerby.

Pripps Bla
The best-selling Swedish beer in all three strength classes. It is a honey-gold sweetish Pilsner. There is also a new Extra Strong Pripps Bla (7.2%) in the strongest beer class.

Royal Pilsner
This is the brand name for a range of hoppy, all-malt Pilsners from Pripps, whose label was designed by Prince Sigvard Bernadotte of Sweden.

Spendrup's Old Gold
This deep-gold, hoppy, all-malt Pilsner-style lager (5%) comes in a distinctive, ridged brown bottle. It is produced by the Spendrup's brewery in Grangesberg.

Spendrup's Premium
This flavoursome, full-bodied, all-malt premium Pilsner comes from the Spendrup's brewery in Grangesberg.

Tom Kelley
This is a potent and flavoursome brew (7.5%). Tom Kelley was introduced by Pripps when the regulations on strong beers were relaxed.

CARNEGIE PORTER – A SCOTTISH BREW IN SWEDEN

Many Swedish beers carry English names, but one of Pripps' more distinctive brews poured out of Scotland. A Scot called David Carnegie emigrated to Gothenburg in the early 19th century, setting up his own brewery there in 1836 to produce the popular porters of the day. The company was eventually absorbed by Pripps, but they never stopped brewing the top-fermented dark drop. Today, Carnegie Porter is brewed in Stockholm in two strengths – a richly roasted 5.6%, and a thin shadow of the full-bodied version at 3.6%. It has also introduced a vintage, year-dated stark (strong) porter, which is matured for a full six months. In 1992, the heavy, aromatic brew returned home to Britain to win a gold medal at the International Brewing Exhibition in Burton-on-Trent.

THE BREWERS

Abro
A family brewery at Vimmerby since 1856, Abro is known for its speciality products, notably a powerful Gorilla (7.6%) in the new extra-strong sector. Other brews include Abro Guld and a darker Abro Bayerskt.

Falcon
This large Falkenberg firm has been brewing since 1896. Besides a range of Pilsners, it also offers a malty Falcon Guldol, and a dark, Munich-style Falcon Bayerskt.

Gamla Stans
Sweden's first brewpub opened in Stockholm in 1995 brewing a fresh, unfiltered lager, Faerskoel (5%).

Gotlands
A small brewery in Visby on the island of Gotland which was revived by Spendrups in 1995. Besides a dry Munkeol lager, it also brews two Scottish-style beers, a creamy Oat Malt Stout (4.5%) and Scotch Ale (4.2%) plus the unfiltered, fruity Klosteroel (6%).

Pripps
The dominant force in Swedish brewing has absorbed many smaller breweries. It was founded in Gothenburg in 1828 and merged with Stockholm Breweries in 1963. At the time of the merger the combined company boasted 30 breweries. Its main plant is now at Bromma near Stockholm and the leading brand is the sweetish Pilsner Pripps Bla ("blue").

In 1995, Pripps merged with Norway's major brewer Ringnes. Pripps also has a stake in Hartwall of Finland, and the two companies have expanded heavily eastwards into the new Baltic states.

Spendrup's
In the difficult and restricted trading conditions that have prevailed in Sweden for many years, it seemed that this local brewery in Grangesberg, like a large number of others, was in danger of closing. The brewery, which was then trading as Grangesbergs, revived its fortune when it restored the old family name of Spendrup's and launched a range of all-malt Pilsners in distinctive bottles.

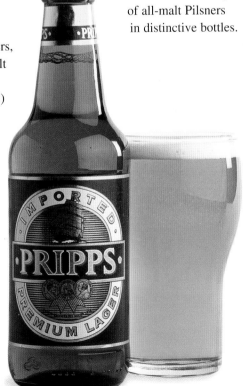

FINLAND

Finland has, more than any other Scandinavian country, managed to retain its ancient brewing traditions, and despite a vigorous anti-alcohol movement in the country, the modern industry is also thriving.

Above: Hartwall, Finland's biggest brewer, produces a golden lager Lapin Kulta, which, in its strongest form (5.3%), may only be sold in restricted outlets.

S UCH IS THE POPULARITY of the traditional Finnish beer *sahti* that it has moved out of remote rural farms into more commercial production. Many Finns like to drink sahti after a traditional sauna, and some households even make it in the sauna. The country also has a long history of more conventional brewing, but the development of the industry was heavily disrupted by anti-alcohol legislation. Like the United States, Finland endured a long period of Prohibition from 1919 until 1932. However, unlike its Scandinavian neighbours, the dry grip of the temperance movement shows little sign of relaxing in Finland and taxes on beer have remained high (as much as 40% on the strongest brews, with an additional value-added tax of around 16%).

Beer is divided into classes according to strength for regulation of sales and for tax purposes. Only the weakest, Class I (beers below 2.8% alcohol by volume), are allowed to be sold through ordinary shops, and may be advertised freely. The popular Class III (3.7–4.7%) is more restricted, through higher taxation and State-regulated distribution. Almost all Class III beer is of the Pilsner style.

As strength climbs, so the State's grip tightens, and sales of stronger beers (to 5.7%) are closely controlled by the State-owned retail monopoly, Alko. These export lagers can only be legally sold through Alko's shops and licensed restaurants. There are also a few speciality brews containing up to 7.8% alcohol. Despite these severe restrictions, the Finnish brewing industry has managed to remain quite vigorous, with two main groups, Hartwall and Sinebrychoff, dominating the tightly controlled market, and a growing number of small "restaurant-brewers" are now springing up all the time.

THE BEERS

Cheers

A copper-coloured, bottom-fermented ale, produced by one of the Finnish giants, Sinebrychoff.

Jouloulot Christmas Beer

A reddish-coloured, rich-flavoured, seasonal winter brew (5%), produced by Sinebrychoff.

Karhu 3

A dark, brownish lager (4.6%), with a strong, full flavour. This is one of a range from the Sinebrychoff's second brewery at Pori.

Karjala

This tawny-coloured, richly flavoured, spicy, hoppy Pilsner is brewed by Hartwall and is their best-selling brew after Lapin Kulta. The company have recently added Hartwall 1836 Classic, a full malt ale to their range, first produced in 1996.

Koff

Koff is the abbreviated name which is given to the beers from the Sinebrychoff brewery, these include a popular, light-brownish, pleasant-tasting Pilsner (4.5%), a powerful pale Extra Strong (7.5%) and an export lager (5.2%).

Koff Porter

The Sinebrychoff brewery still brews one of its oldest beers (7.2%), a dense dark ale which was only revived after the Second World War, using a top-fermenting yeast cultured from a bottle of Guinness. Centrifuged but not filtered, it has a rich, roasted flavour. Four different malts are used in the mash, and the beer is conditioned for six weeks before it is pasteurized. It was once exported to the US under the name Imperial Stout.

Lammin Sahti

The best-known commercial sahti producer sells the Finnish speciality in a container resembling a wine box. The reddish, hazy drink (8%) has a spicy, tart taste.

Lapin Kulta

Hartwall's leading Pilsner from its most northern brewery trades on its fresh image using the icy waters of Lapland. Its strongest form (5.3%) is smooth and malty.

Leningrad Cowboy

This unusually named, golden export lager (5.2%) is brewed by Sinebrychoff and reflects the brewery's Russian connections.

Pilsner Nikolai

A sweetish, premium Pilsner (4.5%) brewed by the Sinebrychoff brewery. It is named in honour of the brewery's founder.

Postin Oma

Michael Jackson (*The Beer Hunter*) described this dark brew from the small Ravintola Wanha Posti brewery very favourably when he visited in 1995, saying, "It has a very attractive copper-brown colour and a good, dense head. The flavour has some nuttiness and some dark chocolate with a good development of malt flavours. It is very easily drinkable and soothing." The brewery was so pleased that it has immortalized Mr Jackson's complimentary write-up of their brew on the back of its beer mats!

Sahti

This is the traditional beer style of Finland. It is strong (usually around 8%), unfiltered, hazy, reddish-amber in colour and quite flat, with a spicy, bittersweet flavour. Rye, rather than barley, is used as the main component in the mash. This, combined with the main seasoning of juniper (rather than hops), gives the finished product a refreshingly tart tang. Juniper twigs are also traditionally used to strain the brew, and saunas are sometimes used to kiln the grains. Sahti production was originally a domestic enterprise, and the fact that baking yeast is often used in the recipe reflects its homely origins.

Sandels

Olvi's lightly hopped, light brown, traditional Finnish lager which has a smooth, malty taste. It is named after Colonel Sandels, a famous soldier in the Russian-Finnish War.

Vaakuna

This dark, golden, malty, toffeeish, Bavarian Märzen-style lager (4.5%) is produced by the Olvi brewery.

Sowing the seed

Finland's cold climate is well suited to cereal production, and it is one of the major barley growers of the world. Its malted grain is exported widely and may even end up in brews as far afield as Japan.

Above and below: The colours of Lapin Kulta's label are inspired by Finland's midnight sun.

THE BREWERS

Hartwall

The Hartwall company controls more than half of the beer market in Finland, with breweries in Helsinki, Lahti and Tornio. The brewery in Tornio was founded in this trapping and gold-rush town in 1873 and the Lapin Kulta name, meaning "Lapp Gold", was taken from an old mine. This brewery is one of the few breweries in the world to take its water from rivers.

Hartwall was a soft drinks manufacturer until 1966 when it bought its first brewery. Its main Pilsner brand is Lapin Kulta. but it also produces Karjala and Hartwall 1836 Classic. In 1991, Hartwall set up a joint venture with Pripps of Sweden, Baltic Beverage Holdings (BBH), to expand into the Baltic states, buying into breweries in Estonia, Latvia, Lithuania and Russia.

Kappeli Brasserie

The Kappeli Brasserie in Helsinki produces unfiltered lagers and seasonal specials.

Olvi

The third-largest brewing group in Finland is based in Iisalmi. Besides a range of Pilsners it produces a malty export lager, Vaakuna and the light brown Sandels.

Sinebrychoff

Finland's oldest brewery was established by a Russian merchant, Nikolai Sinebrychoff, in 1819 in Helsinki. Originally the brewery made porter, mead and top-fermenting beers, then it introduced lager to its range in 1853. It still trades on the Russian connection. The beers are mainly sold under the abbreviated Koff name, but there is also a premium Pilsner Nikolai and oddities such as an export lager called Leningrad Cowboy.

A northern industry

There are thousands of local sahti producers, churning out about four million litres (900,000 gallons) each year. The majority is made in the region the Finns call "the north" – the area stretching 150 km (100 miles) or so to the north-east and north-west of Tampere. The best-known commercial producers are Joutsa, Sysmä and Honkajoki.

ICELAND

The small, northerly island of Iceland has a tradition of producing very weak beers as a result of prohibitive legislation that placed an effective brake on normal beer production for 74 years.

IN 1989, ICELAND finally came in from the cold when it ended a 74-year ban on beer imposed in 1915. Previously, companies such as the family-run Egill brewery of Reykjavík, produced only soft drinks and low-alcohol beers, but since the relaxation of the ban they have added a number of stronger brews for the country's tiny population of 250,000, half of whom live in the capital, Reykjavík. Since the repeal of the ban on beer, Reykjavík is fast gaining the reputation of being a fun-loving town, and an increasing number of well-heeled younger Europeans now visit to experience the hedonistic nightlife, particularly during the summer months. At the same time alcoholism is a growing social problem, which perhaps can be partly attributed to the long, dark winters during which there can be as little as four hours' daylight.

Above: Viking is a new beer that has appeared in Iceland since the repeal of the beer ban.

A Viking toast

Iceland is the home of the oldest "parliament" in the world – the Thingvellir. The ancient sagas handed down from Viking times tell of the annual meeting there to make laws, resolve disputes and strike deals. It was a great occasion accompanied by feasting and of course copious beer drinking.

THE BEERS

Dökkur
This stronger (in Icelandic terms) beer (3.8%) was introduced by Egill after the ban on producing alcoholic drinks was lifted in 1989. The name means dark.

Egils Malt
This old-fashioned style of low-alcohol beer (1%) is still brewed by Egill of Reykjavík.

Egils Pilsner
The weak, pale-gold Pilsner (2.25%) is produced by Egill brewery of Reykjavík. The refreshing beer is brewed with pure Icelandic water and is the most popular light beer in Iceland.

Gull
This golden, Pilsner export lager (5%) was introduced by Egill brewery following the repeal of the ban on strong beers. It is now the most popular beer in the country.

Viking Bjór
This pale-gold, clear Pilsner-style lager (5%) is produced by Viking.

THE BREWERS

Egill
Run by the Tomasson family since 1913, Egill concentrated on the production of low-alcohol beers such as Egils Malt until 1989. It still markets these, but since the repeal of the beer ban it has added the stronger Dökkur and Gull to its range, besides brewing Tuborg under licence.

Viking
Originally a soft drinks producer called Sanitas. Viking built a new brewery at Akureyri in 1988 to meet the demand for stronger beer when the ban was lifted in 1989.

BELGIUM

Belgium is the land of beer. No country offers such a rich variety of styles – from wild, spontaneously fermenting brews and fruit beers to spiced beers and blessed Trappist ales still produced in monasteries.

Above: Belgium's speciality beers have earned acclaim throughout the world. Cherry-flavoured kriek beers, with their luscious dark, red colour, are usually made using whole fruit.

ON ONE LEVEL the Belgian beer market has become concentrated over the last century. The number of breweries has declined from around 3,000 in 1900 to little more than 100 today. Pilsner-style beers, such as Stella Artois and Jupiler, from the major brewers Interbrew and Alken-Maes, dominate domestic consumption, and while they are fine brews, they do not match the top-quality lagers available in the Czech Republic and Germany.

However the joy of Belgian beer lies not in its pils but in the fascinating range of other beers which can be found in its bars. What France is to wine, Belgium is to beer. It may be a small country, but it is vast in what it has to offer those thirsting after new tastes. For the adventurous, Belgium is heaven on earth, a beer drinkers paradise.

There are monasteries still producing strong, richly favoured, Trappist ales such as Chimay and Orval, which are now copied by some commercial breweries and sold as abbey beers. Near Brussels a region creates wild lambic beers which are allowed to ferment spontaneously. Some breweries add fruit to these ancient wheat brews to produce beers such as the deliciously dark kriek made using cherries, while others add spices or sour their beers in special ways.

It is in this colourful and complex speciality section that Belgium has earned its reputation. The speciality beers can be divided into seven main groups – lambic (sometimes spelled lambik), white beer, brown beer, red beer, ales, Trappist and saison. Within these categories the range of flavours, styles and strengths is bewildering and some brews are unique and defy categorization. Many cafés and bars offer a staggeringly long beer menu for the customer to choose from, and each beer is often served in its own special glass.

THE BEERS

Abbaye d'Aulne
This is the name used by the de Smedt family brewery in Opwijk for some of its commercially produced abbey-style beers.

Abbaye de Bonne Espérance
This bottle-conditioned, cloudy golden tripel (7.5%) is better known as Floreffe tripel from the Lefebvre brewery in Quenast.

Adler
The third largest lager producer in Belgium, Haacht brews this strong, golden, premium lager (6.5%).

Affligem
The abbey beers from the De Smedt brewery of Opwijk are brewed according to original recipes from the ancient Benedictine Affligem Abbey in the region of Aalst. It produces a brown, dry Affligem Dubbel, a golden blonde (both 7%) and a fruity, amber tripel (8.5%).

Agnus Dei
A complex, strong, pale tripel (8%). This abbey-style beer is sold under the Corsendonk name. The brew, which dates from 1982, is brewed at the Du Bocq brewery. It is the brainchild of Jozef Keersmaekers.

Augustijn
The strong abbey-style beers from the Van Steenberge brewery of Ertvelde include Augustijn (8%) and a Grand Cru (9%).

Avec les Bons Voeux de la Brasseries
A strong, gold, spicy (9.5%) New Year beer with a long title. This brew comes from Dupont in Hainaut. An organic (biologique) version is also available.

Bel Pils
Considered one of Belgium's better Pilsners, Bel Pils (5.3%) is pale gold with a hoppy flavour. It is produced by the independent family brewery Moortgat, which also makes Duvel and Maredsous abbey beers.

Belle-Vue
Gueuze, kriek and frambozen (5.2%) from this large-scale brewer of lambic beers are pleasant but a little undemanding.

Blanche de Namur
This pale wheat beer (4.3%) with a spicy, fruity flavour is brewed in Namur province by the family brewery Du Bocq.

Blanche des Honnelles
A cloudy wheat beer (6%) that incorporates malted oats in the mash and is spiced with juniper, coriander and orange peel. Produced by Abbaye des Rocs.

Block Special 6
Brewed in Peizegem, Block produces this unique sour beer, Block Special 6 (6%), which is a blend of lambic and young and old pale ales. It also brews the range of Satan ales.

Bokkereyer
A strong (5.8%) Vienna-style lager from a Limburg family brewery, St Jozef, on the Dutch border at Opitter.

Bourgogne des Flandres
Lambic brewer Timmermans of Itterbeek produces this lambic-based, plummy, sour, red ale (6.5%).

Brigand
A robust, bronze-coloured ale (9%) with a sweetish taste. It is served in corked bottles by the Van Honsebrouck brewery of Ingelmunster, West Flanders. Brigand has gained a cult following.

Brugs Tarwebier
Also known as Blanche de Bruges, this cloudy wheat beer (5%) is the best-known brew from Gouden Boom in Bruges. Tarwe means wheat.

Brugse Straffe Hendrik
See Straffe Hendrik.

Brugse Tripel
This strong, golden beer (9.5%) comes from the small Gouden Boom brewery in Bruges (the brewery also boasts its own beer museum).

Right: Transferring casks of craft-brewed Belgian ale from the lorry to the bar earlier this century.

Bush

The strongest beer in Belgium, Bush (12%) is an amber-coloured, English-style barley wine from the Dubuisson brewery in Pipaix, Hainaut. Originally brewed in 1933, this dry, warming brew with a mellow, oaky taste, became the family firm's only regular beer. It is sold as Scaldis in the US in order to avoid confusion with brewing giant Anheuser-Busch. Dubuisson also brews a dark amber Bush Noël (12%) at Christmas. In 1994, the brewery marked its 225th anniversary with the launch of a weaker hoppy Bush Beer (7%).

Celis White

This wheat beer (5%) is now brewed by De Smedt under licence from the original producer of Belgian wheat beer, Pieter Celis, who now brews in America.

Chapeau

This range of weak, lambic fruit beers, including banana, strawberry and pineapple, is produced by De Troch.

Charles Quint

This strong, sweetish brown ale (7%) is produced by Haacht.

Chimay Blanche

See Chimay Cinq Cents.

Chimay Bleu

See Chimay Grande Réserve.

Chimay Cinq Cents

A golden, amber Trappist tripel with a malty flavour (8%). It is the hoppiest, driest offering from the Abbaye de Notre-Dame de Scourmont, near Chimay. In the smaller bottle size it is known as Chimay Blanche, and is so called after the white colour of the bottle cap.

Chimay Grande Réserve

This rich, fruity Trappist ale (9%) is the strongest and most complex ale from the Abbaye de Notre-Dame de Scourmont. The bottle has a blue cap and label. It was originally introduced as a Christmas beer, but has been brewed regularly since 1958. It is vintage-dated and benefits from being laid down for a few years. In the smaller size it is known as Chimay Bleu.

Chimay Première

A rich, red-brown Trappist ale (7%) with a spicy, fruity flavour from the Abbaye de Notre-Dame de Scourmont. The bottle has a red label and top. In the 33cl bottle is called Chimay Rouge.

Chimay Rouge

See Chimay Première.

Cochonne

An annual ale (9%) from the small Vapeur brewery in Pipaix in Hainaut.

A SINGULAR ALE

The Antwerp brewery De Koninck was founded in 1833. It uses a traditional Flemish brick-clad kettle with a hop sieve that is removed by a pulley system. The recipe is all malt (using no adjuncts) and incorporates Saaz hops. The best way to enjoy a glass of De Koninck is on draught in the Pilgrim café opposite the brewery, where locals often add an extra shot of yeast to their glass.

Corsendonk

These two abbey beers in their stylish brown bottles date from as recently as 1982. They are named after the former Corsendonk Augustinian priory near Turnhout, which was established in the 15th century and recently restored. The brews are the brainchild of a member of the well-known brewing family, Jozef Keersmaekers. The dark, chocolatey dubbel, Pater Noster, is brewed by the Van Steenberge brewery. The stronger, pale tripel, Agnus Dei (8%), is brewed at the Du Bocq brewery.

Cristal Alken

This unpasteurized beer is generally regarded as the hoppiest of the main Belgian Pilsners (4.8%). Brewed by the Alken-Maes group, it is the best-selling beer in its home province of Limbourg.

Cuvée d'Aristée

Unusual honeyed ale (9.5%) from the tiny Praille brewery in Peissant near Mons.

Cuvée de l'Hermitage

Cuvée, like the terms luxe and spéciale, has largely become a meaningless title, but this rich, russet ale (8%) from the Union brewery in Jumet deserves the accolade.

De Koninck

This all-malt, top-fermenting ale (5%) has been described as a cross between an English bitter and a German alt. It is matured in the cask, then pasteurized in the bottle. There is also a stronger version available, called Cuvée de Koninck (8%).

Delirium Tremens

This aptly named, notoriously strong, golden, spiced ale (9%) from the Huyghe brewery near Ghent is served in a glass painted with pink elephants.

Dentergems Wit

The Riva brewery of Dentergem launched this, one of the first rival white beers to Hoegaarden, in 1980. The pale, cloudy brew (5%) is more in the German wheat-beer style, with a delicate, wheaty, lemony taste.

Doppelbock Bugel

This is one of the strongest (8%) bottom-fermented beers in Belgium. A heavy Christmas brew, it is produced by Domus, the first home-brew house in Belgium, set up in Leuven in 1985 by a former Cristal Alken brewer. Other beers include a tasty, fresh lager and a cloudy wheat beer, Leuvens Witbier (5%).

Double Enghien Brune

This interesting, creamy, walnutty, strong, dark ale (8%) and the amber blonde come from the Silly brewery in the town of Silly.

Duivelsbier

An unusual beer (6%), produced by the Vander Linden brewery by blending a conventional pale ale and a lambic.

Duvel

This is a beer with a devil of a reputation, one of the best-known and most celebrated drinks in Belgium. A golden ale with a frothy white top, it appears attractive but unremarkable in its balloon goblets apart from its surging lines of bubbles. However, just one sniff of its heady hop aroma and one taste of its complex fruity flavour, together with its sustaining strength

(8.5%), make the beer drinker appreciate that this is a glass apart.

Duvel is brewed by the Moortgat brewery in Breendonk. After the First World War, the brewery attempted to brew a Scotch ale. The Moortgat brewers examined bottles of McEwan's ale from Edinburgh and made a dark ale using the McEwan's yeast. "It's a devil of a brew," claimed one taster, and the name Duvel was born in 1923. In 1968 Moortgat perfected a golden version.

Today, the devil appears in two guises: the delicious bottle-conditioned brew has a red-lettered label; a blander, filtered version has green letters. Other Belgian brewers have tried to copy the beer, but none can match the original.

Ename

A range of abbey beers brewed by the Roman brewery in East Flanders which includes a dark Dubbel (6.5%) and a golden Tripel (8%).

Felix

The Clarysse brewery of Oudenaarde produces this range of sweetish East Flanders brown ales. Beers include Felix Oud Bruin (5.5%), Special Oudenaards (4.8%), plus two kriekbiers (6% and 5%).

Floreffe

This range of quality bottle-conditioned abbey beers from the Lefebvre family brewery at Quenast, south-west of Brussels, is named after the Norbertine abbey at Floreffe.

The best, a mahogany-coloured spicy ale, is simply called La Meilleure (8%). A golden tripel (7.5%) is also sold as Abbaye de Bonne Espérance. Additional beers include a tasty dubbel and a blonde (both 7%).

Gildenbier

This strong, sweetish brown ale (6.6%) is produced by Haacht.

Goudenband

See Liefmans Goudenband.

Gouden Carolus

A distinctive, smooth, dark ale (7%) from the family-run Anker brewery of Mechelen, its name derives from a gold coin of the Holy Roman Emperor Charles V who grew up in the city. There is also a lighter, less spicy Mechelsen Brune (5.5%) and a yellow, pale ale, Toison d'Or Tripel (7%).

Grimbergen

This range of abbey beers from the large Alken-Maes group is brewed at its Union brewery in Jumet. They include a warming Optimo Bruno (10%), a sweet, winey, golden tripel (9%) and blonde (7%) and a dark,

fruity dubbel (6.5%). The beers are named after the abbey of Grimbergen in the northern suburbs of Brussels.

Hapkin

The Louwaege brewery of West Flanders produces this strong, bottle-conditioned golden ale (8.5%), which seeks to rival Duvel.

Het Kapittel

The Van Eecke brewery of Watou produces this range of quality abbey beers. Brews include a strong abt (10%) and darkly delicious prior (9%), plus a dubbel (7%) and pater (6.5%).

Hoegaarden

The renewed interest in cloudy wheat beers began with this beer, first brewed by Pieter Celis at his De

Kluis Brewery in Hoegaarden in 1966. It revived the art of brewing "white" beers spiced with coriander and curaçao. Hoegaarden's chunky glasses have become a familiar part of Belgian bars. Besides the refreshing cloudy, lemon-coloured Hoegaarden (5%), the brewery also produces a stronger, golden Grand Cru and a spicier orangey-coloured Julius (both 8.7%), plus a rich, fruity brown ale, Verboden Vrucht (8.8%). All are bottle-conditioned.

Horse-Ale
This is an English-style pale ale (4.8%), with an aromatic hop character brewed by Interbrew.

Ichtegems Oud Bruin
A refreshing, Flemish red ale, with a sweetish, malt taste from the Strubbe brewery of Ichtegem.

Jacobins
This range of sweetish lambic beers – Jacobins amber, sweet-and-sour gueuze, the red, cherry-flavoured kriek and raspberry frambozen (all 5.5%) – comes from the Bockor brewery of Bellegem.

Jupiler
Belgium's best-selling beer, the popular malty Pilsner (5.2%) comes from Jupille

near Liège. Founded in 1853, the brewery is now part of Interbrew.

Kasteel
A very strong, amber-coloured, bottled, rich dark ale (11.5%). It is laid down to mature by the Van Honsebrouck brewery in the cellars at Ingelmunster Castle, an 18th-century moated mansion owned by the brewing family. The taste is rich, almost like a port.

La Chouffe
This golden ale (8%) from the Achouffe brewery is spiced with coriander.

La Divine
This interesting, strong, dark, amber-coloured ale (9.5%) with a full, spicy flavour, is brewed by the Silly brewery.

La Gauloise
The distinctive strong ales from the Du Bocq brewery of Namur include an ambrée (6.5%), blonde (7%) and dark, red-coloured brune (9%). The larger-size bottles are corked.

La Meilleure
This mahogany-coloured, bottle-conditioned spicy ale (8%) is, as the name implies, the best brew from the Floreffe range of abbey ales.

Leffe
Interbrew produces this range of abbey beers, named after the Leffe abbey at Dinant, near Namur. Besides an amber-coloured blonde and a dark-brown, malty, fruity brune (both 6.5%), there's a golden tripel (8.4%) and two brown ales, Vieille Cuvée (7.8%) and Radieuse (8.2%).

Liefmans Frambozenbier
This pale-pink, sour, raspberry fruit beer (5.7%) can be served as an aperitif in place of champagne.

Liefmans Goudenband
An acidic, chocolate-brown-coloured, sweet-and-sour Belgian brown ale (8%) that is brewed by Liefmans using four different hop varieties and a 100-year-old yeast strain. Part of the brew is matured for six to eight months, then it is mixed with a younger version to make the distinctively flavoured finished product.

Liefmans Kriekbier
This traditional tart, cherry fruit beer (6.5%), produced by the Liefmans brewery in Oudenaarde, is a deep, cloudy red-brown colour. It is suitable for keeping for up to four years and will age and mature with time.

Limburgse Witte

This tasty wheat beer (5%) is produced by the family-owned Martens brewery.

Lucifer

This is one of the rival brews to Duvel. It is a strong, golden ale (8%) brewed by the Riva brewery in Flanders.

McChouffe

A complex, copper-coloured, creamy, malty Ardenne strong ale (8.5%) with a vague Scottish ancestry, from the Achouffe brewery.

McGregor

A dark, whisky-malt brew (6.5%) from the Huyghe family brewery in Melle.

Maes Pils

This popular, mass-market, deep golden Pilsner with a big hoppy flavour (5.1%) comes from the Maes brewery near Antwerp.

Marckloff

A hazy Walloon pale ale (6.5%) which comes from the homebrew café La Ferme au Chêne in Durbuy.

Maredsous

The range of abbey ales from the Moortgat brewery in Breendonk includes a strong, black quadrupel (10%), a dark tripel (8%), a mild-tasting blonde dubbel (6%) and a dark dubbel (6%) and a golden ale with an orange colour. These beers are identified by degree numbers, 10, 8 and 6. They are named after a Benedictine abbey at Denée, south of Namur.

Moinette

These strong ales from the Dupont brewery in Hainaut include a spicy, complex blonde and brune (both 8.5%) and an organic biologique (7.5%).

Mort Subite

These sweet, commercial lambics from the De Keersmaeker brewery include the gentle, amber Mort Subite gueuze, a sweet, cherry-flavoured kriek (both 4.5%), sweet framboise and pêche (both 4%) and a cassis (4%) made with blackcurrant juice. The name means "sudden death" after a card game.

Oerbier

This popular, dark, hazy amber, Scottish-style ale (7.5%) was the first brew produced by De Dolle Brouwers.

Op-Ale

This pale, sweetish, malty ale (4.8%) is produced by the De Smedt family brewery in Opwijk.

Optimo Bruno

This warming Grimbergen abbey beer (10%) comes from the Alken-Maes group's Union brewery.

Orval

This Belgian classic Trappist ale (6.2%) is the only brew made by the Abbaye d'Orval. It is orange, with a heady, hoppy aroma and an intense, dry flavour. Its complex character is in part due to three separate fermentations and dry-hopping.

Oud Beersel

These traditional unfiltered lambics, from the tiny Van-dervelden brewery at Beersel, near Brussels, include Oud Beersel Lambik (5.7%), gueuze (6%) and kriek (7%).

Oud Kriekenbier

This is the only non-lambic cherry beer (6.5%) to be made completely with whole cherries rather than using juice. It is produced by the small Crombe brewery.

Oudenaards Wit Tarwebier

This white wheat beer (4.8%) is produced by Clarysse at Oudenaarde in East Flanders.

Palm

Palm Spéciale (5.2%) is the biggest-selling ale in Belgium. It is brewed by the independent Palm brewery of Steenhuffel. It is an amber, fruity, refreshing beer. A darker version called Dobbel Palm (5.5%), is produced at Christmas. The village brewery, which dates back to 1747, also brews a more powerful, copper-coloured, bottle-conditioned ale, Aerts 1900 (7%), and a wheat beer, Steendonk (4.5%).

Pater Noster

A dark brown, smoky, malt-tasting dubbel (7%) from the Van Steenberge brewery sold under the Corsendonk name.

Pauwels Kwak

This warming, garnet-coloured ale (8%), named after an innkeeper, is served in a distinctive round-bottomed Kwak glass which has to be supported on a wooden stand.

Petrus

The top-fermented beers from the Bavik brewery include a dark imitation of Rodenbach which is matured in oak casks (5.5%). Bavik also brews a golden spéciale (5.5%) and tripel (7.5%).

Poperings Hommelbier

A creamy, hoppy, amber ale (7.5%), this seasonal drink is brewed by the Van Eecke brewery of Watou to celebrate the hop harvest in nearby Poperinge.

Primus Pils

A highly regarded, dry, yellow, hoppy Pilsner (5%), produced by Haacht.

Rodenbach

This distinctive ale (5%) is made by blending a vintage brew, which has been matured in oak casks for over a year, with fresh, young beer, which has only been matured for five to six weeks. A quarter of the old ale is mixed with three-quarters of the new. The resulting beer is so tart that it is sweetened with sugar to produce a refreshing sweet and sour taste. Some of the vintage brew is bottled

unsweetened and undiluted to create the much-bolder Grand Cru (6.5%). There is also a sweeter version, blended with cherry essence, called Alexander (6.5%).

Rose de Gambrinus

The most celebrated lambic frambozen (5%), which comes from the Cantillon brewery in Brussels. It contains a small proportion of cherries and a dash of vanilla, as well as raspberries. It is blood-orange-coloured, wih a tart, fruity flavour.

St Benoît

The fine abbey beers from the Du Bocq brewery of Namur include a yellow, wheaty St Benoît Blonde and amber-brown brune (both 6.5%) with a fresh, dry, woody flavour, besides a hoppy golden tripel (8%), which is also sold as Triple Moine.

St Idesbald

These unusual, sour abbey beers come from the Damy brewery in east Flanders and include a licht and dubbel (both 6%), as well as a dark tripel (8%).

St Louis

The Van Honsebrouck brewery produces this range of sweet commercial lambics, including a gueuze, kriek, framboise and cassis (all 5%). There is also a more characterful, unfiltered Gueuze Fond Tradition (5%).

St Sebastiaan

These abbey beers from the Sterkens brewery of Meer, close to the Dutch border, are sold in distinctive pottery bottles. The beers include a Grand Cru (7.6%) and a dark (6.9%) which is also sold as Poorter.

St Sixtus

See St Bernardus.

Saison de Pipaix

The small Vapeur brewery produces this refreshing spicy saison (6.5%).

Saison Régal

A spicy, hoppy saison-style, amber-coloured beer (6%) from Du Bocq in the province of Namur.

Saison de Silly

A fruity saison beer (5%) produced by the Silly brewery in Hainhaut.

THE LAMBIC HELPER

Thousands of tiny yeast organisms are carried on cool evening air currents through the open windows of lambic breweries. Inside the dark, dusty interiors (for lambic brewers know better than to remove the cobwebs and moulds from the brewery walls) the yeasts settle on cobwebs and into damp nooks and crannies. Some find their way into the open vats of cooling beer, where they begin to feast on the sugars and ferment the brew. These untamed, wild helpers produce an ale that is tart and refreshing. Trusting to the action of wild yeasts borne invisibly in the air is the oldest fermentation method in the world, and their effect was once regarded by brewers as nothing short of magical. The lambic brewers of Belgium, though they now understand the source of their help, have maintained this ancient tradition.

Satan

Strong red, gold and brown ales (all 8%) from the Block brewery of Peizegem.

Sezuens

A hoppy, sunny, gold-amber, saison ale (6%) which comes from the Martens brewery of Bocholt. It follows the saison style of thirst-quenching beers, which are brewed during the winter for drinking in summer. Martens also brews a stronger, amber-red Sezuens Quattro (8%) and the less-powerful Sezuens Europe (6.5%).

Silly Brug-Ale
This fruity beer (5%) comes from the Silly brewery in the town of the same name.

Sloeber
The Roman brewery produces this rich, malty, strong, golden ale (7.5%) in the Duvel style. The name means "joker".

Steenbrugge Dubbel
This abbey ale (6.5%) comes from the small Gouden Boom brewery in Bruges.

Steenbrugge Tripel
This creamy, golden abbey beer (9%) from Gouden Boom is less heavy than the brewery's Brugse tripel.

Stella Artois
Belgium's best-known, golden lager is the flagship Pilsner (5.2%) of the brewing giant Interbrew.

Stille Nacht
Dolle Brouwers produces this strong, orangey, seasonal, bottle-conditioned ale (9%) in winter. The name comes from the German title for the popular carol, "Silent Night".

Straffe Hendrik
This heavily hopped pale ale (6.5%) is the only beer produced by Straffe Hendrick, Bruges.

Titje
A distinctive, cloudy, gold wheat beer (5%) with a fruity, spicy flavour from the Silly brewery.

Tongerlo
Abbey beers from Haacht brewery include a double blonde (6%), brune (6.5%) and amber tripel (8%).

Unic Bier
A characterful, weak table beer (3.2%) from Gigi, a fine example of this style.

Verboden Vrucht
The name of Hoegaarden's distinctive, strong, orangey-coloured dark ale (9%) means "forbidden fruit", and it is also sold as Fruit Défendu in France. When customs officials in the United States saw the sexy label of Adam and Eve, based on a Rubens painting, they tried to ban bottles of the revealing brew.

Vieille Provision
An excellent, hoppy, saison-style ale (6.5%) which comes from the farmyard Dupont brewery. It is also known as Saison Dupont and Vieille Réserve. This classic country beer has a complex, refreshing taste and a solid creamy head.

Vieux Temps
Interbrew's malty, pale ale (5%) from Leuven, is popular in the south of the country. Its name means "old times".

Vigneronne
A tart lambic (5%) made from green grapes and blended lambic beers, from the Cantillon brewery.

Westmalle
Both the dark dubbel (6.5%) and the golden tripel (9%) from this monastic brewery have a secondary fermentation. They are then primed with sugar and given a dose of yeast before being bottled. The dubbel is complex and surprisingly dry. The tripel has many imitators. It is extremely pale with a delicious citric and honeyed flavour.

Westvleteren
A range of much-sought-after beers produced by the small Westvleteren monastery, including a dark, fruity special (6.2%) and a similar and stronger extra (8%) leading up to a stern but rotund abt, which at 11.5% is one of the strongest beers in the country. All are on the sweetish side for Trappist ales. The bottles are identified by the colour of their crown corks – red for special, blue for extra and yellow for abt.

Witkap
This range of quality abbey ales, named after the monk's cowl, come from the Slaghmuylder brewery in Ninove, which was founded in 1860. The Witkap beers include the hoppy pale Stimulo (6%), a rich Dubbel Pater (7%) and a golden, bitter, fruity tripel (7.5%).

Yperman
A robust pale ale (6%), from the Leroy family brewery near Ypres.

THE BREWERS

Abbaye d'Orval

Abbaye d'Orval is the most attractive of the Trappist monasteries, set in woodland above a lake in the rolling hills of the Ardennes. Though an abbey has stood on this site near Florenville since 1070, it was repeatedly sacked and the present stone buildings were only planned in 1926. Five years later, construction was still not finished, so, to provide funds to complete the grand scheme, the community decided to add a brewery, the outside of which is designed like a chapel. It opened in 1931, and drinkers have been giving thanks for this brew ever since.

Orval means "Vale of Gold", and the true treasure of the Orval monastery is its one precious beer. Unlike the other Trappist breweries, Orval does not brew a range of beers, but produces one delicious, intensely dry ale. The monks at the monastery also produce a crusty bread and a fine cheese which go well when eaten as accompaniments to a bottle of Orval.

Abbaye des Rocs

This commercial brewery in Montignies-sur-Roc has been producing strong Walloon ales since 1984. It is best known for its dark, spicy Abbaye des Rocs and golden La Montagnarde (both 9%).

Achouffe

This farm brewery in the Ardennes uses its own spring water for brewing. Its bearded gnome symbol has been a familiar sight in this holiday area since 1982.

Alken-Maes

The Belgian arm of the French brewing giant Kronenbourg controls a fifth of the Belgian beer market through its Cristal Alken and Maes Pilsners, as well as other brands such as Grimbergen abbey ales and Mort Subite lambics.

Artois

Best known for its international Pilsner brand, Stella Artois (5.2%), Artois was founded in Leuven in 1366. Now it is part of Interbrew, the second-largest brewing group in Europe. A massive new brewery opened in Leuven in 1995, alongside the huge original plant.

Bavik

A regional brewery in Bavikove in West Flanders, Bavik was founded in 1894. It produces a range of Pilsners and a witbier, plus top-fermented ales under the Petrus name.

Belle-Vue

The largest brewer of lambics, Belle-Vue has two breweries on the edge of Brussels – a traditional plant at Molenbeek and another operation at Zuun. The Molenbeek brewery has more than 10,000 wooden casks filled with maturing lambic. The quality of these brews is largely unknown because they are diluted with immature young lambics which have been brewed in steel cylinders at Zuun. Since 1990, the Molenbeek plant has also produced an excellent, unfiltered Séléction Lambic (5.2%). Belle-Vue exports its beers to France under the Bécasse brand name.

Binchoise

This small Hainaut brewery was founded in 1989 in an old maltings. It produces a range of strong, spiced ales, notably the citric blonde, which is also sold as Fakir (6.5%) and a honey beer, Bière des Ours (9%).

Block

Brewers at Peizegem in Brabant since 1887 who are best known for their wide range of Satan ales.

Bockor

This regional brewery in Bellegem, West Flanders, founded in 1892, is best known for its Pilsner and Jacobins range of lambic beers. It also brews a brown beer, Bellegems Bruin (5.5%), in which corn is added to the mash and mixed with a lambic brew.

Boon

The pioneering brewer, Frank Boon, helped to revive interest in the ancient lambic style when he started to brew and blend in Lembeek in 1975. His beers include a sweetish Boon gueuze, kriek and frambozen, plus a sourer range which is sold under the Mariage Parfait label. He also brews a weak table beer (2%) called Lembeek and a heavy mix of lambic, pale ale and sugar called Pertotale Faro (6%).

Bosteels

The Bosteels family brewery has been operating in Buggenhout, East Flanders, since 1791. It is famous for its garnet-coloured Pauwels Kwak beer (8%) drunk from its distinctive round-bottomed glass. Bosteels also brews Prosit Pils (4.8%).

Brunehaut

A former African brewer, Guy Valschaerts, established this brewery in 1992 at Rongy in the Hainaut region of Belgium. Brunehaut's beers include an organic wheat Blanche de Charleroi (5%), a juniper brew Abbaye de St Amand (7%) and a golden Bière du Mont St Aubert (8%), besides its original blonde and ambrée ales.

Cantillon

This working brewery museum produces true lambics in the back streets of Brussels. Run by the Van Roy family since 1900, it is famous for its brewing open days. Its uncompromisingly sour beers include a Cantillon lambic, kriek, super gueuze and a gueuze matured in port casks, called Brabantiae (all 5%).

Caracole

A small brewery in Falmignoul, near Namur, Caracole produces a wide range of Walloon strong ales under the sign of the snail, including Caracole ambrée and brune (both 6.5%), an annual Cuvée de l'An Neuf for the New Year, and a good wheat beer called Troublette (5%).

Clarysse

Clarysse has been brewing in East Flanders at Oudenaarde since 1946. It produces mainly brown ales under the Felix name, and is a local rival to the neighbouring Liefmans Brewery. It also brews a wheat Oudenaards Wit Tarwebier (4.8%).

Crombe

A small village brewery in Zottegem near Ghent which dates back to 1798. Crombe is best known for its Oud Kriekenbier (6.5%), the only non-lambic cherry beer to be made completely with whole cherries rather than juice.

De Dolle

See panel opposite – *The Mad Brewers*

De Keersmaeker

This lambic brewery in Kobbegem mainly brews commercial lambics under the Mort Subite brand, but also produces a more traditional gueuze (5%) which is marketed under its own name.

De Koninck

The De Koninck brewery was founded in 1833 in Antwerp. It stuck to producing ale when most of its rivals switched to brewing Pilsners, and it has thrived.

CHIMAY

Chimay is the largest and most internationally famous of the Belgian Trappist breweries. It has been brewing beer on a commercial scale at the Abbaye de Scourmont near Chimay since 1862. The brewery is located behind the walls of the abbey and uses its wells, but the work, as at other Trappist breweries, is carried out largely by secular staff under the monks' supervision. Bottling is handled at a modern plant in nearby Baileux. Chimay brews three distinctive ales, each known by the red, white or blue cap on the bottle. Chimay Rouge, or red (7%), was the original beer produced at the monastery, and was the only product for almost a century.

The quality of the beers owes much to a Belgian scientist, Professor Jean De Clerck of Leuven University, who helped the monastic brewery get back on its feet, after the disruptions of the Second World War, by developing its distinctive yeast strain. When he died in 1978, he was buried at the abbey.

The monastery also produces a range of foods, including some excellent cheeses, which go well with Chimay beer. One, called Chimay à la Bière, has a rind steeped in hops.

De Smedt

A wide range of abbey beers, notably the Affligem range but also Abbaye d'Aulne, are produced by this enterprising family brewery which has been based in Opwijk since 1790. Other beers include a pale Op Ale and the wheat beer Celis White.

De Troch

One of the oldest lambic brewers, De Troch dates back to 1820 in Wambeek. It produces a rare orangey-coloured, sour gueuze and a sweet, fruity kriek (5.5%), but concentrates on a range of weak lambic fruit beers under the Chapeau brand.

Du Bocq

This family brewery, located at Purnode in Namur province since 1858, brews an excellent, if confusing, range of ales, often under a variety of labels. Best known for its La Gauloise beers, it also produces abbey ales under the St Benoît name, a wheat beer Blanche de Namur (4.3%) and a spicy, hoppy Saison Régal (6%).

Dupont

This family farmhouse brewery at Tourpes in Hainaut has been operating since 1850. It produces an excellent saison Vieille Provision (6.5%) and a range of Walloon strong ales under the Moinette label. It also brews organic (biologique) versions of these beers, as well as a strong New Year beer.

Eupener

An old brewery in the border market town of Eupen which has its roots firmly in Germany. This small German-speaking area east of Liège was taken over by Belgium after the First World War. Besides a pleasant pils (4.7%), Eupener brews a sweetish, tawny bock called Klosterbier (5.5%) and two dark, low-alcohol, table beers in the German Malzbier style.

Facon

A family brewery at Bellegem in West Flanders since 1874, which until recent years concentrated on Pilsners and weak table beers. Today it also brews specialist ales, including a dark Scotch Ale (6.1%) and an Extra Stout (5.4%).

Friart

An attractive, old, red-brick Hainaut brewery in Le Roeulx, which was closed in 1977 but reopened in 1988, Friart mainly brews abbey beers under the St Feuillien name. These include a heavy, roasted Cuvée de Noël brewed for Christmas. Some beers are sold in huge six-litre Methuselah bottles.

THE MAD BREWERS

When three brothers rescued an old brewery from closure in 1980 in Esen, near Diksmuide in West Flanders, their bank manager thought they were insane, but the success of their dark Scottish-style ale, Oerbier (7.5%), proved otherwise. De Dolle Brouwers now produce a range of strong and seasonal bottle-conditioned ales including the strong Christmas brew, Stille Nacht (9%), Ara Bier, Boskeun and Oeral.

Gigi

This old Gérouville brewery in Luxembourg province produces the best weak table beers in Belgium, notably the lightly hoppy Double Blonde (1.2%) and the characterful Unic Bier (3.2%). It also sells pale and brown ales (5%) under the La Gaumaise label.

Girardin

This small traditional farm brewery at St Ulriks Kapelle produces fruity lambics from its own wheat, notably Girardin lambic, gueuze and kriek (all 5%). It also produces an aromatic Framboos using raspberries in the brew.

Haacht

The largest independent brewery in Belgium has been operating in Boortmeerbeek in Brabant since 1890. It mainly produces a range of lagers, notably Primus Pils (5%) and a premium Adler (6.5%). It brews a wheat beer Haacht (4.7%), two strong, sweetish brown ales – Charles Quint (6.7%) and Gildenbier (6.6%) – plus a range of abbey beers under the Tongerlo name.

Interbrew

The Belgian brewing giant was formed in 1988 by the merger of Artois and Jupiler. It has bought up several smaller Belgian brewers and produces a large range of brews on home soil. Following the takeover of Canadian brewers Labatt in 1995 and expansion into Eastern Europe after the fall of the Iron Curtain, it is now one of the largest brewing groups in the world, with interests around the globe.

KWAK

The story of Kwak is a marketing lesson in how to make your beer stand out at the bar. In a land where every brew seems to have its own distinctive glass, the Bosteels brewery of Buggenhout went one better and designed a glass which could not stand up on its own. Every time a customer asks for a Kwak, it is served in a tall glass with a round bulbous bottom held erect by a wooden stand. Everyone in the bar knows at a glance when you order a Kwak. Pauwels Kwak (8%) is a warming, garnet-coloured ale named after a famous innkeeper who used to serve beer in stirrup cups to horsemen, for drinking in the saddle.

Lefebvre

Brabant brewery in Quenast since 1876 which produces a wide range of ales, notably the Floreffe abbey beers.

Liefmans

Liefmans is the classic producer of East Flanders brown ales. Its stronger beers are sold in corked bottles, tissue-wrapped for laying down in the cellar to improve with age. All the beers are matured for three months in the bottle before leaving the brewery.

Lindemans

A farmhouse lambic brewer in Vlezenbeek since 1816, Lindemans now sells its beers as far from home as the US. The demands of the world market have led to a range of sweetish lambics including Lindemans faro, gueuze, kriek and framboise. It has recently launched a more distinctive range called Cuvée René, named after the owner.

Martens

This is one of the largest independent breweries in Belgium, but it is still family-owned. Martens has brewed at Bocholt in Limburg since 1758 and is best known for its Sezuens beer, though it also brews a wheat beer, Limburgse Witte (5%), a range of Pilsners and a tafelstout.

Moortgat

A family-owned brewery in Breendonk, north of Brussels, famous for its delicious flagship ale, Duvel.

Riva

Ambitious Flanders brewing group based in Dentergem which includes Liefmans. Best known for its Lucifer ale (8%) and Dentergems witbier.

Rochefort

The least known and most secretive of the Trappist breweries is situated deep in the Ardennes, at the Abbaye de St Rémy near the town of Rochefort.

The first brewery at the abbey, which used its own hops and barley grown in the grounds, dated from 1595, but the present one was built in 1960. More of the monks are involved in day-to-day brewing than at other blessed breweries, and three typically rich, dark Trappist beers are produced. These are all in the same basic style, but increasing in strength from the 6 (7.5%) through the 8 (9.2%) to the ultimate 10 (11.3%), and are known by their degree numbers.

Until quite recently, labels were not used; instead, the three beers were identified by the colour of their bottle caps – red for the 6, green for the 8 and blue for the 10. The chestnut-coloured and powerfully fruity 8, a complex, richly textured and richly rewarding beer is the most popular by far. The lighter, drier 6 is sold only locally, while the near-black 10 is overpowering in its heavy intensity.

Roman

A large, family brewery near Oudenaarde, Roman dates back to 1545. It brews a range of East Flanders brown ales including Oudenaards (5%), the soft, bitter special (5.5%) and bottle-conditioned Dobbelen Bruinen (8%). It also brews a Christmas ale and various Pilsners mainly under the Romy brand, a wheat beer, Mater, and abbey beers under the Ename name.

St Bernardus

This West Flanders brewery, founded in 1946 at Watou specializes in producing abbey beers, both under its own name and that of St Sixtus, after the nearby brewing monastery at Westvleteren. The beer is matured for three months and then bottled without filtering. At one time the monastery used to licence the brewery to produce imitations of its own beers. St Bernardus brews a dark pater (6%), prior (8%), a golden tripel (7.5%) and a strong abt (10%).

St Jozef

Limburg family brewery in Opitter which produces a strong reddish lager Bokkereyer (5.8%).

Silly

Brewery in the Hainaut town since 1950 which brews a vast range of beers including Saison de Silly (5%).

Slaghmuylder

Ninove brewery best known for its quality abbey beers sold under the Witkap label.

Straffe Hendrik

This small brewery in the centre of the city of Bruges brews one ale, Brugse Straffe Hendrik (6%), the classic, hoppy Belgian pale ale.

Timmermans

Lambic brewers in Itterbeek since 1888, their range of lambics includes a fine kriek and Gueuze Caveau (both 5%), plus lighter, aromatic framboise, pêche and cassis (all 4%). They also brew a refreshing lambic wheat beer (3.5%) and a red Bourgogne des Flandres (6.5%).

Vander Linden

A small lambic brewer in Halle since 1893, Vander Linden brews a stronger than average range of lambics, which include a frambozenbier (7%), and the Vieux Foudre gueuze and kriek (both 6%). It also produces Dobbel Faro (6%) and an unusual Duivelsbier.

Westmalle

This Belgian monastic brewery, more than any other, has influenced and defined the abbey style. The monastery near the village of Westmalle, close to the Dutch border near Antwerp, was founded in 1794 by monks from the La Trappe monastery in France. It has been brewing since 1836, but only on a commercial scale since the 1920s. It is now the second largest of the five Belgian Trappist breweries. The brothers brew the defining dark dubbel and tripel. There is also a single, but this everyday drinking beer (4%), also known as Extra, is kept mainly for the monks themselves. The monks also produce a range of cheeses for sale.

Westvleteren

The St Sixtus abbey at Westvleteren, near Ypres in West Flanders, has been brewing since 1839. It is the smallest of the Trappist breweries. Its old brewery is small and its brews are much sought after, partly because they are difficult to obtain. The local beer drinkers queue at a hatch when they hear that a batch of bottles is ready for sale.

In order to meet growing public demand after the Second World War, the Westvleteren abbey for a time licensed the commercial St Bernardus brewery in nearby Watou to brew imitations of its St Sixtus beers. This licensing arrangement has now ceased, but St Bernardus still brews Sixtus beers for the nearby St Sixtus abbey.

RODENBACH

Rodenbach is one of the most remarkable breweries of Belgium. When you walk down the lines of upright old oak tuns, it is like stepping back into another age. The great porter breweries of England once looked like this, but only in Rodenbach have the imposing vessels survived to this impressive extent. There are 300 altogether, filling several halls. Some hold as much as 60,000 litres (13,198 gallons) and are over 100 years old.

The brewery, in Roeselare in West Flanders, was founded in 1820 and came to specialize in the region's sour red beers. A reasonably conventional ale is brewed, using Vienna crystal malt to impart a red colour. Rodenbach's distinct character arises from the way it is then matured. After a second fermentation, the beer is left in huge oak tuns for at least 18 months. During this time, it ages and sours. The inside of the tun is bare and uncoated, so the beer is also flavoured through direct contact with the wood.

Rodenbach only produces three beers – Rodenbach, Grand Cru and Alexander – sometimes called the Burgundies of Flanders. Other more conventional breweries have attempted to imitate these classic ales, but rarely use the same demanding craft.

THE NETHERLANDS

Wedged between the quality brewing found in Germany and the rich variety of Belgium, Dutch beer has always been a little flat in comparison. The country is best known for its international brands.

THE NETHERLANDS has suffered more than most countries from the concentration of its brewing industry into just a few hands. In the late 19th century over 1000 breweries existed, mainly concentrated in the south of the country due to the influence of the anti-alcohol Protestant church in the north.

Now only about 30 breweries remain. The standard product of the early breweries was a traditional sweet, weak, brown table lager called oud bruin and brown dark boks (a Dutch style in its own right), but these styles were mostly usurped in the 20th century by a ubiquitous, rather bland, golden lager beer.

The international giant Heineken now dominates the beer market, closely followed by the Belgian giant Interbrew which in 1995 took over Oranjeboom. The Netherlands is also the home of one of the largest privately owned breweries in the world, Bavaria, which produces own-brand lagers for supermarkets around Europe. However, as the Dutch interest in speciality beers grows, small brewers producing more interesting varieties appear all the time, influenced by both the Belgian and German traditions.

Ales are the main area of interest in the Dutch micro-brewery movement, with many new alts, Kölsch-style ales and the occasional wheat beer. Some major producers have also added meiboks and dark boks to their product lines. Abbey-style beers are brewed by some secular breweries, either under licence or independently. The Netherlands is also the home of the Koningshoeven "Schaapskooi" brewery – the sixth Trappist brewer (the other five are in Belgium) producing top-fermented ales.

Above: Dutch lager brands such as Amstel have become familiar in many countries. Their fame is mainly a product of the companies' effective marketing .

THE BEERS

Alfa

A range of all-malt beers from the brewery of the same name, including a full-flavoured Edel (Noble) Pils, which is lagered for two months (5%), and two of the better Dutch boks – Lente Bok, brewed in the spring, and the darker Alfa Bokbier, (both 6.5%), brewed in the autumn. Alfa also produces an unfiltered midzomerbier (3.9%) in June.

Amber

This amber-coloured, top-fermented, alt-style ale (5%) from Grolsch has a good bitter, hoppy flavour.

Amersfoorts Wit

This spicy wheat beer (5%) is brewed by Drie Ringen in Amersfoort.

Ammeroois

A strong, bottle-conditioned ale (7%) from the Kuipertje brewery in Heukelum.

Amstel

Heineken's second-string brand name covers a range of beers, including a light lager, a hoppy Amstel 1870 (5%), the stronger Amstel Gold (7%), a robust dark, malty Amstel bokbier (7%) and the pale Amstel Lentebok (7%).

Arcener

See Arcen.

Bavaria 8.6

The numbers in the name refer to the strength of the beer (8.6%). It is brewed by the independent Bavaria brewery.

Bethanien

The Kölsch-style Bethanien (4.5%) is brewed by the Maximiliaan brewpub.

Brand Dubbelbok

A ruby-red, bottom-fermented, bok-style beer from the Brand brewery. A gold, top-fermented meibok (7%) is also brewed.

Briljant

A malty, mellow dort (6.5%) produced by the Kroon brewery of Oirschot.

Budel Alt

A deep-amber, smooth, strong, German-style ale (5.5%) with a nutty, malt flavour from the Budel brewery.

Buorren

This copper-coloured, sourish ale (6%) is produced by Us Heit.

Capucijn

This opaque-amber, fruity, smoky, abbey-style beer (6.5%) is brewed by Budel. The name – meaning a monk's cowl – is a reference to the religious connection of the abbey beer style.

Casper's Max

A tasty, copper-coloured, malty, sweet tripel (7.5%) produced by the Maximiliaan brewpub in Amsterdam.

Château Neubourg

This "luxury" brew (5%) is the top Pilsner from the Gulpener brewery near Maastricht.

Christoffel Blond

This quality all-malt, bottom-fermented beer (5%) is dry and heavily hopped. It is unfiltered and unpasteurized, and is available in bottle-conditioned form, including 2-litre (3.5-pint), swing-stoppered jugs. The brewery also produces a good Munich-style lager.

Columbus

A strong, blond ale (9%) brewed by the home-brew house t'IJ in Amsterdam.

Dominator

A rich, fruity dort (6%) from the Dommelsch brewery. It is also sold under the brand name Hertog Jan Speciaal.

Drie Hoefijzers

See Oranjeboom Pilsner.

Drie Ringen Hoppenbier

A powerfully hoppy, rich fruit and malt-flavoured beer (5%) from the "Three Rings" brewery.

Egelantier

A copper-coloured, full-bodied, Munich-style lager (5%) which is produced by the Kroon brewery of Oirschot.

Enkel

See La Trappe.

Frysk Bier

This bitter, pale ale (6%) is brewed by Us Heit.

Gladiator

This strong, golden brew (10%) from the Gulpener brewery was launched in 1996.

Gouverneur

A bronze, sweetish Vienna-style lager from the Lindeboom brewery of Neer.

Grand Prestige

This powerful, dark, barley wine (10%) is produced by the Arcen brewery.

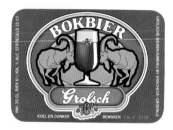

Grolsch Bokbier

This sweet, dark bok (6.5%) is a less well-known, but fine brew from Grolsch. There is also a dry, golden meibok.

Grolsch Pilsner

A fresh, hoppy Pilsner (5%), which is brewed using only malt, hops, yeast and water, and left unpasteurized in the bottle. (The canned premium lager is pasteurized.)

Gulpener Dort

A mellow, malty strong lager brewed using maize and caramel (6.5%) in the mash, which comes from the Gulpener brewery.

Heineken Oud Bruin

This smooth, lightly hopped weak table beer (2.5%) for easy drinking was first brewed over 50 years ago. There is also a stronger Heineken Special Dark (4.9%) for export.

Heineken Pilsner

A universally popular but rather bland Pilsner (5%). This is the Dutch giant's flagship brand.

Imperator

A quality all-malt, amber bokbier (6.5%), brewed using pale, chocolate and Munich malts by the Brand brewery of Wijlre.

Jubileeuw

An all-malt Pilsner (5%) from the Leeuw brewery.

Koningshoeven

See La Trappe.

Korenwolf

An aromatic, spicy, white beer (5%) from the Gulpener brewery. Korenwolf is made not only from wheat and barley but also oats and rye. It is named after the grain-loving hamster.

Kylian

Heineken's newly introduced top-fermented red ale (6.5%) with a smooth, gentle hops flavour, is based on the George Killian's Bière Rousse based on the old Irish recipe that is produced by its French subsidiary company, Pelforth.

La Trappe

A range of four Trappist top-fermenting, bottle-conditioned ales from the Koningshoeven Trappist monastery. The beers rise in strength starting from the pale-amber, fresh, fruity enkel (5.5%). Enkel is one of the few "single" strength Trappist ales brewed for the monks' everyday consumption that is available commercially. The dark, deep-red, dry dubbel (6.5%) is the next strongest brew, followed by a paler, bronze-coloured, spicier tripel (8%). The rich, reddish-coloured, vintage, heavyweight brew quadrupel (10%) makes an ideal nightcap for the dedicated beer drinker.

Lente Bok

One of the better Dutch boks, Lente Bok (6.5%) is brewed by Alfa.

Lingen's Blond

A weak table beer (2%) produced by Heineken.

Maltezer

A strong, malty dort lager (6.5%) from Ridder of Maastricht.

Maximator

A strong, spicy wheat beer (6.5%) produced by Maximiliaan, an Amsterdam brewpub opened in 1992, with the plant actually in the bar.

Maximiliaan Tarwebier

A sweetish tarwebier (5%) is brewed at the Maximiliaan brewpub. "Tarwebier" means "wheat beer".

Mestreechs Aajt

A refreshing sweet-and-sour, low-gravity summer brew (3.5%) from the Gulpener brewery. Mestreechs Aajt is a blend of oud bruin and a wild, spontaneously fermented beer, which has been aged in wooden tuns for a year.

Mug Bitter

This English-style Mug Bitter (5%) is brewed by the t'IJ micro-brewer.

Natte

This dark, abbey-style double ale (6%) is another beer brewed by the t'IJ micro-brewery.

Oranjeboom Pilsner

This mild, golden Pilsner (5%) is the main brew from the Drie Hoefijzers brewery in Breda.

Parel

A flavoursome, pale-gold, creamy, Kölsch-style beer (6%) from the Budel brewery of North Brabant.

Quintus

Rare old brown ale (6.5%) from the tiny Onder de Linden brewery in Wageningen.

Robertus

This reddish, malty bottom-fermenting beer (6%) from Christoffel is sold in bottle-conditioned form, unfiltered and unpasteurized.

Schele Os

This outstanding Belgian-style pale ale (7.5%) is an aromatic, orange ale made from barley, wheat and rye, by Maasland in Oss.

Sjoes

Some Dutch drinkers like to mix their dry Pilsner with a sweet oud bruin. Gulpener produced Sjoes (4.5%) with the two beers ready-mixed in one bottle.

Struis

This spicy, fruity dark brew (10%) is another strong ale from the t'IJ brewpub. The name means "ostrich" which is the brewpub's symbol.

Super Dortmunder

As strong as the name implies, this is the strongest Dutch dort available. At 7%, it is a ripe, fruity, export-style lager, brewed by the small Alfa brewery.

Superleeuw

This strong, rich, malty dort (6.5%) is brewed by the independent Leeuw brewery.

Sylvester

A strong, fruity, copper-coloured, top-fermented, winter ale (7.5%), from the Brand brewery of Wijlre.

Tarwebok

One of Heineken's new, more adventurous range of beers. This rich, dark wheat bok (6.5%) was introduced in 1992.

Urtyp Pilsner

This all-malt Urtyp Pilsner, also known as UP (5%), is brewed by Brand.

Valkenburgs Wit

A fruity, unfiltered wheat beer (4.8%), introduced in 1991, it comes from the Leeuw brewery of Valkenburg.

Van Vollenhoven Stout

Described as a stout, this full-bodied bottom-fermenting beer with added caramel and sugar is really a creamy, dark lager (6.5%). It is brewed by Heineken, and named after a brewery the giant company took over and closed down.

Venloosch Alt

A malty alt (4.5%) from the Leeuw brewery near Maastricht.

Volkoren Kerst

A Belgian-style, malty-brown winter ale (7%) from the Maasland brewery in Oss.

Wieckse Witte

Wieckse Witte is a softly spicy, lemony-tasting cloudy wheat beer (5%) from the Heineken subsidiary brewery, Ridder of Maastricht.

Witte Raaf

A tart, fruity wheat beer (5%) from the Raaf farmhouse brewery in Gelderland. The name Raaf means "raven".

Zatte

This abbey-style tripel (8%) with a spicy, hoppy taste is brewed by the home-brew house t'IJ.

Trading tradition

It should come as no surprise that the world's biggest beer exporter, Heineken, is a Dutch company. The Netherlands has a long history of vibrant overseas trade. It is one of the great maritime nations of the world, and its merchants have been shipping goods across the high seas for centuries.

THE BREWERS

Alfa

This independent family brewery at Schinnen has a reputation for quality all-malt beers, brewed using its own spring water.

Amstel

This Amsterdam brewery was bought by Heineken in 1968. Its name lives on as a Heineken brand.

Arcen

A pioneer of speciality beers in Limburg since 1981, Arcen's early emphasis on ales has recently switched to more mainstream lagers. Its beers appear under both the Arcener and Hertog Jan labels, including an abbey-style dark dubbel (7%) and an amber tripel (8.5%).

Bavaria

The large, independent Bavaria brewery has been brewing at Lieshout since 1719. It has flourished by brewing own-label Pilsners for supermarkets.

Brand

The Brand brewery at Wijlre, with its individual range of beers, claims to be the oldest in the country, dating back to the 14th century.

Budel

The small independent brewery at Budel near the Belgian border has been operating since 1870. It brews a Budel Pilsner and an unusual range of strong ales.

Christoffel

The small brewery was established by Leo Brand of the Dutch brewing family in Roermond in 1986 to brew quality all-malt beers. It is named after the town's patron saint. Its Pilsners are regarded as some of the best in the world.

De Kroon

The small independent brewery at Oirschot dates back to 1627. "The Crown" produces a range of full-flavoured lagers: light and dark bokbiers (all 6.5%), a brown Egelantier and a dort called Briljant.

Dommelsch

The brewery at Dommelen produces mainly Pilsners. Its Pilsner (5%) is also sold as Hertog Jan Pilsner. Dommelsch also brews a darker bokbier (6.5%).

Drie Ringen

"Three Rings" beers have been brewed in Amersfoort since 1989. It is now one of the larger of the new ventures. Its brews include a wheat beer, a pale ale, a meibok and an amber tripel.

Grolsch

Probably as well-known for its bottle as its beer, this large independent brewery in Groenlo was founded in the 17th century by Peter Cuyper. It stuck by its distinctive, swing-stoppered

bottles, which date from 1897, when other breweries were phasing them out, claiming that they had become too expensive. However, the old-fashioned container became the company's most well-known characteristic. Grolsch's bottled Pilsner is sold unpasteurized, even in the export version. The company has been expanding into other countries since the early 1990s.

Gulpener

Brewing in the southernmost tip of the Netherlands, near Maastricht, since 1825, Gulpener is probably one of the most innovative of the country's more established companies. It produces a range of Pilsners, an oud bruin, and a dort. Gulpener has also developed two Dutch versions of Belgian-style beers.

Koningshoeven

The Gospel and the glass have never been more intimately connected than in the birth of the only Trappist brewery outside Belgium, established in 1884 in Koningshoeven, near Tilburg.

The beer came first – the Schaapskooi (Sheep's pen) brewery was originally set up by the monks in order to fund the building of the monastery. Fortunately for the holy community, the blessed beer proved popular. The monastery's initial brews were lagers, thanks to a Bavarian brewmaster. The monastery introduced top-fermenting, bottle-conditioned ales in the 1950s. Today, there are four beers produced under the La Trappe brand, and also sold under the Koningshoeven label.

Leeuw

The independent Lion brewery was established in Valkenburg near Maastricht in 1886 on the site of a former gunpowder factory with a giant waterwheel. Today it brews a range of lagers including an all-malt Pilsner Jubileeuw brewed in honour of the centenary celebration in 1986, as well as an alt, an oud bruin, a winter wit, a meibok and a bokbier (6.5%).

Lindeboom

The small independent Linden Tree brewery was founded in 1870 in Neer, north of Roermond.

Today the brewery produces a variety of lagers including a Vienna-style Gouverneur, a quite bitter, dark, dry Lindeboom bokbier and a sweetish meibok (both 6.5%), as well as a dryish Pilsner (5%) and an oud bruin.

Maasland

This brewery was set up in 1989 in Oss and has been described as the Netherlands' best brewer of spiced ales. Besides the Belgian-style beers, there are two tasty boks.

Oranjeboom

The Orange Tree brewery, founded in Rotterdam in 1671, was once one of the largest breweries in the Netherlands. However, it was closed in 1990 and production moved to the Drie Hoefijzers (Three Horseshoes) brewery in Breda.

Oudaen

A grand brewpub in Utrecht, Oudaen is known for its wheat beers, including a strong tarwebok (6.8%).

Raaf

The Raven farmhouse brewery in Gelderland was revived in 1983, brewing a wide range of beers, including a tasty tripel (8.5%).

Ridder

The Knight brewery was founded in 1857 on the banks of the River Meuse in Maastricht. It brews a cloudy wheat beer, Wieckse Witte, a malty dort, Maltezer, a dark Ridder bokbier (7%) and a Ridder Pilsner (5%).

t'IJ

Probably the most striking home-brew house in the world. t'IJ, situated on Amsterdam's waterfront, is topped by a windmill. Established in 1984, the beers include two abbey-style beers and two strong ales – the blond Columbus and dark Struis. The last name means "ostrich", which is the brewpub's symbol. t'IJ also brews an English-style Mug Bitter.

Us Heit

Founded in a cowshed in Friesland in 1985, the Our Father brewery produces a good range of sourish ales. It also brews a bokbier (6%) and two Pilsners (both 5%).

THE HEINEKEN STORY

Heineken's giant strides through the world of brewing began on December 16, 1863, when 22-year-old Gerard Adriaan Heineken bought the Haystack brewery (founded in 1572) in Amsterdam. His intention, he told his mother, was to tackle the staggering problem of alcoholism by offering the public a light beer as an alternative to the widely consumed strong spirits like gin. He found a ready market. Haystack was the largest brewery in the city, but he soon outgrew it and five years later a larger brewery was opened in Amsterdam. By 1874 the ambitious brewer

was already exporting, and in 1886 Heineken employed Dr Elion, a pupil of Louis Pasteur, to help develop a consistent Pilsner.

Heineken began to export its beers as far as Indonesia after the First World War. In 1933 the brewery made the first legal beer shipment to the United States after Prohibition ended, and today Heineken is the leading imported brand in the United States.

Heineken has acquired stakes in local breweries around the world and built foreign plants, so that Heineken now has over 100 breweries throughout the world.

Only the American giant Anheuser-Busch brews

more beer, but while Anheuser is primarily a US brewer, Heineken is an international force. The vast bulk of its business is outside the Netherlands. It sold 6.7 million hectolitres (147 million gallons) in 1996 in its native land, compared to 1,553 million worldwide. Heineken beer is sold in 170 countries; its second brand Amstel is available in 85.

Heineken in the Netherlands operates two vast plants at 's Hertogenbosch and Zoeterwoude, as well as

owning Brand and Ridder. Its old city brewery in Amsterdam is now a visitor centre.

Heineken concentrates on producing beers which appeal to the widest possible taste. However, since the early 1990s it has started to produce all-malt beers, rejecting the cheaper adjuncts like corn used by many major brewers. It has also extended the variety of its beers.

LUXEMBOURG

The Grand Duchy of Luxembourg, despite its position in the heart of Europe's brewing lands, is not famed for its beers. However, this tiny country has a proud brewing history and rolls out a surprisingly large quantity of beer each year.

A LTHOUGH IT IS BORDERED by Germany and Belgium Luxembourg's brews are more similar to those of its other neighbour, France. Luxembourg beers have neither the exciting variety of Belgium nor the purity of Germany, (brewers often use adjuncts in the mash). Nevertheless, Luxembourg has a long brewing tradition that can be traced back to the abbey at Altmünster in 1083. The abbey is the site of Les Brasseries Réunies de Luxembourg Mousel et Clausen, one of Luxembourg's leading brewers.

BASCHARAGE (Gr. D Luxembourg)

This small country has two other large brewing companies, Bofferding, which merged with Funck Bricher in 1975 to form Brasserie Nationale, the largest group, and Diekirch, which has brewed in the city of the same name since 1871. These breweries mainly brew a mild Pilsner and an export lager, and offer interesting specialities, such as strong seasonal Christmas beers or German-style dunkels.

A major family in the history of brewing in Luxembourg was the Funcks, in particular Henri Funck, whose name is commemorated on the lager Pils produced today by the Mousel group. The Brasserie Henri Funck, which he founded, was in the forefront of brewing technology for years and was among the first brewers to use refrigeration equipment and steel tanks. It became part of the Brasseries Réunies group in 1982.

Above: At the beginning of the 19th century Luxembourg had about 60 breweries. Diekirch is one of the handful of brewers that have managed to survive into the 20th century.

Two of the most interesting small breweries in Luxembourg are the Brasserie Battin, founded by Charles Battin in 1937, which produces four beers sold under the Battin label, and the Wiltz brewery, which has been owned by the Simon family since 1891. This was totally destroyed in the Ardennes offensive at the end of the Second World War and was rebuilt in 1954.

The domestic market in Luxembourg is small, and the main groups survive by concentrating on the export markets, particularly Belgium and France. Almost a third of all the beer produced is exported.

THE BEERS

Altmünster
A firm-bodied, Dortmunder-style beer (5.5%) from Brasseries Réunies.

Bofferding Christmas Béier
This brown, seasonal ale (5.5%) is produced annually by Bofferding.

Bofferding Lager Pils
This refreshing, Pilsner-style lager (4.8%) is brewed using pale malt and corn (maize) and is lagered for a month.

Diekirch Exclusive
A strong, Pilsner-style lager (5.2%) produced by one of the largest brewers in Luxembourg.

Fréijoers
A refreshing, unfiltered beer (4.8%) produced by Bofferding.

Hausbeier
A tasty, all-malt beer (5.5%) brewed by Bofferding.

Henri Funck Lager Beer
This Pilsner (4.8%) is brewed by Mousel to a similar recipe to Mousel Premium. Both use 10% rice in the mash, producing a light, refreshing, bright gold beer.

Luxembourg
Two beers are produced under this brand name, Luxembourg Lager (3%) and the stronger Luxembourg Export (4%). Both are brewed by Mousel.

Mansfeld
A malty Pilsner (4.8%) from Mousel.

Régal
The export-style beer (5.5%) from the Wiltz brewery.

Simon Noël
A rich, dark, Christmas beer (7.5%) from the small brewery in Wiltz, run by the Simon family. They also produce Simon Pils (5.8%) and Simon Régal (5.5%).

THE BREWERS

Battin
This is the smallest of the Grand Duchy's breweries which, along with the similar-sized Wiltz brewery, produces arguably the best beers. Founded in 1937 in Esch-sur-Alzette, it brews an Edelpils, Gambrinus, a fuller-bodied urtyp and darker Battin Dunkel.

Bofferding
The brewery in Bascharge dates back to 1842, and it merged with Funck-Bricher in 1975 to form the country's largest brewing group, Brasserie Nationale. Its main beer is a Bofferding Lager Pils (4.8%), but it also brews an all-malt Hausbeier, a brown Bofferding Christmas Béier (both 5.5%) and the unfiltered, refreshing Fréijoers.

Below: Bofferding, part of Brasserie Nationale, dates back to 1842.

Diekirch
One of Luxembourg's biggest three breweries, this company has brewed in Diekirch since 1871. Besides Diekirch Light (2.9%) and the pale Diekirch Premium Pilsner (4.8%), it brews a mellow, lager, Diekirch Exclusive (5.1%), the amber Diekirch Grande Réserve (6.9%) and a brune (5.2%).

Mousel
Les Brasseries Réunies de Luxembourg Mousel et Clausen brew two similar Pilsners, Mousel Premium and Henri Funck (both 4.8%), and a malty Mansfeld.

Wiltz
This small brewery, founded in 1824, was bought by the Simon family in 1891, who have run it since then. The buildings were totally destroyed during the Second World War.

GERMANY

Drinkers across the world tend to regard Germany as the land of lager, the country where bottom-fermenting beers reign supreme. There is, however, much more to German beer than overflowing steins at the Munich Beer Festival.

N O COUNTRY TAKES more pride in the quality of its beer, and although the rules of the beer purity law the Rheinheitsgebot, mean that German brewers cannot indulge in the wilder flights of fancy of the Belgian brewers, there is still plenty of variety to be found, and excellent quality.

Top-fermenting ales are still brewed, notably the alts of Düsseldorf and kölsches of Cologne. There has also been a revival in demand for wheat beers. Within the lager market, beers vary – from sharp, hoppy Pilsners in the north to the softer, maltier brews of Bavaria. The glasses shimmer with all the colours of the ripening barley field, from pale golden helles through copper-coloured marzens and darker dunkels and bocks to black beers. There are even a few exotic types, such as the smoked beers of Bamberg. All of these brews comply with the rules that prohibit the use of cheap adjuncts and inferior materials.

No people are more loyal to their local beers. The beer marketplace is fragmented, regionally oriented and highly conservative. Unlike most other countries, there are few national beer brands. People stick to their home-town brews. This has meant that many more breweries have survived in Germany than in other European countries, with around 1,200 still steaming away. Cologne, a city of only one million people, has 23 breweries, and there are some 700 in the Bavarian countryside, where the clock appears to have stopped in another era altogether and almost every village has its own brewhouse. Some local breweries have closed, but since the late 1970s a new wave has sprung up, with over 150 brewpubs opening in the last 20 years, catering for a wide range of tastes. About 30% of all the breweries in the world are in Germany.

Above: Much of the revival in the popularity of wheat beers has been due to the perceived health-giving properties of the cloudy, yeasty brew.

THE BEERS

Abtstrunk

The word "Abt" (abbot) reveals the monastic links of the makers of this thick, potent, liqueur-like beer, (11.5%) which is brewed in a former abbey guesthouse at Irsee near Munich.

Achd Bambarcha Schwarzla

The name of this dark, mellow beer (5.3%) means "true Bamberg black". It is produced by the Klosterbräu in Bamberg, the oldest brewer of rauchbier, dating back to 1533. Its small plant was once run by monks.

Aecht Schlenkerla Rauchbier

This is a classic smoked beer (4.8%) from the Bamberg region. It has a light, fresh, smoked flavour and a dry malt aftertaste. It is produced by the Heller Brauerei in Bamberg for the Schlenkerla tavern.

Alt Franken

See Urfrankisch Dunkel.

Altstadthof Hausbier

A fruity, unfiltered but quite flat, dark lager (4.8%) produced by the small Altstadthof brewery in Nuremberg.

Alt Wetzlar

This is not an Altbier in style, but a dark lager, brewed by Euler in Wetzlar, north of Frankfurt.

Apostulator

A dark, ruby-coloured Doppelbock (7.5%) with a fruity, malt taste. This brew is produced by the Eichbaum brewery of Mannheim.

Arcobräu Coronator Doppelbock

An auburn-coloured Doppelbock (7.5%) with a strong malty flavour, from Graf Arco of Bavaria.

Arcobräu Dunkel Weisse

A cloudy, amber-brown wheat beer (5.2%) with a clean, citrus flavour, from this family owned company.

Arcobräu Urweisse

A refreshing, apple-tasting, unfiltered, cloudy, gold Bavarian wheat beer (4.8%) from Graf Arco.

Astra

A range of gold, hoppy Pilsners from the Bavaria St Pauli brewery of Hamburg. The Astra label also has a gold Bock with a light malt flavour.

Aventinus

This classic, extra-strong wheat beer (8%) or Weizen Doppelbock comes from the specialist wheat beer brewers Schneider of Bavaria. Conditioned in the bottle, Aventinus has a deep reddish-brown colour, a creamy head and a warming, rich, fruity taste.

Ayinger Altbayerische Dunkel

A deep-red lager with a malty flavour and pleasant aftertaste, produced by the quality Ayinger brewery.

Ayinger Bräu-Weisse

A pale wheat beer (5.1%) with a tart, fruity taste, produced by Ayinger.

Ayinger Maibock

A pale-gold, traditional maibock with a complex hop flavour, from the Privatbrauerei Franz Inselkammer in Aying.

Beck's

One of Germany's best-known beers on the international market, this crisp, dry Pilsner (5%) has been brewed in the northern port of Bremen since 1874. It is Germany's leading export beer, with more than six million hectolitres sold every year in more than 100 countries. It accounts for more than 85% of German beer exports to the United States. Beck's also brews a deep-amber, dark beer and a dry, malty Oktoberfest brew.

Bernauer Schwarzbier

This is a very dark, creamy, chocolate-tasting, smooth Schwarzbier from the Berliner Bürgerbräu. It is named after the town of Bernau, once known for the black beer style.

Bitburger

Bitburger (4.8%) is a dry, aromatic and hoppy Pilsner from Bitburg in the Rhienland. It is allowed to mature for a three months, making it a classic of its style, and the second-best-selling Pilsner in Germany.

Brauhernen Pilsner

A pale-gold, dry, bitter Pilsner with a hoppy aftertaste (4.9%), produced by Einbecker.

Braumeister

This bright-gold Bavarian Pilsner is produced by the leading Munich brewer Hacker-Pschorr. It has a pleasant, toasted-malt and hop flavour.

Bremer Weisse

This refreshing summer beer with only 2.7% alcohol is a Bremen variation of a Berliner Weisse. The producer, Haake-Beck still delivers its beers locally by horse-drawn drays.

Brinkhoff's No. 1

A smooth, bright-gold, premium Pilsner from DUB of Dortmund, this beer is named after an early brewer.

EINBECKER BEER – A MEDIEVAL TRADITION

The reputation of Einbecker beer is said to have been built on a remarkable communal operation. The Lower Saxony town of Einbeck was once the major brewing centre for the medieval Hanseatic League of north German trading towns. It developed a style of strong beers – bocks – brewed to survive long journeys.

In the Middle Ages, every citizen in the town brewed, using a communal copper which was wheeled around 700 homes. The door arches of the old buildings had to be high to accommodate the vessel. The citizens then sold their beer to the town council, which traded it through the Hanseatic League. The strong beer gained a widespread following – even Martin Luther praised it. Its reputation caused the Bavarian dukes to entice an Einbeck brewmaster to Munich, so spreading the brewing of bock – or beck – beer to southern Germany, where it is mainly brewed today.

Broyhan Alt
A strong, malty Altbeer (5.2%) in the Düsseldorf style. This beer is produced by the Lindener Gilde brewery of Hannover and it is named after a famous Hannover brewer.

Busch Golden Pilsner
A golden Pilsner-style beer produced by the local Busch brewery in Limburg near Koblenz. Despite its name the brewery has no connection with America's brewing giant Anheuser-Busch.

Carolus
This very deep, ruby-brown-coloured strong Doppelbock (7.5%) has an unusual, complex, fruity taste. It is brewed by Binding of Frankfurt.

CD
A popular, brilliant-gold, sweetish Pilsner, named after Carl Dinkelacker, who founded the brewery in Stuttgart in 1888.

Celebrator
This export name is mainly used in the US for the classic, dark-red, velvety Doppelbock, Fortunator (7.2%), from the Ayinger brewery.

Clausthaler
This pioneering non-alcohol lager (0.5%) took Binding of Frankfurt years to develop before it was launched in 1979. It virtually created a whole new beer sector on its own.

Cluss Bock
This malty, dark-copper-coloured Bock is brewed by the Cluss brewery.

DAB Original
This is the premium version of Meister Pils from DAB in Dortmund. It is a golden, grassy, hoppy beer (5%).

Dampfbier
Dampfbier is an unusual top-fermented reddish ale (4.9%) from the Maisel brewery of Bayreuth in Bavaria, which is not unlike a fruity English bitter. The word "Dampf" means steam.

Delicator
This dark, fruity Doppelbock (7.5%) is brewed by the famous Hofbräuhaus of Munich.

Diebels Alt
A brown, biscuity Altbier (4.8%) from the Privatbrauerei Diebel in Issum Weidernhein.

Dom Kölsch
A leading kölsch beer in Cologne named after the cathedral.

Dom Pilsner
This dry Pilsner is brewed by the Euler brewery of Wetzlar.

DUB Export
Dortmunder Union Brewery brews this smooth, malty Export (5%). DUB also produces Pilsners, most notably its hoppy Siegel Pilsner and the premium Brinkhoff's No. 1.

Duckstein
An unusual, fruity, amber ale, matured over beechwood chips. It is produced by the Feldschlösschen Brewery of Brunswick.

Echt Kölsch
This delicate beer, regarded as the true Kölschbier, was originally produced at a home-brew pub, P. J. Früh's Cölner Hofbräu, near Cologne Cathedral. Demand became so great, however, that Echt Kölsch is no longer brewed behind the tavern, but at a brewery outside the city centre.

Einbecker Maibock
A deep, golden-amber-coloured, malty, seasonally brewed spring Bock (6.5%) produced by the Einbecker brewery.

Einbecker Urbock
This bright-gold, smooth, strong, hoppy Bock beer (6.5%) is produced by the Einbecker brewery.

EKU Pils

A soft creamy Bavarian Pilsner (5%) brewed by the Erste Kulmbacher Union of Kulmbach, a brewery best known for its heavy, extra-strong lager, Kulminator 28.

Erdinger Weissbier

This range of top-fermented wheat beers from the Erdinger brewery is brewed strictly according to the Bavarian purity law. It includes a cloudy Hefe (5.3%), a sparkling Kristallklar (5.3%) and a reddish-brown, strong, spicy, dark Dunkel (5.6%).

Euler Landpils

This Pilsner comes from the independent Euler brewery in Wetzlar.

Feldschlösschen

Feldschlösschen Pilsner is a leading Pilsner brand for Holsten. The large north German Feldschlösschen brewery in Brunswick is part of the Holsten group. Feldschlösschen also produces the distinctive Duckstein amber ale and Brunswick alt.

Fest-Märzen

This marzen-style beer (5.8%) is produced by Ayinger of Bavaria.

Feuerfest

This dark, fruity, warming "fire festival" Doppelbock (10%) is produced in limited-edition, wax-sealed bottles by Schäffbräu of Treuchtlingen, near Nuremberg in Bavaria.

First

A popular, pale-gold Pilsner (4.8%) with a grainy flavour, produced by Ritter of Dortmund.

Fortunator

This rich, dark-red, velvety Doppelbock (7.2%) is brewed by Ayinger.

Franz Joseph Jubelbier

This strong, dark lager (5.5%) is named after the monarch. It is brewed by the south Bavarian Altenmünster brewery near Augsburg.

Franziskaner

A range of wheat beers from the famous Spaten brewery of Bavaria. The wheat brews, which now account for more than half of Spaten's production, include the cloudy but refreshing hefe-weissbier, a filtered, grassy Kristallklar and a Dunkel (all 5%).

Freiberger Pils

This hoppy Pilsner is the best-known beer from the sizeable Freiberger Brauhaus in the old colliery town of Freiberg.

Fürstenberg Pilsner

The widely available, bright-gold, hoppy, dry premium Fürstenberg Pilsner (5%) is the best-known beer of the Fürstenberg brewery, which also produces a range of other brews including three wheat beers.

Gatz Alt

The brown, fruity Gatz Alt (4.8%) is produced by Gatzweiler, the family brewers of Alt, in Düsseldorf. There is also a non-alcohol version. The original Düsseldorf brewery was in the brewpub Zum Schlüssel and still brews.

Gilde Pils

This pale-gold Pilsner with a dry finish (5%) comes from Hannover's Lindener Gilde brewery. As its name implies, the brewery was once run by a city guild.

Hacker-Pschorr Edelhell

This is one of the stronger speciality beers (5.5%) from the Hacker-Pschorr brewery in Munich, which dates back to 1417. Its more popular lagers are fruity Hell (5%) and Dunkel (5.2%).

Hacker-Pschorr Oktoberfest Märzen

This Märzen beer (5.8%) is brewed in Munich for the famous Oktoberfest, by Hacker-Pschorr.

HB Hofbräuhaus München

The premium lager (4.9%) brewed at the former Bavarian Royal Court brewery in Munich.

Holsten Pils

The widely available premium Pilsner (5%) from the Holsten brewery is one of that firm's famous dry, hoppy range from Hamburg.

Hopf Dunkler-Bock

This unusually rich and tangy Dunkler-Bock wheat beer (6.3%) comes from the small Hopf family brewery in the Bavarian Alps at Miesbach that specializes in wheat beers.

Hopf Weisse Export

The fruity, but not hoppy, Weisse Export (5.3%) is a wheat beer from Hopf.

Hubertus

Hubertus is a robust, copper-coloured Bock (6.8%) from Hacker-Pschorr of Munich. The brewery's doppelbock is called Animator (7.5%).

Jahrhundert

A golden, export-style beer (5.5%) from Ayinger of Bavaria. It was originally produced to celebrate its centenary in 1978.

KALTENBERG CASTLE

Once upon a time, almost all aristocratic families brewed their own beer, and this tradition continues in the fairy-tale Kaltenberg Castle in the village of Geltendorf, 50km from Munich. The spires of Kaltenberg tower over the cellars where the beer is lagered. However, most Kaltenberg beers, including its Pilsner and Prinzregent wheat beers, are now produced at a modern brewery in Fürstenfeldbruck.

Jever

This is probably the most bitter beer produced in Germany. Jever Pilsner underlines the general German rule that beers become drier as you travel north. The town of Jever is in Friesland. The brewery of the same name, dating back to 1848, is famed for its Pilsner (4.9%), which has a heady, hoppy aroma and an intense bitterness. Owned by Bavaria St Pauli of Hamburg since 1923, a modern brewery was built in 1992 in this old North Sea resort. Its other brews include Jever Light (2.7%) and the alcohol-free Jever Fun.

Kaiserdom

The most widely available Rauchbier (4.8%) (smoked beer) from Bamberg has been brewed by the Bavarian town's Bürgerbräu brewery since 1716. Although it is not the most intensely smoky beer of its type, it will still surprise the unsuspecting drinker with its fume-filled flavour. The Bamberg brewery also produces more conventional lagers, Extra-Dry (4.9%) and Pilsner (4.8%), as well as a delicious apricot-coloured Weissbier (5.3%).

Kaiser Pilsner

The black-labelled bottles of this premium Pilsner (4.8%) from Henninger of Frankfurt have become familiar around the world.

Kaltenberg

See König Ludwig.

Kapuziner

A range of wheat beers from the Mönchshof brewery of Kulmbach in Bavaria which has monastic origins. The name means "monk's hood" and the beers include two heady, unfiltered brews, Kapuziner Dunkel and Hefetrub (both 5.2%).

Kindl Berliner Weisse

The pale, sour, refreshing wheat beer (2.5%), once called "the champagne of the north" is a speciality of Berlin. It is often laced with fruit juices. The large Kindl brewery was founded in Berlin in 1872 and brews several conventional beers, including Kindl Schwarzbier. The main rival brewer of Berliner Weisse is Schultheiss.

Kloster-Urtrunk

The tasty, unfiltered marzen Kloster-Urtrunk (5.6%) is brewed by Irseer Klosterbräu near Munich.

Kloster Urweisse

Kloster Urweisse (5.2%) is a tasty wheat beer from Irseer Klosterbräu near Munich. The name means "original white".

König Ludwig

König Ludwig Dunkel (5.1%) is named after "mad" King Ludwig II of Bavaria. The Dunkel is one of the beers still brewed by Prince Luitpold, heir to the throne of Bavaria, at his Kaltenburg Castle brewery in Geltendorf.

König-Pilsener

A pleasant, dry Pilsner (4.9%), with a faintly appley flavour, from the König brewery, Duisberg.

Korbinian

This dark-amber Doppelbock (7.4%) with a rich, malt flavour, is produced by the Weihenstephan brewery, a former monastery brewery at Freising.

Köstritzer Schwarzbier

Köstritzer Schwarzbier (4.6%) is a smoothly chocolatey, bitter, bottom-fermented beer with a 450-year-old reputation as a sustaining drink for invalids. Goethe drank the revered drop while recovering from illness. It comes from the Köstritz black beer brewery in the former East German spa town of Bad Köstritz in Thuringia.

Kräusen

Kräusen is an unusual, unfiltered, cloudy version of the standard Pilsner, brewed by Haake-Beck of Bremen. It was introduced to the north German market in 1985.

Kronen Classic

This is the golden premium Pilsner (5.3%) with a slightly sour, hoppy taste, from the popular independent, family-owned Kronen brewery in Dortmund. It also brews a robust, malty export.

Kulminator 28

One of the strongest beers in the world, the threateningly named Kulminator 28 has an alcohol content of more than 12% – the highest gravity of any bottom-fermenting beer. The brew is matured for nine months, including a short period of freezing, to produce this intensely malty, heavyweight, amber beer.

There is a less threatening and darker conventional Kulminator Doppelbock (7.6%) without the number. Both of the beers are brewed by EKU in the Bavarian town of Kulmbach, and are widely exported.

Küppers Kölsch

This deep-gold sweetish kölsch comes from the largest brewer of kölsch in Cologne.

Kutscher Alt

A malty, copper-coloured Alt (5%) that is smooth and gently warming. This beer is brewed by Binding of Frankfurt. It is top-fermented, then cold-conditioned in the classic Altbier style.

Lammsbräu Pils

Lammsbräu's pale, amber, delicately fresh and citric organic Pilsner (5%) was introduced in the late 1980s. It is brewed by the small Lammsbräu brewery at Neumarkt, near Nuremberg, using barley and hops grown without artificial fertilizers or pesticides. Some claimed that it was purer than the requirements of the Rheinheitsgebot – much to the annoyance of larger brewers, although this did not prevent others trying their own "bio beers".

Leichter Typ

This light, low-calorie beer from Eichbaum has a strength of just 2%.

Löwenbräu Hefe Weissbier

An unpasteurized, unfiltered, slightly cloudy, wheat beer (5.0%) which comes from the best-known of the Munich breweries. The Hefe Weissbier is produced using Löwenbräu ale yeast, malted wheat, spring barley and Hallertau hops. A filtered version of the Hefe style, which is clear, is also available, called Klares Weissbier. This version has a distinctive flavour rather like a wheaty lager.

Löwenbräu Oktoberfest

A subtle, light, bottom-fermented Reinheitsgebot beer (6.1%) that is specially brewed each year for the Munich Oktoberfest.

Löwenbräu Premium Pils

This light, refreshing, golden lager is made in Munich under the Bavarian purity law, with Hallertau hops, spring barley and yeast.

Maisel Pilsner

This pale-gold, aromatic Pilsner with a good malt and hops taste (4.8%) is brewed by the Maisel brewery, the largest brewery in the famous Bavarian opera town of Bayreuth, which also produces a good range of fruity wheat beers.

Meister Pils

This gold Pilsner with a fresh, zesty taste, comes from DAB of Dortmund. The name, which means champion, is also used by the Schwaben brewery of Stuttgart for its Pilsner.

Mönchshof Kloster Schwarzbier

This deep-copper-coloured Schwarzbier with a smooth, malt flavour comes from the old Mönchshof brewery in Kulmbach, Bavaria. The brewery has monastic origins and is known for its strong, dark lagers.

Oberdorfer

This is a range of wheat beers from the Franz-Joseph Sailer brewery in Marktoberdorf in Bavaria, one of which is sold mixed half and half with lemonade.

Optimator

An orangey-coloured, strong Doppelbock (6.8%) with a smooth, roasted, malt flavour, brewed by Spaten of Munich.

Pikantus

This strong, russet-coloured Weizenbock (7.3%) is brewed by wheat-beer specialists Erdinger of Bavaria.

Pilsissimus

This hoppy Pilsner (5.2%) is very highly thought of by the patrons of the Forschungs brewpub

Pinkus Hefe Weizen

This cloudy, gold, unfiltered wheat beer (5%) with a citrus and wheat flavour is an organic beer which is produced by the Pinkus Müller home-brew house in Münster.

Prinzregent

This range of wheat beers, named after Prince Luitpold, includes an unfiltered hell, and a brown, spicy, malt-flavoured Dunkel Weissbier (both of them 5%). They are brewed by Kaltenberg in Bavaria.

Radeberger Pilsner

This bright-gold, hoppy Pilsner is the flagship brew of the Radeberger brewery near Dresden in the former East Germany. It was once supplied to the King of Saxony.

Ratsherrn

A brand name that is applied to a hoppy, dry Pilsner and malty Bock from the Elbschloss brewery of Hamburg on the River Elbe. Both beers are unpasteurized.

Ratskeller Edel-Pils

This bright-gold, hoppy, premium Pilsner is brewed by the Lindener Gilde brewery of Hannover.

Rauchenfelser Steinbier

This unique speciality is brewed using an ancient process. When all brewing vessels were made of wood, it was risky to use direct flames to heat them, so instead rocks were fired to high temperatures and then placed in the wort to bring it to the boil. In 1983, Gerd Borges revived this process at Neustadt near Coburg. The white-hot stones not only make the brew bubble, but also cause sugars to caramelize on their surface. The top-fermented beer is then matured for two to three months with the sugar-coated rocks. The result is a tawny-coloured Steinbier (4.8%) that is both smooth and smoky. There is also a Steinweizen made using the same process. In 1993, as part of the Franz Joseph Sailer group, the brewing was moved to Altenmünster in southern Bavaria.

Reichelbräu Eisbock

This is a Bockbier (10%) that is strengthened by freezing for two weeks and removing the ice. The dark, warming brew is then matured in oak casks for two months. It is brewed by Reichelbrau in Kulmbach, Bavaria.

Romer Pilsner

A popular, yellow-gold, dry Pilsner (5%) with a classical image, brewed by the giant Binding brewery of Frankfurt. It is a quality brew with a dry, hop finish.

St Georgen Keller Bier

This is the speciality of the St Georgen brewery, an unfiltered lager (4.9%) bursting with hops, which is even exported in bottle to the United States. The small Bavarian village brewery in Buttenheim brews some of the hoppiest beers in the region, including a very dry marzen (5.6%).

St Jakobus

This quality pale Bock (7.5%) is produced by the Forschungs brewpub in the Perlach suburb of Munich. The brewpub is only open in summer.

Salvator

The pioneer of the Doppelbock style from the famous Paulaner brewery of Munich. This rich, ruby brew (7.5%) is overpowering with its fruit-cake aroma and deep, warming flavour.

Sanwald

The wheat beers from the Dinkelacker brewery of Stuttgart include a bright-gold, light, dry hefe weiss and a sparkling, tawny-amber Weizen Krone.

Schierlinger Roggen

This rare, red-amber rye (Roggen) beer (4.7%) is brewed by the local brewery in Schierling, Bavaria. Launched in 1988, it is similar to a dark wheat beer, but with a more tangy, grainy taste. The mash contains 60% rye. The brewery was once part of a convent.

Schlenkerla

The classic and most uncompromising Rauchbier (4.8%), this smoked speciality of Bamberg in Bavaria is brewed from malt kilned over beechwood fires. The result is a pitch-black brew with a pungent flavour of burnt malt. This dry, smoky beer used to be brewed on the premises at the Schlenkerla tavern in Bamberg, but is now produced at the nearby Heller brewery dating back to 1678.

Schneider Weisse

A refreshing, yeasty wheat beer (5.4%) brewed by the Schneider brewery. This is the classic example of the Weisse style. Besides the Original Hefeweizenbier the brewery also produces a filtered Kristall, a weaker Weizen-hell (4.9%), and a light (2.9%).

OKTOBERFEST

Mention Germany and beer, and many people envisage Munich's famous Oktoberfest, when in just 16 days, around six million litres (1,319,814 gallons) of beer will be drunk in huge canvas beer halls by thousands of visitors. It is the world's biggest beer festival – though it is not in October, but in the last two weeks of September. This mad annual party began when the Bavarian Prince Ludwig married Princess Theresa in 1810, and the city threw a huge celebration. It was such a success that it has been repeated ever since. Only the six major breweries in Munich are allowed to supply beer – to the annoyance of many other Bavarian brewers. In 1882 Spaten created the amber-coloured, Oktoberfest beer which caused such a sensation that it has been served ever since!

Above: A happy participant of the Munich Oktoberfest at the end of the 19th century, complete with his stein of beer and tobacco pipe.

Left: The Hacker-Pschorr beer tent at the Oktoberfest. Only the six main breweries of Munich are allowed to supply beer at the festival.

Below: One of six million litres of beer being drunk at the Oktoberfest. In fact, the festival takes place at the end of September.

SPATEN AND THE LAGER REVOLUTION

Spaten is a Munich brewery whose name means "spade". It was at the heart of the bottom-fermenting lager revolution, which swept the world in the 19th century. Brewer Gabriel Sedlmayr pioneered the production of dark and amber lagers in the 1830s and later developed the use of refrigeration and steam power. Spaten is still justly proud of its lagers today, notably its malty Münchner Hell (4.8%) and dunkel (5%) and its classic, full-bodied Ur-Märzen (5.6%). It also brews a dry Pilsner (5%), a golden maibock (6.5%) and a strong Doppelbock called Optimator (6.8%). Its range of wheat beers under the Franziskaner label now accounts for more than half of all production.

Schöfferhofer
The range of Bavarian-style wheat beers from Binding of Frankfurt includes a tasty and lively Hefeweizen, a filtered golden, yeasty kristall and a dark dunkel (all around 5%).

Schultheiss Berliner Weisse
This is one of the most distinctive examples of the Berliner Weisse style, the pale, sourish, weak type of wheat beer that is favoured in the north. Major Berlin brewer Schultheiss blends fresh and more mature brews in order to create its bottle-conditioned Weisse (3%).

Schultheiss Pilsner
This hoppy Pilsner is the best-known brew in Germany from the Berlin Schultheiss brewery.

Starkbier
This strong, brown Starkbier (6.8%) has a dry, malty flavour. It is brewed by Irseer Klosterbräu just outside Munich.

Stauder TAG
This is a strong, dry, hoppy Pilsner (5.3%). The initials stand for Treffliches Altenessen Gold. It is brewed by a family brewery in Essen, which was founded in 1867. It also brews a soft standard Pilsner (4.6%).

Stephansquell
An amber, full-bodied Doppelbock (6.8%). This beer is brewed in Freising by the Weihenstephan brewery.

Triumphator
A seasonal, strong Doppelbock brewed by Löwenbräu of Munich.

Ureich Pils
This dry, gold Pilsner (4.8%) with a strong hop taste is the flagship brew from the Eichbaum brewery of Mannheim.

Urfrankisch Dunkel
This dark, malty Dunkel (4.4%) is bottled as Alt Franken. It is produced by the large Nuremberg Tucher brewery, which brews a wide range of traditional Bavarian beers.

Ur-Krostitzer
This crisp Pilsner (which should not be confused with Köstritzer Schwarzbier) comes from the former East German Krostitz brewery in the town of Krostitz near Leipzig.

Urstoff
This heavy, reddish-brown Doppelbock with a smooth, malt flavour, is produced by the Mönchshof Kloster brewery in Kulmbach.

Ur-Weisse
A wheat beer, Ur-Weisse (5.8%) uses 60% wheat in the mash and is bursting with flavour. It is slightly darker and more full-flavoured than the other wheat beers brewed by the Ayinger brewery.

Warsteiner
This bright, pale-gold Pilsner (4.8%) is the best-selling beer in Germany. The family brewery in Warstein has had to double its output over five years to six million hectolitres (1,319,814,000 gallons) in 1995, in order to keep up with demand.

Weizenhell
A slightly hazy, light-coloured wheat beer (4.9%) brewed by Schneider of Kelheim near Regensburg.

Witzgall Vollbier
A sweetish, copper-coloured lager from Schlammersdorf in Franconia.

Würzig
The name, meaning "spicy", is applied to two distinctive bottom-fermenting beers from the Hofmark brewery: Würzig Mild and Würzig Herb (meaning dry), both with a strength of 5.1%.

The former is a malty brew and the latter is sharply hoppy. Known for its distinctive swing-stoppered bottles, the traditional east Bavarian Hofmark brewery dates back to 1590. It still uses beechwood chips to clear its beers.

THE BREWERS

There are so many brewers in Germany that it is impossible even to list every German brewery of note. The following firms are worthy of honourable mention.

MAJOR BREWERIES

Augustiner

This is the least known brewery outside Munich, but possibly the most popular inside the town, probably because it produces lagers most faithful to the Bavarian city's malty tradition. This is especially true of its pale, smoothly soft hell (5.2%). It was once a monastic brewery dating back to 1328. Its connections with the holy order were broken in 1803. Its grand 19th-century brewhouse, built in 1885, is now a protected building. It has its own maltings in cellars beneath. Locally, some of its beers are still served from wooden casks.

Ayinger

"The most beautiful thing about Munich is the road to Aying", claims this well-respected country brewer, and it is not far wrong. This family brewery lies at the heart of a picturesque Bavarian village on the edge of the Alps, with its own guest house and beer garden. The beer matches the surroundings. The brewery produces a wide range of specialities: a Hell, an Altbairisch Dunkel, a Pilsner, three Bocks, a golden export-style beer called Jahrhundert-Bier, a Fest-Märzen, three Ayinger wheat beers, and a standard Hefe Weisse Bräu-Weisse (5%).

Beck's

An innovative brewer, Beck's of Bremen has been brewing its famous Beck's Pilsner in the northern port since 1874. Early in the 20th century it was one of the first breweries to invest in ice machines and to cultivate a pure yeast culture. In 1917 it merged with its main export rival in Bremen, St Pauli. Between the wars the company also built two overseas breweries in Singapore and Djakarta in Malaya, these were lost in 1945 but Beck's licensed a brewery in China in 1992. Its sister company Haake-Beck brews a range of beers for the local market.

Binding

Binding is Germany's second-largest brewing group. The company is based in Frankfurt, where it celebrated its 125th anniversary in 1995.

The large brewing group includes DAB of Dortmund, Kindl of Berlin, and the Radeberg and Krostitz breweries in the former East Germany.

Binding has the distinction of having virtually created the alcohol-free beer market in Germany with its dominant Clausthaler brand, which it launched successfully in 1979. This now contains (0.45%) alcohol. German law specifies that non-alcoholic beer should not contain more than (0.5%) alcohol which is about the same percentage as apple juice.

The company also brews Romer Pilsner, two Binding Exports, a Doppelbock Carolus, a range of popular wheat beers under the Schöfferhofer brand name and Kutscher Alt.

PROTECTING THE CONSUMER

The German beer purity law, the Rheinheitsgebot, was first introduced in Bavaria in 1516 by Duke William IV, only gradually spreading to the rest of the country this century. The ruling – one of the world's first consumer protection laws – insisted that beer should only be made from malt, hops and water (yeast was not at first mentioned, as its working was not understood). It ensured that cheap adjuncts and sugars were not used, and that no beer was as wholesome as German beer. In 1987, the European Court ruled that the law was a trade barrier, preventing foreign beers being imported. Although the German government could not then stop beers which did not conform to the purity law crossing the border, German brewers resolved to stick to the ruling. It was a wise decision, as drinkers voted with their glasses to stay loyal to their pure beer. The Rheinheitsgebot is now seen as giving German beer a vital marketing edge in a competitive world.

THE ROYAL BREWERS

World-famous for its beer hall in the heart of Munich, the Hofbräuhaus (HB) has the distinction of being the royal brewery. The royal connection dates back to 1589, when the Duke of Bavaria, Wilhelm V established the brewery.

Now owned by the state, it has only started to market its beers in recent years, cutting the number of brands down to two main ones – a wheat beer and its golden lager Hofbräuhaus Original München (4.9%), besides a number of seasonal specialities such as a maibock, marzen and Christmas Doppelbock called Delicator (7.5%).

Today, the HB brewing plant is located outside the city, next to the old airport. It is the smallest of the big six breweries in the beer capital.

Hofbräuhaus means "court brewhouse", and since Germany was once divided into many dukedoms and principalities, there are a number of royal breweries. The Hofbräuhaus Freising, originally owned by a bishop, is now run by Count von Moy. Located north of Munich, it claims to be the oldest brewery in Germany, dating back to 1160. It is best known for its wheat beers. Bavaria also boasts a Hofbräu Abensberg and a Hofbräu Berchtesgaden. Hofbräuhaus Wolters of Brunswick, now owned by the Lindener Gilde Brewery of Hannover, brews a hoppy Pilsner.

Brau und Brunnen
Germany's leading brewing group includes DUB of Dortmund, Küppers of Cologne, Bavaria St Pauli of Hamburg, and Einbecker and Schultheiss of Berlin.

DAB
Dortmunder Actien Brauerei, incorporated in 1868, is one of the north German city's three main breweries, all famous for their big, bold Export (or Dortmunder) beers. Dortmund is Germany's largest brewing centre and only beers brewed there are allowed to be called Dortmunder. DAB's Export is malty and dry, but the firm now concentrates more on its DAB Meister Pilsner. It also brews an altbier, a maibock and a DAB Tremanator Doppelbock. Local rival Hansa is now part of DAB.

Diebels
The largest brewer of Alt beers is based not in Düsseldorf but in the village of Issum near the Dutch border. Diebels is still a family firm. Founded in 1878, the brewery also produces light and low-alcohol versions of its well-known Diebels Alt.

DOM
One of the larger Kölschbier brewers in Cologne. The name of the brewery means "cathedral".

DUB
Dortmunder Union Brewery, the main rival to DAB with a towering brewhouse in the centre of the industrial city, was formed from the merger of a dozen breweries in the late 19th century. It brews a smooth, malty DUB Export but recently has concentrated on brewing Pilsner, notably Siegel Pilsner and the premium Brinkhoff's No.1.

Erdinger
Germany's biggest brewer of wheat beers was founded in 1886. The company buys much of the wheat it uses locally and even supplies local farmers with seed to ensure it receives the right kind of wheat. It brews a range of popular, light wheat beers, including Erdinger Kristall, Hefe and Dunkel (all 5.2%) and a stronger Weizenbock, Pikantus (7.3%).

Eichbaum
One of Germany's oldest brewers, established in Mannheim in the heart of the Rhineland in 1679, Eichbaum produces a wide range of beers, including a very dry Ureich Pilsner, Eichbaum Export Altgold (5.3%) and three wheat beers, and range in strength from a light, low-calorie Leichter Typ to a powerful dark Apostulator Doppelbock. Part of the third-largest brewing group led by Henninger, Eichbaum (the name means oak tree) also owns the Freiberger Brauhaus of Freiberg.

Hacker-Pschorr
Late in the 18th century, Joseph Pschorr built huge underground beer stores in Munich, making it possible for beer of consistent quality to be brewed all year round. The brewery was the first to export draught beer to the US in the 19th century. Since 1976, Hacker-Pschorr has been linked to Paulaner. The brewery brews a Hell (4.9%) and a Dunkel (5%).

Henninger

This Frankfurt brewery has an international reputation and its beers are sold in over 60 countries. It is the fifth-largest brewery in Germany. The brewery's 110-metre (361ft) high silo tower, containing 16,000 tonnes of barley, is one of Frankfurt's dominant landmarks.

Holsten

This internationally well-known Hamburg brewery was founded in 1879, and is famous for its dry, hoppy range of Pilsners, including Holsten Pils, the local Edel Pilsner and more widely available Premium Bier. Holsten also brews an export and a maibock (which is exported under the name Urbock).

The company owns a number of other German breweries, including Sächsische in Dresden. Holsten rivals Beck's as the leading beer exporter of Germany.

Above: Löwenbräu beer is famous the world over. The brewery produces wheat beers as well as Pilsners.

Klosterbräu

The name means "monastery brewery". Some German abbeys do still brew, such as the Benedictine Kloster brewery at Andechs in Bavaria, but they do not produce their own distinctive beers like the Trappists in Belgium. The Andechs abbey brews beers in the style of its home region, notably a pale Spezial and a Doppelbock. The Kloster title is also adapted by many commercial breweries with monastic connections, such as Irseer Klosterbräu and the Klosterbräu at Bamberg, which is the oldest producer of smoky Rauchbier.

Krombacher

This prominent specialist Pilsner brewer in Kreutzal-Krombach produces more than four million hectolitres (21,996,900 gallons) a year of its hoppy Krombacher Pils, one of the best-selling brand in Germany.

Löwenbräu

The Munich brewery with the highest international profile. Its beers are brewed around the world. In Bavaria, it brews malty lagers, from a Hell and a Dunkel to a hoppy Pilsner and strong Oktoberfest (6.1%). It also produces a range of wheat beers and runs the largest beer hall in Munich (the Mathäser holds 5,000 drinkers). Löwenbräu means "lion brew" and there are a number of other lesser-known Löwenbräu scattered around the country.

Paulaner

The largest brewery in Munich is also credited with having created the Doppelbock style. First established as an abbey brewery in 1634 by the community of St Francis of Paula, it became known for its powerful Lenten beer. Commercial brewers took over in the early 1800s and developed this rich, ruby brew, calling it Salvator (saviour). Other brewers copied this Doppelbock, using similar names, and a new style was born. This complex dark beer became the standard-bearer of the brewery. Paulaner's firm, dry beers include Münchner Dunkel, an original hell, a pale Pilsner, and a Hefe Weissbier.

Schneider

The most celebrated specialist wheat beer brewers in Bavaria since 1872, Schneider offers the classic example of the cloudy, yeasty style in the spicy Schneider Original Hefe Weizenbier. There is also a sparkling kristall and a light (2.9%). Schneider is still a family-owned company, that brewed first in Munich and then in Kelheim, near Regensburg, from 1928.

Spaten-Franziskaner-Bräu

The famous brewery in Munich, founded in 1397, was originally named after the Späth family. In 1922 it merged with Franziskaner-Leistbräu .

OTHER OUTSTANDING BREWERS

Bavaria St Pauli

This brewery is in the St Pauli area of Hamburg in northern Germany. It brews mainly Astra Pilsner.

Bitburger

This Pilsner specialist was founded in the town of Bitburg in the Rhineland in 1817 and brewed one of the first Pilsners in 1883.

Einbecker

Part of the Brau and Brunnen group, the Einbecker Bräuhaus brews three malty Urbock-style beers – Hell, Dunkel and Maibock (all 6.5%). It also brews a Brauherren Pilsner (4.9%).

Above: The immaculate Schneider Weisse brewery in Kelheim near Regensburg. This family firm of specialist wheat brewers moved to Kelheim from Munich in 1928.

Füchschen

Im Füchschen (The Fox) is one of four home-brew pubs in Düsseldorf brewing its own malty Altbier.

Fürstenberg

The aristocratic family of the Fürstenbergs were first granted the right to brew by King Rudolf of Habsburg in 1283. Based in the Black Forest at Donaueschingen, their brewery uses water from a spring in the grounds of Fürstenberg Castle.

Gaffel

Founded, it is claimed, in 1302, this brewery in the centre of Cologne is known for its kölsch.

Garde

Some believe this brewery produces the definitive, fruity kölschbier at Dormagen-bei-Köln.

Hannen

Hannen, founded in 1725, is one of the leading brewers of Alt in Düsseldorf. It also brews Carlsberg in Germany.

Hansa

The light beers, including an export and Pilsner, of this famous Dortmund brewing name are now made mainly for supermarkets by DAB.

Herforder

Predominantly a Pilsner brewery in Herford near Hannover. As well as its full-bodied Pilsner (4.8%), it brews a malty export, a maibock and sommerbier.

Hopf

The family-owned brewery of Miesbach brews only wheat beers.

Irseer Klosterbräu

The village of Irseer, south-west of Munich, is dominated by the former monastery. Irseer Klosterbräu is a grand guest house with its own brewery, a small beer museum and vaulted Keller.

König

The name means "king". The large family-owned König brewery of Duisburg in the Rhineland hopes to be crowned king of the premium Pilsner. In 1995 its aromatic Pilsner (4.6%) was the fifth-best-selling brand in the country.

Below: The modern plant of Bitburger, the Pilsner specialist brewer. Bitburger Pils is exceptionally dry with a clean finish.

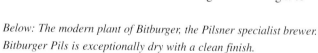

Above: The Pinkus Müller Altbierhaus in Munster in 1928.

Königsbacher

The brewery was founded in 1689 in the city of Koblenz where the Rhine and Moselle meet. It is best known for its hoppy Pilsner, but also produces an Alt and a powerful Urbock (7.3%).

Küppers

This is the largest brewer of kölschbier in Cologne. Besides a sweetish kölsch, it also brews an unfiltered version called Wiess.

Moravia

The name of this brewery in Lüneberg pays tribute to the Czech origins of the Pilsner style. It produces a hoppy, dry Pilsner.

Pinkus Müller

This historic home-brew pub has been brewing and serving beer in Münster since 1816. Pinkus Müller is now run by the fifth generation of the Müller family. Despite its small size, the brewery ships its beers around the world. Since 1990, all Pinkus beers have been produced organically.

The brews include an unusual pale alt beer (5%) brewed using wheat in the mash, which is matured for six months, developing a distinctive sourish, lactic taste. The brewery also produces a bottom-fermenting special (5%) and a golden Pilsner.

Rhenania

This independent family brewer in Krefeld, near Düsseldorf, was founded in 1838. It produces one of Germany's more widely available alts.

Ritter

This Dortmund brewery is now part of the larger Dortmund giant DUB. The brewery produces a good range of fruity beers, including a strong, flavoursome export and a golden-coloured, hoppy First Pilsner (4.8%).

Below: Brass bands, national costume and beer are essential parts of the Oktoberfest.

St Pauli Girl

The sister brewery to Beck's in Bremen, St Pauli Girl produces a similar beer. The odd name is derived from its Girl brand featuring a popular German barmaid. The beer is very popular in the US.

Spezial

The oldest Rauchbier (smoked beer) brewer in Bamberg, dating back to 1536, Spezial produces a lightly smoky brew called Lagerbier (4.9%) plus a more intense Märzen and a Bock at its home-brew pub.

Thurn und Taxis

An aristocratic Bavarian family brewery in Regensburg, Thurn und Taxis dates back to 1834. It produces a Pilsner (4.9%), a pale export (5.5%) and hell hefe weissbier (5.5%). The family still lives in the ornate Schloss St Emmeram in Regensburg. The brewery, which owns a number of other Bavarian breweries, was sold to Paulaner in 1997.

.Uerige

The high altar of Alt. This rambling Düsseldorf tavern, Zum Uerige, has, since 1862, brewed the definitive version of this copper-coloured, top-fermenting beer, deep in flavour and bitterness. In the town it is known by the locals as "dat leckere Droppke" – that fine drop. The shining brewery can be seen from one of the many bars in the tavern.

Unertl

This tiny Bavarian brewery in Haag, east of Munich, has developed a big reputation for its delicious dark, organic wheat beers, notably its sourly fruity hefe weissbier (4.8%) and hefe weizenbock (6.2%).

Veltins

This specialist Rhineland Pilsner brewer led the fashion for premium brands with its sweetish Pilsner.

Weihenstephan

This brewery has long been a Bavarian institution. The former monastery brewery at Freising not only claims to be the oldest working brewery in the world, going back more than 950 years to 1040, it is also the home of Munich University's internationally famous Faculty of Brewing.

The modern hill-top brewery is now owned by the Bavarian Government, and sells its extensive range of excellent beers commercially. The brews include a malty hell, a dark, flavoursome dunkel, a hoppy, dry Edelpils and a range of deliciously fruity wheat beers.

Zum Schlüssel

The Schlüssel brewpub was the first Düsseldorf home of the Gatzweiler Alt brewery. Zum Schlüssel (the name means "The Key") still brews its own malty Schlüssel Alt.

Above: Serving beer in a hotel in Germany. The waitress appears to have four hands!

SMOKY SECRET

The Franconia region of Germany, in particular the small, beautiful medieval town of Bamberg, has maintained a smoky tradition. Here malt is produced for local brews over beech-wood fires, giving it and the final beer a lightly smoked taste.

Bamberg has nine breweries for only 70,000 people. The classic producer is probably the Brauerei Heller Trum, which makes Schlenkerla.

Right: The Schlenkerla Tavern is the main outlet for the Heller Trum brewery's smoked beers.

AUSTRIA

Pilsners may rule the world, but in the mountain fastness of Austria it is a different story. Most Austrian beer follows the style pioneered by Anton Dreher in 1841 – a darker, reddish-amber lager.

THE BULK OF AUSTRIAN BEER still draws on the original malty style, which was a halfway house between bottom-fermenting, brown beers of Munich and the golden Pilsners of the Czech Republic. This beer is known simply as lager or sometimes Märzen, indicating its darker origins in the old, dark lager styles, though it is now more like a deeper Bavarian Hell in colour. A fuller-bodied version is called Vollbier. Between them lager and Vollbier account for almost 80% of the Austrian beer market. The hoppier, drier Pilsner takes little more than 6%, while wheat beers, so popular in nearby Bavaria, manage just over 1%. Stronger lagers are referred to in ascending order of strength as Spezial, Bock and Starkbier. Weaker, low-alcohol styles are usually called Leichtbier or Radler.

Austrian beer is distinct from German brews. The country is not governed by a beer purity law, and allows the use of adjuncts (unmalted cereals) such as rice or corn in its brews, which tend to give Austrian beers a cleaner, less complex flavour. The structure of the Austrian brewing industry is much simpler than that of Germany. Although there are some 60 breweries, including a few new brewpubs and micro-breweries, two groups dominate: Brau AG in the west and north, and Steirische in the south. Schwechater, the brewery where Anton Dreher worked his magic, once controlled Vienna. Each of the two main groups courted this family firm with its aristocratic connections, and it was finally taken over by Brau AG in 1978. High society in the capital was shocked – the beer-brewing family of Mautner-Markhof had fallen.

Since 1993, Brau AG and Steirische (made up of Gösser and Reininghaus) have combined with other Austrian breweries in a new Brau Union to expand into Eastern Europe, buying up breweries in Hungary and the Czech Republic.

Above: Austria is famed for its unique reddish-amber lagers, but Zipfer's pale lager appeals to more modern Austrian taste buds.

THE BEERS

Adam Spezial
See Adambräu.

Adambräu
A refreshing alpine lager (5.2%) that is now brewed in Brau AG's Bürgurbräu brewery in Innsbruck. There is also a stronger Adam Spezial (5.7%), and a brown, malty festbier.

Columbus
A rich, malty, well-hopped lager (5.3%) from the Stiegl brewery.

Edelweiss
Austria's most popular range of wheat beers is produced for the Brau AG group by Hofbräu Kaltenhausen of Hallein near Salzburg. The beers tend to be lighter in flavour than their Bavarian counterparts and there is a full range: cloudy-gold Edelweiss Hefetrüb with a spicy, malt taste; filtered (and therefore clear), bright Edelweiss Kristallklar; and darker-amber Edelweiss Dunkel (all 5.5%). There is also a stronger Edelweiss Bock (7.1%).

Gold Fassl Pils
This crisp, dry, pale-gold, hoppy Pilsner (4.6%) is one of the range of beers produced by the Ottakringer brewery of Vienna, a local independent brewery.

Gold Fassl Spezial
A full-bodied, meaty, malty Spezial (5.6%) produced by the Ottakringer brewery.

Gosser
This is probably Austria's best-known international brand name. It is produced by the Gosser brewery in Leoben-Goss. The range includes a light lager Gosser-Gold, the gold, malty Gosser Märzen, a fruity, malty Gosser Spezial and a deep-brown, full-bodied, sweet Gosser Export.

Hirter
This is a range of beers from the brewery of the same name. The golden Export Pils (5.8%) is probably the best-known, but there is also a Märzen (5%), an unfiltered Zwickl (5.2%) and a hefty, strong Festbock (7%).

Hopfenperle
A hoppy premium Pilsner (5.4%) from the Schwechater brewery near Vienna. It should not be confused with the Swiss brewery of the same name.

Kaiser
Kaiser is Austria's leading beer brand. Besides a standard Kaiser draught, the range also includes a malty Vollbier called Kaiser Märzen (5.2%), a Spezial Kaiser Goldquell (5.6%), and a hoppier Pilsner called Kaiser Premium (5.4%). Other Kaiser beers include the dark Doppelmalz (4.7%) and the strong Kaiser Piccolo Bock (7.1%). The Kaiser beers come from the Brau AG group which is the leading brewing group in Austria.

Keller Bräu
This is a range of seven quality beers from the private Kellerbrauerei of Ried. It includes a Märzen, a Pils, a Spezial, a Dunkel and a Festbock.

MacQueen's Nessie
This strong brew (7.5%) claims to be a whisky-malt beer. Nessie does not contain any of the Highland spirit, however, but uses imported peaty Scottish whisky-malt in the mash in order to produce a smooth, smoky, reddish-coloured beer with a biscuity, malt character and a smoky finish. It is one of the speciality brews produced by the Eggenberg brewery.

Morchl
An unpasteurized, malty, dark lager (5%), produced by the Hirter brewery.

Naturtrub
This is the unfiltered version of Keller Bräu's Annen-Bräu.

Nussdorf Doppel Hopfen Hell
A top-fermenting, dry, hoppy brew (3.8%). Hopfen Hell is one of a range of brews from the Nussdorf castle brewery.

Old Whisky
This strong, seasonal (5.5%), top-fermented beer uses whisky malt and is produced by Nussdorf.

Ottakringer Helles
This brew is a distinctive light-gold-coloured lager (5.1%) with a malty flavour, produced by Ottakringer, Vienna's local independent brewery.

Paracelsus
This unfiltered Vollbier (4.9%) comes from the Stiegl brewery of Salzburg.

Privat Pils
A strong, dry, golden Pilsner (5.2%) with a malty flavour, brewed by Hirter.

Ratsherrn Trunk
This tasty Vollbier (5.3%), which is produced by the Bräucommune Freistadt brewery, won a gold medal at the International Monde Sélection competition in Rome in 1995.

St Thomas Bräu
This is a dry, fruity top-fermented Altbier (4.6%) from the Nussdorf castle brewery.

Schlank & Rank

This dry, hoppy, golden Pilsner (4.9%) is produced at Brau AG's Bürgurbräu brewery in Innsbruck under the Adambrau label. The name means "Slim & Trim".

Sigl

A standard bottled lager (4.9%) from the Sigl brewery. It is known for its unusual "beer bop" characters on the labels.

Sir Henry's Stout

This distinctive, hearty, chocolatey stout (5.2%) was the first beer produced by the Nussdorf brewery.

Steffl

This is a gold, malty premium lager (5.4%) from the Schwechater brewery near Vienna.

Vienna brewpubs

The Austrian capital has a number of cellar bars brewing their own tasty, unfiltered lagers, notably Salmbräu which produces a Hell, a Pilsner and a dark malty Bock.

Stiegl Goldbräu

This amber, malty Vollbier (4.9%) is the best-known brew from the Stiegl brewery.

Stiftsbräu

This malty, softly sweet, deep-brown, dark Stiftsbräu (3.6%) is produced by the Gosser brewery.

Trumer Märzen

This classic Vollbier (4.8%) is produced by the Josef Sigl brewery of Obertrum.

Trumer Pils

An excellent extra-dry Pilsner (4.9%), produced by the Josef Sigl brewery. It is traditionally served in a tall, narrow glass.

Urbock 23

This strong, creamy, golden, slightly oaky Bock (9.9%) with a rich malt and hops flavour is allowed to mature for a full nine months in the Eggenberg brewery.

Weihnachtsbock

A deep-gold, rich, malty winter Bock (7%) from the Stiegl brewery in Salzburg. A darker version is brewed as Freistadter.

Weizen Gold

This range of wheat beers produced by the Josef Sigl brewery of Obertrum includes an unfiltered, hazy, gold, spicy Weizen Gold Hefe Hell, a dark-amber-coloured, malty Dunkel and a sparkling malty, Weizen Gold Champagner (all 5.5%).

Wieselburger Stammbräu

A traditional, pale-gold malty Austrian lager (5.4%). This beer emphasizes its history – the Wieselburg brewery dates back to 1770 – both on the label, which shows old lagering casks, and through its use of old-fashioned traditional swing-stoppered bottles.

Wieselburger Spezial

This strong Austrian lager (5.7%) is produced by the Wieselburger brewery.

Zipfer Märzen

A pale-gold, hoppy marzen (5.2%) with a pronounced sour, malt flavour, produced by the Zipfer brewery, part of the Brau AG group.

Zipfer Urtyp

This hoppy, pale-gold Vollbier (5.4%) is produced by the Zipfer brewery in the town of that name.

THE BREWERS

Augustiner

This Salzburg brewery dates back to 1621. It is still owned by the monks of Kloster Mullen, although it is now run by a secular company. The monastery has its own large beer hall where Augustiner Bräu is served in large, stone steins.

Brau AG

The full name of Austria's leading brewing group is Österreichische Brau-Aktiengesellschaft (the Austrian Brewing Corporation). This large company is a major player in the Austrian market and brews every third glass of beer that is sold in the country. The company is based in Linz and has breweries at Schwechat, Wieselburg, Zipf, Hallein (Kaltenhausen) and Innsbruck (Bürgerbräu), which produces regional beers. Its main brand is Austria's most popular draught lager, the sweetish Kaiser Draught. It also sells a wide range of other beers under the Kaiser brand name.

Eggenberg

This small brewery in the town of the same name which lies halfway between Linz and Salzburg produces some rare Austrian speciality beers, most notably the monstrously named MacQueen's Nessie. made with imported Scottish whisky malt in the mash. It also brews one of the strongest beers in the country, the creamy, golden Urbock 23, (9.9%) and a popular gold lager Hopfenkönig (5.3%).

Freistadter

The independent brewery, based in Freistadt since 1777, brews according to the stricter German beer purity law. Best known for its award-winning Vollbier Ratsherrn Trunk (5.2%), it also produces a Freistadter Märzen (4.9%), a dark Freistadter Spezial Dunkel (5.1%), a Freistadter Pils (4.5%) and a Freistadter Weihnachtsbock, which is a robust, full-flavoured, dark winter Bock (6.6%).

Hirter

The independent brewery in Hirt, Karnten, claims to date back as far as 1270. It is best known for its Hirter Export Pils.

Hubertus

The family brewery at Laa an der Thaya, close to the Czech border, is now run by the sixth generation of the Kuhtreiber family. Its well-matured beers, which are brewed to the German beer purity law, include Hubertus Märzen, the dark Hubertus Dunkel, two Pilsners and a strong Hubertus Festbock.

Keller Bräu

The private Kellerbrauerei of Ried, Hochfeld, dates back to 1446. The brewery has been run by the Mitterbucher family since 1926.

Nussdorfer

Baron Henrik Bachofen von Echt established this brewery in the wine cellars of his grand castle at Nussdorf in Vienna in 1984.

Ottakringer

Vienna's local independent brewery is a family firm that dates from 1837. It produces one of the more distinctive Austrian lagers in its Ottakringer Helles. It also brews a speciality Bräune, a Dunkel and a Bock.

Puntigamer

The brewery, based in Graz, produces a range of soft, mild beers, besides two stronger bocks.

Reininghaus

This Graz brewery produces a range of fruity beers.

Schlägl

Abbey in Upper Austria which brews its own beers including a top-fermenting rye beer Goldroggen (4.9%).

Schwechater

Anton Dreher's original brewery on the edge of Vienna betrays its old aristocratic links through grand pavilions and tree-lined courtyards in the brewery grounds. Besides a soft lager, Schwechater Bier (5.2%), it also brews a Schwechater Pils (5.2%), a premium Pilsner Hopfenperle and a Schwechater Festbock (7.1%).

Sigl

There has been an independent Josef Sigl brewery at Obertrum near Salzburg since 1601. It produces probably the best Pilsner in Austria, the deliciously dry Trumer Pils. It also brews a pioneering range of wheat beers under the Weizen Gold brand, a Sigl Bockbier (7.3%) and a bottled lager (4.9%), famous for its odd labels that feature different trendy characters in a "beer bop collection".

Stiegl

Austria's biggest private brewery dates back to 1492. As well as Goldbräu and Pils, it also produces a quality spezial and a winter Bock. Stiegl also has a brewing museum, along with a Bräu Welt (Beer World) experience for visitors, showing how beer is brewed.

Steirische Bräuindustrie

The second largest brewer in Austria is based in Graz. Many of its beers are brewed uner the Gösser label.

Zipfer

This brewery in Zipf, founded in 1858, produces probably the hoppiest beers in the Brau AG group. It produces a range of beers, including a Pilsner and two strong, malty bocks.

Anton Dreher

In the 19th century Anton Dreher, a brewer in Vienna, worked with Sedlmayr in Munich to develop lager brewing. He was the father of Vienna-style lager – an amber-coloured, subtly malty, sweetish, bottom-fermented lager, which is made using "Vienna malt". The pioneering brew was introduced in 1841 (just before the first Pilsner Urquell was brewed). The style proved a popular export, and Dreher went on to found breweries throughout the Austrian Empire – Italy, Hungary, Mexico and Bohemia – and the popular style reached out across the globe. The beer's prominence faded almost in parallel with the decline of the Austrian Empire, and Dreher's Vienna company closed in the 1930s, Vienna-style lager is still brewed in parts of South America and Scandinavia as well as in Europe.

POLAND

Poles enjoy a glass of beer, but for many years small, unmodernized breweries struggling to match demand. In addition to this handicap, the hoppy drop has always struggled to match the dominance of the national drink – vodka.

IN SHARP CONTRAST to its beer-loving neighbours to the west, Germany and the Czech Republic, Poland is a light imbiber, with Poles consuming less than 40 litres (70 pints) per head a year. This is partly because of a strong spirit-drinking tradition (especially in central and eastern areas), and partly because of the tax system that makes beer expensive compared to spirits.

At the turn of the century, Poland boasted more than 500 breweries. Lack of investment, however, meant that many closed. By the late 1980s a common sign in many shops and cafés was "Piwa Brak" – "no beer". Apart from a handful of larger companies like Okocim and the leading exporter Zywiec, most of the 80 or so breweries that remained were small and served a local area. Since the end of Communist rule, however, there have been fundamental changes in the Polish brewing industry. A growing number of breweries have been privatized, often linking up with western breweries to get funding for modernization. Most of the beer is still unpasteurized, although this is rapidly changing as modern processing techniques are introduced. By 1996, seven of the top 10 Polish breweries had some degree of foreign ownership, and the capital was bustling with many brands at higher prices. However, the government is trying to keep control of the industry in Polish hands by restricting foreign ownership of brewing companies to minority holdings.

A light, Pilsner-style of lager dominates, but there are also some fuller-bodied, export-style lagers and a few strong, bottom-fermenting dark brews called porters. These reflect the historical British influence throughout the Baltic. When the Napoleonic Wars stopped the export of British beers, local brewers responded to the existing demand by brewing their own dark beer.

Above: EB is one of the few Polish beers that is regularly exported. It is particularly popular in countries with large Polish communities.

THE BEERS

Dojlidy Porer

A strong, dark porter (9%) that is a typical example of the Polish porter style.

EB Specjal Pils

The mild, fresh, yellow-coloured lager (5.4%) from Elblag's brewery is triple-filtered. The liquor (water) with which it is made is drawn from the brewery's own deep wells.

Eurospecjal

This full-bodied, strong, golden lager (7.5%) is brewed by Zywiec in the city of Kracόw.

Gdańskie

This is one of the leading lagers (5.6%) from the Hevelius brewery which is situated in the shipbuilding city of Gdańsk.

Grodzisk

This rare, top-fermenting beer is said by the brewers to have been brewed since the 14th century in the town of Grodzisk Wielkopolski, near Poznań. It uses a high proportion of smoked wheat and is spontaneously fermented before being bottle-conditioned. The result is a tart, refreshingly sour, hazy golden ale with a heavy, smoky aroma. It is sold in a variety of strengths, the weakest of which is 5%.

Herbowe

A deep-gold, Pilsner-style lager (5.6%) from the Dojlidy brewery.

Hevelius

This super-premium, tasty lager (6.1%) is brewed by the firm of the same name in city of Gdańsk.

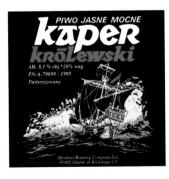

Kaper

A special, extra-powerful, malty, deep-gold lager (8.1%), which is brewed in Gdańsk by the Hevelius company.

BEER POWER

Poles undoubtedly love their beer. A political party, the Polish Beer Drinkers Party (PBP), which campaigned on a ticket of loving beer, holds several seats in the Polish parliament. The party, which started as a joke, now campaigns to deregulate the beer trade, and it publishes a weekly newspaper, *Kurier Piwny (The Beer Courier)*.

Karmelowe

Adark, low-gravity beer (3.5%) from the Okocim brewery.

Krakus

The soft, malty lager (5.4%) from the Zywiec brewery is named after the old name for the city of Kracόw.

Krolewskie

Krolewskie is brewed by the city of Warsaw's local Warszawski brewery. Before the end of Communist rule, this full-bodied lager (5.6%) was almost the only one that drinkers could find in the shops of Warsaw.

Lech Pils

A yellow-gold, hoppy, malty Pilsner (5.3%) from the Lech brewery.

Lech Porter

A strong, dark, cherry-coloured beer (7.4%) from the Lech brewery.

Lech Premium

This strong, malty, golden lager (5.4%) is one of Lech's leading brands.

Magnat

A full-bodied, strong golden lager (7.4%) from the Dojlidy brewery.

OK Jasne Pelne

Okocim's yellow-gold, malty "full light" lager has a strong, hoppy finish. It comes in various strengths.

Okocim Porter

A strong, dark, bottom-fermented porter (9%) from Okocim.

Warszawski Porter

A rich, dark, bottom-fermented porter (9%) from the Warsaw brewery.

Zywiec Full Light

This is a hoppy, fruity golden lager (5.6%), from Poland's famous Zywiec brewery, using fresh mountain water from Mount Skrzyczne.

Zywiec Porter

This rich, mahogany-coloured beer (9.2%) from Zywiec has heavy hints of roasted coffee and currants in the flavour.

THE BREWERS

Dojlidy

Located in Bialystok since 1891, this local brewery is typical of many of the smaller Polish breweries. It produced less than 200,000 litres (14,200 gallons) in 1992 while waiting to be privatized. Besides its main lagers, Zlote and Herbowe, it also produces Gotyckie, Magnat and Dojlidy Porter.

Elbrewery

This is now the largest brewing company in Poland, and it controls nearly one fifth of the beer market. Elbrewery was founded in 1872 as the Brauerei Englisch Brunnen Elbing in the northern town of Elbing. The original name of the brewery demonstrates the early influence of English merchants in the Baltic beer trade.

The company, which also has a second modernized brewery in nearby Braniewo, really took off with the involvement of the Australian company Brewpole in 1991, followed by investment by the large Grolsch company of the Netherlands in 1995. Its flagship brew is the golden EB Specjal Pils.

Hevelius

Founded in 1871 as the Danziger Aktien-Bierbrauerei-Kleinhammer in the port of Gdańsk, it was nationalized after the Second World War as Gdańskie Zaklady Piwowarskie. It was modernized in 1991 and renamed Hevelius that year, after the Polish astronomer. In 1996 the German brewers Binding took a 49% stake.

Above: The Old Town marketplace in Warsaw with open-air cafés and an old-fashioned horse and carriage designed for tourists.

Lech

Founded in 1951 in Poznań in west Poland, Lech also has a second brewery in Ostrow Wielkopolski and substantial maltings, making it the fifth largest brewer in the country. Following privatization in 1993, the firm is now owned by a Polish investor EAC, with a 15% share stake held by South African Breweries. It is best known for the golden lagers it produces – Lech Pils and Lech Premium – as well as the special, cherry-coloured Lech Porter.

Okocim

After Zywiec, this is the best-known Polish brewing company, with plants in Okocim, Kraców and Jedrezejow. The brewery was founded by an Austrian, Jan Gotz, in 1845. Since privatization in 1992, when German giant Bräu und Brunnen gained a quarter share, Okocim has linked up with Danish brewer Carlsberg. Its OK Jasne Pelne (full light) lager appears in varying strengths. Dark beers include a low-gravity Karmelowe and a powerful Okocim Porter.

Warszawski

Founded in 1846, this is the leading brewer in the capital of Warsaw. Besides standard lagers under the names Krolewskie (5.6%) and Stoteczne (5.4%), it also brews Warszawski Porter. The bottles give a nod towards beer's Egyptian origins with a Sphinx on the label.

Zywiec

Poland's most famous brewery had noble origins. It was founded in 1856 in Zywiec near Kraców, by Archduke Charles Olbracht Habsburg, adopting a crown as its emblem. It was owned by the Habsburg family until the Second World War. Under state control, it became Poland's leading beer exporter. On privatization in 1991, the Zywiec plant was extensively modernized. The company also runs smaller breweries in Cieszyn and Bielsko. In 1994, Heineken took a 25% stake in the company. Its main beer is Zywiec Full Light. There is also a softer Krakus and much more full-bodied Eurospecjal. Zywiec also brews one of Poland's most distinctive porters.

EASTERN EUROPE

The common Communist heritage of Hungary, Bulgaria, Romania, Latvia, Lithuania and Estonia has now been shaken off. The nationalized industries, which for a long time struggled to meet even the modest demand from the region, have been thrown open to investment from the West.

THE FORMER COMMUNIST countries of Eastern Europe consume relatively little beer, in part due to a strong spirit-imbibing tradition, but also because of inadequate brewing capacity and a shortage of raw materials.

Although Hungary, Bulgaria and Romania are best known for their wine, they have a healthy appetite for light lagers. Hungarians drink about 80 litres (17½ gallons) of beer per head a year. Foreign companies have shown great interest in the region since the move away from Communism, and many countries have been welcoming foreign investment with open arms. Hungary's brewing industry is now almost entirely foreign-owned. In Bulgaria some 13 breweries were struggling to keep up with demand, but now foreign investors have poured in, and by 1996 western companies had an interest in more than a third of the industry. In Romania too, a wide range of companies from the West have obliged with investment. In 1996, South African Breweries took a major share of the Romanian market.

Since 1991, a joint company called Baltic Beverages Holding (BBH), established by Scandinavian brewers, has taken a major stake in the leading breweries of the three small Baltic states of Estonia, Latvia and Lithuania. The breweries have since been heavily modernized and the beer ranges revamped to a more international style of Pilsners, moving away from traditional beers.

In Russia and the Ukraine, at the start of the 20th century, there were about 1,000 home-owned breweries producing a range of German, Czech and even English-style beers. The beer industry was severely damaged during the Revolution and two world wars, and was slow to recover. It was then hit by Gorbachev's drive against alcohol when breweries were mothballed or turned into soft drinks factories, and the barley farming areas were badly hit by the Chernobyl nuclear disaster. But despite acute beer shortages, the former USSR has been wary of foreign involvement, and only 6% of production in 1995 was foreign-controlled, though imports, especially from the Czech Republic, are increasing and now account for about 10% of the market.

Above: One of the yeasty lagers, brewed by Aldaris, the biggest brewer in Latvia. The brewery was modernized in 1991 by the BBH group.

THE BEERS

Aldaris
This range of sweetish, yeasty lagers produced by Latvia's biggest brewery includes the light Aldaris Pilznes (4%), a hoppier Baltijas, a smoother Zelta (5%) and the more powerful Jubilejas and Latvijas (both 6%).

Amber Pilsner
This light, dry, unpasteurized Pilsner (4.5%) is brewed using rye and sugar in the mash as well as barley malt. It is produced by the Amber brewery in Nikolayev, in the Ukraine.

Astika Lager
This golden, soft, mild and refreshing lager (4.5%) is widely available in Bulgaria. It is produced by the country's best-known brewery, Astika of Haskovo.

Bak
Köbányai's Bak is Hungary's version of a German Bock. This beer is strong (7.5%), dark and sweet.

Baltijas
This hoppy, yeasty lager (4.5%) is produced by the Aldaris brewery in Latvia.

Bergenbier
This popular, standard, golden-coloured, Romanian lager has a refreshing alpine image, with a snowy mountain peak on the label. A deep-amber Bergenbier Bruna has also been added to Bergen's range.

Birziecie
This strong, malty, dark lager (6.1%) is brewed by Ragutu, Lithuania.

Burgasko Lager
This light lager comes from the Burgasko brewery at Burgas on the Black Sea coast of Bulgaria.

Dreher
The Austrian pioneer of Viennese red beers, Anton Dreher, bought the leading Budapest brewery Köbányai Serhaz in 1862 and so gave his name to Hungary's best-known beer brands.

After a gap of some 40 years during Communist rule from 1948, the Dreher name was revived for Köbányai's premium range of beers – including a refreshing, dry, hoppy Pilsner (5%), the fuller-bodied golden-coloured Export and a Bavarian-style bock called Bak.

Dvaro
This is a premium lager (5.2%) from Kalnapilis, Lithuania.

Ekstra
Like Dvaro, this is a premium lager (5.2%) produced by the Kalnapilis brewery, in Lithuania.

Gocseji Barna
This relatively dark lager, which is something like a German Dunkel, is produced by the Konizsai brewery in west Hungary.

Kamenitza Lager
Kamenitza is a regional lager brand produced by the Kamenitza brewery in Plovdiv, Bulgaria.

Kanizsai Korona
The Kanizsai brewery in Hungary brews this malty, export-style lager.

Lauku Tumsais
This hazy, amber brew (6%) has a warming, malty taste. It is produced by the Lacplesis brewery in Lielvarde, Latvia.

Moskovskoye
This fruity lager is the leading beer brand produced by the Moscow brewery.

Nikolaevskyi
An amber-coloured beer (5%) with a spicy hop character, brewed with rye and sugar as well as barley in the south Ukraine by the Amber brewery, built by the Czechs in 1973.

Palmse
A dark, malty lager brewed by Viru in Estonia.

Porteris
The ruby-black beer (7.4%), with a rich, liqueur-like texture from Aldaris, is reputedly the only porter brewed in Latvia.

Reval
A golden, all-malt, hoppy lager, produced by the Saku brewery of Estonia.

Ruutli Olu
A rich, dark, spicy bock (7.5%), which is lagered for 70 days. It is produced by the Estonian Tartu brewery. This strong, dark, cold-weather beer was introduced by the brewery in 1995. It is the strongest beer brewed in Estonia.

Below: A beer stall in Riga, Latvia, in summer.

Above and left: Pilsner-type lagers, typical of the Saku brewery in Estonia, which was founded in 1820.

Talleros

This is the local lager brewed by the Heineken-owned Komaromi, Hungary.

Tartu Olu

This rich lager (6%) is one of the beers brewed by Tartu in Estonia.

Tume

A reddish-coloured, malty lager, Tume is brewed by Saku, Estonia.

Zagorka Lager

The light, golden Zagorka lager is produced by the Zagorka brewery, Bulgaria.

Zhigulevskoe (Ziguli)

One of the main Soviet lager brands, which, under Communist rule, was brewed right across the USSR from Moscow to the Far East. A premium version (4.4%), produced by the Obolon brewery of Kiev, uses a proportion of rice in the mash. This lager has sometimes been exported to the West.

Saku Originaal

Smooth-tasting Originaal is the premium, all-malt lager from Saku, Estonia.

Saku Pilsner

This fresh-tasting, golden, all-malt Pilsner is the main lager from Saku of Estonia.

Siraly (Seagull)

Siraly is a light, malty lager brewed by Kanizsai, Hungary.

Sirvenos

The leading lager (4.2%) from the Lithuanian brewer Ragutus, which, unusually, uses local peas in the mash to help with head retention and to give the beer a more rounded, full-bodied flavour.

THE BREWERS

Aldaris

Latvia's biggest brewery has been based in the capital Riga since 1865. It brews a range of sweetish, yeasty lagers. Aldaris controls more than half the country's beer market and has been owned by Baltic Beverages Holdings since 1992. In 1995, BBH introduced a cleaner-tasting Pilsner, Aldara Luksusa.

Amber

Like many regional breweries in the former Soviet Union, this is a fairly new Czech-built brewery. It was constructed in 1973 in Nikolayev in the southern Ukraine. It produces two main beers, Amber Pilsner and spicy, amber-coloured Nikolaevskyi. Hops are grown locally around Zhitomir, but a shortage of barley malt means rye and sugar are also used. Roasted malt particularly is in short supply, which limits the chance to brew darker beers. All production is bottled and unpasteurized, with a shelf-life of seven days.

Baltika

Work only began on this St Petersburg brewery in 1990 and had still not been completed in 1993 when the unfinished plant was taken over by Baltic Beverages Holding, a joint venture by Scandinavian brewers Pripps of Sweden and Hartwall of Finland. Baltika has since grown rapidly to become one of the largest brewers in Russia, selling 120 million litres (26 million gallons) in 1995, the bulk of it around St Petersburg where it controls two-thirds of the market. It

produces a range of light lagers, including the premium Parnas and Baltika Export on draught.

Bergenbier

The Romanian Bergenbier brewery is owned by Belgian giant Interbrew, which completed a new brewery at Blaj in 1995.

Borsodi

Part of the Belgian Interbrew empire since 1991, the Borsodi brewery in Bocs is the second largest in Hungary, controlling around a quarter of the market. Its main local lagers are Borsodi Vilagos and Rakoczi.

New brewpubs

Hungary's rapidly advancing economy has embraced the western trend for micro-breweries. Since 1989, the pioneer brewer, Zsolt Gyenge, has set up around 50 pub plants. Most of the micros brew all-malt beers according to the German beer purity law.

FARMHOUSE BEER

The Baltic states still retain a local, farmhouse brewing tradition, producing rye and juniper beers similar to the Finnish sahti in the north, as well as other refreshing country brews. On a more commercial scale they produce a variety of lagers, some using unusual brewing materials such as peas, besides a few stronger porters.

Russia also has a tradition of producing its own country beer – a nourishing home-made rye brew called kvass, sometimes sweetened with local fruit juices, such as bilberries. Some breweries produce this relatively low-alcohol beer commercially.

Burgasko
This Bulgarian brewery was taken over by Belgian giant Interbrew in 1995.

Kalnapilis
This large brewery in Panevezys, Lithuania, complete with its own maltings, was founded in 1902 and was acquired by the huge Scandinavian conglomerate, BBH in 1994. Since then, the brewery has launched a new range of international-style lagers, led by the premium Dvaro and Ekstra brands.

Kamenitza
Interbrew's first grip on the Bulgarian market began when it took over this brewery early in 1995.

Kanizsai
The Kanizsai brewery in Nagykanizsa in western Hungary dates back to 1892. The German brewing giant Holsten of Hamburg has had an interest in the brewery since 1984. It is best known for its light Siraly (Seagull) lager and malty Korona (Crown), a common name for Hungarian beers. It also brews a darker lager, called Gocseji Barna.

Köbányai
First opened in 1855, this plant was bought by the Austrian brewer, Anton Dreher in 1862. Although he died the following year, his son made the Köbányai the largest brewery in Hungary. After merging with its main local rivals Reszveny and Haggenmacher in 1933, and Fovarosi in 1934, Dreher controlled three-quarters of the beer market. With nationalization in 1948, the Dreher name disappeared, but it was revived some 40 years later after privatization. South African Breweries gained control of the brewery in 1993. The Dreher range of beers, based on old recipes, uses a high proportion of malt. Some lagers from the Communist period are still produced.

Komaromi
Heineken bought this modern brewery at Komarom in 1991, primarily to brew Amstel for the Hungarian market. Nevertheless, it also continues to brew a number of local lagers, such as Talleros.

Lacplesis
This small country brewery in Lielvarde, Latvia, brews on a former collective farm, where it grows its own grain.

Magadan
This brewery is located in the east in the Stalinist city of Magadan on the Sea of Okhotsk. It still produces the four standard brands once widespread across the former Soviet Union. These are Zhigulevskoe (Ziguli), Moscovskoe (Moscow), Russkoe (Russian) and Ukrainskoe (Ukrainian). All are similar, light, pale lagers that vary in recipe depending on the brewing materials available. The main difference is in their lagering times. Ziguli is lagered for 21 days, and Moscow for double that time, giving it a drier more acidic taste than the fresher Ziguli. This acidic flavour is not due to production problems in the run-down plant, but because many Russians like a sour edge to their beer. All brews add sugar to beef up the limited malt mash. Magadan also produces several commercial brands of kvass, the cloudy, unhopped rye country-beer, which is indigenous to Russia – one kvass is flavoured with lemon. In summer, this refreshing brew is sold unfiltered direct from tanker trucks in the streets.

Above: Shady outdoor tables in a Budapest café are a pleasant place to enjoy a relaxing beer in the heat of the summer months.

Moscow

The Moscow City Brewery, next door to Tolstoy's House, has been brewing since 1863 and was once the main testing plant for beer in the Soviet Union. Its leading lager is the fruity Moskovskoye (4.6%). An all-malt August (4.5%), named after the month of the failed army coup in 1991 that led to Boris Yeltsin's revolution,is exported.

Proberco

This brewery at Baia Mare in Romania is owned by Interbrew.

Ragutus

Like some other Lithuanian breweries, the Ragutus company in the major city of Kaunas uses a proportion of local peas in the mash for its main lager, Sirvenos, to help head-retention. It also brews a dark, malty Birziecie.

Saku

Estonia's leading brewery was founded in 1820 on a former nobleman's estate outside the capital Tallinn. It was taken

Above: Gleaming copper vats at the modernized plant of the Saku brewery in Estonia.

over by BBH in 1991. A new brewhouse was completed in 1992, and Saku now controls more than half of the Estonian beer market. Its main all-malt lagers are Saku Pilsner, a hoppier Reval, the premium Saku Originaal, and the reddish, malty Tume. Saku also brews a coffee-like porter each Christmas.

Tartu

This brewery in Tartu, Estonia, dating back to 1826 has impressive castellated, tower maltings. It was once famous for its Imperial Extra Double Stout, sold to the Russian court when the company was owned by the Belgian merchant Le Coq, who exported the stout for Barclay Perkins of London. It produces a range of lagers including a Pilsner, Rae, a firm-bodied, export-style

Alexander and the richer Tartu Olu, as well as a dark bock called Ruutli Olu.

Viru

The Viru brewery was built on a former collective farm in Estonia in 1975. It is now owned by the large Danish brewer, Harboe.

Zagorka

Heineken has a large interest in this brewery in Stara Zagora, Bulgaria.

Fragmented market

Altogether, there are about 250 breweries in Russia and the Ukraine. They mainly produce light lagers containing adjuncts, such as corn and rice, that are matured for little more than two to three weeks. Breweries primarily serve a local market, but there are some more widely available brands – Ziguli is probably the best example.

Above: A modern brewery in Russia that was built using Austrian investment.

THE CZECH REPUBLIC AND SLOVAKIA

The Czechs have a long and proud brewing tradition and are the biggest beer drinkers in the world. They were among the first to use hops, and their pioneering golden lager has become the most popular beer style in the world.

SINCE THE BREAK-UP of the old Czechoslovakia into the wine-drinking Slovakia and the beer-loving Czech Republic, the Czechs now officially drink more beer per head of population than any other country.

Czech beer sprang to international fame when the citizens' brewery in Plzen developed the first golden lager in 1842. The town – Pilsen in German – gave its name to what was to become the world's leading beer style, Pilsner or just pils – an aromatic, hoppy, bottom-fermented pale beer.

Above: Budweiser Budvar is an internationally known, classic example of the Czech all-malt lager style.

In 1938 Czechoslovakia still boasted more than 300 breweries. But, some 60 years later, the brewing craft is at a crossroads. During the long period of Communist rule, little changed in what had become a nationalized industry. Ironically, the lack of investment in new technology meant that the traditional brewing methods were preserved almost intact. Since the "Velvet Revolution" of 1989 there has been a rush to modernize, with tried and trusted traditional methods often replaced by gleaming new plants. Plzen's dark cellars of wooden conditioning casks, for instance, have been replaced by stainless-steel conical vessels. Character and quality are declining. There are still 70 breweries in the Czech Republic, plus a few brewpubs, but as the larger groups expand and smaller plants are expected to close.

Most Czech beers today are divided into Pilsners of differing strengths, usually indicated by the old degree method of measurement, with 8 indicating a weak brew, 10 an everyday beer and 12 a premium. Before 1989, 12-degree beer was the most popular, but since then, as prices have risen, drinkers have switched dramatically to the weaker 10-degree brews.

THE BEERS

Alt Brunner Gold

This is the malty premium 12 Pilsner (5.1%) brewed by Starobrno.

Bernard Granat

A full-bodied, 11-degree, dark beer (4.9%), produced using two different types of malt, by the family-run Bernard brewery at Humpolec (founded in 1597), which also brews a golden, dry 12% beer (5.1%). The brewery has been one of the leaders of the movement to gain tax concessions for small-scale breweries.

Bohemia Regent

This is a popular, fruity 12 (4.9%), produced by the Regent brewery.

Black Regent

A full-bodied, ruby-red dark beer (4%) with a dark-malt and coffee flavour, produced by the historic Regent brewery.

Budweiser Budvar

This is the most famous of all Czech lagers internationally and perhaps now the classic example of its style. The all-malt Budvar (5%) still retains its soft fruitiness and heady aroma. The Budweiser brewery was founded in the town of Ceske Budejovice (Budweise in German) in 1895, using water from an underground lake. It rapidly became a major exporter, particularly to Germany and the US (where its beer was sold as Crystal). Since 1989 the company has doubled in size, with annual production

THE BATTLE FOR BUDWEISER

Such is the fame of Budweiser Budvar that many of the leading breweries around the world have proposed mergers or other trading arrangements, but none have been as persistent as Anheuser-Busch of the United States, which sells its own leading beer under the Budweiser name. Over the last century, the two have frequently clashed in and out of court over the rights to the title. Anheuser-Busch argues that Budvar was not founded until 20 years after the American brewer launched his Bud, but the Czechs contend that, since the Samson brewery was operating in Budweis since 1795, this is irrelevant. Besides, any brewery in the town of Budweis should have the right to market its beers as Budweiser, as the word means "from Budweis". Nevertheless, Budweiser Budvar has been unable to market its beers under its own name in the United States (calling it Crystal instead), and Anheuser-Busch has to sell its flagship beer as Bud in countries like Spain, where the Czech company registered the Budweiser name

first. The situation has intensified since the "Velvet Revolution", as exports were less of a priority under Communism. The American giant would like to resolve the long-running dispute by taking over the Czech brewery. However, the Czech Government, which owns the brewery, is wary of the overtures, not wanting to be accused of selling off the crown jewel of the nation's brewing industry.

rising from 450,000 to 900,000 hectolitres (10 million to 22.5 million gallons). Traditional horizontal lagering tanks are still used, and the export beer is matured for more than 60 days. This export beer accounts for 60% of the brewery's export sales. New conical fermenters are used for producing a weaker 10-degree version (4%) with a blue label for consumption in the domestic market.

Cassovar

A rich, ruby-black, dark lager (5.5%) with a smooth cocoa and cream flavour, brewed in the Slovak town of Kosice.

Cernohorsky Granat

This dark, malty beer (3.5%) is brewed in Moravia by Cerna Hora.

Cernohorsky Lezak

An quality, golden Pilsner (3.5%) from Cerna Hora.

Chmelar

This pale, but relatively strong, hoppy beer (4.2%) is brewed by the small Zatec brewery. The name means hop-picker.

Crystal

Budweiser Budvar and Samson use this name for their premium beers when sold in the United States.

Drak

A rare, rich, dark, 14-degree Christmas brew (5.7%) from the Starobrono brewery. The name means dragon.

Dudak

A full-bodied premium pale 12 (5%) from the Stakonice brewery of South Bohemia.

Eggenberg

This is the name for a range of beers brewed at Cesky Crumlov in South Bohemia, which includes a pale and dark 10-degree (4%) and a full-bodied 12 (5%). The brewery, which dates back to 1560, is in an old armoury.

Gambrinus

The best-selling Czech beer is brewed by the brewery of the same name in Plzen. Gambrinus is restricted to domestic consumption, but still produces over 1.5 million hectolitres (33 million gallons) a year of a pale, aromatic 10-degree beer (4.1%) with a good,

hoppy character. A small amount of a stronger Gambrinus 12 (5.1%) is also brewed, mainly for export.

Granat

Granat is a popular name for a dark beer, which is used by a number of brewers including Olomouc, Cerna Hora and Hostan.

Herold Dark

A pitch-black, full-flavoured 13-degree brew (5.2%) which comes from the Herold brewery in Breznice. A pale 10-degree beer (3.8%) and stronger 12 (4.8%) are also available.

Holan 10

This hoppy, pale, unfiltered lager (3.5%) is brewed by Olomouc, for the local market.

Karamelové

The malty, dark, 10-degree lager (3.8%) comes from Starobrno of Brno.

Karel IV

A gold, fruity, pale 11-degree lager (4%) with a malty flavour. This is produced at the Karlovy Vary brewery in the famous spa town of that

name in western Bohemia, better known as Carlsbad. The beer is named after the king who founded the spa

Konik

This best-selling, hoppy, pale-gold Pilsner beer (3.8%) is produced by the Ostravar brewery.

Kozel

This range of beers from the Velke Popovice brewery near Prague gained notoriety in the mid-1990s with their raunchy advertising. The name means goat. Its popular beers include a hoppy, pale-golden Kozel 10 (4.3%) with a fruity, sweet, malt flavour, a deep-golden, hoppy 12 (5%) and a dark, deep-brown 10 (4.3%) with a rich, malt flavour.

Krusovice

These include a dark, malty 10 (3.7%) with a very bitter flavour and a pale, thirst-quenching 12 (5.1%) with an aromatic, hoppy, sweet-malt flavour.

Lobkowicz

The pale, hoppy 12 (5%), from this family-run brewery is exported as Lobkov. A malty, dark 12 (4.6%) and a weaker, pale 10 are also available, and a 14 (5.5%) is occasionally produced.

Lucan

This pale, hoppy beer (3.6%) is brewed by the small Zatec brewery.

Martin Porter

This richly roasted, bitter-sweet porter (8%) is the strongest beer brewed in Slovakia. It is produced in the town of Martin, by the brewery of the same name.

Martinsky Lager

A malty, amber lager from the small Martin brewery in Slovakia.

Mestan Dark

This is the dark-amber, award-winning, malty beer (4.6%) produced by the Mestan brewery in the Prague suburb of Holesovice.

Nectar

This range of three fruity beers (10, 11 and a dark 10) comes from the Strakonice brewery of South Bohemia.

Novomestsky

This unfiltered, fruity, pale 11 (4%) is brewed in a rambling brewpub in the heart of Prague, established in 1993 in a shopping arcade.

Ondras

This premium, hoppy, pale, Pilsner beer (5%) is produced by the Ostravar brewery.

Osma

This weak, pale, 8 Pilsner (3.2%) is brewed by Starobrno.

Pilsner Urquell

The original flagship Pilsner of the Czech brewing industry. Its development in Plzen launched golden lager on the world for the first time in 1842. Pilsner Urquell (4.4%) is still a quality beer by any standards, particularly when fresh, with its delicate hop aroma and deep soft fruitiness. Urquell means original source.

Pivo Herold Hefe-Weizen

This spicy, fruity, top-fermented wheat beer (5.2%) is brewed in the Bavarian style by the Herold brewery. The style, long dead in the Czech Republic, has been revived by this brewery in Breznice.

Platan

Three pale beers are produced under this title – 10 (3.9%), 11 (4.4%) and 12 (5%), besides a dark beer (3.6%). All these beers are pasteurized.

Ponik

This is the weakest of the hoppy, pale Pilsners (3%) produced by the Ostravar brewer in Moravia.

Pragovar

A hoppy, premium, golden lager (4.9%) from the Mestan brewery of Prague.

Primator

This range of distinctive dry beers is brewed by the Nachod brewery in north-east Bohemia, which is owned by the town of Nachod. The Primator beers include a pale 10 and 12 and a chocolatey, dark 12 (5.1%).

Primus

A pale-gold, cut-price brew (3.8%) from Gambrinus.

Prior

An unfiltered, yeasty wheat beer (5%), introduced by Pilsner Urquell in 1995.

Purkmistr

One of the best Czech dark lagers (4.8%) from the Pilsner Urquell group, Purkmistr has a bitter-chocolate flavour balancing the initial malty sweetness. It is brewed at Domazlice.

Radegast

The range of beers from the Radegast brewery includes a popular, pale-gold 10 (3.8%) with a dry, hop flavour. The 12 (5.1%), which is sold as Premium light, has a golden hue and a dry hops and malt taste. The brown Premium Dark (3.6%) has a light, malt flavour.

Rezak

This is a half-and-half pale and dark lager, (4.1%), produced to satisfy the demands of drinkers who often mix their pale and dark lagers. It is brewed by Starobrno.

Samson

A range of crisp, dry, pale beers, produced by the brewery of the same name. The 10 (4%) has a bright-gold colour and a clean, crisp hops flavour. The 11 (4.6%) is a tawny-gold-coloured beer, with a creamier, sweeter hop flavour. A hoppier version of the 11 is sold in England under the name Zamec, and the sweet, ripe 12 (5%) is sold as Crystal in the US.

Starobrno 10

This deep-golden, hoppy 10 (4.3%) with a rich, bold flavour is a popular beer from the Starobrno brewery's range.

Staropramen 10

Besides a fresh and hoppy pale 10 (4.2%), this major Prague brewery produces a full-bodied 12 (5%) and a mellow dark (4.6%). The quality of the beers reflect the fact that the brewery has retained traditional methods of brewing.

Tas

A light, golden, tasty Pilsner (2.8%) brewed by the Cerna Hora brewery in Moravia.

Tatran

A range of lagers from the Vega brewery of Poprad in the Tatran mountains, Slovakia. It includes a Tatran export (8%) and a lighter Kamzik (4.1%).

Urpin Pils

The deep-gold, hoppy, Pilsner with a light, malt flavour from the Urpin brewery in Slovakia.

Vaclav 12

A hoppy, pale lager (5.6%), brewed by Olomouc.

Velke Popovice

See Kozel.

Vranik

A delicate, malty, dry, dark 10 (3.8%) from Ostravar.

Zamek

Export name for Samson 11.

Zatecka Desitka

A pale, hoppy beer (3.1%) from the Zatec brewery.

Zlaty Bazant

This gold-coloured, firm, dry Pilsner (4.4%) with a sweet, creamy, malt flavour is one of the popular lagers produced by the Slovakian Zlaty Bazant brewery.

THE BREWERS

Bernard

This family-owned brewery at Humpolec on the main road between Prague and Brno was founded in 1597.

Branik

Originally established by a group of innkeepers in 1900, Branik is now part of the Bass-owned Prague Breweries group led by Staropramen. The dramatic brewhouse and maltings lie among trees in the south of the city. Unfortunately, much of the traditional equipment inside was replaced with conical fermenters and a pasteurization plant in 1992 before Bass took over. Once famous for a strong 14-degree dark lager, it now brews a sweetish pale 10 and 12, and a dark 10.

Budweiser Budvar

The world-famous Budweiser brewery was founded in the town of Ceské Budejovice in 1895, using water from an underground lake. It rapidly became a major exporter, particularly to Germany and the US. Since 1989 the company has doubled in size, with annual production rising from 450,000 to 900,000 hectolitres (10 million to 22.5 million gallons).

Cerna Hora

The small Moravian country brewery at Cerna Hora, north of Brno, built in 1896, produces a range of light but tasty Pilsners.

Chodovar

This small brewery with a long history dates back to 1573. It is located close to the Bavarian border at Chodova Plana, and brews three pale and one dark, nutty 10-degree beer.

HOPPING WITH HISTORY

The Czech Republic hop-growing tradition dates back to the 9th century, making it one of the longest-standing hop producers in the world. The area around the town of Zatec – better known under its German name of Saaz – became world-famous for the quality of its hops. One Bohemian king, Vaclav IV, even forbade growers from selling cuttings abroad on penalty of death to try to protect the green crop which was worth its weight in gold.

For much of the 19th century, Bohemian hops ruled the world, dictating quality, standards and prices. The town of Zatec was at the heart of a global business, only losing its dominant position after the First World War and the break-up of the Austro-Hungarian Empire.

Even today, major brewers like Anheuser-Busch of the United States still import large amounts of Czech hops. Their quality is so widely respected that the vast bulk of the crop is exported.

Gambrinus

This brewery, in Plzen, was once restricted to domestic production, but now produces over 1.5 million hectolitres (33 million gallons) a year of the best-selling Czech beer – a pale, 10-degree lager. It is part of the Pilsner Urquell group.

Herold

This ancient brewery in Breznice, south of Prague, came back from the dead and is now going strong. It was closed down by the Communist authorities in 1988, but brewer Stanislav Janostik rescued the baroque buildings that date back to 1720, and started up brewing operations there again in 1990. The traditional plant now produces a dark 13-degree, a pale 10-degree and a 12-degree, as well as a wheat beer.

Jihlava

The south-Moravian brewery in Jihlava dates back to 1860. In 1995 it was bought by the Austrian brewer Zwettl and it is now being modernized. However, it is uncertain whether its Jezek (hedgehog) beer brand will survive this restructuring.

Above: This promotional postcard from Ceske Budejovice acknowledges beer's Egyptian origins.

Krusovice

This historic brewery to the west of Prague in the Zatec hop-growing region was taken over by the German brewing group, Binding of Frankfurt, in 1994. The German giant has since invested heavily in modernizing the plant – and in the brewery's ancient heritage, calling its products the beers of King Rudolf II. Krusovice, dating back to 1581, was once part of the royal estate.

Lobkowicz

A family brewery south of Prague near Sedlcany.

Mestan

Part of the Bass-owned Prague Breweries group led by Staropramen, this plant in the suburb of Holesovice is best known for its award-winning, malty, dark 11.

Olomouc

The Moravian brewery, north-east of Brno, typifies the present contradictions in the Czech brewing industry. On the one hand it offers a tasty, unfiltered lager for Czech locals; on the other it now brews American beers under licence.

Ostravar

This substantial brewery in the mining town of Ostrava in northern Moravia was bought by Bass in 1995. The brewery, which dates back to 1897, received the last new brewhouse installed by the Communists in 1987. It produces a wide range of local beers, including three hoppy pale Pilsners called Ponik, Konik and the premium Ondras. It also brews Staropramen 10.

Pilsner Urquell

For 150 years Pilsner Urquell in Plzen has managed to maintain its traditional brewing methods, using huge wooden casks to mature each batch of its revered beer for three months. Watching these massive barrels being rolled out of the underground tunnels and into the brewery for repitching and repair was once one of the famous sights of the old brewing town, along with the grand gates to the brewery. Now only the triumphal arches remain, but behind, everything else has changed. Stacks of conical fermenters have replaced the old casks in a bid to increase the brewery's production and efficiency – and with them has gone a little of the complexity of the famous brew. Pilsner Urquell is the largest brewing group in the Czech Republic by far, producing 72.5 million gallons in 1994, almost double the output of its nearest rival. Pilsner Urquell accounts for about a fifth of the total Czech beer market and a large part of the country's exports. Besides the Urquell brewery itself, the brewing group also includes the neighbouring, larger plant of Gambrinus in Plzen, Domazlice and Karlovy Vary.

Platan

The Platan brewery is part of the South Bohemia breweries group along with Regent and Samson. Platan was originally developed by aristocratic landowners in Protivín, with records dating back to 1598. It takes its name from the local plane (platan) trees in its parkland home.

Radegast

Radegast has risen from being a distant local brewery in north-eastern Moravia, at Nosovice, to become the third largest national concern in the Czech Republic. Built in 1971, mainly to supply the Slovak and Polish markets, the privatized company markets its beers under the symbol of Nordic the god of hospitality, Radegast.

Regent

One of the oldest and most historic Czech breweries, Regent dates back to the 14th century in Trebon. Behind its fine facade, however, it is switching to conical fermenters.

Samson

This is probably the brewery in Ceské Budejovice (Budweis in German) that inspired Adolphus Busch to call his American beer Budweiser. Samson dates from 1795. Its heavily modernized brewery produces a wide range of crisp, dry, pale beers.

Starobrno

This is the major brewery in the Moravian city of Brno. It was founded in 1872 and brews a wide range of beers.

Staropramen

Staropramen – the name means "old spring" – has been brewing in the Smichov district of Prague since 1869. Taken over the the English brewers Bass in 1993, it has retained its open fermenting vessels and traditional lagering tanks.

U Fleku

Probably the most famous home-brew pub in the world, U Fleku also claims to be the oldest. U Fleku has been brewing in Prague since 1499 and its softly spicy, dark brew (5.5%) and wood-panelled rooms and courtyard are one of the taste-and-see attractions of the grand city.

Zlaty Bazant

This is Slovakia's best-known brewery. It produces the popular Golden Pheasant brand of lagers, in the southern town of Hurbanovo. The company is now controlled by the Dutch giant Heineken.

ITALY

The Mediterranean countries of Europe have traditionally been lands flowing with wine. At best, beer is viewed as a summer thirst-quencher. Italian consumption of beer might still be one of the lowest in Europe, but unlike most other markets it is expanding.

B REWING, IMPORTED FROM OVER THE ALPS, did not appear in Italy on any significant scale until the 19th century, and then it was limited mainly to the northern region. The Wuhrer brewery of Brescia, founded in 1828 by an Austrian, claims to be the first large commercial concern in the country. The number of breweries grew to about 100 by the end of the century, but then it rapidly declined as production was concentrated in the hands of a few leading companies such as Peroni and Moretti. Brewing – nearly all in a light Pilsner style – was still very small beer until the 1960s. Annual consumption in 1950 was no more than three litres (five pints) a head. However, in the next few decades demand surged, reaching 26 litres (46 pints) by 1995. Most of this (nearly 80%) is sold in bottles. Younger people began to regard beer as a fashionable drink; wine was for their parents or peasants. English-style pubs opened and imports from countries such as Germany and England rocketed, accounting for about one-fifth of all beer sales.

Altogether there are about 20 breweries in Italy today, and many of the major brewers of northern Europe have stepped into this land of expanding opportunity, exporting enthusiastically and buying into the native breweries. Heineken, for example, now controls 40% of production since its purchase of Moretti and the Dreher Group. The French giant BSN (which produces Kronenbourg) has a stake in the country's top brewer Peroni, and through this accounts for 36% of the market. Carlsberg of Denmark also has an interest in the Poretti company.

Above: Italian beer may not have the cachet of the country's wine, but it is an increasingly popular drink. Peroni, the leading brewer, is making the most of the expanding market.

THE BEERS

Birra Moretti
A light, crisp, yellow-gold lager (4.6%) from Moretti.

Birra Peroni
A pale-gold lager with a malt and hop aroma and a hoppy taste, from Peroni.

Bruna
A reddish, all-malt, strong Munich-style lager (6.25%), with a smooth, spicy, roasted flavour. Brewed by Moretti.

Crystal
Peroni's range of draught premium lagers includes a Speciale and a darker, Viennese-style, malty Crystal Red (both 5.6%), plus an even stronger Crystal Gold (6.6%). Crystal Speciale is a clear, yellow-gold lager (5.6%) with a smooth, rich barley and malt flavour.

Forst Sixtus
This unusual, dark, abbey-style beer (6.5%) is brewed by the Forst family brewery in Lagundo.

Gran Riserva
Strong beers in Italy are known as double malts, and in 1996, to mark its 150th anniversary, Peroni introduced one in distinctive, tall, embossed bottles. Gran Riserva is a deep-gold, full-bodied lager (6.6%).

Italia Pilsner
This yellow-gold, light Italian Pilsner (4.7%) has a dry, bitter flavour. It is a leading brand in the north-west of the country. Itala Pilsen of Padua was taken over by Peroni in 1960.

Kronen
This bright-gold, export-style lager (5%) with a malty taste, from Forst, shows a Viennese influence.

McFarland
Despite its Irish image, this bottom-fermented red beer (5.5%) from Dreher is more a Viennese-style lager.

Nastro Azzuro
Peroni's pale-gold, clean, sweetish premium Pilsner (5.2%) was introduced in 1964. The name means "Blue Ribbon".

Raffo
A light, golden-yellow, dry, mildly bitter Pilsner (4.7%) from Peroni. Raffo is sold mainly around its home city of Taranto in southern Italy.

Right: A Roman relief of a tavern scene. The Romans preferred wine to beer.

Rossa
This is probably the most characterful of Italy's red beers. The rosy-amber-coloured, richly flavoured, all-malt La Rossa (7.5%) from Moretti of Udine gives a robust reminder of northern Italy's former connections with Vienna and its Märzen-style brews.

Sans Souci
A pale-gold, malty export-style lager (5.6%) brewed by Moretti of Udine. It has a good hop balance.

Splügen
The brand name for this range of speciality lagers produced by the Poretti Brewery of Varese is taken from the name of a high mountain pass. The most celebrated of the beers is the deep-copper-coloured, faintly smoky Splügen Fumée, which is made with Franconian malt. There is also a coppery-red, robust, fruity Splügen Rossa (7%) and a German-style, black beer Scura (6%).

Werner Brau
A light Pilsner (4.5%) brewed by Poretti.

Wuhrer Pilsner
This pale Pilsner (4.7%) with a light, hoppy taste, is produced by the Wuhrer brewery in Brescia.

THE BREWERS

Dreher

Italy was once part of a vast Austrian empire, and the celebrated brewer Anton Dreher of Vienna crossed the Alps to establish a brewery in Trieste in the 1860s. Today, the Dreher name lives on in a Milan-based group owned by Heineken. Besides a range of light lagers, its beers include a Vienna-style red lager called McFarland.

Forst

The medium-sized brewery in the mountains at Lagundo is owned by the Fuchs family. It brews beers that show an Austrian influence, notably in the export-style lager Kronen. Forst means "forest" in German.

Moretti

Founded in Udine in 1859, the Moretti brewery became well known on the international markets despite its relatively small size. This is helped by its appealing labels showing a moustachioed man blowing the froth off his glass of beer. Besides a light, crisp Birra Moretti there is also a more malty export Sans Souci and two more characterful, darker brews – an all-malt Moretti Bruna and the richly flavoured red Moretti Rossa. In recent years, the company has changed hands at a dizzy rate and is now owned by Dutch giant Heineken.

Peroni

Until Heineken combined Dreher with Moretti in 1996, Peroni was the leading Italian brewer. Founded in Vigevano in 1846, it soon concentrated its activities in Rome then spread out, taking over breweries throughout the peninsula. Since merging with Wuhrer in 1988, it has concentrated production at five plants. Its leading blue-ribbon brand is Nastro Azzurro, but it also brews a lighter Peroni Birra. Other similar regional brands include Itala Pilsen, Raffo and Wuhrer. There is also a "Crystal" range. In 1996, Peroni added a more full-bodied bottled Gran Riserva.

Poretti

The Poretti company was founded in 1877 in Varese, north of Milan. It now has a second brewery in Ceccano, south of Rome. Besides a light Pilsner – Werner Brau – it also produces a number of distinctive specialities under the Splügen brand name. Carlsberg has now bought the brewery.

Wunster

Wunster is another Italian brewery that has Germanic origins. The brewery was founded by the Bavarian Heinrich von Wunster and is based in Bergamo. For many years it was a family concern, but it is now part of the large Belgian Interbrew group.

MALTA AND THE ENGLISH CONNECTION

The tiny island country of Malta off the coast of Sicily has a distinctive brewing tradition and is something of an anomaly in the Mediterranean region.

The legacy of the British Empire still lingers over this independent Mediterranean island. Its one brewery, Simonds, Farsons, Cisk (which is now commonly known as Farsons) started up to brew beers for the sailors at the British naval base there, in the top-fermenting ale styles that they enjoyed back home. Simonds of Reading, England exported ale and stout to Malta in the 19th century, then helped to set up a brewery in cooperation with a local company Farrugian and Sons. Although the British are long gone, the brewery remains, still producing these English-style, top-fermenting ales and a range of lagers under the Cisk brand name.

The Farsons brewery now produces a darkish, soft, mild ale (3.6%) called Blue Label and a stronger ale (5%) called Brewer's Choice. It also brews a hoppy pale ale (4%), Hop Leaf and a creamy, milk stout (3.4%) with a dry finish,, Lacto, which is brewed using lactose (milk sugar) and claims to be "Milk Stout with Vitamin B for Extra Energy". The brewery at Mriehel also produces lagers under the Cisk label. As well as alcoholic drinks, Farsons is the island's main soft drink producer.

Water is a scarce resource on the rocky island of Malta so Farsons collects every spare drop of rainwater in huge rooftop reservoirs, to be stored in underground tanks.

GREECE AND TURKEY

Civilized chat over a drink is a key part of both Turkish and Greek social customs. But on these occasions beer has always come a rather ragged second to wine, or strong coffee and potent aniseed ouzo or raki.

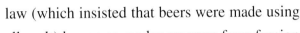

CONTROL BY breweries from northern Europe has reached saturation point in Greece, virtually wiping out the local industry. The only large, Greek-owned brewery – Fix – closed in 1983, and foreign companies and brands now dominate the market. The country's Bavarian-influenced beer purity law (which insisted that beers were made using all-malt) has gone, under pressure from foreign brewers. However, the island of Cyprus has managed to maintain a popular local lager – Keo.

Turkey, in contrast, has a thriving local producer in the shape of Efes, which worked hard to develop the market for international-style light lager after the state brewing monopoly, Tekel, was relaxed in 1955. The Danish-owned Turk Tuborg and state-run breweries in Istanbul, Ankara and Yozgat compete, but Efes dominates the Turkish market.

Above: Keo, from Cyprus, won a Gold Medal for Excellence at the 1987 World Bottled Lager Competition.

THE BEERS AND BREWERS

Aegean
This sweetish, malty Pilsner (5%) is produced in the north of Greece by Athenian Breweries, which is wholly owned by the Dutch giant Heineken. It has a hint of toffee and a slightly bittersweet edge.

Efes Pilsener
This golden, sweetish, full-bodied premium lager (5%), produced by Efes in Turkey, is widely exported. The company takes its name from the ancient Roman city of Ephesus, and its full title, Efes Pilsen Bira Fabrikasi, indicates an intention to brew a dry, hoppy Pilsner. The company also brews Efes Light, an Extra and an alcohol-free Alkolsuz Efes.

The Efes brewery has branched out in recent years and as well as running four breweries in its home country, it now also runs two malting plants and a brewery in Romania.

Keo
This sweetish, full-bodied, Pilsner-type lager (4.5%) is brewed in Lemesos, southern Cyprus, by the Keo brewery. It is bottled fresh and unpasteurized. Keo is one of the few remaining local brewers.

FRANCE

France is mainly associated with some of the great wines of the world, and French beer is rarely given a second thought. Beer in France is treated as a refreshment, not as a serious drink in its own right, and the industry is dominated by a few large companies.

D ROP INTO MOST FRENCH cafés and ask for *une bière* and you will be served a *pression* (draught) of light, refreshing but undemanding lager. Most of this beer is brewed in the Alsace region, close to the German border in the east of the country. The German influence is obvious in the place-names and the cuisine of the area, but most of the beer is a pale shadow of the better-quality brews across the border. The French do not have a beer purity law but use a variety of adjuncts, and have been the most vigorous campaigners against the German Rheinheitsgebot, claiming that it restrains trade. In addition, they allow their lagers much less time to mature than German brewers and they tend to use a relatively small quantity of hops.

The centre of the French lager brewing industry is Strasbourg and the major names are Kronenbourg and Kanterbräu, both owned by the same BSN conglomerate, which dominates about half the domestic beer market. The Dutch giant Heineken also has a major stake in the French market, owning the "33", Mutzig and Pelforth brands and controlling almost a quarter of the trade. In 1996, they added to this by taking over the sizeable Fischer group.

One region of France, the Nord-Pas de Calais in the north-east close to Belgium, does boast its own distinctive traditional beer style. A number of small breweries in this region, especially around Lille, brew "bières de garde" (keeping beers), which are strong, top-fermenting, bottle-conditioned ales. These were traditionally made in farmhouses in the winter and spring before the heat of summer made brewing too unpredictable. More commercial versions are now produced, some of which are bottom-fermented and filtered, but still retain an ale-like fruitiness through warm fermentation. They are often sold in champagne-style wired and corked bottles. The brewers who use barley and hops from the region are entitled to use the appellation "Pas de Calais/Région du Nord".

Above: Bière de garde from the rural north of France is still sold in large corked bottles. Jenlain is probably the most famous example of the type.

THE BEERS

Abbaye de Vaucelles

Not so much a Belgian abbey-style beer as a French bière de garde (7.5%), this amber-coloured, honey-like drink is brewed with herbs by the Choulette brewery for an abbey near Cambrai.

Ackerland

Two strong, malty lagers – the rich, malty, amber-coloured Ackerland Blonde (5.9%) and the dark Ackerland Brune (6.3%), which has a sweeter flavour – are sold under this brand name. Both are produced by the independent Meteor brewery of Hochfelden in Alsace. The name is taken from the agricultural area which lies around the village.

Adelscott

Labelled a "Bière au Malt à Whisky", this faintly smoky, amber-red, pale lager (6.4%) from the Adelschoffen brewery, is made using peaty Scottish malt. It created a niche market when it was launched in the early 1980s.

Adelscott Noir

This is another (6.6%) Bière au Malt à Whisky from Adelschoffen. It is almost black, with red highlights, and has an intense, peaty, slightly smoky flavour.

Amberley

Pelforth brewery of Lille introduced this whisky malt beer (7.3%) in 1993 as a rival to the popular brews produced by Adelscott.

Ambre de Flandres

A mellow, oaky, bottom-fermented bière de garde (6.4%) from the Jeanne d'Arc brewery at Ronchin, near Lille, sold under the Orpal brand name.

Ancre

A popular Alsace lager (4.8%), Ancre is brewed by Heineken at Schiltigheim.

Bière des Templiers

A dark, fruity, sedimented bière de garde (8.5%) from the Saint Sylvestre brewery.

Bière du Désert

This strong, pale-yellow-gold, fruity beer (7%) is brewed by Gayant.

Breug

See Terken.

Brune Spéciale

A deep, amber-brown dark lager (6.7%) with a roasted malt flavour, produced by the Terken brewery.

Certa

This alcohol-free beer was the first of its kind to be produced in France. Unusually, it is available on draught. Certa is brewed by Les Brasseurs de Gayant, a firm normally famous for its strong beers.

Ch'ti

The name is local Picardy patois for a French north-easterner and is the brand name for the bières de garde produced by the Castelain brewery of Bénifontaine, near Lens. The richly fruity beers from this coal-scarred region, featuring a rugged miner on the label, include a deep-gold, malty-fruity blonde and a darker brune version (both 6.5%) as well as a deep-amber-coloured Ch'ti Amber (5.9%).

Choulette Framboise

A seasonal, speciality, top-fermented, unpasteurized bière de garde (6%). It is flavoured with natural raspberry extract to produce a tart, fruity flavour and is brewed by La Choulette farmhouse brewery.

Cuivrée

Cuivrée is a powerfully smooth, Vienna-style reddish lager (8%) with a strong, fruity, malty flavour brewed by the independent Schutzenberger brewery of Schiltigheim.

Cuvée de Jonquilles

This is a golden-coloured, flowery, fruity, top-fermented, bottle-conditioned spring brew (7%) produced by the Bailleux family brewery in the Café Restaurant au Baron in Gussignies.

Démon

La Bière du Démon from Les Brasseurs de Gayant of Douai claims to be the strongest blonde beer in the world, with 12% alcohol. Brewed with extra malt and a special lager yeast, it has a fiery but rather heavy, honeyish character with a small head.

Fischer Gold

A strong lager (6.5%) with a perfumy aroma and a hoppy flavour from Fischer. It is sold in a distinctive swing-stoppered bottle.

Goldenberg

A strong, malty, golden beer (6.4%) from Gayant of Douai.

Goudale

Goudale is a pale top-fermented traditional bière de garde (7.2%) with a full, fruity flavour, from Les Brasseurs de Gayant. The beer is bottle-conditioned and wire-corked in the traditional manner.

Jade

This is a *bière biologique* or organic beer. Jade is a refreshing, pale-yellow, fruity lager (4.6%) that is produced using only organically grown malt and hops by the Castelain brewery of Bénifontaine, near Lens. The unpasteurized, fresh, hoppy brew can be sold in a large, champagne-style bottle.

Jenlain

This strong, reddish-amber, all-malt bière de garde (6.5%) is the best-known of its type. It is a top-fermented brew, packed with spicy, fruity flavours. The Duyck brewery of Jenlain, near Valenciennes, still sells Jenlain in classic corked and wired bottles, but it is also available in smaller, capped bottles.

Jubilator

Jubilator is a golden, aromatic, full-bodied, pale doppelbock (7%) in the German style, from the Schutzenberger brewery of Schiltigheim.

Killian

George Killian's Bière Rousse (6.5%), an Irish-style, strong, malty red ale, is brewed by Pelforth of Lille. The beer is sold in the Netherlands as Kylian.

Kronenbourg

The main Kronenbourg beer (5.2%) is a light-tasting lager and the stronger 1664 (5.9%), popularly known as "soixante-quatre", is smoother but a little more full-bodied. There is also a weaker Kronenbourg Légère (3.1%). A hoppier variant of the standard lager is called Kronenbourg Tradition Allemande, while Kronenbourg Tradition Anglaise is softer and deeper amber in colour. There is also a maltier, dark version of 1664 called Brune, and two seasonal brews, a rosy La Bière de Noël and a golden Kronenbourg Bière de Mars.

L'Angélus

The label for Annoeullin's hazy golden-bronze wheat bière de garde (7%) features J. F. Millet's painting of pious peasants at prayer in the fields. The beer has a very fresh, fruity, creamy flavour.

La Bière Amoureuse

This is a distinctly un-beerlike lager (4.9%). It is flavoured with ginseng and herbs. According to the brewers Fischer these "natural plant extracts" produce an aphrodisiac effect on the lucky drinker.

La Choulette

This is an amber-coloured, soft, fruity bière de garde (7.5%), produced by La Choulette farmhouse brewery using a blend of top and bottom-fermenting yeasts at warm temperatures. Local malts and Flemish and Hallertau hops are used in the brew, and the beers are roughly filtered in order to leave some yeast in the bottle. A blonde version is also available. Both are bottle-conditioned. The name comes from a traditional local game similar to golf.

Lutèce

This powerful, malty sourish bière de garde (6.4%) is produced by the Enfants de Gayant brewery in Douai.

Meteor

This light, hoppy, unpasteurized, Pilsner-style lager (4.6%) is produced by the Alsace brewery, Meteor.

Mortimer

Meteor's fruity, all-malt, copper-coloured, Vienna-style strong lager (8%) was first brewed in Hochfelden in 1993. It is bottled and packaged to look like a malt whisky.

Mutzig Old Lager

A strong, characterful, amber lager (7.3%), with a rich malt-and-hops flavour, produced by the Mutzig brewery in Alsace near the French-German border.

Mutzig Pilsner
A standard, golden, hoppy Pilsner (4.8%) brewed by the Mutzig brewery, Schiltingheim, Alsace.

Noordheim
A creamy, pale lager (4.7%) brewed by Terken of Roubaix for sale in supermarkets. It is sold in small 25 cl bottles.

Pastor Ale
Subtitled "C'est une symphonie", this all-malt, amber-coloured bière de garde (6.5%) hits all the right tart, fruity, hoppy notes. It is brewed using bottom-fermenting yeasts and Saaz and Flemish hops by one of the classic bière de garde producers, the Annoeullin farm brewery near Lille. It can be bought either unfiltered in tall, wire-corked bottles or in more conventional small capped bottles in packs. The name is a pun on Beethoven's *Pastorale Symphony.*

Patriator
Darker and fruitier than its sister beer Jubilator, Patriator (7%) is a doppelbock which is produced by the Schutzenberger brewery of Schiltigheim.

Pêcheur
See Fischer.

Pelforth Brune
A strong, sweetish, dark lager (6.5%) with a warm, rich, chocolatey-malt flavour, produced by the Pelforth brewery.

Pelforth Blonde
A light, fruity lager (5.8%) from the Pelforth brewery near Lille.

Pelican Lager
A standard, golden lager (4.8%) with a malty flavour, from the Pelforth brewery near Lille.

Porter 39
A rich, strong, roasted porter (6.9%), produced by the Pelforth brewery.

Saaz
A hoppy lager (5.2%) brewed by Gayant of Douai.

Saint Arnoldus
A fruity, abbey-style sediment beer (7.5%) from the Castelain brewery of Bénifontaine, near Lens. The beer is filtered, then yeast is added again before bottling.

Saint Landelin
A range of French top-fermenting abbey-style beers from Les Brasseurs de Gayant of Douai named after the founder of L'Abbaye de Crespin. The range includes: a sweet, creamy Blonde (5.9%), which has a rich-gold hue and a fruity flavour; a reddish-brown Saint Landelin Ambrée (6.1%), with a full, biscuity-malt

flavour; and a richer, dark Brune (6.2%), with a coffee-chocolatey flavour. All the beers are matured for two months before bottling.

Sans Culottes
There is nothing missing from this classic, golden bière de garde (6.5%) produced by La Choulette brewery of north-eastern France. Top-fermented and bottle-conditioned, it is full of yeasty character. The name, usually interpreted as meaning "without trousers", refers to the French revolutionary soldiers.

Schutz Deux Milles
This richly fruity, bottle-conditioned brew (6.5%) from Schutzenberger was originally brewed to mark the 2,000th anniversary of Strasbourg.

Sebourg
The blonde sister to Jenlain from the Duyck brewery of Valenciennes, this full-flavoured, aromatic bière de garde (6%) also comes in tall

corked and wired bottles. It is not brewed in Jenlain, but in the neighbouring village of Sebourg.

Septante Cinq
This powerful, reddish-amber-coloured lager (7.5%) is described as a bière de garde. It is the flagship brand of the Terken brewery.

Tourtel
This low-alcohol lager (1%) from Kanterbräu comes in blonde, amber or brown versions.

Trois Monts
This classic, harvest-gold, top-fermenting bière de garde (8%) is produced by the Saint Sylvestre brewery near the Belgian border. This complex, dry and winey brew is named after three local hills which stand out in the flat Flanders landscape.

Upstaal
A mild, pale lager (3%) with a sweet, appley taste, from Terken.

Wel Scotch
This dark-amber-coloured lager (6.2%) is produced by Kronenbourg, using Scottish whisky malt.

Willfort
A malty, dark lager (6.6%) from the Kronenbourg group.

"33"
Trente-trois is a popular number in France, south-east Asia and Africa, where this light export Pilsner (4.8%) with a malted cereal flavour has developed a large market in the old French empire. Originally brewed near Paris, it is now comes from Marseilles.

THE BREWERS

Adelschoffen

The Alsatian brewery in Schiltigheim, near Strasbourg, founded in 1864, has been described as a brewing laboratory. Its most famous creation is the Adelscott whisky malt beer.

Castelain

Specialist brewer of the Ch'ti bières de garde based at Bénifontaine near Lens.

La Choulette

La Choulette farmhouse brewery began to market the traditional, fruity La Choulette bière de garde in 1981. They are top-fermented and bottle-conditioned, and there are also seasonal specials. The brewery in Hordain, near Valenciennes, dates back to 1885.

Deux Rivières

Two Bretons set up this micro-brewery in 1985 in Morlaix in Brittany, inspired by tasting traditional Welsh

ales. Its two main bitters are Coreff Red Label (4.6%) and Black Label (6%).

Duyck

The family farmhouse brewery near Valenciennes, near the Belgian border, has brewed the best-known bière de garde, Jenlain, since 1922. Duyck kept the style alive when most other brewers in the region were abandoning these traditional beers. It also markets another golden country beer called Sebourg and two seasonal specialities, Duyck Bière de Noël (6.8%) and a refreshing pale Duyck Bière de Printemps.

Above: Bière du Démon.

Above: The handsome Duyck brewery in the hamlet of Jenlain.

Fischer

Founded in 1821, the brewery in Schiltigheim, near Strasbourg, also sells its beers under a French version of its name, Pêcheur. It brews a variety of lagers, such as Poussez, the cherry-flavoured Fischer Kriek and the so-called aphrodisiac lager – La Bière Amoureuse.

Gayant

Les Brasseurs de Gayant at Douai was formed in 1919 from a merger of four family breweries. Named after the two giants who traditionally protected this French Flanders town near Lille, the firm is famous for its strong beers. It produces a bière de garde, the top-fermented speciality of the region, called La Goudale (7.2%) but is better known for its devilishly powerful Bière du Démon (12%), which claims to be the strongest blonde beer in the world. It also brews a less strong, but far from arid, fruity Bière du Désert, and a rare abbey-style range of beers, Saint Landelin, and some more standard lagers which are marketed under the Saaz and Goldenberg brands.

Kanterbräu

Now seen as Kronenbourg's second-string brand, at one time Kanterbräu was the largest brewing group in France. Its main brewery at Champigneulles, near Nancy in Lorraine, dates back to 1887 and it also has a second smaller plant at Rennes in Brittany. Besides a light lager Kanterbrau (4.5%), it also brews a stronger Kanterbräu Gold and a low-alcohol lager called Tourtel. The brewery is named after a German brewmaster, Maître Kanter. In 1994 Kanterbräu formally combined with Kronenbourg under the name Les Brasseries Kronenbourg.

Kronenbourg

France's dominant beer brand takes its name from the Cronenbourg quarter of Strasbourg (the use of the K was felt to be more beerily Germanic). The company grew after the Second World War by selling its premium Bière d'Alsace across France in small bottles, at a time when most take-home lagers were low in strength and sold in litre bottles. In 1952 a "super premium" Kronenbourg 1664, named after the firm's founding date, was added. In 1969 a vast brewery was opened at Obernai, and shortly afterwards the company became part of BSN.

Meteor

Probably the best of the Alsace lager brewers, this family company in Hochfelden, dating back to 1640, asked the Czechs if they could use the term Pilsner in 1927 and received a written agreement from Pilsner Urquell. Météor sells more than half its beers on draught in bars where it is unpasteurized. It also sells two strong lagers, Ackerland Blonde and Brune.

Mutzig

An Alsace brewery, that brews its beers at Schiltigheim.

Pelforth

This brewery near Lille, with its pelican trademark, has become famous for its strong speciality beers, notably its Pelforth Brune which was introduced in 1937. There's also a Pelforth Blonde and a standard Pelican lager. The name Pelforth is an anglicized abbreviation of "pelican" and "forte" (strong), which was adopted in 1972. It also brews George Killian's Bière Rousse, a porter, a whisky malt brew called Amberley, a rich bière de Noël (both 7.3%) and a seasonal spring bière de Mars (5.3%).

Saint Sylvestre

One of the classic country brewers of French Flanders, it has been brewing in the village of Saint Sylvestre Cappel near Hazebrouck for over a century. It produces a traditional bière de garde, Bock du Moulin, and the seasonal brews Bière de Mars and de Noël.

Schutzenberger

The only independent brewery left in the famous brewing town of Schiltigheim, near Strasbourg, was founded in 1740. It brews some of the most distinctive beers in Alsace, notably two French bockbiers, a pale Jubilator and the darker Patriator and a stronger-still Cuivrée (8%). Other beers include the bottle-conditioned Schutz Deux Milles and two seasonal brews for Christmas and spring.

Terken

Roubaix's independent brewery produces a wide range of beers under various brand names. It is best known for its flagship Septante Cinq, but it also brews Brune Spéciale, a blonde lager called Orland (5.9%), the festive Terken Bière de Noël (7%) and a low-alcohol brew called Elsoner. Its supermarket brands include Breug, Noordheim, Ubald, Überland and Upstaal.

BREWPUBS

Brasseurs

Les Brasseurs is a chain of home-brew pubs in northern France, which started with a palatial pub by the main railway station in Lille. The colourful, unpasteurized, all-malt beers include a Brasseurs ambre – blonde and brune – and a cloudy, fruity wheat beer, blanche.

Frog & Rosbif

The Paris home-brew pub in the Rue St Denis has been brewing English-style ales with Anglo-French punning names since 1993. The beers include a bitter Inseine, a stronger ale Parislytic and a stout Dark de Triomphe. In 1996 it opened a second brewpub, the Frog & Princess, across the Seine in St-Germain-des-Prés.

SWITZERLAND

Despite having one of the earliest-known, large-scale breweries in Europe – the Abbey of St Gallen, which dates back to the 9th century – the Swiss were predominantly wine drinkers until well into the 19th century.

Above: The Swiss beer market is dominated by two big names – Feldschlösschen and Hürlimann. Feldschlösschen's hoppy lager is a best-selling brew.

S WISS BEERS tend to be as clean as the mountain air, but less breathtaking than the scenery. Little malting barley and few hops are grown in the rugged country. Led by the German-speaking areas of the north, however, in the mid-1800s the Swiss began to adopt the new bottom-fermenting lager beers from Bavaria. Some enterprising brewers in Zurich even chipped away their ice supplies from the Grindelwald glacier. Between 1850 and 1885 the number of breweries snowballed from 150 to 530. Since that date, much of the choice has melted away, leaving little more than 30 breweries remaining today. Once sales agreements helped to keep local breweries alive but now, like its alpine neighbour Austria, the country is dominated by two main groups – Feldschlösschen (which also controls Cardinal, Gurten, Valaisanne and Warteck) and the more internationally known Hürlimann (which includes Löwenbräu of Zurich). Heineken of the Netherlands also owns Haldengut and Calanda.

Like Austria, the main beer in Switzerland is a fresh, clean-tasting, malty lager. Although there is no complete beer purity law, most beers are all-malt and most brands are fairly similar in taste. Pilsners are barely mentioned. The Swiss prefer to ask for blonde lagers. Dark beers account for little more than 1% of sales. Most of the so-called specialities are just stronger, golden lagers, and only a few wheat beers are produced.

On international markets, Switzerland is probably best known for two distinctly different products. On the light side are low or no-alcohol brews, such as Birell, while at the heavyweight end of the market there is Samichlaus from Hürlimann , one of the strongest beers in the world. A recent innovation is the establishment of a chain of home-brew pubs, Back und Brau (Bake and Brew) which, as the name suggests, bakes baguettes and quiches while brewing fresh, unfiltered Huus (house) lagers and other beers, such as an Altbier.

THE BEERS

Anker

A rare, dark, top-fermenting Altbier (5.8%) that was launched by the Cardinal brewery of Fribourg in 1980 in a bid to develop the limited speciality beer trade. It was marketed as a move back to tradition – "the way beer used to be".

Barbara

The patron saint of the artillery has given her name to this deep-golden-coloured "de luxe" strong lager (5.9%), produced by the Eichhof brewery in Luzern . It is a smooth, slightly sweet beer with a hint of malt.

Birell

Hürlimann of Zurich's golden, low-alcohol lager is now brewed around the world. Unlike many other near beers, the alcohol is not removed by distillation after fermentation, or by osmosis. Instead it uses a special yeast strain, which produces just 0.8% alcohol.

Braugold

This light, clear-gold premium lager beer (5.2%) is brewed to a special recipe using only the best ingredients. Eichhof claims that it is the best-selling premium brand beer in Switzerland.

Calanda Weizen

One of the few Swiss wheat beers, Calanda Weizen is a lightly fruity brew in the Bavarian style. It comes from the Calanda brewery, based in Chur in the eastern side of the country, and it was founded in 1780.

Cardinal Lager

A light, tawny-gold lager (4.9%), with a smooth, malt and hops flavour, produced at the Fribourg brewery.

Cardinal Rheingold

An amber, malty, strong lager (6.3%) with a gentle perfumed aroma, from the Fribourg brewery.

Castello

This strong, full-bodied, sweetish lager, has a malty flavour. It is brewed by Feldschlösschen.

Dreikönigs

Hürlimann's stark (strong), sweetish pale lager (6.5%) is brewed in Zurich. The name of this rich, malty beer means "Three Kings", from the coat of arms of a Zurich district.

Dunkle Perle

A dark, malty lager (5.2%) brewed by Feldschlösschen.

Eichhof Lager

This standard, refreshing, clear-gold lager (4.8%) is the flagship brew of the Eichhof brewery in Luzern . It is available on tap and in bottles and cans.

Hexen Bräu

A creamy, amber-brown Dunkel (5.4%) with a chocolatey flavour produced by Hürlimann. Its name means "witches' brew" and brewing coincides with the full moon. (See Swiss Moonshine panel.)

Hopfenperle

Feldschlösschen's hoppy lager (5.2%) from Rheinfelden is probably the most widely distributed beer in Switzerland.

Hubertus

This is a dark, strong, deep-amber-coloured, premium lager (5.7%) brewed by

Eichhof in Luzern . The unusual colour comes from the roasted malts used in the mash. Its smooth, malty, slightly sweet flavour goes well with cold meats, especially game.

Hürlimann Lager Bier

This malty, golden, standard lager (4.8%) is the main brew from the Hürlimann brewery.

Löwenbräu

A malty, golden Pilsner-style lager (4.7%) with a light, hoppy flavour, from the Löwenbräu subsidiary of Hürlimann (no connection to the famous German, international brewing giant).

Moussy

A deep, bright-gold, alcohol-free beer with an intense malt flavour, from the Cardinal brewery, Fribourg.

Pony

This clear, sparkling deep-golden Pilsner-type of beer (5.7%) with a strong, but well-balanced, bitter, hoppy flavour, is produced by the Eichhof brewery, Luzern .

Rheingold

This is a strong, full-bodied golden-coloured lager (6.3%). Rheingold is produced by the Cardinal brewery of Fribourg.

highly alcoholic cognac and cough-mixture character, it is a smooth beer to sip and savour before going to sleep.

Spiess Edelhell
This pale-gold lager (4.8%) is brewed to the original recipe of the Eichhof brewery's founder in 1834, and the label has changed little since then. The beer's smooth, well-rounded flavour is not too bitter, and the Eichhof brewery attributes this to the "secret" mix of cereals in the mash.

Sternbräu
A golden-amber, full-bodied Spezial (5.2%) with a malt and hops flavour, brewed by Hürlimann. The name means "star beer" and is inspired by the brewery's five-pointed star emblem.

Tambour
A strong, golden Starkbier (Starkbier means "strong beer") produced by the Wartek brewery.

Vollmond
See panel.

Wartek Lager
A hazy, golden lager, with a good malty flavour, produced by the Wartek brewery, Basel. There is also a malty Wartek Brune, and a fruity, copper-coloured, top-fermenting Wartek Alt.

THE BREWERS

Cardinal
The Fribourg brewery, founded in 1788, originally developed its Cardinal beers to celebrate the election of the bishop of Fribourg to the Papacy. It is one of the few national brands.

Eichhof
This is Switzerland's largest independent brewery, commanding a market share of 7%. The name Eichhof was born in 1937, but the company's origins can be traced back to a brewery set up by Traugott Spiess in Luzern in 1834.

Feldschlösschen
Switzerland's largest brewer, based at Rheinfelden, near Basel since 1874, merged with Cardinal of Fribourg, in 1992 and Hurlimann in 1996 to become Feldschlösschen-Hurlimann, the biggest brewer in the land by far.

The Feldschlösschen castle-like plant at Rheinfelden, set in grand grounds, looks a fitting home for the country's ruling beer dynasty. Its polished brewhouse even comes complete with stained-glass windows and marble pillars.

Feldschlösschen's main lager is the hoppy Hopfenperle. There is also a darker Dunkle Perle, a stronger, sweeter Castello and an alcohol-free Ex-Bier.

Hürlimann
Hürlimann was founded in 1836 in Zurich, where it now dominates the market. It is Switzerland's best-known brewery abroad.

Löwenbräu
No relation to the Munich giant, this lion brewery is a subsidiary of Hürlimann, producing a range of similar lagers, as well as a Celtic Whisky Brew.

Ueli
This small brewery, established behind the Fischerstube café in Basle in 1974 was Switzerland's first micro-brewery. It brews a fruity Ueli Weizenbier, a malty Ueli Dunkel and a light Ueli Lager.

Wartek
This is the leading brewery in Basel, established in 1856.

SWISS MOONSHINE

The Swiss may have a rather conservative image, but one beer casts them in a totally different light. In 1992, the family-run Locher brewery of Appenzell, near St Gallen, revived an old tradition when it started brewing beers at the full moon, reflecting local beliefs about the effect of the moon's pull on earthly, particularly biological, events. Brewer Karl Locher claims that beer brewed at this time ferments more quickly. His golden Vollmond (full moon) lager, produced in two strengths (4.8% and 5.2%), caught the public's imagination – so much so that Hürlimann of Zurich began to brew its chocolatey, dark lager Hexen Bräu (5.4%) on the same monthly night shift when the full moon was peering through the clouds. The name means "witches' brew".

Samichlaus
Classed as the world's strongest lager at a staggering 14%, Samichlaus (Santa Claus) is brewed just once a year at the beginning of December by Hürlimann of Zurich and then left to mature for 12 months before being ready to redden Father Christmas's nose the following festive season. This reddish-brown brew, first introduced in 1980, is testimony to the gutsy fighting qualities of Hürlimann's quality yeast strain, and a constant contender for the *Guinness Book of Records*. With its

SPAIN

Recently, chilled, thirst-quenching, pale lager has taken a firm hold on the wine-drinking Spanish. Few other beers are now brewed or drunk there, and consumption has been rising rapidly over the last 20 years.

Above: The best-known brand outside Spain, San Miguel, was originally brewed by a Filippino company.

THE SPANIARDS HAVE a brewing tradition going back centuries. The Romans were impressed by the grain-based brews of the Iberian peninsula. The 16th-century King of Spain, Charles I, was a great lover of beer, and under his influence the first commercial Spanish breweries were set up by Flemish and German members of his court. However, it is only in the last few decades that beer has become a truly popular drink. Spain has witnessed a remarkable revolution. In 1948, drinkers in this country of robust wines drank less than three litres (five pints) of beer per head, per annum. Now, however, the Spaniards are the keenest imbibers in the Mediterranean region, consuming about 70 litres (125 pints) per person each year – considerably more than either France or Italy. Most of the beer that is drunk is a light, thirst-quenching lager – cerveza Pilsner that is brewed with a mix of malt and corn grits and matured for a short period, with a strength of about 4.5%. The bulk of this is sold in bottles, with a substantial amount on draught in bars and cafés. In recent years, influenced by the demands of northern European tourists and the growing amounts of imported beers, there has been a switch to a stronger, more malty, full-bodied "especial" beer (around 5.5%) approximately in the Dortmunder style, or a stronger-still "especial extra". A few dark lagers and some low or no ("sin") alcohol brews can also be found.

The country is dominated by five major breweries – Cruzcampo, Aguila, San Miguel, Damm and Mahou – and there is a strong international presence. Guinness owns the largest brewer, Cruzcampo, while Heineken controls its main rival, Aguila. Since Franco's demise in 1975 opened the door to foreign investors, international companies have been active in Spain, making the most of the boom in beer consumption.

THE BEERS

Adlerbräu

The copper-coloured, sweetish, fruity, malty cerveza especial (5.5%) with the German-sounding name is influenced by the style of Munich dunkels. It is brewed by Aguila (the Eagle).

Aguila Pilsner

Aguila's standard golden lager (4.5%) with a full-bodied, corn-sweet taste. It is allowed to mature for three weeks during its production.

Aguila Reserva Extra

At 6.5%, this is a powerful, malty "extra" from Aguila.

Alhambra

The refreshing Alhambra Pilsen (4.6%), which is also sold as "Star", the more malty Especial (5.4%), and dark Alhambra Negra (5.4%) all come from the brewery of the same name based in Granada.

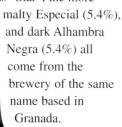

Ambar

A refreshing, golden lager (4.2%) and stronger deep-amber-coloured especial (5.2%) with a malty flavour, from La Zaragozana.

Bock-Damm

This is a deep, black-brown, malty, German-style bock beer (5.4%) with a thick, pale-cream head, produced by Damm. It is a specialist beer in Spanish terms, as well as a reminder of the Damm brewery's Germanic origins.

Cinco Estrellas

The name means "five stars" and this is the strong, darker, malty especial (5.5%) produced by the Mahou brewery of Madrid.

Cruzcampo

The Cruzcampo brewery is breaking out of its traditional market in Andalucía in the south of Spain, to launch national brands, including this pale-gold lager (4.7%) with a dry, sourish, citrus flavour.

Edel

This light-golden, all-malt, refreshing Pilsner (4.8%) is produced by Spain's pioneering lager producer, Damm. It is a premium product and is aimed at the quality end of the beer market.

Estrella Damm

This bright-gold, honeyish, premium-quality Pilsner (5.4%) is one of Damm's best-known beers. This "star" lager is a thirst-quencher, intended to be served cold on a hot day. A "light", low-calorie version is also available (3.2%).

Mahou Classic

This sweet, malty beer with a hoppy finish is the standard lager (4.8%) produced by Madrid's main brewery of the same name.

Marlen

A malty, Dortmunder-style lager (5.8%), Marlen is brewed by Zaragoza's La Zaragozana brewery.

Nostrum de San Miguel

This lager is smoother and richer than its stablemate San Miguel. It is an amber-gold-coloured, full-bodied, strong especial lager (6.2%).

San Miguel Premium

The malty, hoppy flagship lager of the San Miguel company is a relatively strong lager (5.4%) with light, citrus notes and good body. Like much of the company's output, it is aimed at the quality end of the market.

Estrella

Estrella, meaning "star", is a popular name for lagers, including Estrella del Sur from Cruzcampo, especials from Damm and Mahou (Cinco Estrellas) and an extra-powerful Estrella Extra from Coruna.

Voll-Damm

This tawny golden, full-bodied, robust, strong lager (7.2%) with a creamy, hop flavour is produced by Damm. It is much more similar to a Dortmunder Export lager than to the dark, Franconian Vollbier it is named after.

Xibeca

This popular, refreshing light-golden Pilsner (4.6%) is brewed by Damm of Barcelona. It is mainly produced and sold for home consumption in large 1-litre bottles as well as cans.

Zaragozana Export

This rich, reddish, extra-strong export lager (7%) is brewed by La Zaragozana brewery in the town of Zaragoza.

THE BREWERS

Aguila

A famous Spanish brewery dating back to 1900, Aguila (the Eagle) for many years flew high above the rest of the industry. Aguila had its roots in Madrid, but by 1980 the company was running eight breweries across the country and was half as big again as any of its rivals. By 1987, however, the rival Cruzcampo group was threatening to ease the eagle off the top perch, and Aguila came under the control of international giant Heineken. The number of plants was reduced from seven to four – in Madrid, Valencia, Córdoba and Zaragoza. Aguila, always well-known for its draught beer, brews a light Pilsner, a sweeter especial called Adlerbräu and more full-bodied Reserva Extra. Like many Spanish lagers, the beers are brewed with corn grits as well as barley malt and lagered for three weeks. Production is now concentrated in two large, modern breweries in Madrid and Valencia.

Alhambra

This is one of Spain's smaller breweries. It was founded in 1925 in the far south of the country in Granada. It has links with Damm in Barcelona.

Cruzcampo

Spain's largest brewing group was formed through the merger of a number of regional breweries in 1987. Since 1990, it has been owned by Irish stout brewers Guinness, who added Union Cervecera in 1991. The combine now controls about

Above: Cruzcampo is now owned by Guinness of Ireland.

a quarter of the market, with its traditional heartland in Andalucía in the south. It has five breweries in Seville, Jaen, Madrid, Valencia and Navarra. The group is building national brands, notably its main beer Cruzcampo. More local lagers include Keler, Alcázar, Victoria, Calatrava and Estrella del Sur.

Damm

The firm that pioneered lager-brewing in Spain was introduced by an Alsatian brewer Auguste Damm in 1876. The company later absorbed other breweries such as La Bohemia. Damm dominates Catalonia in north-eastern Spain and has breweries in Barcelona and nearby Llobregat, besides

plants in Murcia and at Palma on the island of Majorca. As well as a popular Pilsner Xibeca and especial Estrella, it brews a number of speciality beers, which reflect its Germanic roots, including an all-malt Edel, a dark Bock-Damm and a robust Voll-Damm. There is also a golden Estrella Light (3.2%) and a non-alcoholic Damm-Bier.

Mahou

The dominant brewer in the Spanish capital Madrid dates back to 1890. It has two breweries, one in Madrid and the other in Abrera.

San Miguel

The Asian brewing giant of the Philippines entered the Spanish market in 1956, building a plant in Lerida in Catalonia. From the start it concentrated on the premium end of the market and led the move to stronger especial beers. The company

also developed barley growing in Spain and the brewing of near all-malt beers. Its two main brews are the malty San Miguel and smoother, richer Nostrum de San Miguel. The Spanish San Miguel, with additional breweries in Burgos and Málaga, is now linked to Kronenbourg of France.

La Zaragozana

This small brewery has been operating in Zaragoza since 1900. Besides an Ambar lager (4.2%) and especial (5.2%), it also brews a German-style Dortmunder called Marlen (5.8%) and an extra-strong Export (7%).

Above: La Zaragozana uses horse-drawn drays to promote its beers.

PORTUGAL

Beer drinking has only become popular in Portugal in recent years, though breweries were founded on the Iberian peninsula in the 19th century. Golden lagers predominate, but there is an occasional native dark beer to be found.

Above: Portuguese brewers concentrate on stronger lagers, such as Sagres.

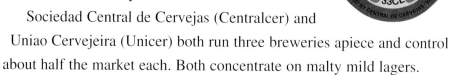

THE PORTUGUESE DICTATOR Salazar kept the country in isolation for many years, shutting the local brewing industry off from foreign influence and investment. In 1889, seven small companies in Oporto combined, followed by another merger in 1934 based in Lisbon. These two groups dominated the country and survived nationalization (1977–1990) to form the basis of the modern industry.

Sociedad Central de Cervejas (Centralcer) and Uniao Cervejeira (Unicer) both run three breweries apiece and control about half the market each. Both concentrate on malty mild lagers.

Portugal's beers tend to be good-quality interpretations of German styles and there are also a few dark lagers. Most beer is bottled. There are separate breweries on the islands of Madeira (Empresa) and the Azores (Melo Abreu).

THE BEERS

Cergal
A mildly bitter, Pilsner-style lager (4.6%) with a light dry taste from Centralcer.

Coral
The main brand from Madeira's Empresa brewery is a light, golden lager with a light malt and hops flavour and a dry aftertaste.

Cristal
Unicer's deep-yellow-coloured, hoppy, sweetish lager (5.2%) also comes in a dark version, Cristal Brown.

Melo Abreu Especial
This orangey-coloured lager (5%) has a sweet, malt flavour. It is the main brand from the small Melo Abreu brewery in the Azores.

Sagres

The Sagres brew from Central de Cervejas is named after the old, beautiful cape on the south-western tip of Portugal, where Prince Henry, the Navigator started his naval school in the 15th century.

Onix
A mild, dark, Vienna-style lager (4.3%) with a medium body and pleasant caramel and hoppy flavour which comes from Centralcer.

Sagres
Central's best-selling fruity lager (5.1%) is sold in both popular, pale-yellow blonde (Sagres Pale) and rarer brown versions. The smoother, dark-brown-coloured, chocolatey, molasses-flavoured, dark beer is in the style of a Munich Dunkel. There is also a premium Sagres Golden.

Super Bock
Unicer's pale, robust, malty, fruity lager (5.8%) is one of the most popular brands drunk in Portugal.

Topazio
A deep-gold, malty lager with a sweet aftertaste. It is a regional brand from Sociedad Central de Cervejas.

AFRICA

The Egyptians were the earliest recorded beer makers, and the tradition of brewing is widespread across the African continent. Local beers, made from fermented maize or millet, are still commonly brewed and enjoyed.

Above: Tusker is a well-known, malty lager beer from Kenya, one of the few African countries where barley and hops are grown.

DRINKING POTENT, cloudy home-brew has been a communal occasion for centuries across Africa. Thanksgivings, initiations, marriages and births have all long been celebrated around a pot or two of home-brewed beer. The enduring popularity of these native, top-fermented brews has meant that Africa is one of the areas of the world where the increasing dominance of bottom-fermented lagers has been kept partially at bay.

European settlers in Africa brought their own beer and brewing tradition to the continent. Africa's first commercial brewery was set up by a sailor from Antwerp, Pieter Visagie, in Rondebosch in the Cape of Good Hope as early as 1655. It took more than a century after that before local commercial production in southern Africa posed a challenge to imported beer but leading breweries, such as the Cape brewery and the Mariedahl brewery in Newlands, South Africa, were established in the early 1820s. European brews made their mark across the continent, and stouts from England remain an enduring favourite. However, once lager brewing arrived in the 1890s, pioneered by Castle Lager from South African Breweries, it rapidly replaced the earlier top-fermenting ales in the commercial market.

In the north of the continent, breweries tended to arrive later. More recent ventures have been set up by international groups such as Heineken and Interbrew, often as joint ventures with local companies. Carlsberg, for example, established Carlsberg Malawi Ltd in partnership with the Malawi Government in 1968. Virtually all these breweries produce local versions of international Pilsners, often made by mixing in local cereals such as maize, since little barley is grown in Africa.

THE BEERS

Allsopp's White Cap

A sweetish, fruity, aromatic lager (4%) from Kenya Breweries. White Cap is named after the snowy peak of Mount Kenya. This lager was originally brewed by Allsopp, East Africa, but the company merged with Kenya Breweries in 1962.

Asmara Lager

The golden Asmara Lager, which is matured for more than four weeks, has a firm, malty flavour and excellent body. It is the only beer produced by the Asmara brewery in Eritrea.

Bière Bénin

This light, French-style lager comes from the Bénin brewery in Togo.

Bohlinger's

Bohlinger's is a dry, golden lager brewed by National Breweries of Zimbabwe, which was founded in 1911, and for many years was known as Rhodesian Breweries.

Bosun's

This light, fruity, golden bitter (4.5%) is brewed by the first European-style micro-brewery to be established in Africa – Mitchell's of Knysna in South Africa.

Camel Beer

This is the Blue Nile brewery's famous Sudanese lager brand. It was first launched in 1955. The recipe was originally based on an early English lager, brewed by the Barclay Perkins company, and was widely exported to Africa from London at the time.

Castle Golden Pilsner

This light lager from South African Breweries is brewed using barley malt and maize.

Castle Lager

This pale, lemony-tasting lager (5%) with a dry, hoppy finish is the leading beer brand from South African Breweries. It is brewed using barley malt, maize and sucrose. The name comes from the Castle brewery founded by Charles Glass in Johannesburg in 1884.

Castle Lager was the first bottom-fermenting beer produced in Africa, using plant bought by the South African Breweries pioneer, Frederick Mead, from the

Pfaudler Vacuum Company of the US. Once introduced in 1898, the lager proved to be such a popular refreshing drink in the hot African climate that South African Breweries decided to adopt the Castle name for all of its beers and breweries. Rival breweries, impressed by the success of the golden brew, rushed to imitate the trend and brew lager as well.

Castle Milk Stout

South African Breweries' full-bodied, dark, smooth milk stout (8%) is brewed using milk sugar (lactose), The range of Castle beers are also produced by National Breweries of Zimbabwe in which SAB has a stake.

Chibuku

A fast-fermenting, cloudy, traditional beer (3.5%) from Zimbabwe, with a chewy, cereal consistency. Chibuku has a refreshing, sour taste and a shelf-life of 3–4 days. It is sold as a value-for-money, low-cost product, particularly on draught in large, communal beer halls. In 1991 a premium version was introduced in a plastic bottle and because of its shape it was nicknamed "the Scud" after the missiles used in the Gulf War.

Club Pilsner

This light, refreshing Pilsner (4.5%) is lagered for an average of three weeks and uses cane sugar in the mash. It comes from Nile Breweries of Uganda.

ESB

One of the strongest beers in the whole of Africa. This smooth, golden, chill-filtered lager (7%) is produced by Nile Breweries of Uganda. It is made using cane sugar as well as barley malt in the mash. The beer's full name is Chairman's Extra Strong Brew.

Flag

This range of popular local light lagers is produced by Brasseries du Maroc (of Morocco). It includes Flag Pilsner, Flag Spéciale and a golden, hoppy, malty Flag Export.

Forester's

Following the world trend for real beers, this unfiltered and unpasteurized, full-bodied lager (5%) is brewed by the Mitchell's micro-brewery in Knysna, South Africa.

Gulder

A refreshing, slightly hoppy, dry lager (5%) that is the flagship brand of Nigerian Breweries. Gulder is also brewed in the company's plant in Ghana.

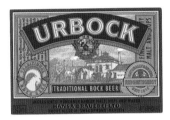

Hansa Urbock

The rich, reddish Urbock (6%) is brewed by the German-founded Hansa brewery in Swakopmund. Like all Namibian beers, it is brewed according to the German beer purity law. The warming winter brew provides Africa with a rare, German-style, dark lager.

Hunter's

A pale-gold, refreshing lager that is nevertheless full of flavour. Hunter's is brewed by a Czech brewmaster in accordance with the German beer purity law, using only malt, hops, barley and yeast. It is produced by the private Nesbitt brewery of Zimbabwe.

Legend Stout

A strong, rich stout (7%), with a roasted-chocolate flavour, produced by Nigerian Breweries. It is a rival to Guinness in the country that is the third largest market for stout in the world.

Lion Lager

Another leading lager (5%) from South African Breweries. It is slightly sweeter than SAB's other major brand, Castle. The Lion brand has been roaring since a Norwegian merchant Anders Ohlsson, who had been involved in beer brewing in Africa since 1862, established the Annaberg brewery in Cape Town in 1883.

Mamba Lager

This bright-gold, malty lager is probably the best-known beer from French West Africa. It has been brewed by Solibra in Abidjan in the Ivory Coast since 1960. The Solibra brewery also produces a Mamba Bock and a rich, tawny Mamba Brune.

Ngoma

A range of beers from Brasseries du Bénin of Lome, Togo. It includes a light, hazy-gold Pilsner with a well-balanced, hoppy flavour, and a darker, more malty, amber-coloured Special with a sourish malt flavour. The brand name Ngoma means "a drum".

Nile Special

This full-bodied lager (5.6%) is brewed by Nile Breweries, using cane sugar as well as barley malt. It is lagered for an average of three weeks.

Ohlsson's Lager

A golden lager (5%) named after the Ohlsson's brewery that is now owned by SAB.

Above: The Nile snakes through the African continent for over 4,000 miles (6,500 km). At its source in Uganda, Nile Breweries is now flourishing thanks to help from overseas. The great river slows as it nears the end of its course in Egypt, the country where the world's earliest brewers once produced their beer.

Raven Stout

This dark, rich, heavy stout (6%) is brewed by the Mitchell's micro-brewery of Knysna in South Africa.

Rex

A dry, golden lager produced by Nigerian Breweries.

Simba Lager

A popular golden lager in Zaire (formerly the Belgian Congo) Simba has been produced by the Brasimba brewery (in which the Belgian giant Interbrew has a stake) since 1923.

Tafel Lager

A refreshing, standard lager (4%) with a slightly bitter flavour, brewed according to the German beer purity law. Tafel is produced by the Hansa brewery in Swakopmund on the Namibian coast.

Windhoek

The Windhoek beers include a low-alcohol light (1.9%), a refreshing Windhoek lager (4%), a more hoppy export (4.5%) and a fuller-bodied, malty special (5.3%). The range of lagers, all brewed according to the German beer purity law, comes from Namibia Breweries' modern plant in Windhoek. The brewery opened in the outskirts of the town in 1986 when the old Garten Street premises were closed.

Zambezi

A pale-gold, light, refreshing lager (4.5%) with a sweet-sour flavour, from National Breweries, Zimbabwe.

Star

A sweetish, hazy, golden, hoppy lager (5%). Star lager beer was first produced in 1949 in a Lagos brewery that is now owned by Nigerian Breweries. This most popular lager brand is now brewed and sold all the way across West Africa – from Sierra Leone to Ghana.

Tusker

Kenya Breweries' creamy, dry, golden lager appears in a variety of strengths. Tusker Premium, a strong, all-malt beer (5%), is brewed for international export. According to legend, it was named after the angry elephant which trampled to death one of the two brothers who founded the brewery.

DARKEST AFRICA

Some areas of Africa have a strong stout-drinking tradition. Nowhere is this more true than in Nigeria, the third-largest stout market in the world. Guinness Nigeria alone boasts four breweries in this heavily populated country. Local rivals to Guinness in Nigeria include Legend Stout by Nigerian Breweries, Power Stout by North brewery of Kano, Eagle Stout by Golden Guinea brewery of Umuahia, and Lion Stout by the Mopa brewery. The stouts produced by these breweries are much more than faint shadows left over from the British Empire. The Guinness sold here, for instance, is not the standard Guinness brewed in Ireland or even the more substantial Foreign Extra Stout sold elsewhere in Africa, but a stronger version still, weighing in at 8% alcohol by volume. This rich, bitter-sweet brew is a blend of a strong local pale beer and concentrated dark wort supplied from Dublin. It is sold as an energy-giving stimulant, "Guinness for Power", with potent properties. Advertising campaigns, free from the restrictions of Europe or America, once even suggested the possibility of "a baby in every bottle".

THE BREWERS

Asmara

An Italian, Luigi Melotti, originally set up this company in Asmara, Eritrea, in 1939 to produce pure alcohol and spirits. It began to produce lager three years later. In 1984, it changed its name from Melotti to Asmara.

Blue Nile

This was the first brewery in the Sudan. It was built in the early 1950s and was established by the English brewing company Barclay Perkins. It brewed a little stout and brown ale (known as dark) when it opened in 1955. Today, however, production is mainly devoted to its main beer – a bottom-fermenting lager, Camel.

Brasseries du Bénin

Brasseries du Bénin of Togo in the former French West Africa produces a light, French-style, Bière Bénin lager and also markets beers under the Ngoma (Drum) brand name.

Brasseries du Maroc

Breweries of Morocco in north-western Africa is one of the few thriving brewing groups in a Muslim country. It runs three modern breweries in Casablanca, Tangier and Fès, alongside an extensive soft drinks operation. Brasseries du Maroc produces its own popular range of light lagers in bottles and cans, mainly under the Flag brand name. These account for four-fifths of production and also include the Bock 49 and Stork brands, besides the non-alcoholic Crown.

Chibuku

Chibuku is the leading commercial producer of traditional native beer in Zimbabwe. It has 16 breweries scattered around the country in order to ensure fresh, live beer in each local market. It is sold mainly on draught in large, communal beer halls.

By 1995, a newly introduced take-home bottle accounted for 40% of the brewery's production.

East African Breweries

See Kenya Breweries.

Hansa

The Hansa brewery was founded in 1929 in the picturesque Namibian coastal town of Swakopmund. In 1968, it was taken over by South West (later Namibian) Breweries. As well as a refreshing Tafel Lager, it also produces a rich, reddish urbock and a refreshing golden Pilsner. Like all Namibian beers, these beers are brewed according to the German beer purity law Rheinheitsgetbot.

Kenya Breweries

Kenya Breweries was founded by two brothers in Nairobi in the early 1920s, using equipment from England. It was for many years known as East African Breweries. Some English-style ales and stouts were produced initially, using locally grown barley, but the company soon concentrated on a golden lager called Tusker. In 1952, the company opened a second brewery on the coast at Mombasa. It was bad timing, though, as the country exploded in the Mau Mau rebellion against British rule, and the African population boycotted European beers. As independence approached, the company merged in 1962 with its local rival, Allsopp, East Africa. Seven years later, the combine added another Nairobi brewery, City. In 1982, the group opened a new brewery in Kisumu near Lake Victoria. Today, the main lagers are Tusker and the more fruity White Cap (both around 4.2%), and a slightly more hoppy Pilsner. Unmalted barley is added as an adjunct to all three. Less full-bodied "export" versions are also produced using cane sugar, and a stronger, nearly all-malt, Tusker Premium (5%) for international sales.

Mitchell's

Africa's first micro-brewery was set up in 1984 by a former SAB brewer Lex Mitchell in Knysna on the southern coast of Cape Province, South Africa. His unfiltered and unpasteurized malty beers include a lightly fruity Bosun's Bitter (4.5%) and fuller-bodied Forester's.

Namibia

The Namibia Company was founded in 1920 as South West Breweries, when four German colonial breweries in the area amalgamated. In 1968, the Windhoek-based group absorbed its rival, Hansa of Swakopmund. When Namibia gained independence in 1990, the group was renamed Namibia Breweries. The company brews quality lagers such as Windhoek Export Lager following the beer purity law.

National

Founded in 1911 and known for many years as Rhodesian Breweries, National Breweries of Zimbabwe has two plants in Harare and Bulawayo.

Nesbitt

Zimbabwe's first independent brewery was founded at Chiredzi in 1990 and employs a Czech brewmaster, F. Mrazek, to brew its all-malt beers. Its main beer is the crisp Hunter's Lager.

Nigerian Breweries

The largest brewing company in Africa's leading brewing nation is Nigerian Breweries, with plants in Iganmu, Ibadan, Aba and Kaduna. Nigerian opened its first brewery in 1949 with the support of Heineken. It began by brewing a sweetish Star lager. Other lager brands have now been developed, notably the drier Gulder and Rex beers. The Nigerian Breweries group also produces a rich rival to Guinness – Legend Stout.

Nile Breweries

This Ugandan brewery was built with German investment and assistance in the town of Jinja in 1954, close to the source of the Nile. The brewery flourished until 1972, but it struggled in the years that followed. For 20 years, during and after Idi Amin's regime, the brewery was allowed to disintegrate.

The Nile brewery was revived in 1992 with help from the international giant Carlsberg. Three main lagers are produced: a light Club Pilsner, the fuller-bodied Nile Special and the extra-strong ESB. All of the brews use cane sugar as well as barley malt and are lagered for an average of three weeks. Nile Breweries controls more than 60% of the Ugandan beer market.

Solibra

This brewery was set up in the Ivory Coast in 1960. Its beers include the rich, the golden, malty Mamba, a bock and a brune. Mamba beer is now exported.

South African Breweries

This was the first brewing giant of the African continent. The company's roots lie in the Natal brewery of Pietermaritzburg, which was set up by Frederick Mead in 1891. In 1892 Natal took over Glass's Castle Brewery in Johannesburg to form South African United Breweries, which then became South African Breweries (SAB) in 1895.

SAB was not to dominate the country, however, until 1956 when it merged with its two main rivals, Ohlsson's (Lion), which controlled the Cape, and Union Breweries (Chandler's).

Today the main lagers that it produces – Castle and Lion – reflect this history. SAB also offers a wide range of other lager brands which includes Ohlsson's, Chandler's, Rogue and Old Dutch.

The company now holds substantial share stakes in many other African breweries and and has expanded into breweries in Eastern Europe.

Above: Even in bygone days, the need to supply beer to a thirsty nation meant that Namibia Breweries had to expand its brewery.

SOUTH AFRICAN SORGHUM BEERS

Beer brewing using sorghum and relying on spontaneous fermentation has long been a domestic industry in Africa, and it is not unusual to find women still selling home-brewed beers in the marketplaces. These thick, tawny brews or "porridge beers" are cheap and must be consumed within two or three days. They are generally regarded by African drinkers as more nutritious than pale European lagers.

Commercially brewed sorghum (millet) beers have been produced in South Africa from the early 20th century to meet the demands for beer from the black, urban population. They originated in Natal.

Their popularity, however, is partly due to the fact that until 1962 the majority of the black population was not allowed to buy European-style beers. Sorghum beers, which were called "Kaffir beers" by white South Africans, were sold in special bars reserved only for blacks, in open-air "beer gardens" or at roadside stalls.

Since the collapse of the apartheid regime, although the consumption of golden lagers has certainly soared, there has been no mass switch. In the late 1970s there were 32 commercial sorghum beer breweries in South Africa, and new ones are still being opened.

Above: Enjoying a sorghum beer in an open-air bar.

Above: A Zulu woman in South Africa prepares the mash for a sorghum brew. The thick, porridge-like mixture will be left open to the air and the action of wild yeasts for a few days in order to ferment, and will then be drunk within two or three days.

CHINA

Although the Chinese have been making alcoholic drinks for centuries, they have no real beer-brewing tradition. However, this is not going to stop China becoming the largest beer-brewing nation in the world by the year 2000.

FOREIGN EXPERTISE played a great part in the initial development of the beer-brewing industry in China. The trend started at the beginning of this century – the Russians brewed in Harbin and the Germans in Tsingtao. Today, joint venture partners are bringing in new technology and capital to modernize the creaking Chinese industry. Some sources estimate that by the year 2000 China will be the world's largest beer producer in terms of volume.

Official estimates of the number of breweries in China put it at approximately 850, though there are probably hundreds more "unregistered" breweries. No single brewer has a market share larger than 4%. The breweries fall into three main categories – joint-owned Chinese and foreign ventures, large national breweries and local breweries. They are owned and run in a bewildering diversity of ways – publicly quoted companies (such as Tsingtao), town breweries run by local entrepreneurs and state-owned concerns run by government agencies.

Although the current consumption of beer is relatively low, this seems set to change. Personal disposable income is rising steeply among some of the population, and at least some of this money seems to be being spent on beer.

Most beer is sold in the form of "value for money" brands. Large, returnable bottles of local brews make up the majority of sales. Most consumers are fiercely loyal to their local beer – seemingly no matter what the quality. Regional markets are often protected by official and unofficial restrictions – such as fines levied on "substandard" beers imported from other areas and charges to retailers for each crate of beer brought in from outside the region. In their protected markets, substandard local brewers have little incentive to improve.

Above: Germany leased the port of Tsingtao (now called Quingdao) and built a brewery there which still survives today, though it is now Chinese-owned.

THE BEERS

Baiyun Beer

A hazy-yellow lager beer from the Guangzhou brewery, Guangzhou City.

Canton Lager Beer

A gold-coloured, malty lager, from the Guangzhou brewery, Guangzhou City.

Chinese Ginseng Beer

A thin, pale lager (4.1%) brewed under licence in Britain using only natural ingredients and some Ginseng herbal seasoning.

Chu Sing

A pale-gold, malty lager from the Chu Jiang brewery, Guangzhou City.

Double Happiness Guangzhou Beer

A pale-gold, highly carbonated lager with a light, malt flavour. It is produced by Guangzhou brewery, Guangzhou City.

Emperor's Gold Beer

A gold lager with a slightly molasses aftertaste, produced by the Hangzhou brewery, Hangzhou City, using Zhejiang barley.

Five Star Beer

This golden lager has a mild, malty flavour. It is produced by the Shen Ho Shing brewery, Beijing.

Guangminpai

An unusual dark lager produced by the Shanghai brewery.

Hua Nan Beer

A pleasant, refreshing, yellow-gold lager beer, from the Guangzhou brewery, Guangzhou City.

Mon-Lei Beer

A reddish-coloured lager, brewed by the Beijing Wuxing and Shen Ho Shing breweries.

Nine Star Premium

This gold lager beer has a good malt and hop flavour. It is brewed by the Five Star brewery, Beijing.

Peking Beer

A pale-golden lager from the Feng Shon brewery, Beijing.

Shanghai (Swan) Lager

The popular name for lager which in this case comes from the emblem on the label of this malty, lightly hopped lager. It is brewed by the Shanghai brewery and is said to have once been the official drink served at Communist Party conferences.

Song Hay Double Happiness Beer

Gold, well-flavoured lager beer from the Guangzhou brewery, Guangzhou City.

Sun Lik

A traditional Chinese dragon decorates the label of this golden, malty lager (5%), brewed by the Hong Kong brewery.

Sweet China

A pineapple-flavoured, yellow-gold lager which comes from the Guangzhou brewery, Guangzhou City.

Tientan Beer

A hazy, yellow-gold lager from the Beijing brewery. The name means "Temple of Heaven".

Tsingtao Beer

A pale-gold, Pilsner-style lager (5%), with a malt and hops, vanilla flavour, brewed by the Tsingtao brewery in Quingdao, Shandong province. Tsingtao is widely exported around the world in both bottles and cans, partly to fuel the thirst of Chinese populations in other countries. It is also popular among Westerners as an accompaniment to Chinese food. It is something of a cult beer in the US.

There is also a deep-amber Tsingtao Dark Beer.

West Lake Beer

A dark-gold-coloured, light lager beer (3.8%) which has a sweet, fruity flavour, and claims to contain no artificial ingredients – only hops, malt, rice and spring water from the West Lake region. It is brewed by the Hangzhou Zhongce Beer Co Ltd.

JAPAN

The first commercial brewery in Japan, Spring Valley in Yokohama, was started by an American, William Copeland, in 1869, when Japan opened up to trade with the West. At that time the beer was mainly for foreign traders and seamen.

Above: Japanese brewers have long been in the vanguard of technological innovation, producing high-tech beer styles such as dry beer.

BEER IS A RELATIVELY recent arrival in Japan. Gradually, the Japanese tried out the new drink and then embraced it with a passion, so that today the country is one of the leading beer-drinking nations in the world. As has been their way with many outside inventions they have adopted, the Japanese have refined and developed the product. Most of the lagers are ultra-clean, hi-tech versions of golden international Pilsners, using rice in the mash. The Japanese were pioneers in developing new styles, such as dry beers. There is a constant conveyor-belt of ingenious variations on a light lager, along with novelty presentations such as Sapporo's can that turns into a cup. Some dark beers are produced – a legacy from the early German influence.

Today, the brewing industry is dominated by four main groups: Kirin, Asahi, Sapporo and Suntory (with Orion on the island of Okinawa). A ruling that allowed only breweries producing a minimum of 450,000 gallons (two million litres) a year to operate froze small-scale, independent brewers out of the market. This ruling was repealed in 1994. The result was a flood of new micro-breweries and brewpubs producing fresh ji-biru (local beer). A number of these new ventures have been set up by established saké makers. The major brewers have responded to the rising popularity of more unusual brews by producing regional beers and opening their own brewpubs. At the same time, there has been growing demand for imported beers, which has encouraged the large groups to try out new beer styles, such as an alt-style beer produced by Kirin.

Most beer in Japan is sold in bottles or cans, with only a small amount available on draught. Bottled and canned beers marked "draft" are fine-filtered (in a process known as micro-filtration) but the majority are usually sold unpasteurized for the the home market.

THE BEERS

Asahi Black Beer
Many Japanese like to blend this sweetish, red-brown, beer (5%) with a light lager.

Asahi Stout
This richly roasted, top-fermented stout is a potent brew (8%). It also has a hint of lactic sourness, like early English porters and stouts.

Kirin Beer
Japan's best-selling beer (4.9%) is a crisp, full-bodied, fresh-flavoured Pilsner brewed using Saaz and Hallertau hops. It is matured for up to two months before being sold unpasteurized.

Kirin Black Beer
This smoky, traditional, dark beer (5%) has a hint of roasted coffee and hops.

Kirin Ichiban Shibori
Kirin's second-best-selling beer was introduced in 1990. Brewed using just the first liquid run-off from the mash tun, Ichiban Shibori ("first wort") gives a smoother malt taste. It is sold in distinctive, tall bottles. This soft golden

lager (5.5%) has proved a major marketing success.

Kirin Stout
This marvellously rich, complex, bottom-fermenting stout (8%) has a hint of toffee.

Kuro-nama
This light, golden lager is marketed by Asahi as a late-night drink.

Kyoto Alt
See Kirin.

Malt's
Suntory's appropriately named malty, flagship lager is, unusually for a Japanese beer, brewed with 100% malt.

Sapporo Black Beer
Sapporo was the first Japanese brewery to brew a German-style, dark lager in 1892 and this classic, full-flavoured black beer (5%) is still brewed today, using crystal, chocolate and Munich malts as well as rice.

Sapporo Original Draft Black Label
The fourth-best-selling beer in Japan, this lively, light Pilsner (4.7%) was the first to use the micro-filtration technique instead of pasteurization to produce what is called a "draft" beer. It is sold abroad in stylish silver cans as Sapporo Draft.

Shirayuki
Two Belgian-style ales, a soft Shirayuki Blonde and a creamy Shirayuki Dark, are produced in the saké town of Itami, near Osaka, in a brewery restaurant run by the Shirayuki (White Snow) saké firm.

Shokusai Bakushu
Asahi launched this lager in 1996. It was designed to accompany meals and is sold under two different labels, pink and green. The pink version has a milder flavour.

Spring Valley
This hoppy, golden lager takes its name from Japan's first brewery, which was founded in Yokohama in 1869. It is brewed at a pub brewery in a tourist beer village close to Kirin's modern brewery in the port of Yokohama, near Tokyo.

Below: An old beer poster advertising Yebisu and Sapporo beer in the museum at the Sapporo brewery, Hokkaido.

Suntory Daichi

A smooth golden lager (4.8%) from Suntory which emphasizes its natural ingredients. It is brewed with 100% barley malts.

Super Dry

The original pioneer of the dry beer style, Super Dry became fashionable around the world for a brief time in the late 1980s and early 1990s. In the mid-1980s the Asahi brewery was in trouble, with falling sales and a reduced market share. A taste test on 5,000 consumers in 1985 found that people wanted a smooth, light-tasting beer. The resulting Asahi Super Dry was launched in 1987. This is a pale Pilsner, fermented for longer than normal. This reduces the body of the beer while increasing the alcohol content (to 5% from the then more usual 4.5%). The beer is less bitter than usual Pilsners, with virtually no aftertaste and a characteristic, dry, parching effect in the mouth. The intention was to create a thin, clean beer with little flavour, which would leave consumers in need of another drink. In both aims it succeeded beyond Asahi's most extravagant dreams. Since the early 1990s, while dry beers have fallen out of favour elsewhere, Super Dry has remained popular in Japan. In 1995, it was the country's second-best-selling beer after Kirin Lager, selling more than 121 million cases.

Right: The Asahi brewery in Tokyo, designed by Philippe Stark.

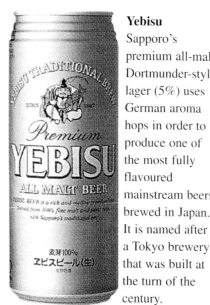

Yebisu

Sapporo's premium all-malt Dortmunder-style lager (5%) uses German aroma hops in order to produce one of the most fully flavoured mainstream beers brewed in Japan. It is named after a Tokyo brewery that was built at the turn of the century.

Z

Asahi brews this faintly fruity, top-fermenting light ale. The company claims that this unpasteurized brew is one of the "most technologically advanced beers" in Japan. In keeping with the Asahi company's policy of linking beers to different occasions, Z beer is marketed specifically as a holiday drink.

THE BREWERS

Asahi

Founded as the Osaka brewery in 1889, Asahi became part of the Dai Nippon brewing company in 1906. This was Japan's first beer giant. After the Second World War, Dai Nippon was split up into Nippon (later renamed Sapporo) and Asahi. The latter was the smaller of the two parts, but this changed dramatically in 1987 when Asahi launched Super Dry. The huge success of this brand rocketed Asahi's share of the market from 10% to 28% in 1995, making it Japan's second-largest brewing group. Other Asahi beers include Z, Double Yeasts and two more traditional brews, a sweetish red-brown, Asahi, Black Beer (5%), and a richly roasted, top-fermented Asahi Stout (8%). In 1996, Asahi launched a new marketing strategy linking such beers as Shokusai Bakushu and Kuro-nama to different occasions.

Kirin

Japan's largest brewer accounts for about half of the country's production, with 14 breweries. The company can trace its history back to Japan's first brewery, Spring Valley of Yokohama of 1869, and was foreign-owned until it was bought by Japanese interests, led by Mitsubishi, in 1970. It brews Japan's best-selling beer, Kirin Lager. Its other main beer is the more malty Ichiban. In 1995, Kirin Lager sold more than 151 million cases; Ichiban 76 million. In the search for a new sales success to equal Ichiban, the company has launched a wide range of local and speciality beers including a copper-coloured alt brewed from crystal malt in a micro-brewery in Kyoto. It also brews a slightly smoky Kirin Black Beer and a richer, more chewy bottom-fermenting Kirin Stout.

Sapporo

The oldest continuously operating brewery in Japan was founded in the town of Sapporo in 1876. It became part of Dai Nippon in 1906, before being split up again in 1949 and regaining its original name in 1964. This leading exporter of Japanese beer, has pioneered a number of beer styles and brewing techniques. It was the first Japanese brewery to brew a German-style dark lager in 1892. In 1971, it launched Japan's original all-malt premium beer, Yebisu, and was the first to introduce seasonal and regional beers.

It also pioneered the use of micro-filtration to produce unpasteurized "draft" beers. Today its best-selling beer is its Original Draft Black

Label, a lively dryish Pilsner, which is sold abroad as Sapporo Draft. There is also a low-priced, low-malt lager called Drafty.

The company runs a brewpub in Kawaguchi and popular German-style beer gardens alongside its breweries in Sapporo, Nagoya, Sendai and Shizuoka.

Suntory

The smallest of Japan's four main breweries, Suntory is primarily a wine-maker and distiller dating from 1899. It began brewing in 1963. Its flagship beer, the softly sweetish all-malt Malt's. A lighter brew named Super Hop's is also available. In addition there is a North American-style lager, Dynamic (brewed with Canadian yeast).

MICRO-BREWERIES AND BREWPUBS

Since 1994, Japan has seen a boom in micro-breweries and brewpubs. The result is more variety of beer styles.

Akasaka

A soft-drinks company set up this micro-brewery in a suburb of Tokyo. It brews a Pilsner and a dark Kuro Half.

Doppo

This micro was set up by the Miyashita saké company in Okayama. It brews German-style beers – Doppo Pilsner and a reddish Doppo Dunkel.

Gotenba Kohgen

The hot springs tourist town of Gotenba is home to a beer hall and brewery. It offers a light Pilsner, a malty Gotenba Dunkel and a fruity Weizen.

KIRIN

The Kirin is a legendary animal of ancient China – half dragon, half horse – which appeared to the mother of Confucius just before his birth 2,500 years ago. The sight of this benevolent creature was supposed to herald the arrival of great men, and it is regarded as a symbol of good luck, a harbinger of happy events to come. The name was first adopted by the Spring Valley Brewery for its beer in 1888, and the fabled animal still appears on Kirin's main brands today.

Kizakura Kappa

The Kappa saké company set up this brewpub in Kyoto. Its German-style ales include a Kappa Alt, a fruity kölsch and a sweeter Kölsch Mild, all brewed using saké yeast.

Kyoto

See Kirin.

Moku Moku

This rural micro-brewery in Nishiyubune, near Ueno, was set up by a farming co-operative. It brews a variety of country beers, including a Pilsner, a fruity amber ale, a peaty smoked ale and a tart Biscuit Weizen.

Okhotsk

This brewpub in Kitami on the island of Hokkaido is named after the nearby Sea of Okhotsk. Its wide range of beers includes a finely balanced Okhotsk Bitter.

Otaru

This brewpub in the port of Otaru, near Sapporo, produces German-style lagers, including a hoppy Otaru Helles and a malty, dark dunkel.

Sandaya

This brewpub near Osaka is run by a smoked meat company. The unfiltered beers include a yeasty Pilsner, a malty Festbier, a black beer and a well-roasted Sandaya Smoked Beer, which is served to accompany the smoked meat produced by the parent company.

Sankt Gallen

This small Tokyo brewpub was one of the first to open. It brews a range of seasonal, spiced ales including a hoppy Sankt Gallen Spring Ale and the sweeter St Valentine's.

Sumida River

Asahi's brewpub in its Tokyo office complex makes three German-style draught beers: a mild Altbier, a Kölsch called River Beer and a full-bodied, unfiltered Zwickelbier.

Uehara

One of Japan's first micro-breweries was set up in the Echigo pub in Makimachi. Its wide range of beers includes a fruity Uehara Pale Ale, a cloudy Uehara Weizen and a very powerful Old Ale.

Above: The beautiful stained-glass window in the Sapporo brewery.

THE REST OF ASIA

In the booming economies of the Far East, the beer market is expanding. There is a strong European influence on the industry in the shape of machinery and investment, and in the predominance of lagers.

ASIA'S BREWERIES are spread far and wide – from the far north of India, through Sri Lanka, Thailand, Malaysia and Vietnam, to Singapore and Indonesia. As a result, the influences are wide-ranging, and the brewers have to contend with a diversity of laws, even within some country boundaries. Some states of India, for example, are strictly prohibitionist, while others are very relaxed in their attitude to alcohol.

The colonial heritage has had a profound influence on beer drinking and brewing. Adventurers from Europe brought their technical brewing knowledge and their own particular tastes with them, and these in turn were adopted by the local drinkers. British ales have made their mark on the Indian subcontinent, particularly in the form of India Pale Ale and rich, dark stouts. Despite its distance, the Pilsner revolution in Europe, which has transformed the beer-drinking landscape into one of pale lagers, has taken a grip on Asia too.

Beer consumption per head is relatively low in the region. Singaporeans for example, who are believed to be among the highest consumers of beer in Asia, drink a meagre 25 litres (5½ gallons) per head per annum, compared to 130 litres (28½ gallons) in England. Nevertheless, the large population of the region means that there is still scope for the marketing muscle of international companies such as Heineken to be flexed, and for the development of large "local" brewers. San Miguel of the Philippines has been brewing for over 100 years and is one of the major players in the Asian market, with joint ventures throughout the region. Asian Pacific Breweries from Singapore is also a large-scale producer, with hundreds of breweries throughout Asia. The strong, golden lagers that the region's brewers tend to produce are now bouncing back across the globe on the coat-tails of Asian cuisine to become household names in the West.

Above: Indonesia's most famous brew is the award-winning Bintang. The Dutch influence is apparent both in its taste and in the squat bottle design.

THE BEERS

ABC Stout
This powerful, creamy bottom-fermenting stout (8.1%) is produced by Asia Pacific Breweries.

Amarit
A malty, sweet, pale-gold lager from Thailand, brewed by Thai Amarit Bangkok.

Anchor Beer
This dry, hoppy Pilsner was introduced by Asia Pacific Breweries in 1941.

BGI
A golden lager brewed in My Tho, Vietnam, by a joint venture between the French BGI group and the Vietnamese Government.

Bintang
A light, malty lager (5%) from Bintang in Indonesia.

Cerveza Negra
A black beer (5.2%) with a roasted malty taste, from San Miguel in the Philippines.

Cobra
One of the best-known lagers from India and a successful export to the West.

Flying Horse
A premium, golden lager beer (5%) from the Vinedale Breweries, Hyderabad, India.

Hite
A pale-gold, dry, hoppy Korean lager (4.5%).

Jubilee
A premium, amber-gold lager (5%) from the Vinedale Breweries, Hyderabad, India.

Kingfisher
This sweetish, malty draught lager (5%) from the Vinedale Breweries, Hyderabad, India, is brewed under licence in England. There is also a pleasant Kingfisher stout.

Lion Stout
A top-fermenting stout (7.5%) produced using Czech, British and Danish malt, Styrian hops and an English yeast strain. The ingredients are transported to the Ceylon brewery in Nuwara Eliya high in the tea-planting area of Sri Lanka. It is served by handpump in the Beer Shop in the town, and in UKD Silva in the holy city of Kandy.

Red Horse
A bock-style, pale-gold lager (6.8%) with a full-bodied flavour, from San Miguel in the Philippines.

Sando Stout
A rich, fruity, bottom-fermented stout (6%) from the Three Coins Brewery in Colombo, Sri Lanka. It is named after a Hungarian circus strongman.

San Miguel
This golden, Pilsner-style beer, made with 80% malt, is lagered for a month by the Filipino giant San Miguel.

Singha
A bright-gold lager (6%) with a hoppy flavour, brewed by the Boon Rawd Brewery in Thailand. It is named after the mythical half-lion creature shown on the label.

Tiger
This refreshing, gold-coloured lager (5.1%) is one of the best-known Asian beers. It is brewed in Singapore and Kuala Lumpur by Asia Pacific Breweries. Its marketing slogan, "Time for a Tiger", was even the title of a novel by the British writer Anthony Burgess.

Tiger Classic
A mellow, golden, seasonal beer, brewed by APB using crystal malt, in time for each New Year's festivities.

THE BREWERS

Asia Pacific Breweries
APB is a regional giant based in Singapore. It was formed in 1931 as a joint venture between Fraser & Neame and Heineken, and was originally called Malayan Breweries. It is involved in many joint ventures in the region.

Boon Rawd Brewery
This Thai brewery was set up in Bangkok in the 19th century using German technology.

Mohan Meakin
Edward Dyer established a brewery at Kasauli in 1855. In 1935 this company merged with the Meakin brewery, set up by Mr H.G. Meakin, to become Dyer Meakin Breweries Limited. The Mohan Meakin company's main brewery is the Solan Brewery in the Simla Hills.

San Miguel
This Filipino giant producer was the first brewery in South-east Asia. It was established as La Fabrica de Cerveza de San Miguel in a small brewery next to the colonial mansion of the Spanish governor-general in the heart of Manila in 1890. It is now responsible for 85% of the Filipino beer market and has many breweries in other countries in the region, including ventures in Guangzhou and Guangdong, China, and a brewery in Hong Kong. It has also set up joint ventures in Vietnam, Indonesia, Nepal and Cambodia. In total, San Miguel has over 250,000 retail outlets in Asia.

AUSTRALIA

The image of beer drinking in Australia has often been ice-cold lager firmly clenched in the fists of macho men. But, like the legendary six o'clock swill that forced drinkers to knock back their beers in double-quick time, this hard-drinking reputation is now gradually draining away.

SINCE 1975, BEER DRINKING in Australia has remorselessly declined from almost 140 litres (30¾ gallons) per head in 1975 to less than 100 litres (22 gallons) 20 years later. Sharp rises in excise duty, together with the spectacular growth of an enterprising Australian wine industry and increased consumption of wine, have hastened this dramatic drop. The fall has had far-reaching effects. Australia is a huge country with a relatively small population of about 18 million. Once domestic consumption started to slide, the large, well-developed brewing industry had to look elsewhere for markets.

Two major Australian brewing groups led by Elders IXL (Foster's) and the Bond Corporation (Castlemaine and Swan) began to scour the globe. Elders bought up breweries such as Courage of England and Carling of Canada, making Foster's an international brand. Bond moved into the United States when it snapped up Heileman and eventually claimed to be the fourth-largest brewing company in the world. The two groups had overreached themselves, however, and struggled under heavy debt burdens. Elders was eventually reconstructed as Foster's Brewing and sold off some of its earlier acquisitions. Bond collapsed in a spectacular fashion, and New Zealand's leading brewer, Lion Nathan, then picked up the pieces of the brewing business in Australia.

These two combines still completely dominate the country. Foster's, which trades in Australia through its subsidiary, Carlton and United Breweries (CUB), controls 54% of the beer market, while Lion Nathan now controls almost 44%. This leaves little more than 2% for the two remaining independent breweries, Boag of Tasmania and Coopers of Adelaide, plus a handful of new micro-breweries and brewpubs.

Above: Most people equate Australian beer with Foster's or Castlemaine mass-market lagers, but there are a number of independent breweries, notably Coopers of Adelaide.

THE BEERS

Abbots Invalid Stout

CUB's strong stout (5.6%) is a rare reminder of Australia's early brewing links with England. Although now bottom-fermented, it still has a creamy, coffee character. Only found in Victoria, it is named after the co-operative Abbotsford brewery of Melbourne, which was taken over by CUB in 1925. The site now houses one of CUB's largest and most modern plants.

Black Crow

A fruity, all-malt dark ale (3.6%) from Coopers of Adelaide. Unlike the company's more celebrated brews, it is filtered before being bottled.

Blue Label

See Tooheys.

Broken Hill Draught

A dry, malty lager (4.9%) from the South Australian brewery of Adelaide, this beer is named after the famous mining town. It is one of Australia's truly regional brews and has been produced for the "Silver City" and surrounding areas for nearly 80 years. It is only available in kegs in the Broken Hill area.

Carbine Stout

Castlemaine's full-bodied dark beer (5.1%) from Brisbane was introduced in 1925. Despite the name, it is a bottom-fermented lager with a roasted-malt flavour.

Cascade

The Cascade range of bottom-fermented beers, produced at the Cascade brewery, includes a full-bodied Cascade Pale Ale (5.2%), a lighter Cascade Bitter (4.8%) and a pleasantly roasted Cascade Stout (5.8%). They also produce a crisp Cascade Lager (4.8%), a darker, Cascade Draught (4.7%) and the fuller-flavoured Cascade Premium (5.2%).

Castlemaine XXXX

Still described in Australia as a bitter ale, Castlemaine XXXX is a malty golden lager (4.8%), which uses whole hops rather than pellets or hop extracts. The brewery also brews an all-malt Castlemaine Malt 75 (4.8%), a Castlemaine Special Dry (5%), a low-carbohydrate Castlemaine DL (4.1%), XXXX Gold (3.5%), a low-alcohol Light (2.7%) and XL (2.3%).

Coopers Sparkling Ale

Coopers' best-known, yeasty, cloudy brew (5.8%) is a full-flavoured, bottle-conditioned strong pale ale. Coopers also brews two other bottle-conditioned beers – a richly roasted, robust Coopers Best Extra Stout (6.8%) and a fruity middle-strength Coopers Original Pale Ale (4.5%). The company also produces the filtered ale, Coopers Premium Clear (4.9%). All the beers are free of additives and preservatives.

Crown

This sweetish brew (4.9%) comes from Carlton.

D-Ale

See Diamond Draught.

Diamond Draught

A more fully fermented, low-carbohydrate beer (4.6%) than others from Carlton, this is also known as D-Ale.

Dogbolter

A powerful ale (7%), Dogbolter was initially brewed at the Sail and Anchor brewpub in Fremantle in 1983, but is now a bottom-fermenting, creamy, dark lager from the CUB-owned Matilda Bay Brewing Co. of Perth. The beer is cask-matured before bottling and takes twice as long to brew and ferment as most Australian beers.

Eagle Blue

This deep-amber-coloured low-alcohol beer (2.7%) is refreshingly bitter. The ice-brewing process has also been used to produce another low-alcohol alternative in the light-amber lager, Eagle Blue Ice (2.7%). Both are produced by the South Australian Brewing Company.

Eagle Super

This golden-amber, full-strength lager (5%) produced by the South Australian brewery, is available in bottles and cans.

Emu

Swan's Emu beers take their name from a Perth brewery taken over by Swan in 1928. The range includes four lagers, Emu Pilsner, Emu Export (4.9%), a hoppier Emu Bitter (4.6%) and the darker, more malty Emu Draft (3.5%).

Export Mongrel

This bronze-coloured wheat beer (5.1%), produced by the Traditional Brewing Company, is a variation on Yellow Mongrel, using a light crystal malt as well as wheat and barley malts.

Foster's Beer

This light, fruity lager (4%) has a worldwide reputation and is the beer most drinkers abroad associate with the Foster's name.

Foster's Light

A low-alcohol brew (2.5%) from Foster's.

Foster's Special
A bright-gold low-alcohol lager (2.8%) from Foster's.

Fremantle Bitter
This full-bodied, amber-coloured, bottom-fermenting beer (4.9%) is brewed by Matilda Bay.

Hahn Gold
A mid-strength lager (3.5%) with a smooth, hop and malt flavour and sweetish finish, from the Hahn Brewery.

Hahn Premium
A full-strength, straw-coloured, European-style lager (5%) with a balanced character and bitter taste, created by late-hopping with Tasmanian hops.

James Boag's Premium
The pale, full-flavoured premium lager, with a fresh, hayfield aroma, is lagered for more than 60 days. Like all Boag lagers, it is batch-brewed and made from Tasmanian malt and Pride of Ringwood hops. It was voted Australia's best beer in 1995.

Kent Old Brown
One of Australia's rare, top-fermented beers, this dark, fruity ale (4.9%) is one of the Tooth brewery's KB range.

Loaded Dog Steam Beer
A deep-copper, lager-style beer (4%) with a smooth, wheaty flavour and biscuity overtones. The "steam" style comes from the burst of gas released when the cask is tapped. The logo of a snarling dog comes from a short story, in which a mongrel wanders into a pub carrying a stick of dynamite. Brewed by the Traditional Brewing Company.

Longbrew
A speciality lager produced by Lion under the Hahn name, this is a more fully fermented beer (4.5%) than most Australian brews.

Matilda Bay Bitter
An amber, all-malt, bottom-fermenting, Australian-style bitter (3.5%) from the Matilda Bay brewery in Western Australia.

Melbourne Bitter
This dryish lager (4.9%) comes from CUB. It is quite similar to Victoria Bitter (Victoria's best-selling beer), also brewed by CUB.

Moonshine
The strong, spirited barley wine called Moonshine (8%) is produced by the small Grand Ridge brewery in rural Victoria.

COOPERS ORIGINAL

Thomas Cooper, a shoemaker, emigrated to Australia from Yorkshire in England in 1852 with his wife Alice. She was the daughter of a publican and when she fell ill, asked her husband to make her some beer as a tonic, giving him the recipe from her sickbed. According to family legend, this brew was so successful that Thomas Cooper went into brewing full-time in 1862. However, as a devout Wesleyan, he regarded pubs (but not beer) as evil, and so restricted his trade to direct deliveries to private houses. The brewery moved to its present site in Upper Kensington in 1880.

O'Flanagan's
The Swan brewery of Perth sells this draught stout (4.8%) as a rival to Guinness.

Old Southwark Stout
See Southwark Old Stout.

Original Chilli Beer
The Traditional Brewing Company in Melbourne brews this fiery chilli beer (4%). It is a smooth lager, but chilli is added at the second fermentation in the bottle to give an unmistakable bite.

Power's Bitter
A light-amber bitter (4.8%) with a dense, creamy head and a hoppy flavour.

Power's Gold
This light-gold, full-bodied, mid-strength lager (3.4%) from the Power brewery, has a hoppy aroma.

Power's Light
A pale-amber, low-alcohol lager (2.8%) with a full-bodied flavour and a clean, crisp aroma.

Razor Back
A creamy, roasted stout, named after a local pig, brewed by Traditional Brewing Company of Melbourne.

Red Ant
A hearty, robust red lager (4.5%) in the Australian style, produced by the Jerningham Street brewery.

Redback
Australia's first wheat beer (4.8%) was introduced by the pioneering Matilda Bay Brewing Co. of Perth. Named after a local spider, it is brewed using 65% wheat. Since being taken over by CUB, this filtered, fruity, golden brew is less spicy than before. Besides Redback Original, there is also now a lower-alcohol Redback Light. An associated brewpub in Melbourne, also called Redback, produces a more distinctive, unfiltered Redback Hefe-Weizen.

Red Bitter
Sometimes called Tooheys Red, this is a light-gold, dry lager (5%) that uses a high proportion of malt and hops in the brewing process.

Reschs DA

Dinner Ale is a deep-amber, full-strength lager (4.9%) with a robust, aromatic flavour and a sweet aftertaste, produced by the NSW brewery.

Reschs Draught

This fruity, golden lager (4.7%) is one of the distinctive range of lagers produced by the Resch brewery. There is also a lighter lager called Reschs Real Bitter.

Reschs Pilsner

A light, golden Pilsner (4.6%) with a distinct bitterness, from the Resch brewery in NSW.

Sheaf Stout

This dry, bitter, top-fermented stout (5.7%) from Tooth's brewery in Sydney is one of Australia's most distinctive beers.

Southwark Old Stout

This reminder of the English origins of many people in South Australia is a heavy, chocolatey brew (7.4%), reminiscent of a 19th-century London-style stout.

Southwark Premium

The South Australian brewery produces its sweeter beers under the Southwark label. These include Southwark Bitter (4.5%), the full-bodied, fruity Premium lager (5.2%) and Southwark Old Black Ale (4.4%).

Swan Draught

This crisp, gold, malty lager (4.9%) is the best-known beer produced by the Swan plant at Canning Vale. Others include Swan Export lager and Swan Gold (3.5%), for the low-calorie market.

Swan Lite

An ultra-low-alcohol, golden, lightly malted brew (0.9%) where the alcohol is removed by vacuum distillation.

Sydney Bitter

Despite its name, this is a pale, golden lager (4.9%) with a lightly hopped flavour and a light, bitter finish. It was one of the first speciality brews from Hahn.

Tooheys Draught

This pale, sweetish lager (4.6%) is one of Tooheys most popular brews.

Tooheys Old Black

A dark, fruity ale (4.4%) from Tooheys brewery. It is one of the few surviving "Old" top-fermenting beers produced by this concern.

Victoria Bitter

Despite the international reputation of Foster's Lager, this is the best-selling beer in Australia (4.9%). It accounts for a quarter of the total beer market and 60% of CUB's output. A similar brew is sold as Melbourne Bitter.

EARLY BREWS

Brewing arrived in Australia with the first European settlers. John Boston, who landed in Sydney in 1794, manufactured the first recorded beer. It would have been an interesting drink, as it was made from maize and flavoured with the leaves and stalks of the Cape Gooseberry. In 1804, the government set up the colony's first commercial brewery in Parramatta.

The early brews had a poor reputation. Good-quality ingredients were difficult to obtain, and fermentation of English-style, top-fermenting ales was difficult to control in the hot, harsh climate. Yeast deteriorated rapidly, and even if the brewing process could be controlled, the beer itself quickly went off once it was hauled away by bullock cart. The laxative effects of this warm, sour soup earned it the unsavoury nickname "swipes". Most drinkers preferred rum or strong imported beer.

The quality of the beer improved in the 1860s, with the founding of the Swan brewery in 1857 and Coopers brewery in 1862, but the real breakthrough came with the introduction of refrigeration in the 1880s. This allowed the controlled use of yeast, as well as bottom-fermentation, and meant that more reliable beers could be produced. In 1885, two German immigrants, Friedrich and Renne, set up the first lager brewery in Melbourne. Foster's was established nearby by the American Foster brothers in 1888. Although now famous throughout the world, the two brothers only stayed in Australia for 18 months, selling their Collingwood brewery within a year before returning to New York.

West End

South Australia's drier, slightly more hoppy lagers include West End Draught (4.5%), Export Bitter (4.9%) and West End Light (2.6%).

Yellow Mongrel

The rare, golden-straw-coloured, refreshingly fruity Australian wheat beer (3.5%) comes from Traditional Brewing Company of Sydney. Green Bullet hops are used to offset the natural sweetness of the wheat, and give a characteristic bitter finish.

1857

These two lagers, the crisp 1857 Pilsner (4.8%) and more malty 1857 Bitter (3.5%) from Swan are named after the founding date of the brewery on the Swan River in Western Australia.

THE BREWERS

Boag's

Scottish immigrant James Boag and his son bought the Esk brewery on the island of Tasmania at Launceston in 1881. From 1922 until 1993, Boag's was linked with rival island brewers, Cascade of Hobart. This partnership was broken when CUB took over Cascade. Since then, Boag's has taken on new life as one of the few remaining independent breweries, and has revamped its range of beers with a Boag's Original Bitter (4.7%) and a cold-filtered Boag's Classic Bitter (4.9%). All use local Tasmanian malt and Pride of Ringwood hops. Unlike many Australian beers, the beers are batch-brewed in the traditional way. The company's lagers are also matured for 30 days instead of the more usual ten.

Carlton United Brewers

Victoria's leading brewery was founded in Melbourne in 1864 as Carlton and merged with five local rivals including Victoria and Foster's to form Carlton and United Breweries in 1907. In 1990, the combine was renamed the Foster's Brewing Group, but the CUB subsidiary remained in charge of brewing in Australia. Today, it brews in five of the country's seven states, producing 950 million litres (209 million gallons) a year.

Many of CUB's national brands are sold under the Carlton name, including the dryish Carlton Draught, Crown, the more fully fermented Diamond Draught or D-Ale, the extremely clean-tasting Carlton Cold Filtered Bitter (4.9%) and Carlton Light (3.3%).

Cascade

Founded by a Frenchman in 1824, Cascade is the oldest continuously operating brewery in Australia. It also has the grandest location. The fine front of the stone brewhouse in Hobart, Tasmania, is set against the soaring cliffs of the Cascade Mountains. Cascade was badly damaged by bush fires in 1967, but within 12 weeks was brewing again. In 1993, Cascade, then part of Tasmanian Breweries, was bought by CUB. It still produces Cascade beers.

Castlemaine

This Brisbane brewery began life many miles away in the town of Castlemaine in Victoria, where the Fitzgerald brothers had established a brewery in 1859. They set up another Castlemaine brewery in Melbourne in 1871 and then expanded across the country to Brisbane, converting a distillery in Milton into a brewery in 1878. The Victoria interests were later sold to become part of CUB, but the Castlemaine brewery in Brisbane remained part of the rival group, merging with local brewers, Perkins, in 1928 to form Castlemaine Perkins. The main beer, Castlemaine XXXX, introduced in 1924, became Queensland's favourite beer and an international rival to Foster's. Castlemaine's other famous beer is the heavy, dark Carbine Stout. Castlemaine controls 65% of the Queensland market, but is now part of Lion Nathan.

Cooper's

When most other Australian brewers were switching wholesale to producing pasteurized, continuously brewed, pale mass-market lagers (even if some were called bitters), Coopers of

Above: Boag's advertising plays on the Australian image of hard drinking macho beer drinkers.

Adelaide stuck to its guns and continued to brew traditional, top-fermenting ales, which are still sold unfiltered, allowing the beer to mature in the bottle. The Cooper's brews remain the classics of the continent.

Founded in 1862 and still run by the Coopers family, the Upper Kensington brewery in the suburb of Leabrook still ferments its ales in open vats made of native jarrah wood using a distinctive yeast strain that is at least 85 years old. Extra wort is added to the beer on bottling in order to ensure a secondary fermentation of the beer in the bottle. Given the sediment that this process leaves in the bottle, it is surprising that Cooper's best-known yeasty, cloudy brew is called Sparkling Ale.

Coopers introduced their own lagers in 1969 and now use stainless-steel conical fermenters to produce a Draught Lager, a Dry Lager (both 4.5%), Coopers Light (2.9%) and the malty, dark Black Crow (3.6%).

The firm began exporting its ales in 1963 and now they are famous around the world. As a result, today less than a third of total production is sold in South Australia.

Foster's Brewing Group

The international name for Australian beer is also now the overall title of the country's leading combine. The Foster's Brewing Group includes Australia's leading brewer CUB as well as its international arms including Foster's Asia. Originally founded in Melbourne in 1888, Foster's was a lager pioneer, importing ice-making equipment from America. It was also a bottled-beer specialist and leader in the export field.

Grand Ridge

A small brewery in rural Victora at Mirboo North. It brews an Australian-style bitter ale (4.9%) – Gippsland Gold; a hoppy Pilsner (4.9%) – Brewer's Pilsner; an Irish-style stout (4.9%) – Hatlifter Stout; and a powerful extra-strong, pure-malt barley wine (8.5%) – Moonshine.

Hahn

Dr Charles Hahn founded a new brewery in Camperdown, Sydney, in 1988. Hahn had worked in New Zealand where he helped to develop Steinlager. His new brewery produced an all-malt Hahn Premium lager and a Sydney Bitter. It gained such a reputation it was bought by Lion Nathan

in 1993. Its name is still used for speciality lagers, including Hahn Dark Ice (5.2%) and a cold-filtered Hahn Gold (3.5%).

Lion Nathan

In 1992, New Zealand's leading brewery group bought up Bond Brewing in Australia (Castlemaine, Swan and Tooheys) and has since added South Australian and Hahn. It now dominates the Australian industry alongside Foster's CUB.

Matilda Bay

This pioneer of the new brewery and speciality beer movement was founded at Nedlands in Western Australia in the mid-1980s by Philip Sexton, a former brewer with Swan in Perth. Matilda Bay launched the country's first wheat beer called Redback and also a strong ale, Dogbolter. The company accepted substantial investment in 1988 from CUB, which acquired a controlling interest, to expand and build a new brewery in Perth. Matilda Bay still brews Redback and Dogbolter, Matilda Bay Bitter and a Fremantle Bitter.

Power

Hotel owner Bernard Power decided to challenge the might of the two big groups and set up his own large brewery at Yatala, near Brisbane, in 1988. However, after early success, his Power Brewing venture was taken over by CUB in 1992. The Queensland plant still brews Power's creamy, full-bodied Bitter, the weaker Power's Gold, and Light, and Brisbane Bitter and Pilsner.

Reschs

Edmund Resch bought the New South Wales Lager Company in Waverley, Sydney, in 1900 and soon established a sound reputation for his beers. The company merged with Sydney rivals Tooth's in 1920. Today, Resch beers are still brewed at Tooth's Kent brewery, now part of CUB.

South Australian

This major Adelaide brewery was founded in 1888 by the amalgamation of the city's Kent Town and West End breweries. In 1938 it bought the Southwark brewery and all production is now concentrated there in a modern brewery. The company controls almost 70% of the state market. The beers are sold under three main brands, Southwark, West End and Eagle.

Swan

Beer in Western Australia has traditionally been all about the birds. The Swan brewery was built in Perth by the Swan River in 1857 and in 1928 took over the rival Emu brewery. Now part of Lion Nathan, it controls almost three-quarters of the state market. In addition to the well-known Swan lagers, the company also markets a strong, top-fermenting dark Swan Stout (6.8%) and a smooth O'Flanagan's Cream Stout. Other lagers include 1857 Pilsner and 1857 Bitter, and a range of Emu lagers.

Tooheys

Sydney's Catholic Irish brewery was founded in 1869 when John Thomas and his brother James bought the Darling brewery. They moved to a new site to build the Standard brewery, used

until 1978 when production was moved to a modern site at Lidcombe in Sydney. It is now part of Lion Nathan. Tooheys' first beers were top-fermenting darkish ales. When the company started producing bottom-fermenting, golden lagers in the 1930s, it called these "new" beers as opposed to the "old" style ales. Lagers now dominate, notably Tooheys Draught (4.6%). Since 1985 Tooheys has pioneered the development of full-bodied, low-alcohol beers using crystal malt, through its Blue Label.

Below: Brisbane, home of Castlemaine brewery, showing the modern skyline and Brisbane River.

Tooth's

Merchant John Tooth founded the Sydney brewery in 1835. He called it the Kent brewery, after the English hop-growing county he came from. Its beers were sold under the KB brand. Tooth's absorbed its local rival, Reschs of Waverley, in 1929 but was taken over by CUB in 1983. Its beers are still brewed in NSW, including a soft malty KB Lager (4.7%) and two top-fermenting beers – a dark, rich Kent Old Brown and a full-bodied Sheaf Stout.

Traditional Brewing Company

This small brewery at the Geebung Polo Club pub in Hawthorn, Melbourne, has developed a reputation for brewing tasty, stylishly bottled ales. It started in 1985 and claims to be Melbourne's oldest established "boutique brewer".

ICE BEER

As the alcohol content rises in a brew, fermentation becomes more difficult because the action of the yeast is subdued by the alcohol it produces. One way around this difficulty is to freeze the brew. The water freezes before the alcohol and can then be removed to produce a concentrated, purified beer. However it is the effect of the freezing process on the flavour of the beer that has become popular, and few of the fashionable, ultra-smooth lagers weigh in at more than 5.5%. The ice beer craze has certainly arrived in Australia, with most of the main brewers introducing their own brands over the last couple of years.

BREWPUBS

Lion
This small brewery in North Adelaide was built in a pub complex in the mid 1980s. Its Old Lion beers include a hoppy Pilsner, a Sparkling Ale and a Porter.

Lord Nelson
Sydney's oldest hotel is home to a brewery which produces English-style ales, including Trafalgar Pale (4%), Victory Bitter (4.8%) and a rich, dark, malty Old Admiral (6.5%).

Port Dock
The Port Dock Hotel, a brewpub in Port Adelaide, was built in 1855. It uses malt extract to produce golden Lighthouse Ale (3.9%), creamy Black Diamond Bitter (4.9%) and strong Old Preacher (6%).

Pumphouse
A waterside brewpub in Sydney, Pumphouse's beers include the hoppy, English-style Bull's Head Bitter and the darker, more malty Federation.

Redback
This Melbourne brewpub is associated with the Matilda Bay Brewing Company and produces its own distinctive, unfiltered Redback Hefe-Weizen. It also offers Redback Original wheat beer (4.8%) and a lower-alcohol Redback Light.

Rifle Brigade
One of Australia's smallest breweries was installed in the Rifle Brigade pub in the central Victoria mining town of Bendigo in 1986. Its malt extract plant produces seven

Above: An outback pub in Toncoola, South Australia. The rail was originally used for tethering horses.

different beers, including the full-bodied Old Fashioned Bitter (5.3%), the richly roasted Iron Bark Dark (5.3%) and a wheat beer called Platman's (5%).

Sail and Anchor
Australia's first modern brewpub was set up in 1983 by Philip Sexton, a former brewer with the Swan brewery in Perth, when he bought the Freemason's Hotel in Fremantle, renamed it the Sail and Anchor, and installed a brewery on the premises. Later he went on to found the Matilda Bay Brewing Company in nearby Perth. The Sail and Anchor brews several top-fermenting ales served on a handpump, including a fruity English-style bitter called Seven Seas Real Ale (4.6%), a Brass Monkey Stout (6%) with a coffee character and a warming, rich, dark ale, Ironbrew (7%).

Scharer's
The small New South Wales brewery based at the George IV pub in Picton has been brewing German-style lagers since the mid-1980s, most notably a creamy, malty Burragarang Bock (6.4%), an amber Scharer's Lager (5%) and D'lite (3%).

The Inn, which is said to have been built in 1819, originally catered for "Officers and Gentlemen" passing through the town. Convicts, road gangs and future inmates of Berrima and Goulburn jails were often held in what are now the lagering cellars.

NEW ZEALAND

New Zealand has had a long love-hate relationship with beer. Although it is one of the world's top beer-drinking nations, the country has also been the home of a powerful temperance movement.

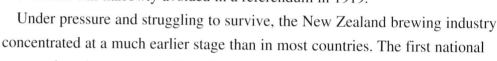

IN 1885, THE SCATTERED POPULATION of New Zealand boasted one brewery for every 6,000 people. These early breweries brewed British-style ales in a climate not far removed from that of northern Europe. Lager was not introduced until 1900, and then only in Auckland in the warmer north. This industry served hotels, which were more like American wild-west saloons than English pubs. Heavy drinking provoked a powerful temperance movement, which closed down hotels and introduced six o'clock closing during the First World War. This lasted for 50 years, and total Prohibition was narrowly avoided in a referendum in 1919.

Under pressure and struggling to survive, the New Zealand brewing industry concentrated at a much earlier stage than in most countries. The first national brewing company, New Zealand Breweries (later Lion Breweries), was formed in 1923 when ten of the largest breweries joined forces, thus controlling 40% of the trade. Seven years later, the rival Dominion Breweries group was formed. Today, the two combines, known as Lion Nathan and DB, dominate the beer market.

The early concentration of the brewing industry meant it invested heavily in research, influenced by the high standards of cleanliness in New Zealand's dairy industry. In the 1950s, Morton Coutts of Dominion developed continuous fermentation whereby beer is produced from a never-ending flow of wort and yeast through four aligned vessels. Rival New Zealand Breweries soon also adopted this cost-efficient system, replacing the traditional batch method. The result was that all beers were chilled, filtered and bottom-fermented. Most draught beers also abandoned the barrel in favour of large tankers that deliver beer direct to hotel cellar tanks. These mild, full-coloured lagers – often referred to as "brown" beers or ales – are sweet, most being primed with sugar and served very cold and highly carbonated.

With the removal of strict licensing restrictions in 1967, New Zealand has gradually adopted a more relaxed attitude to beer drinking. Since the 1980s, a few brewpubs and micro-breweries have appeared.

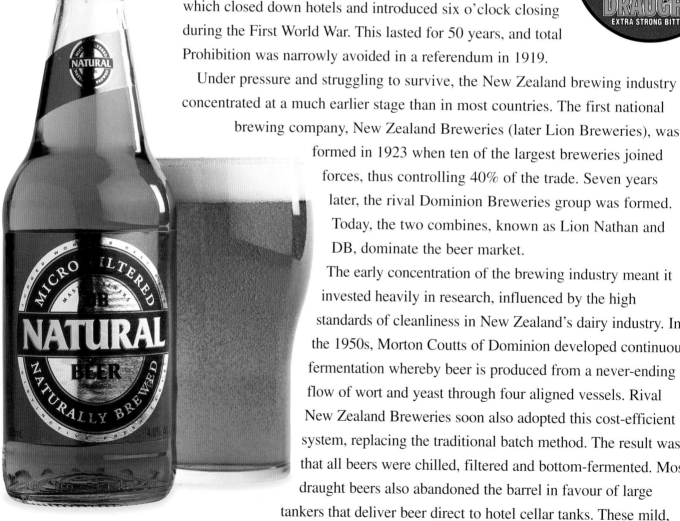

Above: New Zealand brewing is dominated by two groups. Many of the beers have their origins in Britain, and ale and stout are brewed as well as lager.

THE BEERS

Canterbury

A regional, amber-coloured "brown" beer (4%) with a malty, smooth flavour, barley overtones and a dry finish. It comes from Lion's Christchurch brewery on the South Island.

Coromandel Draught

A full-flavoured bitter beer (4%) is brewed by the Coromandel Brewing Company.

DB Export Dry

A pale-gold, hoppy, crisp beer (5%) from Dominion Breweries with a smooth, light, malt taste. It is lagered for longer than most New Zealand brews.

DB Natural

A fresh, unpasteurized, amber-coloured ale (4%) with a sweetish, roast-malt taste and a hoppy finish. It is bottom-fermented and micro-filtered by Dominion Breweries (DB).

Double Brown

A full-flavoured, amber-gold, bottom-fermented speciality beer (4%) with a fruity-malt flavour, brewed by Dominion.

Flame

This amber-gold lager with a smooth finish (5.2%) is produced by the Black Dog brewery in Auckland using the extreme brewing process. This first heats the malt and hops to 106°C (223°F) and then crash-cools the beer to emphasize the flavours.

Hawkes Bay Draught

This amber-coloured ale (4%) with a dry, malt taste, is a regional beer, brewed by Leopard in Hastings. Leopard, now part of Lion, was once New Zealand's third brewing force, behind Lion and Dominion.

Leopard Black Label

A golden-amber lager (4%) with a crisp, fruity flavour. It is brewed by Lion, using the traditional Leopard Brewery's batch-brewing process and a combination of New Zealand hops and a new, recently developed "black label" yeast.

Lion Brown

This amber-gold, sweet and fruity, malt-flavoured ale (4%) is one of Lion's best-selling brews.

Lion Ice

This light-golden-amber modern lager (4.7%) is a smooth, easy-drinking beer from Lion Breweries.

Lion Red

A deep-gold, malty, hoppy, sweetish beer (4%) with a good body. It is one of the leading brands in New Zealand produced by Lion Breweries.

Mainland Dark

Described as a dark ale, this is a richer lager (4%) than others from Dominion, brewed using a blend of roasted malts and barleys by DB's South Island brewery at Timaru.

Mako

This low-alcohol, light beer (2.5%) is brewed by Dominion. It is an authentic, bitter-style beer, brewed with extra hops.

Monteith's Black Beer

This black-coloured beer (5.2%) is stronger than an ale, yet it is lighter than a stout. It is produced by Monteith's using the traditional batch-brewing method and combining five crystal and chocolate malts in a special mash.

Monteith's Original Ale

The Monteith label is used for Dominion Breweries' new "boutique" range of beers, including the malty Monteith's Original Ale (4%), which is brewed from an original 1860s recipe.

Nugget Golden Lager

A crisp speciality lager (5%) from Monteith's.

Rheineck Lager

Relatively light, this golden lager (3.8%) is drier than most New Zealand brews.

Cook's special

Captain Cook, the English explorer who literally put New Zealand on the map, is credited with being the country's first beer brewer. Concerned about scurvy on his second visit in 1773, he brewed "beer" for the ship's crew by boiling up spruce and tea shrub leaves and twigs, mixed with molasses. The concoction was served to the sailors with a shot of rum and brown sugar stirred in, perhaps to help disguise the flavour!

Speight's Gold Medal Ale

A deep-gold, fruity, malt-and-hop-tasting ale (4%). It is still a major malty "brown" beer brand on the South Island. Speight's, established in Dunedin in 1876, was New Zealand's largest brewery before the First World War and the leading company in the merger that formed New Zealand Breweries (Lion) in 1923. The Lion group still brews in Dunedin.

Steinlager

Lion's premium, pale-gold, international lager (5%), much drier and more aromatic than its other beers, is mainly sold abroad. This sweetish, hoppy brew was originally introduced as Steinecker in 1958, named after the new, German-made, Steinecker continuous-fermentation brewing plant that had been installed in its Auckland brewery. After a legal challenge in the US from Dutch giant Heineken, the name was changed to Steinlager in 1962.

Steinlager Blue

Lion introduced this variant on its premium lager in 1993. It is a golden, medium-dry, malty lager with a light hop aroma.

Taranaki Draught

A dark, full-bodied, malty regional lager (4%) with a bitter flavour. It carries the name of the Taranaki brewery of New Plymouth, which was taken over and closed in the 1960s by Dominion Breweries (DB).

Trapper's Red Beer

Monteith's of Greymouth on the South Island produces this deep-red, speciality beer (4.4%), brewed with roasted crystal malt, using a batch-brewing method.

Tui

Although described as an East India Pale Ale, this is a sweet, golden-reddish lager (4%) with a clear, hoppy flavour and malty aftertaste from DB's Tui Brewery at Mangatainoka. The brewery itself dates back to 1889. It is most closely associated with the Hawke's Bay region on the North Island.

Vita Stout

The name of Dominion's smooth, sweet, dark-brown beer (4%) with a chocolate-malt and roasted-barley flavour hints at health-giving properties. Faced with a strong temperance movement in the early part of the 20th century, Kiwi breweries regularly claimed that their beer was full of health-giving properties and should be drunk regularly. Dominion's early Waitemata beer was sold as "The Secret of Good Health and Long Life" and "As Nourishing as Bread or Milk".

THE BREWERS

Dominion Breweries (DB)

Formed in 1930 in Auckland, Dominion Breweries has prided itself on its technological advances, notably the introduction of continuous fermentation in the 1950s. Besides its modern Waitemata brewery in Auckland, it also runs the Tui brewery at Manga-tainoka, Monteith's at Greymouth and the Mainland brewery at Timaru. The main beers are the best-selling, sweetish DB Draught, which uses the company's famous Clydesdale horses in its promotion, and the drier DB Bitter. Regional brands include Tui and Taranaki.

Although described as brown beers and ales, these are mid-strength, reddish-tinted and softly sweet lagers (all 4%). Paler lagers are led by DB Export Gold (4%) and the crisper Export Dry (5%). The company also produces a low-alcohol light beer, Mako (2.5%). Speciality brews, all bottom-fermented, include a fresher-flavoured, unpasteurized DB Natural, a fuller-flavoured Double Brown, a smoothly sweet Vita Stout and richer, more roasted Mainland Dark. DB have recently promoted a range of "boutique" beers, which are sold under the Monteith label in the speciality beer market.

Harrington

The Christchurch micro-brewery produces a rare New Zealand wheat beer and a tasty Dark Beer, besides more conventional lagers.

Lion

New Zealand's largest brewing company controls almost 60% of the domestic market. The overall group, which also owns substantial brewing interests in Australia, is called Lion Nathan. In New Zealand the company trades as Lion Breweries in the North Island and under its older name of New Zealand Breweries in the South Island. The group runs two breweries in the North Island, in Auckland and Hastings, and two in the South Island, in Dunedin and Christchurch. Its main brand is the best-selling, malty Lion Red and the sweeter, fruity

Salvation

The birth of New Zealand's second-largest brewing group sums up the country's love-hate relationship with beer. When the Coutts family opened the Waitemata brewery in Auckland in 1929, the Women's Christian Temperance Movement marched to the site and prayed that the new brewery be turned into a food factory. In part their prayers were answered, for the new venture struggled to find a market and only survived by merging with a drinks wholesaler in 1930 to form Dominion.

Lion Brown. There are also regional bottom-fermenting "brown" beers, including Hawkes Bay and Waikato Draught and, in the South Island, Speight's and Canterbury Draught. More golden, drier brews include a light Rheineck Lager and the company's international flagship brand, the crisp Steinlager (5%). In the 1980s, Lion abandoned the continuous fermentation system and reverted to more traditional batch methods to meet the demand for a wider variety of beers.

Mac's
When the Prime Minister Sir Robert Muldoon opened New Zealand's first micro-brewery in Stoke, in 1981, he described it as a David in an industry of two Goliaths. Nevertheless, the venture launched by former All-Black rugby player Terry McCashin has survived, and has even set up its own maltings to ensure supplies. The marketing for the all-malt beers, brewed to the German beer purity law using a bottom-fermenting lager yeast, emphasizes that no chemicals or preserv-atives are added. The main brews are a malty Mac's Ale, a hoppy Gold, a darker, fuller-bodied Black Mac (all 4%), a more powerful lager Extra (7%) and a Mac Special Light (1%).

Monteith
Dominion took over the Westland brewery in Greymouth in 1969, renamed it Monteith's Brewing Co. in 1995 and began to brew beers for the speciality market. These include the malty Monteith's Original Ale, a deeper-coloured Trapper's Red Beer and a crisp Nugget Golden Lager. The Westland brewery, established in 1858, retains open fermenting vessels, coal-fired boilers and traditional batch brewing. Greymouth, a mining area of the west coast of the South Island, has a large Irish population and prides itself on its pubs and beer.

Newbegin
Established in Onehunga near Auckland in 1987, this micro-brewery produces an all-malt lager, Silver Fern (4%) and a dark more robust Old Thumper.

New Zealand Breweries (NZB)
New Zealand's largest beer company, Lion, trades under its older name of New Zealand Breweries in the South Island. NZB was formed in 1923 when ten of the country's largest breweries merged, including Speight's of Dunedin, Staples in Wellington, Ward's of Christchurch and the Great Northern brewery (Lion) of Auckland.

Petone
Two former Lion employees set up this "boutique" brewery in Petone, near Wellington. They imported yeast from Britain to start fermenting the malty Strongcroft's Bitter.

Shakespeare
The country's first brewpub was founded in Auckland in 1986. Its beers include the soft, malty Macbeth's Red Ale, bitter Falstaff Real Ale, Barraclough Lager, pale gold with a light hop finish, and lightly bittered Willpower Stout, as well as the dramatically rich, hoppy King Lear Old Ale (7.5%).

Stockan
Henderson, near Auckland, is home to this brewery, which was partly financed by a vineyard. Set up in the mid-1980s on a larger scale than most micro-breweries, its beers include a spicy Stockan Ale and the chocolatey Dark Ale.

BREWING IN THE PACIFIC

The vast Pacific Ocean is peppered with hundreds of tiny islands, and on some of these there are brewers gallantly turning out brews for their small populations.

The South Pacific brewery in Papua New Guinea was set up in the 1940s by Australians who travelled to Papua New Guinea to work in the gold fields. They were frustrated by the lack of good quality beer, all of which was imported, so they built their own brewery in Port Moresby and used rain water collected in tanks to produce their own beers. Production started in 1952. Sales soared in the 1960s when Prohibition was ended for the islanders. The brewery is still going strong. It produces a malty, dry, golden lager (4.5%) called SP Lager and South Pacific Export Lager –a delicate malt lager (5.5%) that won the Brewex international gold medal award in 1980. There is also a deep-brown-black stout (8%) called Niugini Gold Extra Stout.

Western Samoa Breweries boasts Vailima, a smooth, refreshing lager (4.9%), which is actually brewed in Auckland, New Zealand, and the small Pacific islands of Tahiti and Fiji also have their own breweries. On Tahiti the Brasserie de Tahiti produces a prestigious, pale-gold Hinano Tahiti lager (4.9%), which won a World Gold Medal for quality in 1990, as well as two local beers, Hei Lager Gold, a premium lager (5%), and Vaita, a virtually non-alcoholic lager (0.8%). The Calton brewery in Fiji makes a tawny brew with a malty flavour called Fiji Bitter Beer.

The Kona Brewing Company on Hawaii, the 52nd State of the US, brews Fire Rock Ale, a dark amber beer (4.1%), using pale and Munich malts and Cascade, Galena and Mount Hood hops, while the same company's Pacific Golden Ale (3.5%) is a golden-amber pale ale, created with a blend of pale and honey malts, hopped with Bullion and Willamette varieties.

CANADA

Prohibition hit Canada hard, and as a result the industry is dominated by the few big names that survived. The Canadians are not big beer drinkers, but the picture is now changing slowly and more small breweries are appearing.

BREWING IN CANADA has run parallel with its big neighbour south of the border, although technically Canada has often led the way. The first commercial brewery in Canada was set up in Montreal in 1786, by English immigrant John Molson, making it the oldest brewery in North America. He was followed by two other familiar names, Thomas Carling who started his brewery in London, Ontario, in 1840, and John Labatt who founded his brewery in the same town seven years later. Canada has had a love-hate relationship with alcohol, and, following the passing of the Scott Local Option Law in 1878, a nightmare cobweb of regulations ensnared the production and sale of beer. There was also the dry period of national Prohibition, which lasted from 1918 until 1932. When that ended, each province developed its own set of rigid rules – many of them are still in existence. In Ontario, for example, the Liquor Control Board is one of the biggest purchasers of alcohol in the world, and it has a monopoly on selling beer throughout its 585 stores. Also, taxes on alcohol in Canada are the highest of any nation, with tariffs making up 53% of the price in 1995. As a result of all this, beer in Canada is relatively expensive.

Local laws in Canada require beer to be brewed in the area where it is sold, so the three large groups which dominate brewing in Canada – Molson, Labatt and Carling – have breweries scattered across the provinces, often producing beers under a myriad of local labels. Originally the beer they produced was typical of the top-fermenting ales that reflected the English origins of the founding brewers, but they soon switched to bottom-fermenting lagers, and Labatt's pioneered the introduction of "ice beer" in 1993 which has proved so popular.

Since the early 1980s there has been a small-scale brewery revolution, particularly in British Columbia, Ontario and Quebec. By 1995, some 40 micro-breweries had been set up, bringing a new wave of beers to the bar. But many of these small breweries have had to struggle against stifling regulations.

Above: Molson is the oldest brewer on the North American continent. The company merged with Carling in 1989 to form a giant international company.

The Beers

Alpine Lager
This refreshing lager (5%) is produced locally by the independent Moosehead brewery for the Maritime provinces.

Anniversary Amber Ale
A red-amber, Bavarian-style, all-malt brew (5.5%) was created to celebrate 10 years of production at the Granville Island micro-brewery.

Arkell Best Bitter
Wellington County produces this light, bitter ale (4%) with a malt aroma in the brewing town of Guelph in the state of Ontario.

Big Rock Pale Ale
This quality pale ale (5%) is brewed at the Big Rock brewery in Calgary, which was founded by Ed McNally in 1985. Big Rock has created its own stampede, with demand rising for its tasty, all-malt, unpasteurized ales brewed by Bernd Pieper, who was formerly a head brewer with Löwenbräu in Zurich.

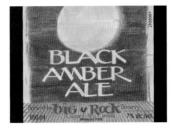

Black Amber
An extra-strong, amber ale (7%) from the small Big Rock brewery.

Blanche de Chambly
A cloudy, spicy, bottle-conditioned wheat beer (5%) from the Unibroue micro-brewery. This tart, refreshing brew won the Silver Medal in the 1995 World Beer Championship.

Brador
A rich, fruity, top-fermenting specialist ale (6.5%) from Molson.

Brasal Bock
An amber-brown, sweet-roasted, hoppy bock (7.8%), which is matured in oak barrels for three months.

Brasal Légère
The lightest lager brewed by the Brasal micro-brewery of LaSalle. The companion brew Brasal Hops Bräu (4.5%) is also quite light.

Brasal Special Amber
A malty, strong, German-style lager (6.1%).

Brick Bock
A strong, unpasteurized German-style bock (6.5%) from the Brick micro-brewery.

Brick Premium Lager
This excellent, hoppy, golden lager (5%) is one of the award-winning brews from the Brick micro-brewery of Waterloo, Ontario.

Brick Red Baron
An unpasteurized ale (5%) produced by the Brick micro-brewery.

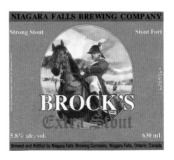

Brock's Extra Stout
Brock extra stout porter (5.8%) is one of the specialist beers brewed by the innovative Niagara micro-brewery.

Canadian Lager
An unexciting, but not unpleasant, standard lager (5%) produced by Moosehead.

Carling Black Label
A light-tasting, pale-gold, standard lager (5%) from Molson, which has proved to be a best-selling export to the UK.

Colonial Stout
This stout porter (4.8%) comes from the Upper Canada micro-brewery.

County Ale
This excellent, amber, malty, traditional ale (5%) with a hoppy aftertaste is a slightly stronger ale produced by the Wellington County micro-brewery.

Frontenac
This light ale (5%) comes from the popular small brewery, McAuslan, which is based in Ontario.

Granville Island
Dark Bock
This delicious, amber bock (6.5%) brewed by Granville Island Brewing Company in Vancouver, British Columbia, is one of the finest beers in Canada. It has a rich, malt nose, a hearty, roasted-malt and hop flavour, good balance and an exceptionally long and well-balanced finish.

Grasshopper Wheat
This all-malt, unpasteurized wheat beer (5%) is produced by Big Rock of Calgary.

Griffon Brown Ale
A mahogany-brown, complex, full-bodied, slightly sweet, hoppy ale (4.5%) produced by Brasserie McAuslan.

Griffon Extra Pale Ale
This bright-gold, pale ale (5%) has a hoppy, fruity-malt flavour. It comes from the Brasserie McAuslan.

Gritstone Premium Ale
This strong ale (5.5%) is produced by the Niagara Falls Brewing Company.

Imperial Stout
This dark stout (5.5%) from Wellington County has a faint chocolate-malt nose, a light but complex malty flavour and a hoppy finish.

Island Lager
A full-bodied, hoppy, deep-gold lager (5%), from Granville Island Brewing.

John Labatt's Classic
This gold, highly carbonated lager (5%) from Labatt has a mild, hoppy aroma and a dull, malt and hop flavour.

La Fin du Monde
Unibroue produces this deep-yellow, fruity, spicy, extra-strong, triple-fermented ale (9%). It is conditioned in the bottle.

La Gaillarde
This unusual bottle-conditioned beer (5%) from Unibroue uses herbs and spices in place of hops.

Labatt Ice Beer
This pioneering ice beer, with a golden, malt and hop flavour and full body, weighs in at 5.6%.

Labatt's Blue
This grainy, deep-amber, slightly dry lager (5%) is Labatt's flagship brand.

Labatt's 50 Ale
This refreshing, bright-gold ale (5%) has a medium body, a light hop nose with fruity hints and a crisp, fresh flavour with a slightly sour malt finish.

Lord Granville Pale Ale
This all-malt, copper-red, fruity pale ale (5%) from the Granville Island brewery is brewed in accordance with the German beer purity law, using only barley malt, hops, water and yeast in the brew.

McAuslan Pale Ale
This zesty pale ale (5%) from Brasserie McAuslan has a smooth, well-balanced hop and malt flavour.

McNally's Extra Pure Malt Irish Style Ale
This deep-amber, extra-strong, unpasteurized, all-malt beer (7%) from Big Rock brewery has a powerful, roasted-malt nose, a rich malt flavour, and a hop and malt aftertaste with hints of caramel.

Magpie Rye
This is an unpasteurized, tart-flavoured rye beer (5%), which comes from the Big Rock brewery in Calgary.

Maple Wheat Beer
A strong, syrupy wheat beer (8.5%) from the Niagara Falls Brewing Company.

Maudite
A warming, mellow, bottle-conditioned red ale (8%), from the Unibroue micro-brewery.

Mitchell's ESB
A copper-coloured, English-style ale (5.5%) from the Spinnakers brewpub.

Molson Canadian Lager
The most famous of Molson's products (5%) is pale gold with a dry malt nose and hints of hops. Its flavour is smooth and well-balanced with malt and hops and a long, dry finish.

Molson Export Ale
This light, brownish-gold ale (5%) is a little fuller than the lager, with a crisp, hoppy taste, good body and a long malt and hop aftertaste.

Molson Special Dry
A slightly stronger lager (5.5%) from Molson.

Moosehead Lager
This is the popular, mild, pale-malt lager (5%) that gave its name to the brewery.

Moosehead Pale Ale
This pale-gold ale (5%) has a yeasty, malt-hop nose, a well-hopped, slightly sweet malt flavour, and a dry malt-hop finish. It is brewed at the Moosehead brewery.

Mount Tolmie

This dark ale (4.2%) is brewed by the Spinnakers brewpub, using four malt types and Mount Hood hops.

Ogden Porter

This strong porter (6.2%) comes from the Spinnakers brewpub in Victoria, British Columbia.

Okanagan Spring Brown Ale

A deep-brown, top-fermented ale (5.6%), brewed with two-row barley malt and Hallertauer hops by the Okanagan Spring brewery, British Columbia.

Okanagan Spring Pilsner

A light, golden, hoppy Pilsner (4.5%) from the Okanagan Spring brewery, British Columbia.

Pacific Real Draft

This light, pleasant lager (5%) is the best-known brew from the Pacific Western brewery.

Publican's Special Bitter

The Upper Canada micro-brewery produces this special top-fermented, amber-brown, English-style bitter (4.8%).

Raftman

This gold, smoky, bottle-conditioned beer (5.5%) is brewed using peat-smoked whiskey malt by the Unibroue micro-brewery.

Rebellion Malt Liquor

This deep-gold, malt liquor (6%) has a sweet, full, honey taste with a malty hop finish. It is a very pleasant, well-rounded beer from the Upper Canada Brewing Company.

Red Baron

This pale-gold lager (5%), brewed by the Brick Brewing Company, has a light hop and malt aroma, a mild malt flavour and a hoppy finish.

Red Cap Ale

The Brick Brewing Company produces this classic beer (5%) using the original Carling recipe.

Red Dog

A golden, German-style ale (5.5%) with a faint malt and hop nose and a dry, malty flavour.

St-Ambroise Framboise

A Belgian-style, light, pink-red, raspberry fruit beer (5%), from the Brasserie McAuslan.

St-Ambroise Oatmeal Stout

A black, chocolatey, malt and roasted barley, traditional, dry stout (5.5%), brewed using oatmeal in the mash by McAuslan Brasserie, St Ambroise, Quebec.

St-Ambroise Pale Ale

A reddish-gold, robust, malty ale with a clean taste – a characteristic of the Cascade hops used in the brew by Brasserie McAuslan.

Signature Amber Lager

This amber, all-malt lager is brewed under the Signature label by Molson.

Signature Cream Ale

A characterful, all-malt ale. It is one of Molson's prestige Signature brews.

Sleeman Cream Ale

As with all Sleeman brews, this tawny-gold, malty cream ale (5%) is sold in a distinctive embossed bottle.

Sleeman Original Dark

This dark-amber ale (5.5%) has a malty aroma and is lightly hopped. It comes from the Sleeman brewery.

Spinnaker Ale

An amber, English-style ale (4.2%) from Canada's first brewpub, Spinnaker.

Spinnaker Hefe-Weizen

This spicy, cloudy beer is a speciality brew from the Spinnaker brewpub.

Trapper Lager

A deep-gold lager with a grapey nose and a thin, sweet taste from the Niagara Falls Brewing Company.

True Bock

This is a red-amber German-style bock beer (6.5%) with a complex, warm, soft malty flavour and a pleasant hop nose. It is the most interesting beer from the Upper Canada micro-brewery in Toronto. The brewery also produces a light wheat beer (4.3%) with a tart, fruity aroma, a standard lager (5%) and an English-style IPA (4.8%).

Warthog Ale

The Big Rock Brewery in Calgary produces this all-malt, unpasteurized ale (4.5%).

Waterloo Dark

An unpasteurized dark draft ale (5.5%) from the Brick Brewing Company.

Wellington Imperial Stout

A rich, brown-black, top-fermented stout (5.5%) brewed using speciality malts by the Wellington County Brewery.

Legal restrictions

The legal restrictions on the Canadian brewing industry stem from the Prohibition of the 1920s and rigid state laws. Micro-breweries have had to struggle against these barriers. In spite of this, Canada has always been at the forefront of brewing developments.

THE BREWERS

Big Rock
Founded by Ed McNally in 1985, the Big Rock brewery is dedicated to the batch-brewing of premium beers following the German beer purity law. It uses a cold multi-microfiltration system rather than pasteurization. Among its best-known brews are Buzzard Breath Ale, a light to medium-bodied ale, McNally's Extra Pure Irish-style Ale, Warthog Ale, which is copper-coloured and nutty, Magpie Rye Ale and Grasshopper Wheat Ale.

Brasal Brasserie Allemande
This is Quebec's largest micro-brewery. It was founded in the city of LaSalle, Montreal in 1989, by the Jagerman family to brew German-style lagers according to the German beer purity law.

Brick
The Brick Brewing Company was established in 1984 in Waterloo, Ontario. Brick laid the foundations for the new brewery movement in eastern Canada. Its unpasteurized beers, many of them award-winners, are mainly European-style lagers developed by founder Jim Brickman.

Carling
One of Canada's leading international brewing names, Carling was founded in Ontario in 1840 by Sir Thomas Carling. Later in the 19th century Carling merged with the rival brewery O'Keefe, founded by Eugene O'Keefe in 1862, forming Carling O'Keefe. The company was taken over by the Australian giant, Foster's, in 1987, but that company overreached itself and Carling was merged with Molson in 1989. They then formed the largest brewing group in Canada, with vast overseas interests. The flagship brew, Carling Black Label, is one of the best-selling lagers in the UK. Because of the state laws in Canada that stipulate that beer must be brewed within the state boundaries, the company runs a large number of breweries, which produce local beers under various labels.

Granville Island Brewing
Businessman Mitch Taylor set up Canada's first micro-brewery in Vancouver's waterfront crafts area in 1984. It brews Bavarian-style all-malt lagers, notably Island Lager.

Labatt
One of Canada's two brewing giants, Labatt was taken over by the Belgian brewing company Interbrew in 1995. It also owns Latrobe (Rolling Rock) in the US.

The brewery was founded in London, Ontario, in 1847 by John Labatt. Despite the brewery being burned down twice in the 19th century, the company persevered, surviving Prohibition to take over many rival regional brewers after the Second World War.

Today it runs seven breweries across Canada, and at one time it marketed almost 50 brands. Its main lager is Labatt's Blue (5%). Local beer brands include Kokanee and Kootenay in the West and Schooner and Keith's IPA in the East, besides Blue Star in Newfoundland.

Labatt pioneered ice beer (introduced in 1993). During the brewing process the beer is chilled to 4°C (39.2°F) to form ice crystals, which are then removed leaving a stronger (5.6%) but rather bland brew behind.

McAuslan
After two years preparation this small brewery in Montreal began brewing in 1989. The famous British brewer Alan Pugsley helped to formulate the recipe for its first brew – St-Ambroise Pale Ale. The brewery has since gone from strength to strength, and in the seven years since launching, it has introduced four new beers, St-Ambroise Oatmeal Stout, Griffon Extra Pale Ale, Griffon Brown Ale and Frontenac, a golden, lightly hopped extra pale ale.

Molson
The oldest brewer in North America dates back to 1786 when English immigrant John Molson set up the Molson brewery in Montreal. Now based in Toronto, it is the rival giant to Labatt, with nine breweries and about 50 brands. Molson merged with Carling O'Keefe in 1989 to make it

the brewmaster Conrad Oland was killed in an explosion in 1917 when two ships collided in Halifax harbour – the company moved to St John's, New Brunswick. In 1931 George Oland renamed his main beer Moosehead and this proved to be such a successful innovation that the company name was changed to Moosehead in 1947.

The beer is enormously popular in the US. It also brews local Alpine Lager (5%) for the Maritime Provinces, and a dry Moosehead Pale Ale.

Niagara Falls
This innovative micro-brewery on the Canadian side of the Niagara falls produced the first North American ice beer, the smoothly malty Niagara Eisbock (8%) in 1989. It was inspired by the local Eiswein.

Niagara was set up by the Criveller brothers, Mario and Bruno, after their Ethiopian brewery in Addis Ababa was nationalized. Since then the brewery has added an Apple Ale and a Kriek (both 6.5%) made with cherries.

the largest Canadian brewer, with 53% of the market. Best known for its Molson Canadian Lager (5%) and Molson Special Dry (5.5%), it introduced a new range of all-malt beers in 1993, which are marketed under the Signature brand name. These brews have found a ready acceptance in the home market.

Moosehead
Moosehead, Canada's oldest and largest independent brewery, was founded by Susannah Oland in Halifax, Nova Scotia, in 1867. The company used old family recipes from Britain and then won the contract to supply beer to the Canadian forces. It became known as the Army and Navy brewery.

After a troubled history –

Okanagan Spring Brewery
A small, specialist brewery established in Vernon, British Columbia. Their most prestigious brew is the Old English Porter, full-bodied and rummy (8.5%), but the company also produces a golden, malty Premium Lager, a Pale Ale and an Old Munich Wheat Beer that has a dry cider aroma and roasted-malt flavour.

Sleeman
The fourth-largest brewer in Canada (behind Molson, Labatt and Moosehead), Sleeman was first founded in Guelph, Ontario, in 1834, but closed in 1939. In 1985, John Sleeman decided to resurrect the family brewing business, opening a new plant in Guelph in 1988. Its beers are sold in distinctive embossed bottles.

Spinnakers
Canada's first brewpub had to overcome a succession of legal hurdles before opening in Victoria, British Columbia, in 1984. Permission to brew and sell beer on the same premises required a change to federal law and a local referendum. Spinnakers had to make the bar into a restaurant and build another storey to house the bar. Paul Hadfield brews mainly English-style ales and some lambic-style brews.

Unibroue
Quebec's largest micro-brewery was founded in 1991 in Chambly, Montreal, by Belgian beer enthusiast André Dion. It produces a range of characterful beers, such as Eau Bénite, that are even exported to France.

Upper Canada
Frank Heaps founded this Ontario micro-brewery in 1985 in a Toronto warehouse. It is now one of the largest new breweries in North America, and exports its beers to Europe. It uses water from the Caledon Hills 48 km (30 miles) away, trucking it in daily to ensure the purity of its beers.

Wellington County
The small Wellington County plant was set up in the Ontario brewing town of Guelph in 1985 to brew English-style ales, including some of the first cask-conditioned beers in North America to come from a commercial brewery, besides an Imperial Stout (5.5%) and Iron Duke strong ale (6.5%).

UNITED STATES OF AMERICA

The United States is the largest brewer in the world and its big-name lagers are famous the world over. Recently it has become the land of the born-again brewer, as micro-breweries spring up to meet the growing demand for variety.

ONCE THE US heaved with Europe's best beers – from English ales and Irish stouts to Czech Pilsners. Many of the leading brewers were German immigrants and brought with them that country's rich range of styles. Then came Prohibition. The Volstead Act of 1919 destroyed a thriving and colourful brewing industry by outlawing the manufacture and sale of alcohol. By the time Prohibition was repealed 14 years later in 1933, most of the original companies had vanished. The way was open for a few combines to dominate the trade – with a much-reduced range of beers.

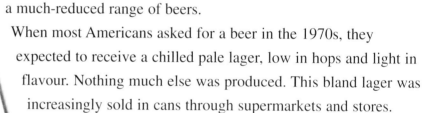

Above: Anchor Steam Beer, brewed in San Francisco, was one of the pioneering brews of America's modern beer renaissance.

When most Americans asked for a beer in the 1970s, they expected to receive a chilled pale lager, low in hops and light in flavour. Nothing much else was produced. This bland lager was increasingly sold in cans through supermarkets and stores.

With little to distinguish between beers in taste, the emphasis was on marketing. The brand image became bigger than the beer, and the big brands gradually squeezed out those with less marketing muscle.

America is the home of light beer, a low-calorie lager launched by Miller in 1975. By 1995, three of the top four best-selling beers were light beers.

At the end of the 1970s, new small-scale breweries began to appear. Some, like New Amsterdam, used the spare capacity at established breweries to brew their beer. This contract brewing system helped struggling regional breweries to survive, while launching colourful new beers. By the 1990s new brewery business was booming. Some micro-breweries produced draft and bottled beers for local bars and stores, while others set up brewpubs to serve their beers direct to the customers. There are now about 1,000 new ventures with 92 micro-breweries and 138 brewpubs opening in 1995 alone. This speciality market is relatively small, but it is growing all the time.

THE BEERS

Abita Amber

This light-amber, sweetish, malty European-style beer (3.8%) is brewed by Abita Brewing Co. Inc., Louisiana's first micro-brewery. Abita also brews a Golden Lager, a brilliant-amber, hoppy Fall Fest, an amber Bock Beer and Purple Haze Raspberry Wheat Ale.

Acme Pale Ale

This famous Californian brand was revived in 1996 by North Coast, the award-winning Californian brewery in Fort Bragg, which began as a brewpub in 1988. Other beers include Scrimshaw Pilsner (4.5%) and Blue Star Wheat (4.8%). It also brews a rich, intense Old Rasputin Russian Imperial Stout.

Adirondack Amber

This amber-coloured, Bavarian-style lager (5%), with a classic Pilsner flavour, is part of the Saranac range from FX Matt.

Alimony Ale

This famous nut-brown, orange-tinged ale ("the bitterest beer in America") is brewed by beer enthusiast Bill Owens. Alimony's bitter finish is complemented by a sweet-malt entry. Owens originally brewed the beer in honour of an employee who was going through a divorce. Bill Owens opened America's third brewpub, Buffalo Bill's, in Hayward, California, in 1983.

Amber

This unpasteurized, golden, smooth, malty lager (4.5%) is brewed by the Thomas Kemper Brewing Company.

American Originals

Anheuser-Busch sells its speciality beers, based on turn-of-the-century recipes, under the American Originals name. Beers include Muenchener Amber and Black and Tan Porter.

Anchor Steam Beer

A bright, copper-coloured cross between an ale and a lager (5%) with a well-rounded, malty taste and a crisp finish. Fritz Maytag's brewery revived this gold-rush-era beer, produced using a shallow-fermenter brewing method, perfected by forty-niners when no refrigeration was available.

Apricot Ale

This mild ale (3.5%) has a subtle apricot taste from start to finish. It is made with real apricots by Hart Brewing.

Auburn Ale

This ale is brewed by the family-run Leinenkugel lager brewery in Chippewa Falls, Wisconsin.

Augsburger

This is the brand name for speciality German-style beers from the US's fourth largest brewer, Stroh. Augsburger beers were originally developed by the Wisconsin brewer, Huber.

Bachelor Bitter

This copper-coloured, cold-conditioned, English-style ale (5%) with hints of grapefruit and evergreen is brewed by Deschute's brewery in Bend, Oregon. This Pacific Northwest brewery began life in 1988 as a brewpub but has expanded rapidly to meet demand.

Baderbräu

These German-style lagers from Chicago's Pavichevich brewery (set up in 1989 in Elmhurst, Illinois) comply with the German Reinheitsgebot beer purity law. The beers included a hoppy, bronze-coloured Pilsner (4.8%) and a light-brown, malty bock (5.4%).

Ballantine's Ale

Once one of the best-selling ales in America, Ballantine's was originally brewed in Albany, New York, in the 1830s before moving to Newark, New Jersey. In the 20th century, the beers have been brewed by a variety of companies, but are now produced by Pabst in Milwaukee. The best-known Ballantine beer is the copper-coloured hoppy IPA, but there is also a lighter Ballantine Ale.

Ballard Bitter

This strong, caramel-coloured bitter (5.9%), brewed by Redhook, is aggressively hopped, but offers some maltiness and a dry finish.

Banquet Beer
This pale-gold lager put Coors on the map when it was launched in the 1960s.

Bert Grant's
A range of "real ales" from the Yakima Brewing and Malting Co. brewpub in Yakima, WA. The brews include an English-style IPA (4.2%), a fruity, malty Scottish Ale (4.7%), a chocolatey Imperial Stout (6%), a hoppy Hefe Weizen (4.2%), a rich Perfect Porter (4%) and the flowery Amber Ale (5.5%).

Big Butt Doppelbock
A German-style doppelbock from Leinenkugel, Wisconsin.

Big Shoulders Porter
This chocolate-brown porter has a slightly roasted taste with a good hops balance. It is produced by the family-run Chicago brewery, the only commercial brewery left in the "windy city".

Bigfoot Barley Wine
This powerful, bottle-conditioned, russet barley wine (10.6%), brewed by Sierra Nevada, has a fruity, bittersweet taste.

Black and Tan
A dark-brown mix of a specially made stout and Saranac Adirondack Lager. The Black and Tan has a chocolate-malt nose, a medium body and roasted barley flavour with hints of fruity hops.

Black and Tan Porter
This dark-amber-coloured speciality beer by Anheuser-Busch has a toasted-malt aroma, a smooth, dry malt flavour and a dry malt finish.

Black Butte Porter
A dark-reddish-brown, cold-conditioned, unfiltered porter (5.5%), with a tan head and a rich, roasted-malt taste with a touch of chocolate, was a surprise success for Deschute's in Bend, Oregon.

Black Chocolate Stout
This potent stout (8.3%), produced annually by the Brooklyn brewery, is a classic imperial stout with a rich, creamy texture and a deep-malt, burnt-coffee taste.

Black Hawk Stout
This light-bodied stout, brewed by Mendocino – California's first micro-brewery – is fruitier than either Irish or English stout, with a flavour of chocolate, caramel and coffee.

Blackened Voodoo
This dark, ruby-brown beer (5%) with a light, malt aroma and slightly sour tang, brewed by Dixie, caused some outrage and was banned in Texas when launched in 1992, with allegations that it was the devil's brew.

Blackhook Porter
This dark-chestnut porter (4.9%) has a robust malt and coffee nose and a bitter, roasty finish with hints of coffee. It is brewed by the Redhook Ale brewery in Woodinville, WA.

Blue Fin Stout
This ebony stout (5%) has a roasted malt nose with hints of molasses. It has a medium body and a bitter coffee finish. It is brewed by Shipyard in Portland, Maine.

Blue Heron Pale Ale (Bridgeport)
This attractive, copper-coloured, malty American pale ale (5.8%) with a white head has a sweet malt and complex, bitter flavour and a dry finish. It is available in cask-conditioned form in the brewery bar of Oregon's oldest micro-brewery, Bridgeport.

Blue Heron Pale Ale (Mendocino)
This excellent, hazy-gold, English-style pale ale (5.9%) from Mendocino Brewing has a dry, hoppy character and a touch of fruit and sweet maltiness.

Blue Moon
In 1995, the brewing giant Coors launched this range of speciality beers with a Belgian White, Nut Brown and Honey Blonde Ale. They were developed in its Sandlot micro-brewery in Denver, Colorado. The beers are brewed under licence by F.X. Matt of Utica, New York.

Blue Star Wheat Beer
A good version of American wheat beer (4.8%) brewed by North Coast. It is a pale, clean, dry brew with a soft, refreshing flavour.

Bohemian Dunkel
This rich, well-rounded, unpasteurized, dark lager (5.6%) is brewed by Kemper, using chocolate-malt and Styrian hops.

Boulder Amber Ale
A robust, bright-amber ale (4.5%) with a yeasty, malty nose and a well-balanced malt and hop taste. It is brewed by Rockies Brewing in Boulder, Colorado.

Brooklyn Lager
Dubbed the pre-Prohibition beer, the dry-hopped Brooklyn Lager (4.5%) was launched in 1987 in New York. Originally all the beer was contract-brewed upstate by F.X. Matt of Utica, but in 1996 the company opened its own brewery in Brooklyn, reviving the area's brewing traditions. Once Brooklyn was one of the country's top beer towns with breweries like Piels, Shaefer and Rheingold. It also brews a

strong Brooklyn Brown Ale (5.5%), a dry Brooklyn IPA (7.4%) and an annual Black Chocolate Stout (8.3%).

Budweiser
The world's leading beer brand from Anheuser-Busch of St Louis was first launched in 1876 and named after the famous brewing town in the Czech Republic. Budweiser is the epitome of a light American lager, using rice in the mash to give a crisp, clean taste that belies its alcohol content of 4.7%. Despite using eight hop varieties, it is very lightly hopped. Anheuser-Busch also takes pride in maturing the "King of Beers" in tanks containing beechwood chips to smooth out the flavour. In 1995, about one in four beers sold in America was a Budweiser.

Cascade Golden Ale
Another unfiltered, cold-conditioned, English-style ale (4.1%) from Deschute's.

Celebration Ale
This is one of the best of the American IPAs. It is a copper-coloured ale (5.1%), brewed by Sierra Nevada Brewing. It has a pungent,

floral nose with hints of caramel malt and a roasted malt and earthy hops flavour and a long, full-bodied finish. This is a real gem.

Celis White
This is a Belgian-style wheat beer (5%), flavoured with coriander and orange peel, from the Celis brewery in Austin, Texas.

Cerveza Rosanna Red Chili Ale
This odd, slow-burning speciality beer, flavoured with red chillies, is occasionally produced by the Pike Place brewery of Seattle. It goes well with Mexican food.

Chesterfield Ale
A golden, bottom-fermented ale with a flowery hop aroma, from Yuengling, America's oldest brewery.

Christian Moerlein
A malty lager brewed by Hudepohl-Schoenling of Cincinatti, named after an early brewer in the city. A Reinheitsgebot brew with plenty of body and a full, smooth finish.

Cold Spring Export Lager
This mild, crisp, gold lager, brewed by Cold Spring Brewing Company in Cold Spring, Minnesota, has a crisp, malty flavour and a dry, hoppy finish.

Coors
A range of lagers from this American giant. There is a full-bodied Original, a refreshing clean-flavoured Extra Gold, a Light, and a variety of Winterfest beers.

Crazy Ed's Cave Creek Chili Beer
This golden, hot-pepper specialty beer has a nose, taste and finish dominated by jalapeño peppers. It is brewed by Evansville Brewing Company in Evansville, Indiana, for the Black Mountain brewery of Cave Creek, Arizona.

Cream City Pale Ale
This top-fermented amber ale (4.2%) has a complex, hoppy nose with woody and citrus hints, a spicy hop taste and a long, dry hop finish. Brewed by the Lakefront micro-brewery.

Dortmunder Gold
This is a malty, dry, full-bodied, strong, export-style lager (5.4%) in the Dortmunder style. It is brewed by Great Lakes.

Dundee's Honey Brown Lager
A tasty brown lager from Genesee in New York.

East Side Dark
A deep-chestnut bock (6.5%) with a brown head, from Lakefront Brewery in Milwaukee, Wisconsin. This medium-bodied beer is sweet, with a deeply roasted malt flavour and a velvety smooth finish.

Eliot Ness
This amber-red, Vienna-style lager (5.4%) with a roasted-malt, buttery, fruity taste, is named after the man who jailed the notorious 1920s Chicago bootlegger Al Capone, and is brewed by Great Lakes.

Elk Mountain Amber Ale
Made with 100% barley malt, whole cone hops and English sale yeast, this amber ale (4.1%) has a malt and hops nose, a hoppy flavour with touches of sweet malt, and a dry hop and malt aftertaste. Brewed by Anheuser-Busch.

Espresso Stout
In keeping with its name, this deep-brown stout with a dark-brown, creamy head boasts a long coffee-like aftertaste. It has a good thick body, a rich chocolate and charcoal nose and a powerful roasted-malt flavour. It is made by Hart Brewing Company in Kalama, Washington, the makers of the Pyramid line of brews.

Esquire Extra Dry

A deep-gold, rich, malt-flavoured lager from the small regional Jones Brewing in Smithton, Pennsylvania.

Esquire Premium Pale Ale

This straw-coloured pale ale from Jones Brewing in Smithton, Pennsylvania, is hoppy from nose to finish.

Eye of the Hawk

A well-balanced, strong, amber ale (7.6%), brewed by Mendocino. It has a fruity nose, followed by a malty taste with assertive hopping.

Fall Fest

This sweetish, malty, European-style beer (4.9%) is brewed by Abita in Louisiana.

AMERICAN BEERS OVERSEAS

The major American brewers have been relatively slow in going international, mainly due to the attraction of the massive domestic market on their doorstep. This insular attitude is in sharp contrast to the soft drinks industry in which American brands like Coca-Cola dominate the world. The world's largest brewer, Anheuser-Busch of St Louis, only established Anheuser-Busch International in 1981. Its top beer, Budweiser, is now brewed in eight overseas countries and sold in 70 others. Second-placed Miller of Milwaukee only seriously developed overseas interests in the early 1990s, spurred by the realization that, while the beer market has peaked in the United States, it is still growing abroad. The company is now making a major push to double its foreign business by the year 2000.

Full Sail Nut Brown Ale

This English-style brown ale (5.4%) has an auburn colour, a nutty nose and a rich, roasted-malt flavour with hints of fruit and smoke. It is brewed by Full Sail in Hood River, Oregon.

Frontier

A cloudy, dark-amber American pale ale (4.2%) with a spicy, hoppy nose and a big, complex, highly carbonated flavour with a dry finish. An award-winning beer from Alaskan Brewing in Juneau, Alaska.

Genny Bock

An occasional deep-amber, malty bock, brewed by Genesee in Rochester, New York.

George Killian's Red Ale

This pale, copper-red ale from Coors (3.9%) has a light body, a toasted-malt nose and a fresh hop and malt flavour.

Gerst Amber

This malty beer is brewed by Evansville, a small former Heileman brewery in Indiana, which was bought out by its employees.

Grant's Scottish Ale

This reddish-amber American ESB (5%) with an off-white head, a hoppy, fruity aroma, a roasted-malt entry and an earthy hop finish, is brewed by Bert Grant of Grant's Yakima Brewing in Yakima, WA.

Great Northern Porter

A dark, reddish-brown porter (5.4%), brewed by Summit Brewing in Minneapolis, MN, with a rich, dark aroma and a big, fruity, roasted-malt and chocolate flavour, and hints of liquorice.

Growlin Gator Lager

A yellow-gold, light, refreshing lager (3.7%), brewed with pale malt and Yakima and Saaz hops by the August Schell Brewing Company.

Hampshire Special Ale

A strong, intensely malty winter ale (7%) with an earthy nose and a bitter-sweet finish, from Geary's Brewing in Portland, Maine.

Heartland Weiss

This hazy-gold, refreshing white wheat beer with a spicy, malt flavour is produced by the Chicago brewery.

Hefeweizen

This pale-yellow, hazy, unfiltered, unpasteurized, wheat beer (5%) is brewed by Thomas Kemper. It has a crisp, refreshing flavour.

Heimertingen Maibock

This powerfully pale German-style spring beer (7.5%) is brewed by Summit.

Helenbock 1992 Oktoberfest

This amber-coloured, German-style beer (4.2%) is made with Hallertau and Saaz hops and Munich malts. It has good body with a light head, a hearty hop aroma, a powerful malty flavour with a hop bite and a dry finish. It is contract-brewed by August Schell Brewing in New Ulm, MN, for Friends B.C. in Helen, Georgia.

Hell Doppel Bock

This rich and warming Bavarian-style beer (7.2%) comes from Heckler, a Californian venture set up in Tahoe City in 1993 by Keith Hilken after he had trained at a number of German breweries. Heckler produces only Bavarian-style lagers with German ingredients, brewed according to the Reinheitsgebot beer purity law. Hell Doppel Bock, like all Heckler beers, is currently contract-brewed by the Schell Brewery in New Ulm, Minnesota.

Hell Lager

This Bavarian-style lager (4.9%) comes from Heckler of Tahoe City. Made with German ingredients, it complies with the Reinheitsgebot beer purity law.

Helles Gold

This German-style lager (4.5%) is one of a range of German-style beers brewed by Pennsylvania, a pioneer of craft brewing on the East Coast. Set up in 1988 by Thomas Pastorius in the former Eberhardt and Ober brewery in the Deutschtown area of Pittsburgh, the brewery uses imported German plant.

Henry Weinhard's Private Reserve

This medium-gold beer (3.75%) is brewed by the G. Heileman Brewing Company, using Cascade hops. It has a medium body, an inviting hop nose and a well-balanced malt and hop flavour with a light hop finish. Each bottling is numerically identified on the neck of the bottle.

Hickory Switch Smoked Amber Ale

This ale (4.4%) is brewed using cold-smoked malt by Otter Creek in Middlebury, Vermont. It has a beautiful chestnut colour, a delicate smoky aroma and smoked-malt taste.

Honey Double Mai Bock

A golden, refreshing, strong German-style bock (7%) with a tall white head and a blend of sweet malt and tangy hops. It is traditionally brewed to be served in May, hence the name, but Stoudt's Brewing makes it available year-round.

Honeyweizen

Brewed with local honey in Washington State, this unpasteurized beer (5%) is produced by Kemper.

Hudy

This range of beers is produced by the Hudepohl-Schoenling brewery, formed in 1986 by the merger of Cincinnati's last two breweries in a city once famous for its brewers.

Iron City Lager

This lager from the Pittsburgh Brewing Company in Pennsylvania attracts strong local loyalty, despite the fact that it is a very bland American-style lager, in the same vein as Budweiser.

Jax Lager

This golden lager is produced by the Pearl brewery, the Texas rival to Lone Star, based in San Antonio.

Jax Pilsner

This light, refreshing yellow-gold Pilsner is a good thirst-quenching hot-weather drink. It has a pleasant malt nose, a mild but slightly sweet malt and hop flavour and a lot of carbonation. It is brewed by Pearl in San Antonio, Texas – now part of the S & P Company Brewing Group.

Jazz Amber Light

This amber-coloured, light beer (3.2%) is brewed in New Orleans by Dixie.

Jubelale

A mahogany, strong ale (6%) with a tan head, a fruity malt aroma and a roasted-malt, fruit and hops flavour. It is brewed by Deschute's, using an unfiltered, cold-conditioned technique.

Kilsch Lager

A striking German-style Pilsner (6.5%) with a cloudy-gold-coloured body, and a white head. It has a hoppy aroma and a sweet, malt entry followed by a long crisp finish. It is brewed by Lakefront brewery,

Latrobe

See Rolling Rock.

Legacy Lager

A bottom-fermented, German-style Pilsner (4.8%) with a deep-gold body, a tall white head, and a malty taste with a hint of butterscotch. It is brewed by Chicago Brewing, the only commercial brewery apart from Miller that is left in the "Windy City".

Legacy Red Ale

A bright, copper-coloured Irish-style red ale (4.9%) from the Chicago Brewing Company. It has a roasted-malt nose, a full-bodied malty entry and a tangy bitter finish.

Leinenkugel

This light, flowery premium beer is popular in Wisconsin where it is brewed by the family-run Leinenkugel Brewery in Chippewa Falls.

Liberty Ale

A strong, hazy bronze American IPA (6%) with a big malty hop nose, a powerful malt flavour with spicy hops, and a grapefruity finish. This is the first American beer to be dry-hopped in modern times. It is one of the best IPAs available.

Little Kings Cream Ale

This cream ale (5.5%) is brewed by Hudenpohl-Schoenling of Cincinnati.

Lone Star

This gold, crisp, light malt lager (3.5%) from the famous Texas brewery (part of Heileman) is regarded as the state's national beer.

Mactarnahan's Scottish Ale

This bright-copper-coloured, malty American pale ale (4.8%) has a fruity flavour with hints of caramel. Brewed by Portland Brewing.

Meister Bräu

A low-budget beer brewed by Miller. It used to sell itself by saying it tasted like Bud, but cost less.

Michelob

Made with a high percentage of two-row barley malt and imported hops, this gold lager has a balanced hop and dry malt flavour, and a medium long finish with a slight hop character. It is named after a town in Czechoslovakia.

Milwaukee's Best

Another cut-rate beer brewed by Miller. Just like Meister Bräu but with different packaging.

Mirror Pond Pale Ale

A deep-gold, unfiltered, cold-conditioned American-style pale ale (5.3%) with a creamy head and a flowery flavour with earthy hints, from Deschute's.

Moondog Ale

A pale-copper-coloured English-bitter-style ale (5%) with a dry, well-hopped flavour. Brewed by the Great Lakes Brewing Company in Cleveland, Ohio.

Moose Brown Ale

Brewed by Shipyard in Portland, Maine, and available on tap at the Great Lost Bear in Portland, this brown ale has a faint hop and malt nose, and a strong malt flavour balanced with a dry hop aftertaste.

Muenchener Amber

This ale, based on a turn-of-the-century recipe, is one of Anheuser-Busch's speciality American Originals beers.

Mystic Seaport Pale

This English-style pale ale (4.8%) from the Shipyard brewery in Portland, Maine, is bright-amber with a beige head. It has a perfumey, earthy nose, a fruity entry and a dry finish.

Northwoods Lager

This Germanic lager is brewed by the family-run Leinenkugel lager brewery in Wisconsin.

Obsidian Stout

This dark-brown, ruby-tinted, potent stout (6.9%) is brewed by Deschute's using an unfiltered, cold-conditioning method. It has a fresh, full-bodied malty flavour with a dry, roasty finish.

Oktoberfest

This strong, Bavarian-style lager (6%) comes from Heckler of Tahoe City. It is brewed with German ingredients and complies with the beer purity law.

Old Bawdy Barley Wine

A golden, oak-aged barley wine (9.9%) brewed by Pike Place brewery using peated distillers malt, which gives a smoky edge to the taste.

Old Crustacean

A cloudy, copper-coloured, strong, hoppy beer (10.2%) with a creamy head. It has a rich malt and apricot nose, a sweet caramel and roasted-malt entry, followed by fruit and scorched malt. It is one of the most complex and interesting beers available and is brewed by the Rogue micro-brewery, founded in Newport, Oregon, in 1988.

Old Foghorn

A deep-copper barley-wine-style ale (8.7%) with a creamy tan head, a hoppy, malty nose and a taste of fruit, hops and roasted malt. It is Anchor's strongest beer.

Old Knucklehead

A dark-copper ale with a sweet, roasted-malt nose, a malty, bitter-sweet taste and a long warm finish. This ale is produced by the Oregon micro-brewery Bridgeport, and is served in cask-conditioned form in the brewery bar.

Old Milwaukee

A range of lagers from the Stroh Brewery, Detroit. It includes a standard pale-gold Old Milwaukee Beer with a good malt flavour (3.6%), a pale, yellow-gold, clean-tasting Premium Light Beer, the highly carbonated, golden Genuine Draft and a deep-gold, strong Ice Beer.

Old No. 38 Stout

This award-winning stout (5.6%), named after a steam engine, is brewed by North Coast. It is very dark black, with a ruby hue and a dense brown head. The nose is of roasted malt and barley, and it has a rich barley flavour with a bitter, burnt, malt flavour.

Old Rasputin Russian Imperial Stout

A dark, reddish-brown, rich, intense stout (7.8%) with a hoppy roasted malt nose, a roasty flavour and a bitter finish. It is brewed by North Coast.

Old Thumper
This is an American version of the English ale (5.7%), brewed in Portland, Maine, by Shipyard.

Oregon Honey Beer
A pale-gold honey beer (4%) with a gentle, earthy aroma of hops and a malty flavour, from the Portland brewery.

Pearl Lager
This golden lager is produced by the Pearl brewery, the Texas rival to Lone Star, based in San Antonio.

Pennsylvania Dark
This German-style, deep-ruby-brown lager (5%) has a delicious roasted taste with hoppy notes.

Pennsylvania Oktoberfest
A German-style lager (6%) brewed by Pennsylvania.

Pennsylvania Pilsner
This clear-gold, sweet, malty, lightly-hopped German-style lager (5%) is one of a range of German-style beers brewed by Pennsylvania in the Deutschtown area of Pittsburgh, using imported German plant.

Perfect Porter
This rich, dark Scottish-style porter (4%) is brewed by Bert Grant of Yakima.

Pete's Wicked Winter Brew
A delicious, red-amber ale (4.2%) with hints of nutmeg and raspberry in its flavour. It is one of the wide range of speciality brews from Pete's Brewing Company.

Pike Pale Ale
The bold Pale Ale (4.5%) is the best-known brew from the Seattle Pike brewery founded by famous "Marchand du Vin" beer importer Charles Finkel in 1989. Pike also brews a 5X Stout, an IPA and a lusty, oak-aged Old Bawdy Barley Wine. In 1996, Pike opened a new brewery with a pub attached.

Pike XXX
A dense, black stout (6.2%) with a creamy dark-brown head and a malt and coffee nose. The flavour starts off sweet and is then followed by a strong coffee flavour and a bitter, burnt, hoppy finish. This excellent stout has a rich, creamy body and texture.

Pintail
This ale is produced by the Oregon micro-brewery in Bridgeport, and is available in cask-conditioned form in the brewery bar.

Point Special
This better-than-average American lager is brewed at the Wisconsin Point brewery founded in 1857 at Stevens Point.

Portland Ale
This malty ale (5%) was the first beer to be produced by the Portland brewery when it opened in Oregon in 1986. The brewery has two pubs in Portland.

Pottsville Porter
This bottom-fermented, dark porter is produced by America's oldest brewery, Yuengling.

Premium Verum
This malty lager is the most notable beer brewed by the Kentucky brewery, Oldenburg. The Fort Mitchell brewery is famed for its occasional weekend beer camps, when visitors taste the brews, tour the brewery and visit the neighbouring American Museum of Brewing History.

Pullman Pale Ale
This pale ale (5.9%) comes from the Californian Riverside brewery set up in Riverside in 1993.

Pumpkin Ale
This beer is made using huge, home-grown pumpkins and is spiced with cinnamon, nutmeg and cloves. It is another delicious and interesting beer from Bill Owens.

Raincross Cream Ale
This mellow pale ale (5.9%) is produced by the Californian Riverside brewery, which was set up in Riverside in 1993.

Rainier Ale
The fruity Rainier Ale was a much sought-after beer in the years before the micro-brewery revolution hit the north-west.

The ale was known as "The Green Death" owing to the colour of its label and high alcohol strength. It is produced by the Rainier brewery.

Red Bull
A strong, golden, malt-liquor brand (7.1%) produced by Stroh in Detroit for the Canadian market.

Red Hook ESB

This deep-amber, strong extra-special bitter (5.4%) comes from the ground-breaking Red Hook brewery founded in 1981 by Paul Shipman and Gordon Bowker in the Ballard area of Seattle.

Red Hook Rye

This golden, unfiltered beer (5%) with a dry grainy flavour is brewed by Red Hook. Red Hook has embarked on a series of expansions and is rapidly becoming a national brewer.

Red Sky Ale

This amber-coloured, complex, strong ale (5.6%) is produced by St Stan's brewery, whose other beers tend to be German-style alts.

Red Tail Ale

This hazy, copper-coloured, strong English-style ale (6.5%) is brewed by Mendocino.

Riverwest Stein Beer

A striking, bright-copper Märzenbier (6.5%) with a delicate beige head, a buttery caramel nose and a caramel flavour with hints of scorched smoke.

Roggen Rye

This golden, unfiltered, unpasteurized rye beer (5%) is brewed by Thomas Kemper, using flaked grain and pale barley malt.

Rogue-n-Berry

Marionberries are used to flavour this beer from the Rogue micro-brewery.

Rolling Rock

This lager brand revived the fortunes of the Latrobe brewery of Pennsylvania, founded in 1893. The light lager stands out from the crowd due to the fired-on label on its green bottles.

Ruedrich's Red Seal Ale

This rich, amber-coloured, award-winning beer, brewed by North Coast Brewing Company, is the epitome of a good American ale. It is a pleasant combination of hoppy dryness and malty flavours with fruity notes.

Samuel Adams Boston Lager

This bright-amber Pilsner has a fresh, hoppy nose, a sweet-malt entry, a caramel flavour and a dry, malty finish. It is brewed by Boston Beer Company.

Samuel Adams Boston Stock Ale

This bright-amber ale (5%) has a complex, earthy nose and a hoppy, off-dry palate. It is brewed by Boston Beer Company.

Schaefer Beer

A light-gold lager, produced by the Schaefer Brewing company in Detroit and promoted as the US's oldest lager beer.

Schlitz

A range of beers from the Stroh brewing company. Schlitz beer is the standard pale-gold lager; there is also a Light Beer, a Malt Liquor, a Draught and an Ice Beer.

Schmaltz's Alt

This strong, dark alt (6%) is brewed by the family-owned Schell brewery in New Ulm, Minnesota.

Scrimshaw Pilsner

Brewed by North Coast, this well-balanced lager (4.4%) has a sweet, malty entry and a crisp finish.

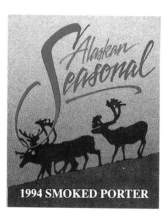

Seasonal Smoked Porter

The distinctive, intense taste of Alaskan's award-winning annual porter (6.4%) comes from using malt kilned over alder wood in the local fish smokehouse.

Shakespeare's Stout

An ebony-coloured export stout (6.1%) with a creamy, dark-brown head. Shakespeare has a complex hoppy, chocolatey, smoky, malt nose and a bittersweet, fruity flavour with a dry, burnt, bitter finish.

Shea's Irish Amber

This traditional East-Coast ale is brewed by Genesee in Rochester, New York.

Shiner Bock

This dark, amber bock (4.4%) is brewed by a small local brewery in Shiner, Texas, called Spoetzl, founded in 1909.

Shipyard Export

This export beer (5.1%) comes from Portland's Shipyard brewery.

Signature

See Stroh's.

Snow Goose

This complex old ale (6.4%) is brewed by the Wild Goose micro-brewery in Maryland. It has a beautiful dark-copper, orangey colour, a pungent, hoppy nose and a caramelized malt flavour, followed by a long, bitter, malty finish.

Stegmaier

Stegmaier lager and porter are the best-known brews from the Lion brewery in Wilkes-Barre, Pennsylvania.

Stoney's Lager

This light lager is produced by the small regional Jones Brewing in Smithton, Pennsylvania.

Stoudt's Festbier

A copper-coloured Märzenbier (5.1%) from the Stoudt brewery in Adamstown, Pennsylvania, which complies with the German Reinheitsgebot beer purity law. Festbier has a beautiful head, a roasted malt nose and a caramel finish.

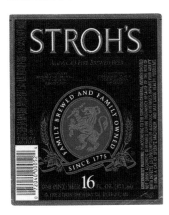

Stroh's

This lager is one of the ranges of beers from the Stroh brewing company. It includes a copper-amber bock, a Light Beer (3.1%), a standard American Beer and Signature lager.

Tabernash

This small Denver micro-brewery produces a range of four beers. The golden Weiss is a top-fermenting German-style wheat beer with a spicy, fruity flavour. It is bottle-conditioned. Golden is a light-gold, hoppy Pilsner.

Munich is a deep-brown, rich, malty, Bavarian-style dunkel, brewed using six different malts in the mash. Amber claims to be a traditional ale brewed according to 19th-century methods to produce a deep-amber ale with a light, crisp lager finish.

Triple Bock

This heavyweight beer (17.5%) is brewed at the Bronco Winery in Ceres, California, using a champagne yeast, primed with maple syrup and matured for three months in former Tennessee whisky casks. It is the most powerful of the contract beers from the Boston Beer Company.

Turbo Dog

This is Abita's deep, ruby-amber, strong, darkish, dry-hopped beer (4.9%) with a roasted-malt flavour and long, dry aftertaste.

Twelve Horse Ale

This bright-gold, refreshing lager (3.8%) with a dry hops finish, is brewed by Genesee in Rochester, New York.

Victoria Avenue Amber Ale

A dark, scarlet-amber ale (5.8%) with a tan-coloured head, from Riverside. It has a malty nose with hints of fruit, a sweet malt and caramel palate and a slightly bitter, malty finish.

Wassail Winter Ale

Brewed by Full Sail, this strong winter warmer (6.5%) is a hazy, dark-amber ale with a fruity nose and a complex malt flavour with a bitter, tangy finish.

Weizen Berry

This rosy-gold, unfiltered, unpasteurized fruit and wheat beer (5%) has a raspberry nose and a malty raspberry flavour. It is brewed by the Thomas Kemper Brewing company in Poulsbo, Washington.

Wheat Berry Brew

This malty beer (4.5%) is made from local Oregon marionberries. It is brewed by Portland.

7th Street Stout

This potent, ruby-black, rich stout (6%) is brewed by Riverside Brewing in Riverside, California. It has a rich, malty aroma and a burnt, bitter, malt, full-bodied flavour.

Above: Customers outside the Second Class Saloon in Alaska, 1899, which was owned by Wyatt Earp during the Gold Rush.

THE BREWERS

Abita

Set up in 1986 at Abita Springs near New Orleans, Louisiana's first new brewery produces sweetish, malty European-style beers.

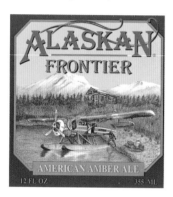

Alaskan

This highly regarded brewery was established in the Alaskan capital of Juneau in 1986. Its rich beers have won many awards.

Anchor

See panel right.

Anderson Valley

The Californian brewery at the Buckhorn Saloon in Boonville has been famous for its richly flavoured beers since 1987.

Anheuser-Busch

The undisputed giant of the American brewing industry has 12 breweries and 44% of the US beer market. In 1995 it sold 87.5 million barrels, nearly double that of its nearest rival, Miller. Its leading brand Budweiser is the biggest-selling beer in the world, brewed in eight overseas countries and exported to more than 70.

Anheuser-Busch is a family company. The story started in 1860 when German immigrant Eberhard Anheuser (1805-80) bought a failed brewery in St Louis, Missouri. His energetic son-in-law Adolphus Busch (1839–1913) turned it into a national success. Busch used the new rail system to introduce the first fleet of refrigerated wagons, he pioneered the use of pasteurization and in 1876 launched the first national beer brand, Budweiser. Twenty years later he added a premium brew, Michelob. Sales reached a million barrels by 1901.

During Prohibition the company brewed the non-alcoholic Bevo. After the Second World War, sales soared, with eight regional breweries built to meet demand.

The original brewery in St Louis is now a tourist attraction and houses the company's Clydesdale horses.

Besides Budweiser and Michelob, the company brews about 30 beers. In response to the micro-brewery movement Anheuser-Busch has introduced its own speciality beers.

Boston Beer Company

The Boston Beer Company has its beers produced to order by other breweries in Pennsylvania, New York and Oregon. Formed in 1985, ten years later the company was the ninth-largest US brewer, with sales of a million barrels per year. The brews are named after Samuel Adams, one of the organizers of the Boston Tea Party of 1773. Jim Koch revived his ancestors' brewing recipes with his Boston Lager and now produces a wide range of beers. The Boston Beer Company also has its own small brewery.

Catamount

A small brewery started in White River Junction, Vermont, in 1985 by Steve Mason, who had trained in England. He named his new enterprise after the cougar or mountain cat – catamount.

Celis

See panel opposite.

ANCHOR

Anchor is the guiding light of the new brewery revolution in North America. When Fritz Maytag, the heir to a washing-machine empire, bought a bankrupt brewery in San Francisco in 1965, his main aim was to preserve a piece of Californian history. The Anchor brewery, founded in 1896, used a unique American method of brewing perfected in the California Gold Rush days when no refrigeration was available. Very shallow fermenters cooled the brew, producing a cross between a lager and an ale. Maytag maintained this tradition and his Anchor Steam Beer (5%) gained a national reputation. It helped inspire the new brewery movement by showing that quality beers of character had a market in America. Maytag has since added a range of other brews, including Liberty Ale (6.1%), Anchor Porter (6.3%) and Old Foghorn (8.7%).

In 1989, Maytag extended his exploration into beers from the past by making a brew using an ancient Sumerian recipe.

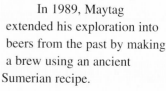

CELIS

The Celis story is one of the most remarkable in the world of beer. Pierre Celis started not one but two pioneering breweries – each on a different continent.

Born in Belgium, Celis grew up next to a brewery. When the local "white" wheat-beer style disappeared, he decided to revive it, setting up the De Kluis (the Cloister) brewery in Hoegaarden in 1966. Its refreshing, spicy Hoegaarden beer proved so popular that, after expanding the brewery a number of times, he sold up to Belgium's largest brewer Interbrew in 1989. He had revived a beer style that was widely copied in his home country.

Hoegaarden had also been successful as an export to the United States. Celis decided to cross the Atlantic, and in 1992, he opened the Celis Brewery in Austin, Texas, to brew his Belgian-style wheat beer now called Celis White. It too proved a huge success and was soon copied by others.

History also repeated itself in another way. In 1995, Celis sold a controlling interest to American brewing giant Miller. In 1996 the company doubled capacity. The Celis brewery also brews other Belgian-style beers, including Celis Raspberry (5%), a richer Grand Cru (8.7%), a Pilsner Celis Golden (5%) and a Pale Bock (5%).

Coors

Coors boasts the biggest single brewery in the world, filling the town of Golden, near Denver, Colorado. The plant is capable of brewing 20 million barrels a year. The US's third-largest brewing company has just one other brewery at Memphis, Tennessee.

A family firm founded by Adolph Coors in 1873, Coors was an unremarkable regional brewery until its Banquet Beer developed a cult following in the 1960s, spurred on by its fresh Rocky Mountain water image. Now Coors Light is its flagship brand. A slightly more malty Extra Gold is brewed under licence by Scottish Courage in England. Coors is noted for its refusal to pasteurize its beers, only chilling and micro-filtering them. Its most distinctive beer is its annual Winterfest. Coors also pioneered the first red ale, George Killian's, which was introduced back in 1978. The brewery launched a range of speciality beers under the Blue Moon name in 1995.

Dixie

This legendary New Orleans brewery was founded in 1907. It still ages its "slow-brewed" beers in cypress wood vessels. Its main beers are the malty Dixie (4.5%) and Jazz Amber Light. It also brews the notorious dark beer, Blackened Voodoo.

Dock Street

An innovative restaurant brewery in Philadelphia, which produces a wide range of beers such as a ginger wheat and a juniper rye. Its bottled beers – notably Dock Street Amber (5.3%), Dock Street Bohemian Pilsner (5.3%) and Dock Street Illuminator (7.5%) – are contract-brewed by F.X. Matt of Utica, New York, for the Dock Street restaurant in Philadelphia.

Frankenmuth

The Michigan town of Frankenmuth was founded in 1845 by Bavarian immigrants from Franconia, in Germany, the world's most brewery-packed region. Inevitably, the town built its own brewery, dating back to 1862. In 1987, the Frankenmuth brewery was rebuilt. Its German-style beers include Frankenmuth Dark (5.2%), Pilsner (5.2%), Old Detroit Amber (5.9%) and Bock (6.4%).

Full Sail

Founded in 1987 at the windsurfing centre of Hood River, Oregon, this brewery's fruity ales have grown in popularity on the West Coast. Bottled beers include Golden (4.4%), Amber (5.9%) and Nut Brown, as well as a range of seasonal beers.

Geary's

New England's first micro-brewery opened in Portland, Maine, in 1986. Its founder David Geary had worked in various Scottish and English breweries and the influence is obvious in the beers.

The flagship beer is Geary's Pale Ale (4.5%), but the brewery also produces a dark Geary's London Porter (4.2%), Geary's American Ale (4.8%) and a warming winter Hampshire Special.

Genesee

The largest independent regional brewery in the US was founded in Rochester, New York, in 1878. It still follows the north-eastern tradition of ale brewing, notably with the soft, sweetish Twelve Horse Ale, Cream Ale and Shea's Irish Amber. It also produces an occasional Genny Bock and other speciality beers such as Dundee's Honey Brown Lager.

Great Lakes

This extensive range of widely acclaimed beers has poured from Cleveland's first micro-brewery, which was set up in an old saloon in Ohio in 1988. The range of beers includes Moon Dog Ale, Dortmunder Gold, a Vienna-style lager Eliot Ness, a Porter (5.9%) and a Great Lakes' IPA (6.9%).

Harpoon

The Mass Bay brewery has been brewing Harpoon ales in Boston since 1987, notably a Harpoon Ale, Light, Pilsner, IPA and Stout. Its bottled beers are contract brewed by F.X. Matt of Utica, New York.

Heileman

The fifth-largest brewing company in the US is based in La Crosse, Wisconsin, where it is known for its Heileman Old Style and Special Export lagers. This brewpub in Davis, California, has been operating close to the university brewing school since 1990. It is known for its extensive range of German-style lagers, including a Hübsch Hefe-Weizen (5%), Märzen (5.5%) and Doppelbock (7.5%).

Matt

F.X. Matt has been brewing in Utica in upstate New York since 1888, originally as the West End brewery. Now it mainly contract-brews speciality beers for other companies. The first was New Amsterdam in 1982. In 1985, the firm also introduced its own successful Saranac range of beers including Adirondack Amber, Pale Ale, Golden (5.2%) and Black and Tan.

Mendocino

Mendocino is one of the standard-bearers of the new brewery revolution in the United States. In 1983 it was California's first brewpub, opened in an old saloon. The brewery in Mendocino County now brews a wide range of excellent English-style ales.

Miller

The second-largest brewer in the United States, Miller has more than a fifth of the beer market and runs the five main brewing plants. Founded in 1855 when German immigrant Frederick Miller bought a small brewery in Milwaukee, the company was taken over by tobacco giant Philip Morris in 1970. Miller Lite, which was launched in 1975, created a huge new market for low-calorie beers. In little more than ten years, production soared from around five million barrels to more than 40 million per year.

Its other high-profile brand is bottled Genuine Draft, launched in 1986 using a special cold-filtered process, which means that the beer does not need to be pasteurized. The oldest brand Miller High Life, is now part of Miller's popularly priced range, which also includes Miller Meister Bräu and Milwaukee's Best. In addition, Miller brews a non-alcoholic beer called Sharp's and a Magnum Malt Liquor.

The Miller company has responded to competition from the fast-growing speciality beer market in a number of ways. In 1990 it introduced a range of all-barley beers under the Miller Reserve brand name, including an Amber Ale. It also markets various brands under the company's original name, Plank Road Brewery. In addition, Miller has also directly taken over smaller breweries. In 1988, for example, it bought the old Leinenkugel brewery of Wisconsin, which still sells its lager under the Leinenkugel name. In 1995 Miller bought a majority interest in the successful Celis Brewery of Texas and Shipyard of Maine.

New Amsterdam

The original contract brewer, New Amsterdam was founded in New York in 1982 by Matthew Reich. He contracted established brewer F.X. Matt of Utica to brew his New Amsterdam beers, selling them as if from a micro. New Amsterdam's best-known beers are its Ale and Amber.

New Glarus

This Wisconsin village brewery was set up in 1993 by a former Budweiser brewer who trained in Germany. In 1996 it revived a famous old Californian brand – Acme Pale Ale. It specializes in European lagers, notably Edel-Pils, Wisconsin Bock and Weiss.

Pabst

The US's sixth largest brewery, Pabst, is best-known for Pabst Blue Ribbon lager, "the working man's beer". Founded in Milwaukee in 1844 as Best Brewing, Frederick Pabst married into the Best family, rapidly expanded sales and in 1889 the company's name was changed to Pabst. After being recognized as America's Best Lager at the World Exposition in 1893, Pabst began fixing blue ribbons to its bottles, giving their flagship beer its name.

Below: A gleaming copper in the modern Pyramid micro-brewery.

Pete's

Home-brew enthusiast Pete Slosberg has been marketing his Pete's Wicked Ale with wicked success since 1986. Contract brewed in St Paul, Minnesota, nine other speciality beers have since joined the original chestnut ale (5.1%) including Pete's Bohemian Pilsner and Pete's Amber (both 4.9%) and summer and winter brews.

TOP TEN BREWERS

This table shows the largest brewers, with their market share and number of barrels sold in 1995. Although the top three brewers account for 77% of the market, their grip is slipping – the previous year they controlled 81%. The new speciality brewers are creating a more diverse market, with one of them, the Boston Beer Company (Samuel Adams) becoming the ninth-largest US brewer.

BREWER	MARKET SHARE	NO. OF BARRELS
1 Anheuser-Busch	44.1%	87.5 million
2 Miller	22.7%	45.0 million
3 Coors	10.2%	20.3 million
4 Stroh's	5.4%	10.8 million
5 Heileman	4.0%	7.9 million
6 Pabst	3.2%	6.3 million
7 Genesee	0.9%	1.8 million
8 Latrobe	0.6%	1.2 million
9 Boston	0.5%	1.0 million
10 Pittsburgh	0.5%	0.9 million

Plank Road Brewery

This was the original name of the Miller brewing giant. It now markets various beers under this brand name, including Icehouse and Red Dog.

new venture in the United States. Pyramid ales include Pyramid Pale Ale, Pyramid Wheaten Ale, Pyramid Best Brown and Pyramid Rye (all 5.1%). It also brews a range of seasonal brews including Porter (5.4%) and Snow Cap (6.9%).

Pyramid

One of the success stories of the craft brewery movement, the Pyramid brewery was set up as Hart Brewing in 1984 in the small logging town of Kalama in Washington State, brewing Pyramid Pale Ale. Since then, Pyramid has grown into the third-largest

St Stan's

Inspired by visits to Germany, Garith Helm built a brewery in Modesto, California. St Stan's is best-known for its original unpasteurized Amber Alt.

Schell

This rare midwest regional brewery was founded in 1858 by German immigrant August Schell in New Ulm, Minnesota, and it is still family-owned. It produces pre-Prohibition-quality lagers. The family's elaborate 1858 mansion and beer garden are now a site of national historic importance. Its lagers include an all-malt Schell Pilsner (5.3%), a Schell Weizen (4.4%) using 60% wheat and an Oktoberfest (5.3%).

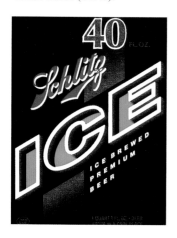

Schlitz

Once one of the best-known breweries – and brands – in the US, "The Beer that made Milwaukee Famous" is no longer brewed in the city since the brewery was taken over by Stroh's in 1982.

Sierra Nevada

One of the leaders of the craft brewery revolution, Sierra Nevada has grown to be the largest in the west. It was founded by keen home-brewers Ken Grossman and Paul Camusi in Chico, California, in 1981. Its flagship beer is the highly acclaimed Sierra Nevada Pale Ale (5.5%). It also brews a Sierra Nevada Porter (5.9%) and Sierra Nevada Stout (6%).

Sprecher

The former Pabst brewer Randall Sprecher revived the German brewing arts that Milwaukee had largely forgotten when he set up his own brewery in the town in 1985. His robust beers include an all-malt Sprecher Special Amber, Sprecher Black Bavarian (6%) and an unfiltered Sprecher Hefe-Weiss. He also brews an occasional Sprecher Irish Stout (6%).

Stoudt's

The first American micro-brewery to be designed and developed by a woman, Carol Stoudt's German-style beers have won about 20 medals at the Great American Beer Festival since she set up her brewery in Adamstown, Pennsylvania, in 1987. Her beers, brewed to the Reinheitsgebot beer purity law, include Stoudt's Gold Dortmunder (5%). In addition, she brews two Belgian Abbey ales, plus English-style ales and stout.

Straub

This small, long-established, family-owned brewery in rural Pennsylvania at St Mary's produces a light Straub Beer.

Stroh's

The US's fourth-largest brewing company was originally founded in 1850 in Detroit. Bernhard Stroh emigrated to America from Germany in 1849 where his family had started brewing in the late 1700s at Kirn. The next year he started a small brewhouse in Detroit, and five generations of the Stroh family have run the brewery ever since. During Prohibition, the company continued to operate producing "near" beers and

alternative products made from brewing ingredients, including a popular malt extract that was a favourite of local home-brewers. Recently the company has expanded with a series of acquisitions, culminating in the takeover of the Heileman Brewing Company of Wisconsin in 1996. A number of the Stroh beers are advertised as being "fire-brewed", meaning that direct heat on the coppers is used to boil the wort, a process that was started by Julius Stroh in the early 1900s. The best-known brands are Stroh's Lager and Signature. The company also produces maltier German-style beers under the Augsburger name and has recently developed a number of low-alcohol beers, especially Stroh's Non-Alcoholic beer.

Summit

This midwest brewery was opened by Mark Stutrud in 1986 in St Paul, Minnesota, and has steadily grown in size and reputation. Best known for its Extra Pale Ale and IPA, it also brews seasonal German-style beers including a Hefe Weizen and a Düsseldorfer Alt (4.9%).

Tabernash

This micro-brewery in Denver, Colorado, concentrates on brewing German-style beers, such as its malt-accented dark Munich lager and an unfiltered Bavarian-style wheat beer, Tabernash Weiss.

Thomas Kemper

Thomas Kemper was founded in Washington State in 1985 specifically to brew German-style lagers, soon establishing itself near the coastal town of Poulsbo. In 1992 it merged with another north-west brewer, Pyramid Ales. It produces a range of unpasteurized beers. Seasonals include a Belgian White (4.4%) and Maibock (6.5%). See also Pyramid.

Twenty Tank

The Twenty Tank brewpub opened in a former sheet metal shop in 1990 in the heart of San Francisco's SOMA club district. The brew-kettle and mash vessels are in plain view for customers in the bar and restaurant. It offers a wide variety of house-brewed ales.

Widmer

North America's first modern Hefeweizen, a cloudy draught beer, surprised drinkers when it was launched by the Widmer brothers, Kurt and Rob, in Portland, Oregon, in 1986. The Widmer brewery uses a top-fermenting German alt yeast, and its original beer was a rich-copper-coloured alt. There is an unfiltered Hefeweizen available, and the brothers also brew an Amber, Blackbier and a fruity Widberry.

Wild Goose

One of the first micro-breweries in the mid-Atlantic states was founded in Cambridge, Maryland, in 1989. It brews a range of English-style ales, including Wild Goose Amber (5%) and IPA (5.3%).

Yakima

The Yakima Brewing Company was set up in 1982 in the heart of the hop-growing area in Washington State by Bert Grant, an engaging ale pioneer who opened the first modern brewpub in the US. Grant was an experienced brewing chemist. In 1982 he branched out on his own to brew better-quality beers, starting with the Yakima brewpub. He built a larger commercial brewery in 1991. Many of the beers produced by Yakima reflect his Scottish ancestry.

Yuengling

The oldest brewery still operating in the United States was founded in 1829 in Pottsville, Pennsylvania, where deep cellars were dug into the hillside to keep the beer cool during maturation. Still family-run, it is best known for its bottom-fermented Pottsville Porter and Chesterfield Ale, which are now enjoying renewed sales with the revival of interest in specialist beers. Yuengling also brews a Premium and Traditional Lager and a blended lager-porter called Black and Tan.

Zip City

This sophisticated New York brewpub and restaurant was established in the former headquarters of the National Temperance Society in Manhattan. It brews mainly unfiltered German-style lagers, including a Märzen and a Dunkel, to accompany its gourmet food.

Below: At the beginning of Prohibition in the US government agents closed down hundred of saloons.

LATIN AMERICA

Now best known for light, thin lager drunk straight from the bottle with a wedge of lime, Central and South American beer has a much richer tradition than is widely appreciated.

THE MAYANS were brewing beer from fermented corn stalks long before Spanish conquistadors made their mark. Meanwhile, in northern Mexico, the Aztecs enjoyed a fermented drink made with sprouted maize. Even after the conquest, peasants in isolated areas remained loyal to pulque, a drink brewed with the juice of the agave plant. It keeps for just a day or two (the name means "decomposed") and can still be found today, along with other indigenous drinks. An Inca legend claims that specially chosen maidens would chew cooked maize to a pulp to prepare it for brewing – their beauty and the purity of saliva were considered an aid to fermentation.

The Spanish conquistadors set up small breweries – cervecería – across the continent from the 16th century onwards. Beer came a poor second to distilled spirits, such as mescal or tequila, however, until Bavarian, Swiss and Austrian brewers introduced lager to Mexico in the 19th century, and ice-making machines arrived on the continent.

During Prohibition, which devastated the North American brewing industry from 1919 to 1933, the sleepy Mexican town of Tijuana became an outpost of alcohol tourism for thirsty Americans. As a result, at one point there were 75 bars on its 200m (600ft) main street.

Mexico remains the leading beer producer in Latin America. Its two biggest breweries, Cervecería Modelo and Cervecería Moctezuma, dominate the home market. Brazil, which was colonized by the Portuguese rather than the Spanish, and has a brewing tradition that looks to Germany, is the second-largest producer. Brazil also produces a traditional black (negra) beer. Lagers are the popular drink of choice in Latin America, with most brewers offering a Pilsner. Light, cheap and cheerful lagers made using rice, corn or other adjuncts in the mash are widely available, although other, more eclectic and traditional brews can also be found.

Above: Dos Equis, "Two Crosses", is a rich, dark, high-quality lager brewed in Mexico which has proved popular in many export markets.

THE BEERS

Africana

This rich, dark lager (5.5%) is a cross between a Munich-style dunkel and a Vienna Red, brewed with hops, rice and maize. It has an aroma of roast malt, a smooth chocolate taste and a hoppy aftertaste. It is brewed by Argentina's Bieckhart brewery in Buenos Aires.

Ancla

Columbia's Ancla brewery offers a range of all-malt beers. These include Cerveza Ancla which is made with German and Canadian hops and matured for four weeks, Ancla Premium (4.8%) and the amber-coloured Ancla Roja (4.1%). Ancla also offers the all-malt Naval Super Premium (4.8%) and an all-malt, alcohol-free beer.

Antarctica Pilsen

This Brazilian beer, the eighth most popular beer in the region, is gold-coloured and highly carbonated, with a strong hop aftertaste.

Bavaria Gold Beer

Golden-coloured and unremarkable, this fruity, slightly malty lager-style beer (3.5–5%) is brewed by Cervecería Costa Rica S.A.

Belikin Beer

The malty, golden, dryish lager (3.5–5%), from the Belize Brewing Company in Ladyville, is a pleasant, fizzy beer, best served cold.

Belikin Stout

A strong, dark-brown, faintly hoppy, rich stout (6–7.5%) with a sweet, malty aroma from the Belize Brewing Company.

Biekhart Cerveza Pilsen

A malty Pilsner-style lager (4.8%), made using pale malt from Argentinian barley, rice, maize and American Cascade hops. It is brewed by the Argentinian Biekhart brewery.

Biekhart Especial

This golden premium lager (5%) is more aromatic and fully flavoured than its sister brand, Cerveza Pilsen, from the Biekhart brewery.

Bohemia

This superior, strong lager (5.4%) from Cuauhtémoc in Mexico is made with Saaz hops, to give it a malty, full-bodied taste with a hint of vanilla. In 1995, Bohemia was the most popular beer in Mexico.

Brahma Chopp Export

From Brazil's Companhia Cervejaría, this yellow-gold, malty, slightly sour beer was the fourth-best-selling beer in South America in 1996.

Brahma Pilsner

This quality, hoppy Pilsner (5%) from Brazil's Companhia Cervejaría, based in Rio de Janeiro, has a rich malty, bittersweet taste with a hint of vanilla.

Corona Extra

Corona Extra (4.6%) is a lager made with about 40% rice and a relatively low proportion of hops. Cheap to make and refreshing when served very cold, this beer was designed for the taste-buds of the Mexican working man, and is served in a distinctive clear bottle. It was taken up eagerly by American tourists, who took to drinking it with lime, much to the amusement of the Mexicans, although the lime and lager fashion is now taking off in Mexico as well. Corona is the best-known brew from the Modelo brewery of Mexico City, one of the country's two major brewing companies. It is now widely exported and is a familiar designer beer which can be found in the bars of many of the European capital cities.

Cuzco

This very pale, yellow-gold, fizzy, malty, Pilsner-style lager (5%) is brewed using 100% barley by the Compañia del Sur del Perú S.A. It takes its name from the ancient Inca city in the high Andes of Peru.

Mexico's malty legacy

One of the few legacies of the Austrian Emperor Maximilian's short and inglorious reign over Mexico between 1864 and 1867 is a strongly Germanic influence on that country's brewing industry. The malty, dark-amber beers of Vienna may be hard to find in Austria today, but the old style is still very popular in the former colony.

Dos Equis

Dos Equis ("Two Crosses") is a rich, dark-red, high-quality, Vienna-style lager (4.8%) with a fruity, chocolatey taste. Brewed in Mexico by Moctezuma, it has also proved popular in export markets.

Kaiser Bock

Introduced by Cervejarías Kaiser in 1994 as a cold-weather drink, this amber-coloured, pasteurized beer was the first bock to be produced in Brazil.

Kaiser Gold

This premium pasteurized Pilsner was initially launched as Kaiser Copa 94, to mark Brazil's entry in soccer's World Cup. Due to their success, it was renamed Kaiser Gold in 1995.

BLACK BREW

Black beer was first produced in the parts of the Upper Amazon Basin in the 15th century, using roasted barley and dark-pigmented grains to give its distinctive colour, and lupins for flavour (the lupin is a distant relative of the hop). A modern version, Xingu, is brewed commercially by Cervejaría Cacador in Brazil.

Naval Superpremium

A Brazilian all-malt beer (4.8%) from Ancla.

Negra León

Brown rather than black, León is made by the Yucatán brewery (owned by Modelo) in Mexico. It is chocolatey in taste and quite similar to its sister brew, Negra Modelo.

Negra Modelo

Despite its name, Negra Modelo (Black Model) (5.3%) is more of a deep amber-brown colour. It is a cross between a spicy Vienna red and a softer Munich dunkel, with a chocolate aroma, a hint of fruit and spices, and a hop finish. This classic, first-rate Mexican beer enjoys a justified reputation among beer connoisseurs both at home and abroad.

Peru Gold

A dry, tart and refreshing lager (5%), Peru Gold has a rich corn-and-vanilla aroma. It is brewed by Peru's Cervesur. The bottle label features a memorable Peruvian Indian face mask.

Polar Lager

Venezuela's leading brand is a light, thin lager (5%) that takes the style of Sol and Corona to an extreme. Despite this, it is the second-best-selling beer in South America, where the Polar Brewing Company sells over 12 million hectolitres (264 million gallons) of it each year.

Porter

A rich, top-fermenting, dark beer (8%) from the Companhia Cevejaría of Brazil. Some say it takes its name from Portugal, the country that colonized Brazil, rather than from the beer style.

Sol

In the 1980s, the Moctezuma brewery's Sol succeeded Corona Extra as the fashionable Mexican beer to drink. Sol (4.6%) is a thin, light lager with a high proportion of adjuncts. Like its arch-rival, it is sold in a distinctive, embossed bottle.

Superior

This pale lager (4.5%) from Moctezuma has more hop character than its stablemate Sol.

Tecate

Launched in the 1950s by Cuauhtémoc of Mexico, this pale, light ("clara") lager (4.5%) is low in flavour, but good for satisfying thirst in a hot climate. It was originally served with salt and fresh lemons – a custom that probably inspired the recent craze for drinking Mexican lagers with a slice of lime.

Xingu

This Brazilian black beer (5%) is a modern version of the historic Amazonian drink. It is brewed commercially by Cervejaría Cacador, using hops rather than lupins to add flavour and act as a preservative. Sweet and malty, Xingu, named after a tributary of the Amazon River, is the fourth-best-selling beer in South America.

THE BREWERS

Ancla

Cervecería Ancla S.A. in Columbia produces a range of quality beers made with 100% pure malt, which come in amber glass bottles as well as in cans. The company has positioned itself at the top end of the domestic market and uses the marketing slogan "Por cultura es colombiana". A modernized plant opened in 1996, with a capacity of 1.2 million hectolitres (26 million gallons) per year.

Bieckhart

Cervecería Bieckhart has a range of German-influenced beers, even though its home is in the capital city of the former Spanish colony Argentina, Buenos Aires. It brews a golden lager and the rich, dark lager Africana.

Cardenal

Venezuela's second beer company after Polar is home to a typical Latin American light, thin lager called Andes, as well as a range of interesting Germanic beers,

among them the golden, malty beer, Tipo Munich (in the Munich style) and an authentic-tasting Nacional "Cerveza Tipo Pilsen" (in the Pilsen style).

Cervecería La Constancia

The San Salvador brewery in El Salvador offers a range of bottom-fermented lager beers: Pilsener of El Salvador Export Beer, Suprema Special Beer, Regla Extra, Noche Buena Special Dark Lager and Cabro Extra.

Cervesur (Compañia Cervecera del Sur del Perú S.A.)

Based in southern Peru, Cervesur has been brewing since 1898, when it was founded in Arequipa under the name Sociedad Industrial Ernesto Günther & Francisco Rehder. It adopted its present title in 1926. It brews using Andes water, barley from its malting plant in Cuzco as well as imported barley, malt and hops. Unusually for Latin America, it concentrates on 100% barley beers and does not use adjuncts. Brews include both

Pilsners and dark beers. Export brews are Cusqueña Pilsner and Cuzco Beer, Cusqueña Dark and Cuzco Dark (both 5.6%), as well as Peru Gold. In 1996, it was the first brewery in Latin America to be awarded a quality certificate by TUV Bayern. Cervesur first began exporting beer to Chile in 1978. By 1995, it controlled 17.5% of the beer market in Lima and accounted for 69% of Peru's beer exports.

Companhia Cervejaría

This Brazilian group brews a quality malty Brahma Pilsner, Brahma Chopp, as well as a top-fermenting, extra-strong porter (8%). The company produces more than 31 hectolitres (660 gallons) of beer annually.

Cuauhtémoc

Now merged with Moctezuma, this brewery offers a pale ("clara") lager called Chihuahua (named for the Mexican state) similar to Corona or Sol, as well as Tecate, another "clara" lager, the best-selling beer in Mexico, and the fuller-bodied, malty Bohemia, brewed with Saaz hops.

Kaiser

Kaiser, Brazil's third-largest brewery, was set up in 1983. The first plant was opened in Divinópolis in Minas Gerais State. Today, it has six plants across the country. The brewery is run by specialist technicians, trained by master brewers in Belgium. Beers, available both bottled and on draught, include Kaiser Cerveja and Premium Pilsner. It was the first Brazilian company to develop a bock, in 1994. In

Beer and chilli

Light, cheap lagers like Sol and Corona are reputed to go well with spicy Mexican food, but Mexico's dark and amber lagers are a better match for hot, robust flavours.

1995, it changed its name to KAC (Kaiser Consumer Relations). The company's marketing strategy has fixed it firmly in the minds of Brazilian beer drinkers in just ten years, partly due to the company's distinctive spokesman, "Shorty".

Moctezuma

Since merging with Cuauhtémoc, the Cervecería Moctezuma of Monterey has since overtaken Modelo and has become Mexico's largest brewery. The merged group, which controls seven breweries in the country, is owned by a large holding company called Valores. Moctezuma was founded in 1894 in Orizaba, Veracruz.

Modelo

The Cervecería Modelo of Mexico City is one of Mexico's two brewing giants. Modelo produces its beers at the single largest brewing plant in the country. Beers include the cheap, refreshing Corona Extra and tasty, Vienna-style dark lagers, Dos Equis and Negra Modelo.

Polar Brewing Company

This Venezuelan company is best known for the extremely light and thin Polar lager which is the country's leading lager brand.

Above: Bars in Mexico tend to be an all-male preserve – a place for a quiet drink after a hard day's work.

THE CARIBBEAN

Rum, fermented from locally grown cane sugar, is the region's favourite tipple but, perhaps surprisingly for an area with a warm climate that grows little grain, there is also a strong beer culture, and drinkers show a marked preference for dark stouts and strong lagers.

Above: Carib is a relatively dry lager from Trinidad that bucks the trend for sweet, strong lagers and dark, heavy stouts throughout the Caribbean.

INHABITANTS OF THE CARIBBEAN islands have been producing beer for centuries, using maize to brew a kind of porridge, which was then left to ferment. The recipe and name may vary from island to island (*chicha, izquiate* and *sendecho,* to name a few), but the technique remains the same.

The arrival of European brews and brewers in the 19th century had a great impact on the drinking and brewing habits of the region. Today in the Caribbean, lager is a popular drink and international giants, such as Heineken, brew many conventional Pilsner-style beers. They are often served ice-cold as a thirst-quencher for the beach, as an alternative to rum and coke, or sipped in relaxed island bars, as an accompaniment to seafood. There are also many strong, relatively sweet, full-flavoured lagers available. Jamaica's most popular exported beer, Red Stripe, which is now a familiar sight in the US and the UK, is a classic example of this Caribbean-style golden brew. Another European beer style that has been wholeheartedly taken into the bosom of the Islands is rich, strong, dark stout. Many in these exotic climes believe dark beers to possess aphrodisiac or virility-enhancing qualities. Guinness Stout, the classic of this type, has been brewed here for over 150 years and is now produced under licence at the Central Village Brewery in Spanish Town, Jamaica. Other breweries in Trinidad, Granada and St Vincent produce similar dark brews. These "exotic stouts", as they are often known, are usually brewed with a higher alcohol content than stouts produced in England or Ireland.

At the other end of the scale, but continuing the theme of rich, dark brews, another popular product from many breweries in the Caribbean is a dark drink made from malt extract. It is more of a soft drink than an alcohol-free beer.

THE BEER

Banks Lager Beer
A pale-gold, sweet, malty lager (4.5%) from the Banks brewery in Bridgetown Barbados.

Bohemia Cerveza
A hazy, pale, amber-gold standard lager (5%) brewed in Santo Domingo, Dominican Republic, by the Cervecería Bohemia.

Caribe
A dry, light-flavoured, pale-yellow lager (4.5%) from the Caribe Development Company, Port of Spain, Trinidad.

Corona
A pale, golden-yellow lager (4.5%) from the Cervecería Corona in Puerto Rico.

Dragon Stout
A deep-brown, sweetish, rich, malty stout (7.5%). It is brewed in Kingston, Jamaica, by Desnoes & Geddes. This potent brew is believed by some to aid virility.

Ebony Super Strength
A deep-brown ale (8%) with a high alcohol content that gives it an almost port-like quality, from the Banks brewery in Barbados.

Kalik Gold
A golden, rich, malty lager which is high in alcohol, from the Commonwealth Brewery in the Bahamas.

Red Stripe
A pale-gold, lightly hopped, strong lager (4.7%) with a full flavour, from the family-run Desnoes & Geddes in Kingston, Jamaica. It is now brewed under licence in the UK, where it is a particular favourite with the West Indian population.

Royal Extra Stout
A deep-brown, classic stout with a malty flavour. Brewed by the Caribe Development Company in Port of Spain, Trinidad.

THE BREWERS

Banks (Barbados) Breweries Ltd
This major player in the Caribbean market is also a familiar name on the South American mainland, where it has a brewery in Guyana.

Desnoes & Geddes Ltd
A family-owned firm set up in 1918 in Kingston, Jamaica, by Eugene Desnoes and Thomas Geddes. Heineken now has a small shareholding.

Granada Breweries Limited
This bright idea by the Caribbean Development Company was first registered as a company in 1960, but it wasn't until the 1970s that it really began to thrive.

St Vincent Brewery Ltd
Set up in 1985 on the island of St Vincent, this small brewery produces its own-brand, Hairoun Lager, as well as brewing Guinness and EKU Bavaria under licence.

Salty liquor
In 1994 Granada Breweries unveiled the solution to its problem of water shortages during the dry season. It had drilled its own borehole to tap underground water and installed a desalination plant.

Left: Enjoying a beer and chewing the fat is part of the relaxed Caribbean way of life. Red Stripe is the region's leading lager.

INDEX

ABC Stout, 211
AK, 87
Aass brewery, Norway, 117
Abbaye d'Aulne, 125
   d'Orval brewery, Belgium, 130
   de Bonne Espérance, 125
   de Notre-Dame de Scourmont brewery,
     Belgium, 15, 126, 134
   de Vaucelles, 185
   des Rocs brewery, Belgium, 125, 133
   d'Orval, 133
Abbey St Gallen, 190
Abbot Ale, 87
Abbots Invalid Stout, 213
Abbotsford brewery, Aus., 213
Abita brewery, US, 231, 234, 239, 240
Abro brewery, Sweden, 119
Abstrunk, 147
Achd Bambarcha Schwarzla, 147
Achouffe brewery, Belgium, 130, 133
Ackerland, 185
Acme Pale Ale, 231, 243
Adam Spezial, 163
Adambräu, 163
Adelschoffen brewery, France, 185, 188
Adelscott, 185
Adirondack Amber, 231
Adler, 125
Adlerbräu, 194, 195
Adnams brewery, England, 15, 87, 89, 98, 101
Aecht Schlenkerla Rauchbier, 147
Aegean, 183
Aerts 1900, 130
Affligem, 125
Africana, 247
Agnus Dei, 125
Aguila brewery, Spain, 193, 194, 195
Akasaka Micro-brewery, Japan, 209
Akershus brewery, Norway, 117
Alaskan brewery, US, 234, 240
Albani brewery, Denmark, 113, 114
Alcazar, 195
Alcolsuz Efes, 183
Aldaris brewery, Latvia, 170, 171
Aldchlappie Hotel brewpub, Scotland, 111
Ale of Atholl, 107
Alfa brewery, Netherlands, 139, 141
Alhambra brewery, Spain, 194, 195
Alimony Ale, 231
Alken-Maes brewery, Belgium, 127, 130
Alko, 120
Allbright, 80, 81
Alloa brewery, Scotland, 107, 108, 109, 110
Allsopp brewery, England, 62, 87

Allsopp's White Cap, 198
Alpine Lager, 225
Alt Brunner Gold, 175
   Franken, 147
   Weltzlar, 147
Altenmünster, 145, 149
Altforster Alt, 139
Altmunster Abbey, 144
Amarit, 211
Amazon Bitter, 87
Ambar, 194
   Lager, 195
Amber brewery, Ukraine, 171
   Ale, 139
   Lager, 231
   Pilsner, 170, 171
Amberley, 185
Ambre de Flandres, 185
American Museum of Brewing History, 237
   Originals, 231
Amersfoorts Wit, 139
Ammeroois, 139
Amstel brewery, Netherlands, 139, 141
Anchor Steam brewery, San Francisco, US, 12,
   66, 240
   Beer, 211
   Steam Beer, 231, 240
Ancla, 247
Ancre, 185
Anderson Valley brewery, US, 240
Andes, 249
Angelus, 185
Anheuser, Eberhard, 240
Anheuser-Busch brewery, US, 19, 42, 60, 175,
   178, 231, 232, 233, 236, 240
Animator, 147
Anker brewery, Belgium, 128
   Ale, 191
Anniversary Amber Ale, 225
Annoeullin brewery, France, 187
Ansells brewery, England, 24, 87, 101
Antarctica Pilsen, 247
A Pint-a Bitter, 87
Apollo Brewpub, Denmark, 114
Apostulator, 147
Apple Ale, 229
Apricot Ale, 231
Aqui mineral water, 29
Arcen brewery, Netherlands, 140, 141
Arcener, 139
Archdruid, 81
Archers brewery, England, 87, 88, 91, 101
Arcobräu, 147
Arctic Pils, 117
Arkell Best Bitter, 225
   Kingsdown brewery, England, 93, 94, 96,
     100, 101
Arrols 80/–, 107
Arthur Pendragon, 87
Artois brewery, Belgium, 133
Arundel brewery, England, 87, 95
Asahi brewery, Japan, 60, 206, 207, 208
   Super Dry, 208
Ash Vine brewery, England, 93
Asia Pacific Breweries, 210, 211
Asmara brewery, Eritrea, Africa, 198, 201
   Lager, 198
Astika Lager, 170
Astra, 147
   Pilsner, 158
Athenian Breweries, Greece, 183
Auburn Ale, 231
Augsberger, 231
August, 173
   Schell brewery, US, 234
Augustijn, 125
Augustiner Bräu, 164
   brewery, Austria, 155, 164
   brewery, Germany, 155
Auld Alliance, 107
Autumn Frenzy, 35
Avec les Bons Voeux de la Brasseries, 125
Aventinus, 147
Ayinger brewery, Germany, 147, 148, 149, 154,
   155
   beers, 147

BBH, 169, 171
BGI, 211
B&T brewery, England, 90, 97, 100
BSN (Kronenbourg), 25, 180
Bachelor Bitter, 231
Back und Brau, 190

Backdykes brewery, Scotland, 108
Baderbräu, 231
Badger brewery, England, 101
Badgers Beers, 87
Bailleux brewery, France, 185
Baiyun Beer, 205
Bak, 170
Ballantine's Ale, 231
Ballard Bitter, 231
Ballard's brewery, England, 87, 99, 101, 231
Baltic Beverages Holdings (BBH), 169
Baltijas, 170
Baltika brewery, Russia, 170, 171
Banks Breweries Ltd, Barbados, 251
Banks brewery, England, 87, 95, 105
Banner Bitter, 87
Banquet Beer, 232, 241
Barbara, 191
Barclay Perkins, 173, 198, 201
Barn Owl Bitter, 87
Barraclough Lager, 223
Barrett, Henry, 53
Bass brewery, England, 62, 101
Bateman brewery, England, 97, 99, 100, 101
Batham's brewery, England, 87, 101
Battin brewery, Lux., 145
Battleaxe, 87
Bavaria, 8,6, 139
   brewery, Netherlands, 139, 141
   St Pauli brewery, Germany, 147, 158
Bavarian Gold Beer, 247
Bavik brewery, Belgium, 131, 133
Beacon Bitter, 87
Beamish and Crawford brewery, Ireland, 77
   Red Ale, 75
   Stout, 75
Bear Ale, 107
Beast, 87
Beaumanor Bitter, 87
Beck's brewery, Germany, 147, 155
Beechwood, 87
beer
   adjuncts, 42
   adulterants, 43
   drinking, 27, 57
   flavour enhancers, 43
   history, 8–27
   ingredients, 15, 29, 34, 42–3
   origins, 10–13
   styles, 58–69
Beijing brewery, China, 205
Bel Pils, 125
Belhaven brewery, Scotland, 108, 110
Belikin Beer, 247
Belle-Vue brewery, Belgium, 125, 133
Bellegems Bruin, 133
Benchmark, 87
Benefontaine brewery, France, 185, 186
Bergenbier brewery, Romania, 170, 171
Bering, 113
Berliner Burgerbräu, Germany, 147
   Weisse, 69
Bernard brewery, Czech., 175, 178
Bernauer Schwarzbier, 147
Berrow brewery, England, 99
Bert Grant's beers, 232
   Yakima Brewing Company, 62, 232
Bethanian, 139
Biekhart Cerveza Pilsen, 247
   Especial, 247
Bière Bénin, 198
   de Garde, 53
   de Mont St Aubert, 134
   des Ours, 133
   des Templiers, 185
   du Démon, 188
   du Désert, 185, 188
Big Butt Doppelbock, 232
   Rock brewery, Canada, 225, 226, 227, 228
   Shoulders Porter, 232
Bigfoot Barley Wine, 232
Binchoise brewery, Belgium, 133
Binding Brewing Group, Germany, 148, 151,
   152, 154, 155
Bintang beer, Indonesia, 210, 211
Birburger, 65
Birell, 64, 190, 191
Birra Moretti, 181
Birziecie, 170, 173
Bishop's Ale, 87
   Finger 87
   Tipple, 88
Bitburger brewery, Germany, 147, 158

Bjørne Bryg, 113
Black Adder, 88
   Amber, 225
   & Tan Porter, 232
   Biddy, 75
   Butte Porter, 232
   Cat Mild, 88
   Chocolate Stout, 232
   Crow, 213, 217
   Diamond, 88
   Bitter, 219
   Douglas, 107
   Hawk Stout, 232
   Jack Porter, 88
   Mac, 223
   Magic, 88
   malt, 35
   Mountain brewery, US, 233
   Regent, 175
   Rock, 88
   Sheep brewery, England, 88, 96,101
Blackawton brewery, England, 90, 92
Blackened Voodoo, 232, 241
Blackhook Porter, 232
Blanche de Chambly, 225
   de Charleroi, 134
   de Namur, 69, 125
   des Bruges, 125
   des Honnelles, 125
Block brewery, Belgium, 125, 131, 133
Blue Fin Stout, 232
   Heron Pale Ale (Bridgeport), 232
   Heron Pale Ale (Mendocino), 232
   Label, 182, 213
   Moon, 232
   Nile brewery, Africa, 198, 201
   Star Wheat Beer, 228, 232
Blunderbus, 88
Boag's Classic Bitter, 216
Bock de Moulin, 189
Bock-Damm, 194
Bockor brewery, Belgium, 129, 133
Boddingtons brewery, England, 88, 101
Bodgers, 88
Bofferding brewery, Lux., 145
Bohemia, 247
   Cerveza, 251
   Regent, 175
Bohemian Dunkel, 232
Bohlingers, 198
Bokkereyer, 125
Bombardier, 88
Bond Corporation, 212
Boon brewery, Belgium, 134
   Rawd brewery, Thailand, 211
Bor Best, 88
Borsodi brewery, Hungary, 171
   Vilagos, 170, 171
Borve Brewpub, Scotland, 107, 110
Boskeun, 62
Bosteels brewery, Belgium, 134
Boston Beer Company, US, 67, 238, 239, 240
   John, 215
Bosun Porter, Poole, England, 88
Bosun's Bitter, Africa, 198, 202
   St Austell, England, 88
Boulder Amber Ale, 232
Bourgogne des Flanders, 125
Brabantine, 134
Brador, 225
Bragot (Bragawd), 82
Brahma Chopp, 249
   Export, 247
   Pilsner, 247
Brains Old brewery, Wales, 80, 81, 83
Brakspear brewery, England, 95, 101
   Bitter, 88
   Special, 88
Brand brewery, Netherlands, 139, 140, 141,
   142
   Oak Bitter, 88
Branik brewery, Czech., 178
Branoc, 88
Branscombe Vale brewery, England, 88, 96, 98
Brasal Brasserie Allemande, Canada, 228
   Bock, 225
   Legère, 225
   Special Amber, 225
Brasimba brewery, Africa, 200
Brass Monkey Stout, 219
Brasserie de Tahiti, 223
   du Bénin, Togo, Africa, 198, 199, 201
   du Maroc, Africa, 198, 201

   McAuslan, Canada, 225, 226, 227, 228
   Nationale, 144, 145
Brasseries Réunies de Luxembourg Mousel et
   Clausen, 144, 145
Brasseurs beers, 189
Bräu AG, 164
   AG brewery, Austria, 163, 164
   und Brunnen Group, Germany, 156
   und Brunnen, 168
Braugold, 191
Brauhernen Pilsner, 147
Brauherren Pilsner, 158
Braumeister, 147
Bremer Weisse, 147
Brenin, 81
Breug, 185
Brew 97, 88
   XI, 88
Brewer's Choice, 182
   Droop, 89
   Pilsner, 217
   Pride, 89
Brewery-on-Sea, Lancing, England, 88, 89, 91,
   96, 97
brewing 45–51
Brick Brewing Company, Canada, 225, 227–8
Bridge Bitter, 89
Brigand, 125
Briljant, 139, 142
Brindle, 81, 83
Brinkhoff's No. 1, 147
Brisbane Bitter, 218
   Pilsner, 218
Bristol Stout, 89
Brno, 178
Broadside Ale, 89
Broadsword, 107
Brock Extra Stout, 225
Broken Hill Draught, 213
Brooklyn brewery, US, 232
Broughton brewery, Scotland, 107, 108, 109, 110
Broyhan Alt, 148
Brugs Straffe Hendrick, 125
Brugs Tarwebier (Blanches de Bruges), 69, 125
Brugse Tripel, 125
Bruna, 181
Brune Spéciale, 185
Brunehaut brewery, Belgium, 134
Buccaneer, 89
Buchan Bronco, 107
Buckley's Best Bitter, 81, 83
Bud Dry, 60
   Ice, 62
Budel brewery, Netherlands, 139, 141, 142
Budweiser, 26, 42, 175, 233
Budweiser Budvar brewery, Czech., 175, 178
Bull's Head Bitter, 219
Bulldog Pale Ale, 89
Bullion, 89
Bullmastiff brewery, Wales, 80, 81, 83
Bunces brewery, England, 87, 89, 95, 98, 99
Buorren, 139
Burgasko brewery, Bulgaria, 170, 172
Burgerbräu brewery, Germany, 150
Burragarang Bock, 219
Burton Bridge brewery, England, 89, 91, 95, 99
Burtonwood brewery, England, 89, 99, 101
Busch, Adolphus, 240
   Golden Pilsner, 148
Bush, 126
Butcombe brewery, England, 89, 100, 101
Butterknowle brewery, England, 87, 88, 89, 92,
   93, 95
Buur, 113
Buzz, 89
Buzzard Breath Ale, 228

CD, 148
Caffrey's Irish Ale, 75
Cains brewery, England, 89, 91, 102
Calanda brewery, Switzerland 191
Calatrava, 195
Calder's, 107
Caledonian brewery, Scotland, 61, 107, 108, 110
Calton brewery, Fiji, 223
Cambrian brewery, Wales, 80, 83
Cambridge Bitter, 89
Camel Beer, 198
Cameron brewery, England, 89, 98, 102
CAMRA, 26–7, 86
Canadian Lager, 225
CanCo, 54
Canterbury, 221

Cantillon brewery, Belgium, 131, 132, 134
Canton Lager Beer, 205
Cape brewery, Africa, 197
Capucijn, 139
Caracole brewery, Belgium, 134
Carbine Stout, 213, 216
Cardenal brewery, Venezuela, 249
Cardinal brewery, Switz., 191, 192
Carib, 250
Caribe Development Company, Trinidad, 251
Carling Black Label, 24, 89, 225
    brewery, Canada, 228
    O'Keefe brewery, Canada, 228
Carlsberg brewery, Denmark, 25, 26, 112, 113,
    114, 115, 168, 180, 197
    Foundation, 115
    Let, 113
    Malawi Ltd, 197
Carlton United Brewers, Aus., 213, 216
Carnegie Porter, 119
Carolus, 148
Cascade, 30, 213
    brewery, Tasmania, 216
    Golden Ale, 233
Casper's Max, 139
Cassovar, 175
Castelain brewery, France, 188
Castello, 191, 192
Castle Eden brewery, England, 89, 90, 91, 102
    Ale, 89
    Golden Pilsner, 198
    Lager, 42, 197, 198
    Milk Stout, 198
    Special Pale Ale, 89
Castlemaine brewery, Aus., 213, 216
    Perkins, brewery, Aus., 216
    XXXX, 213, 216
Catamount brewery, US, 232, 240
Celebration Ale, 233
Celebrator, 148
Celis brewery, US, 233, 240, 241
    Pieter, 69, 126, 129
    White, 126, 233
Central Village brewery, Jamaica, 250
Ceres brewery, Denmark, 113, 114
Cergal, 196
Cerna Horna brewery, Czech., 175, 176, 177,
    178
Cernohorsky Granat, 175
    Lezak, 175
Certa, 185
Cervecería Ancla S.A., Colombia, 247, 249
    Bieckhert, Argentina, 247, 249
    Corona, Puerto Rico, 251
    Costa Rica S.A., 247
    La Constancia, 249
    Moctezuma, Mexico, 246, 248, 249
    Modelo, Mexico, 246, 247, 249
Cervejaría Cacador, Brazil, 248
Cervesur (Compañia Cervecera Del Sur Del
    Peru S.A.), 248, 249
Cerveza, 247
    Negra, 211
    Rosanna Red Chilli Ale, 60, 233
    Tipo Pilsen, 249
Ceske Budejovice, 178
Ceylon brewery, Sri Lanka, 211
Ch'ti, 185
Chairman's Extra Strong Brew, 198
Challenger, 89
Chapeau, 126, 135
Charles Quint, 126
Château Neubourg, 139
Cheers, 121
Chesterfield Ale, 233, 245
Chibuku, 198
    Breweries, Zimbabwe, Africa, 201
Chicago brewery, US, 235
Chicha, 10
Chihuahau, 249
Chiltern brewery, England, 87, 88, 89
Chimay brewery, Belgium, 68, 126, 134
    ales, 15, 126
Chinese Ginseng Beer, 205
Chiswick Bitter, 89
Chmelar, 176
chocolate malt, 35
Chodovar brewery, Czech., 178
Choulette brewery, France, 185, 186, 187, 188
Christian Moerlein, 233
Christmas Juleol, 117
Christoffel brewery, Netherlands, 139, 142
Ch'ti, 185
Chu Jiang brewery, China, 205
Chu Sing, 205
Cinco Estrellas, 194
Clark brewery, England, 92, 99

Clarysse brewery, Belgium, 128, 130, 134
Clausthaler, 64, 148
Club Pilsner, 198, 202
Cluss Bock, 148
Cnudde, 60
Coach House brewery, England, 88, 89, 92, 93
Coachman's Best, 89
Cobra, 211
Cochonne, 126
Cocker Hoop, 89
Cold Spring Export Lager, 233
College Ale, 89
Colonial Stout, 225
Columbus, 139, 143, 163
Companhia Cervejaría, Brazil, 247, 248, 249
Conciliation Ale, 89
coopering, 52
Cooper's brewery, Aus., 213, 216–17
    beers, 213–4
Coopers WPA, 89
Coors, 233
    brewery, US, 30, 62, 232, 233, 234, 241
Coral, 196
Coreff, 188
Coromandel Brewing Co., NZ, 221
Corona, 251
Corona Extra, 247
Corsendonck, 127
Cotleigh brewery, England, 87, 92, 95
Country Best Bitter, 90
    Stile, 90
County Ale, 225
Courage brewery, England, 68, 89, 90, 91, 93,
    102
Coutts, Morton, 50, 220
CPA (Crown Pale Ale), 81
Craftsman, 90
Crazy Ed's Cave Creek Chilli Beer, 60, 233
Cream City Pale Ale, 233
Creemore Springs brewery, Canada, 228
Cristal, 196
    Alken, 127
    Brown, 196
Crombe brewery, Belgium, 130, 134
Cromwell Bitter, 90
Crouch Vale brewery, England, 94, 97, 100
Crown Buckley brewery, Wales, 80, 81, 83
Crown, 213
Drawwell Bitter, 90
Crystal, 176, 181
    malt, 35
Cuauhtémoc brewery, Mexico, 247, 248, 249
Cuillin, 107
Cuivrée, 185
Cumberland Ale, 90
Cusquena, 249
Cuvée d'Aristées, 127
    de Jonquilles, 185
    de Koninck, 127
    de l'An Neuf, 134
    de l'Hermitage, 127
    René, 136
Cuzco, 247, 249
Cwrw Castell, 81
    Tudno, 81

DAB (Dortmunder Actien Brauerei), Germany,
    60, 148, 149, 151, 156
DOM brewery, Germany, 156
    Kölsch, 148
    Pilsner, 148
DUB (Dortmunder Union brewery), Germany,
    60, 147, 148, 156
D-Ale, 213
Daleside brewery, England, 90, 94
Damm brewery, Spain, 193, 194, 195
Dampfbier, 148
Dansk Dortmunder, 113
    LA, 113
Daredevil Winter Warmer, 90
Dark de Triomphe, 189
    Island, 107
Dart, 119
De Dolle brewery, 62, 130, 134
De Keersmaeker brewery, Belgium, 130, 134
De Kluis brewery, Belgium, 129
De Koninck brewery, Belgium, 127, 134
De Kroon brewery, Netherlands, 142
De Smedt brewery, Belgium 125, 126, 130,
    135
De Troch brewery, Belgium, 126, 135
Deacon, 90
Deep Ender's, 233
    Shaft Stout, 90
Delerium Tremens, 127
Delicator, 148
Dent brewery, England, 96, 99
Dentergems Wit, 69, 127

Deschute brewery, US, 231, 232, 233, 235, 236
Desnoes & Geddes brewery, Jamaica, 251
Deuchars IPA, 107, 110
Deux Rivières brewery, France, 188
Devil Gold, 90
Devon Gold, 90
Diamond Draught, 213, 216
Diebels brewery, Germany, 58, 148, 156
Diekirch brewery, Lux., 145
Dinkelacker brewery, Germany, 148, 152
Director's, 90
Dixie brewery, US, 232, 235, 241
Dock Street brewery, US, 241
Dogbolter, 213, 217
Dojlidy brewery, Poland, 167, 168
Doppelbock Bugel, 127
Doppo Micro-brewery, Japan, 209
Dolphin Best, 90
Dominator, 139
Dominion Breweries (DB), N.Z., 220, 221, 222
    beers, 221–2
Dommelsch brewery, Netherlands, 139, 142
Domus brewery, Belgium, 127
Donnington brewery, England, 87, 100, 102
Doppelbock Bugel, 127
Dorset Best, 90
Dort Maltezer, Ridder, 143
Dortmunder Gold, 233, 242
Dos Equis (Two Crosses), 246, 248, 249
Double Brown, 221
    Chance, 90
    Diamond, 90
    Dragon, 81
    Enghein Brune, 128
    Happiness Guangzhou Beer, 205
    Maxim, 90
    Stout, 90
Douglas, 107
Dr Johnson's Draught, 81
Dragonhead Stout, 107
Dragon's Breath, 81
Dragonslayer, 90
Dragon Stout, 67, 251
Drak, 176
Draught Bass, 90
    Burton Ale, 90
Drawwell Bitter, 90
Dreher, Anton, 69, 165, 172
Dreher Bak, 170
Dreher brewery, Italy, 181, 182
    Export, 170
    Pilsner, 170
Dreikönigs, 191
Drie Hoefijzers brewery, Netherlands, 141, 143
Drie Ringen brewery, Netherlands, 139, 142
dry beer, 206
Du Bocq brewery, Belgium, 66, 69, 125, 129,
    131, 135
Dubuisson brewery, Belgium, 126
Duckstein, 148
Dudak, 176
Duffy's, 225
Duivelsbier, 128
Dundee's Honey Brown Lager, 233, 242
Dunkle Perle, 191
Dupont brewery, Belgium, 66, 125, 130, 132,
    135
Duvel, 128
Duyck brewery, France, 186, 187, 188
Dvaro, 170, 172
Dyffryn Clwyd brewery, Wales, 80, 84

EB Specjal Pils, 167
EKU brewery, germany, 149
ESB, 90
    Africa, 198, 202
ESX Best, 90
Eagle Blue, 213
    Blue Ice, 213
    IPA, 90
    Stout, 200
    Super, 213
East African Breweries, Africa, 201
    Side Dark, 233
Easy Street Wheat, 233
Ebony Dark, 81, 83
    Super Strength, 251
Echt Kölsch, 148
Edel, 194
    Pils, 157
Edelweiss, 163
Eden Bitter, 90
Edelwiss, 163
Edinburgh Strong Ale, 107
Edmund II Ironside, 90
Efes brewery, Turkey, 183
Egelantier, 139
Eggenberg, 176

Eggenberg brewery, Austria, 163, 164
Egill brewery, Iceland, 123
Eichbaum brewery, Germany, 147, 151, 154,
    156
Eichhoff brewery, Switz., 191, 192
Einbeck, 59
Einbecker brewery, Germany, 147, 148, 158
Eisbock, 59
Ekstra, 170, 172
Elbrewery brewery, Poland 168
Elbschloss brewery, Germany, 152
Elders IXL, 212
Eldridge Pope (Hardys) brewery, England, 97
Elegantier, 139, 142
Elephant, 113
Elgood brewery, England, 89, 91, 95, 102
Eliot Ness, 233, 242
Elizabethan, 90
Elk Mountain Amber Ale, 233
Emperor's Gold Beer, 205
Empresa brewery, Portugal, 196
Emu, 213
Ename, 135
Enkel, 139
Enville Farm brewery, England, 62, 90, 91
Erdinger brewery, Germany, 69, 149, 151, 156
Espresso Stout, 233
Esquire Extra Dry, 234
    Premium Pale Ale, 234
Estrella del Sur, 194, 195
Euler brewery, Germany, 147, 149
Eupener brewery, Belgium, 135
Europa, 196
European Beer Consumers Union, 27
Eurospecjal, 167
Evansville brewery, US, 234
Everard brewery, England, 87, 90, 95, 99
Exmoor brewery, England, 87, 91, 97, 102
Export Mongrel, 213
Eye of the Hawk, 234

Facon brewery, Belgium, 135
Fäffer beer, 17
Fakir, 133
Falcon brewery, Sweden, 119
Fall Fest, 234
Falstaff Real Ale, 223
Fargo, 91
Farmer's Glory, 91
Farsons Brewers, Malta, 182
Faxe brewery, Denmark, 113, 114
Fed Special, 91
Federation Ale, 219
    brewery, England, 91, 92, 102
Feldschlösschen brewery, Germany, 148, 149
    Breweries, Switz., 190, 191
    Ex-Bier, 192
Felinfoel brewery, Wales, 55, 80, 81, 84
Felix Kriekbier, 128
    Oud Bruin, 128
Feng Shon brewery, China, 205
fermentation, 10, 15
Fest-Märzen, 149
Festive, 91
Feuerfest, 91
Fiji Bitter Beer, 223
Fire Rock Ale, 223
First, 149
Fischer brewery, France, 185, 187,188
Five Star brewery, Beijing, China, 205
Flag, 198
Flame, 221
Floreffe brewery, Belgium, 125, 128, 129
Flowers brewery, England, 91, 102
Flying Herbert, 91
    Horse, 211
Foreign Extra Stout, 67
Forester's 199, 202
Formidable Ale, 91
Forschungs brewery, Germany, 151, 152
Forst brewery, Italy, 181, 182
Fort Mitchell brewery, US, 237
Fortunator, 149
Fortyniner, 91
Foster's Brewing Group, Aus., 25, 213, 214,
    215, 216, 217
Founders, 91
Framboises, 43
Frankenmuth brewery, US, 241
Franklin's Bitter, 91
Franz Inselkammer brewery, Germany, 147
Franz Joseph Jubelbier, 149
    Sailer brewery, Germany, 151
Franziskaner, 149
Fraoch, 12, 107
Freedom Pilsner, 91
Freeminer Bitter, 91
Freiberger Brauhaus, Germany, 149

Freidrich and Renne, 215
Fréijoers, 145
Freistadter brewery, Austria, 164–5
Fremantle Bitter, 214
Friart brewery, Belgium, 135
Frog & Rosbif brewery, France, 189
    Island brewery, England, 94
Frontenac, 225, 228
Frontier, 234
Frydenlund Pilsener, 117
Frysk Bier, 139
Füchschen brewery, Germany, 158
Fuggles Imperial, 91
Full Sail brewery, US, 234, 239, 241
Fuller's brewery, England, 89, 90, 93, 102
Funck, Henri, 144
Fürstenberg brewery, Germany, 149, 158
F.X. Matt brewery, US, 231, 232, 242

GB Mild, 91
GSB, 91
Gaffel brewery, Germany, 158
Gales brewery, England, 93, 96
Gambrinus brewery, Czech., 176, 177, 178
Gamla Stans brewery, Sweden, 119
Gamle Special Dark, 113
Gammel Porter , 113
Garde brewery, Germany, 158
Gargoyle, 91
Gatz Alt, 149
Gatzweiler brewery, Germany, 149
Gayant brewery, France, 185, 186, 187, 188
Gdanskie, 167
Geary's Micro-brewery, US, 241
Genesee brewery, US, 233, 238, 239, 242
Genny Bock, 234, 242
George Killian's Irish Red, 62, 234
Georges Bitter Ale, 91
Gereons brewery, Germany, 158
German Purity Law (see Reinheitsgebot)
Gerst Amber, 234
Gibbs Mew brewery, England, 88, 90, 97, 100
Gigi brewery, Belgium, 132, 135
Gilde Pils, 149
Gildenbier, 128
Gillespie's, 107
Ginger Tom, 91
Gingersnap, 61, 91
Gippsland Gold, 217
Giraf, 113
Girardin brewery, Belgium, 135
Gladiator, 139
Gladstone, 91
Glass's Castle brewery, Africa, 202
Gocseji Barna, 170, 172
Gold Brew, 81, 83
    Fassl, 163
    Label, 91
Golden Amber, 107
    Best, 91
    Bitter, 91
    Brew, 81
    Gate, 234
    Guinea brewery, Africa, 200
    Label, 91
    Mead Ale, 62
    Pale, 107
    Promise, 61, 107
Goldenberg, 185
Gordon's Ales, 107
Gorilla, 119
Gosser, 163
Gotenba Kohgen Brewpub, Japan, 209
Gothic Ale, 91
Gotlands brewery, Sweden, 119
Gotyckie Magnat, 168
Gotz, Jan, 168
Goudale, 185
Gouden Boom brewery, Belgium, 69, 125, 132
    Carolus, 128
Goudenband, 128
Gouverneur, 140, 143
Governor, 91
Graduate, 91
Gran Riserva, 181
Granada brewery, Granada, W.I., 251
Granary Bitter, 91
Granat, 176
Granite brewery, Canada, 228
Grand Ridge brewery, Aus., 217
Grandâ Prestige, 140
Grant's Scottish Ale, 234
Granville Island Brewing Company, Canada,
    225, 226, 228
Grasshopper Wheat, 226
Great Lakes brewery, US, 233, 236, 242
Great Northern brewery, N.Z., 223
    Porter, Ireland, 75

Porter, US, 234
Greene King brewery, England, 87, 98, 102
Greenmantle, 108
Griffon Brown Ale, 226, 228
    Extra Pale Ale, 226, 228
Grimbergen, 128
Gritstone Premium Ale, 226
Grodzisk, 167
Groll, Joseph, 18
Grolsch brewery, Netherlands, 140, 142, 168
Grøn, 113
Growlin Gator Lager, 234
Grozet, 108
Grutzer, Eduard, 15
Guangminpai, 205
Guangzhou brewery, China, 205
Guinness brewery, St James's Gate, Dublin,
    Ireland, 17, 19, 24, 25, 30, 65, 67, 75,
    77, 78–9, 195, 200
    Draught, 75
    Extra Stout, 74
    Foreign Extra Stout, 75
    Special Export, 75
    Stout, 250
Gulder, 199, 202
Gull, 123
Gulpener brewery, Netherlands, 139, 140, 141,
    143
Gulpener Dort, 140, 143
Gunpowder, 92
Gyenge, Zsolt, 171

HB Hofbräuhaus München, 149
HSB, 93
Haacht brewery, Belgium, 125, 126, 127, 131,
    136
Haake-Beck brewery, Germany, 147, 150, 155
Hacker-Pschorr brewery, Germany, 61, 147,
    149, 156
Hahn brewery, Aus., 214, 217
Hall & Woodhouse brewery, England, 87, 90,
    98, 101
Hambleton brewery, England, 94
Hammerhead, 92
Hampshire brewery, England, 87, 90, 93, 100
    Special Ale, 234, 241
Hanby brewery, England, 90, 97
Hancock's brewery, Wales, 80, 84
    HB, 81
Hangzhou brewery, China, 205
Hannen brewery, Germany, 158
Hansa brewery, Germany, 158
    brewery, Namibia, Africa, 199, 200, 201
    brewery, Norway, 117
Hansen, Emil, 41, 115
Hapkin, 128
Harboe, 173
    brewery, Denmark, 113, 114
Harbour Bar brewpub, Scotland, 111
Hardington brewery, England, 95
Hardy brewery, England, 103
Hardys & Hansons brewery, England, 92, 93,
    102
Harp Export, 75
    Lager, 75
Harpoon brewery, US, 242
Harrier SPA, 92
Harrington Micro-brewery, N.Z., 222
Hart brewery, US, 231, 233
Hartwall brewery, Finland, 120, 121,122
Harvest Ale, 92
Harveys brewery, England, 90, 92, 98, 99, 103
    beers, 92
Harviestoun brewery, Scotland, 108, 109, 110
Hatlifter Stout, 217
Hatters, 92
Hausbier, 145
Hawkes Bay Draught, 221
Headstrong, 92
Heartland Weiss, 234
Heather Ale, 107
Heckler brewery, US, 235, 236
Hefeweizen, 234
Hei Lager Gold, 223
Heileman brewery, US, 235, 236, 242
Heimertingen Maibock, 234
Heineken brewery, Netherlands, 25, 26, 138,
    140, 141, 142, 168, 172, 173, 179, 180,
    190, 195, 197, 250
Helenbock 1992 Oktoberfest, 234
Hell Doppel 1992 Bock, 235
    Lager, 235
Heller brewery, Germany, 147
Helles Gold, 235
Henninger brewery, Germany, 157
Henri Funck Lager Beer, 145
Henry Weinhard's Private Reserve, 235
Herbowe, 167, 168

Herforder brewery, Germany, 65, 158
Heritage, 92
Herman Joseph's, 235
Herold brewery, Czech., 176, 177, 178
Herrtua, 121
Hersbrucker Weizenbier, 92
Hertog Jan Pilsner, 142
Het Kapittel, 128
Hevelius brewery, Poland, 167, 168
Hexen Bräu, 191, 192
Hick's Special Draught, 92
Hickory Switch Smoked Amber Ale, 235
High Force, 92
    Level, 92
Highgate brewery, England, 92, 103
Highland Hammer, 108
Hilden brewery, Ireland, 75, 76, 77
Hinano Tahiti Lager, 223
Hirter brewery, Austria, 163, 165
Hite, 211
Hobgoblin, 92
Hoegaardens brewery, Belgium, 43, 69, 128, 132
    Grand Cru, 129
Hof, 113
Hofbräu Abensberg, 156
    Berchtesgaden, 156
Hofbräuhaus Freising, 156
    Oktoberfest, 64
    Original Munchen, 156
    Wolters, Brunswick, 156
Hofbräuhaus, (The Royal brewery) , Germany,
    148, 149, 156
Hoffmans Lager, 76
Hofmark brewery, Germany, 154
Hogs Back brewery, England, 36, 87, 99
Holan 10, 176
Holden brewery, England, 92, 100, 103
Holsten brewery, Germany, 149, 157, 172
Holt brewery, England, 92, 103
Honey Double Mai Bock, 235
Honeyweizen, 235
Hong Kong brewery, Hong Kong, 205
Hook Norton brewery, England, 90, 93, 95, 103
Hop and Glory, 93
Hope & Anchor Breweries, Sheffield, 62
Hopf brewery, Germany, 149, 158
Hopfenperle (Austria), 163
Hopfenperle (Switzerland), 191, 192
hops, 15, 29, 36–9
Horse-Ale, 129
Hoskins brewery, England, 87, 96
Hoskins & Oldfield brewery, England, 91, 100
Hostan brewery, Czech., 176
Hua Nan Beer 205
Hubertus, 191
    brewery, Austria, 149, 165,
Hubsch Hefe-Weizen, 242
Hudenpohl-Schoenling brewery, US, 233, 235, 236
Hudy, 235
Hull brewery, England, 91, 103
Hunter's 199, 201
Hürlimann brewery, Switz., 30, 190, 191, 192
Huyghe brewery, Belgium, 127, 130
Hydes brewery, England, 100, 103

ice beer, 216
Icehouse, 235
Ichiban, 208
    Shibori, 207
Ichtegems Oud Bruin, 129
Imperator, 140
Imperial Extra Double Stout, 173
    Russian Stout, 93
    Stout, Canada, 226
    Stout, Denmark, 113
Ind Coope brewery, England, 24, 87, 90, 103
Indiana's Bones, 93
Innkeeper's Special, 93
Inseine, Frog & Rosbif, 189
Inspired, 93
Interbrew, Belgium, 129, 132, 136, 171, 172,
    197, 228
Irish Festival Ale, 76
Iron City Lager, 235
    Duke, 226
    Strong Ale, 229
Ironback Dark, 219
Ironbrew, 219
Ironbridge Stout, 93
Irseer Klosterbräu, Germany, 14, 149, 150, 158
Island Lager, 226
Isle of Skye brewery, Scotland, 107
Italia Pilsner, 181, 182

Jacobins, 129
Jacobite Ale, 108
Jade, 186
Jahrhundert, 149

James Boag brewery, Aus., 214, 216
Jax Pilsner, 235
Jazz Amber Light, 235, 241
Jenkins, D.T., brewery, Wales, 83
Jenlain, 186
Jennings brewery, England, 89, 90, 93, 97, 103
Jerningham Street brewery, Aus., 214
Jever brewery, Germany, 150
Jihlava brewery, Czech., 178
John Labatt's Classic, 226
John Smith's brewery, England, 93, 94
Joiners Arms Brewpub, Wales, 84
Jolly Jack Tar Porter, 81
Jones brewery, US, 234, 238
Jouloulot Christmas Beer, 121
ju-biru, 206
Jubelale, 235
Jubilator, 186
Jubilee, 211
Jubileeuw, 140, 143
Jupiler, 129
J.W. Lees, 103

kaffir beer, 203
Kaiser Bock , 248
    brewery, Brazil, 249
    Cerveja, 249
    Doppelmalz, 163
    Draught, 163, 164
    Gold , 248
    Goldquell, 163
    Märzen, 163
    Piccolo Bock, 163
    Pilsner, 150
    Premium, 163
Kaiserdom, 150
Kaliber, 76
Kalik Gold, 251
Kalnapilis, brewery, Lithuania, 172
Kaltenberg brewery, Germany, 150, 152
Kamenitza brewery, Bulgaria, 170, 172
Kane's Amber Ale, 108
Kanizsai brewery, Hungary, 172
Kanterbräu brewery, France, 187, 189
Kaper, 167
Kappeli Brasserie, Finland, 122
Kapuziner, 150
Karamelové, 176
Karmelowe, 167
Karel IV, 176
Karhu 3, 121
Karjala, 121
Karlovy Vary brewery, Czech., 176
Karmelowe, 167
Kasteel, 1298
Keersmaekers, Josef, 127
Keith's IPA, 228
Keler, 195
Kelts, König, 159
Kent Old Brown, 214
Kenya Breweries, Africa,198, 200, 201
Keo brewery, Cyprus, 183
Kilkenny Irish Beer, 76
Killian's Irish Red, 62
Killian, 186
Kilsch Lager, 235
Kimberley Best Mild, 93
    Classic, 93
Kindl brewery, Germany, 150, 155
King & Barnes brewery, England, 93, 98, 103
King Alfred's, 93
King Lear Old Ale, 223
Kingdown Ale, 93
Kingfisher, 211
Kirin brewery, Japan, 206, 207, 208, 209
    beers, 207
Kizakura Kappa Brewpub, Japan, 209
Klisch Lager, 235
Kloster–Urtrunk, 150
Kloster Urweisse, 150
Klosterbräu brewery, Germany, 147, 157
Köbányéi brewery, Hungary, 172
Koch, Jim, 240
Koff, 121
    Porter, 121
Kokanee, 228
Kölsch beer, 254
Komaromi brewery, Hangary, 172
Kona Brewing Company, Hawaii, 223
Kongens Bryg, 113
König brewery, Germany, 150, 159
    Ludwig, 150
König Pilsner, 150, 159
Königsbacher brewery, Germany, 159
Konik, 176
Koningshoeven,140
    brewery, Netherlands, 143

Konizsai Korona, 170
Kootenay, 228
Korbinian, 150
Korenwolf, 140
Kostritz brewery, Germany, 150
Köstritzer Schwarzbier, 150
Kozel, 176
Krakus, 167
Kräusen, 150
Kriek, traditional Belgian beer, 42, 43, 124, 229
Krolewskie, 167
Krombacher brewery, Germany, 157
Kronen brewery, Germany, 60, 150, 151
Kronen, Italy, 181
Kronenbourg brewery, France, 186, 187, 189
    beers, 186
Kronenburg brewery, Denmark, 30
Kroon brewery, Netherlands, 139
Krostitz brewery, Germany, 154, 155
Krusovice brewery, Czech., 176, 179
Kulmbacher Eisbock, 61
Kulminator, 28, 151
Küppers brewery, Germany, 62, 151, 159
Kuro-nama, 207, 208
Kutscher Alt, 151, 155
kvass, 172
Kylian, 140
Kyoto Alt, 207

La Biére Amoureuse, 186
La Bière de Noël, Kronenbourg, 186
La Bière du Demon, 185
La Chouffe, 129
La Choulette, 186
La Divine, 129
La Fin du Monde, 226
La Gaillarde, 226
La Gauloise, 129
La Goudale, 188
La Meilleure, 129
La Montagnarde, 133
La Rossa, 181
La Trappe, 140
Labatt brewery, Canada, 25, 62, 136, 226, 228
    John, 224, 228
Lacplesis brewery, Latvia, 172
Lacto Milk Stout, 182
lager, 15, 18–19
Laird's Ale, 108
Lakefront brewery, US, 233, 235
Lammin Sahti, 121
Lammsbräu Pils, 151
Lancaster Bomber, 93
Landlord, 93
Lapin Kulta, 121
Larkins Best Bitter, 93
Larkins brewery, England, 99
Latrobe brewery, US, 235
Lauku Tumsais, 170
Lauritz, 117
Lech brewery, Poland, 167, 168
Lederer brewery, Nurenburg, 17
Lees brewery, England, 91, 92, 94, 103
Leeuw brewery, Netherlands, 140, 141, 143
Lefebvre brewery, Belgium, 128, 136
Leffe, 129
    Abbey, 14, 129
Legacy Lager, 235
    Red Ale, 235
Legend Stout, 199, 200, 202
Leichter Typ, 151
Leinenkugel brewery, US, 231, 232, 235, 236
Lembeek, 134
Leningrad Cowboy, 121
Lente Bok, 140
Leopard brewery, N.Z., 221
Leroy brewery, Belgium, 132
Les Brasseurs brewery, France, 189
Lett's brewery, Ireland, 77
Liberty Ale, 235, 240
Lichfield brewery, England, 91, 93, 98
Liefmans brewery, Belgium, 60, 129, 136
    beers, 129
Lighthouse Ale, 219
Limburgse Witte, 130, 136
Lindeboom brewery, Netherlands, 143
Lindemans brewery, Belgium, 136
Linder Gilde brewery, Germany, 148, 149, 152
Lingen's Blond, 140
Lion Breweries (Lion Nathan), N.Z., 25, 220,
    221, 222
    brewery, US, 238
    Brewpub, Aus., 219
    Ice, 221
    Lager, Africa, 199
    Nathan brewery, Aus., 212, 216, 217
    Stout (Africa), 200
    Stout (Asia), 211

Lion's Pride, 226
Little Kings Cream Ale, 236
Loaded Dog Steam Beer, 214
Lobkowicz brewery, Czech., 176, 179
Locher brewery, St Gallen, Switz., 192
London Pride, 93
Lone Star, 236
Longbrew, 214
Lord Granville Pale Ale, 226
Lord Nelson Brewpub, Aus., 219
Louwaege brewery, Belgium, 128
Löwenbräu brewery, Germany, 25, 151,
    154, 157
    beers, 151
Löwenbräu of Zurich, Switz., 191, 192
Lucan, 176
Lucifer, 130
Ludwig Pils, 117
Lugton Inn Brewpub, Scotland, 111
Lutèce, 186
Luxembourg Export 145
    Lager, 145
Lynesack Porter, 93
Lysholmer, 117

M&B, 94
Maasland brewery, Netherlands, 141, 143
Mac's Micro-brewery, N.Z., 223
MacAndrews, 108
Macardles Ale, 76
McAuslan Brasserie, Canada, 226, 228
Macbeth's Red Ale, 223
McChouffe, 130
McEwan's brewery, Scotland, 108, 110
McFarland, 181
McGregor, 130
Mack brewery, Norway, 117
Mackeson brewery, England, 93
Maclay's brewery, Scotland, 108, 109, 111
McMullen brewery, England, 87, 89, 90, 91,
    98, 103
McNally's Extra Pure Malt Irish Style Ale, 226, 228
MacQueen's Nessie, 163
Mactarnahan's Scottish Ale, 236
Maes Pils, 130
Magadan brewery, Ukraine, 712
Magnat, 167
Magnet, 94
Magnum Malt Liquor, 242
Magpie Rye, 226, 228
Mahou brewery, Spain, 193, 194, 195
Main Street Bitter, 81
Mainland Dark, 221, 222
Maisel brewery, Germany, 148, 151
Mako, 221
Malcolm's, 108
malt, 29, 32–3, 35
Malt and Hops, 94
Malta, 182
Maltezer, 140
malting, 32–3
Malton brewery, England, 90
Malt's, 207
Mamba Lager, 199
Mann's brewery, England, 94, 103
Mansfeld, 145
Mansfield Arms Brewpub, Scotland, 111
Mansfield brewery, England, 94, 95, 103
Maple Wheat Beer, 226
Marckloff, 130
Maredsous, 130
Mariage Parfait beers, 134
Mariedahl brewery, Africa, 197
Marlen, 194, 195
Marston Moor brewery, England, 89, 90
Marston's brewery, England, 30, 68, 94, 96, 103
Martens brewery, Belgium, 66, 130, 131, 136
Martin brewery, Slovakia., 176
Martinsky Lager, 176
Matilda Bay Brewing Company, Aus., 27, 213,
    214, 217
Maudite, 226
Mauldon brewery, England, 88, 94, 103
Mautner-Markhof, 162
Maximator, 140
Maximilaan Brewpub, Netherlands, 139, 140
Mechelsen Brune, 128
Meister Brau, 236
    Pils, 151
Melbourn brewery, England, 103
Melbourne Bitter, 214
Melo Abreu Especial, 196
Mendocino brewery, US, 232, 234, 238, 242
Merlin's, 108
Merman, 108
Mestan brewery, Czech., 176, 177, 178
Mestreechs Aajt, 140
Meteor brewery, France, 185, 186, 189

Michelob, 236
Mikro brewery, Norway, 117
Millenium Gold, 94
Miller brewery, US, 236, 242
  High Life, 26, 242
  Icehouse, 62
  Lite, 64, 242
Milwaukee's Best, 236, 242
Ministerley Ale, 94
Mirror Pond Pale Ale, 236
Mitchells & Butlers brewery, England, 88, 94, 100, 101, 103
Mitchell's brewery, England, 93, 94, 97, 103
Mitchell's ESB, 226
  Micro-brewery, South Africa, 198, 200, 202
Mohan Meakin, India, 211
Moinette, 130
Moku Moku Micro-brewery, Japan, 209
Moles brewery, England, 88, 94
Molson brewery, Montreal, 25, 62, 228–9
  Canadian Lager, 226, 229
  Export Ale, 226
  Special Dry, 226, 229
Mon-Lei Beer, 205
Mönchshof Kloster brewery, Germany, 150, 151, 154
Monkey Wrench, 94
Monteith brewery, N.Z., 223
  Black Beer, 221
  Original Ale, 221
Montrose, 108
Moondog Ale, 236, 242
Moonraker, 94
Moonshine, 214, 217
Moorhouse brewery, England, 88, 96
Moortgat brewery, Belgium, 125, 128, 130, 136
Moose Brown Ale, 236
Moosehead brewery, Canada, 225, 227, 229
  Lager, 226
Mopa brewery, Africa, 200
Moravia brewery, Germany, 159
Morchl, 163
Moretti brewery, Udine, Italy, 181, 182
Morland brewery, England, 95, 104
Morocco Ale, 94
Morrells brewery, England, 89, 91, 94, 99, 104
Mort Subite, 130
Mortimer, 186
Moscovskoye, 172
Moscow brewery, Russia, 173
Moskovskoye, 170, 173
Moss Bay Extra, 236
Moulin Hotel Brewpub, Scotland 111
Mount Tolmie, 226
Mousel brewery, Lux, 145
Moussy, 191
Muenchener Amber, 236
Mug Bitter, 140, 143
Münchner Dunkel, 157
Munich Oktoberfest, 16, 153
Munich Wheat Beer, 229
Murphy's brewery, Ireland, 76, 77
Murray's Heavy, 108
Mutiny, 94
Mutzig brewery, France, 186, 187, 189
My Tho, Vietnam, 211
Mystic Seaport Pale, 236

Nachod brewery, Czech., 177
Nag's Head Brewpub, Wales, 84
Namibia Breweries, Africa, 200, 201
Nastro Azzuro, 181, 182
Natal brewery, Africa, 202
National Breweries of Zimbabwe, Africa, 198, 200, 201
Natte, 140
Natterjack, 94
Naturtrub, 163
Naval Super Premium, 247, 248
Nectar, 176
Neer brewery, Netherlands, 140
Negra León , 248
  Modelo , 248, 249
Nesbitt brewery, Zimbabwe, Africa,199, 201
Nethergate brewery, England, 95, 99
New Amsterdam brewery, US, 242
New Glarus brewery, US, 243
  South Wales Lager Company, Aus., 218
  Zealand Breweries, (NZB), N.Z., 220, 222, 223
Newbegin brewery, N.Z., 223
Newcastle Amber Ale, 94
  Brown Ale, 60, 94
Ngoma, 199
Niagara Falls Brewing Company, Canada, 225, 226, 229
Nigerian Breweries, Africa, 199, 200, 202
Nightmare Porter, 94
Nikolaevskyi, 170, 171

Nile Breweries, Uganda, Africa,198, 199, 202
Nine Star Premium, 205
Noel Ale, 94
Noordheim, 187, 189
Norfolk Nog, 94
Norman's Conquest, 95
Norsemen, 13
North brewery, Africa, 200
  Brink Porter, 95
  Coast brewery, US, 231, 232, 236, 238
  Yorkshire brewery, England, 88, 91
Northwoods Lager, 236
Nostrum de San Miguel, 194
Novomestsky, 176
Nugget Golden Lager, 221
Nuigini Gold Extra Stout, 223
Nuremburger Tucher brewery, Germany, 154
Nussdorf brewery, Austria, 163, 164, 165
Nut Brown Ale, 95

OBJ, 95
Oakhill brewery, England, 104
Oberdorfer, 151
Obsidian Stout, 236
Oerbier, 130
Off the Rails, 81
O'Flanagan's, 214
Ogden Porter, 227
Ohlsson's Lager, 199
OK Jasne Pelne, 167
Okanagan Spring brewery, B.C., Canada, 227, 229
Okhotsk Brewpub, Japan, 209
Okocim brewery, Poland, 167, 168
Oktoberfest, 236
Old Admiral, 219
  Baily, 95
  Bawdy Barley Wine, 237
  Bircham, 95
  Bob, 95
  brewery Bitter, 95
  Buzzard, 95
  Crustacean, 236
  Detroit Amber, 241
  Ebenezer, 95
  English Porter, 229
  Expensive, 95
  Fashioned Bitter, 219
  Foghorn, 236, 240
  Growler, 95
  Hooky, 95
  Jock, 108
  Knucker, 95
  Knucklehead, 236
  Lion Pilsner, 219
  Manor, 108
  Masters, 95
  Mill brewery, England, 89, 95
  Milwaukee, 236
  Nick, 95
  No 38 Stout, 236
  Nobbie Stout, 81
  Original, 95
  Peculier, 95
  Preacher, 219
  Rasputin Russian Imperial Stout, 236
  Smokey, 95
  Southwark Stout, 214
  Speckled Hen, 95
  Spot Prize Ale, 95
  Stockport Bitter, 95
  Thumper, 96, 223, 237
  Tom, 96
  Vienna, 227
  Whisky, 163
Olde Merryford Ale, 96
  Stoker, 96
Olomouc brewery, Czech., 176, 179
Olvi brewery, Finland, 120, 121,122
Ondras, 176
Onix, 196
Op-Ale, 130
Optimator, 151
Optimo Bruno, 130
Oranjeboom brewery, Netherlands, 141, 143
Oregon Honey Beer, 237
Original Chilli Beer, 214
  Porter, 96
Orkney brewery, Scotland, 107, 108, 109, 111
Orland, Terken,189
Orval, 68, 130
  Trappist ale, 53
Osma, 176
Ostravar brewery, Czech., 176, 177, 179
Otaru Brewpub, Japan, 209
Ottakringer brewery, Austria, 163, 165
Otter Creek brewery, US, 235

Oud Beersel, 130
Oud Kriekenbier, 130, 134
Oudaen brewery, Netherlands, 143
Oudenaards Wit Tarbebier, 130, 134
Owd Roger, 96
Oyster Stout, Porter House, 76
  Marston's, 96

Pabst brewery, US, 54, 243
  Blue Ribbon, 26
Pacific Golden Ale, 223
  Real Draft, 227
Palm brewery, Belgium, 130
Palmer brewery, England, 98, 104
Palmse, 170
Paracelsus, 163
Parel, 141
Parislytic, 189
Parnas, 171
Pasteur, Louis, 40–1, 51
Pastor Ale, 187
Pater Noster, 130
Patriator, 187
Paulaner brewery, Germany, 152, 157
Pauls and Sandars, 34
Pauwels Kwak, 131, 134, 136
Pavichevich brewery, US, 231
Pearl brewery, US, 235, 237
Pedigree, 96
Pedwar Bawd, 81
Peking Beer, 205
Pelforth brewery, France, 62, 185, 186, 189
  beers, 187
Pêcheur, 187
Pelican Lager, 187
Pembroke Docks brewery, Wales, 84
Pendle Witches Brew, 96
Penn's Bitter, 96
Pennsylvania brewery, US, 235, 237
Perfect Porter, 237
Peroni brewery, Italy, 181, 182
  Stout, 200
Peru Gold , 248, 249
Pete's brewery, US, 243
  Wicked Winter Brew, 237
Peter's Porter, 96
Petone brewery, N.Z., 223
Petrus, 66, 131
Pfaudler Vacuum Company, 198
Phoenix, 76
Phoenix brewery, England, 96, 100
Pictish Ale, 107
Pieper, Bernd, 225
Pikantus, 151, 156
Pike Place brewery, US, 60, 233, 236, 237
Pilgrim brewery, England, 96
Pilsener Mack-Ol, 117
  Xibeca, 195
Pilsissimus, 151
Pilsner Celis Golden, 241
  Hopfenperle, 163, 165
  Jubileeuw, 143
  Nikolai, 121
  Urquell, 65, 174, 177
  Urquell brewery, Czech., 179
Pinkus Hefe Weizen, 152
  Müller brewery, Germany, 152, 159–60
Pintail, 237
Pittsburgh brewery, US, 235
Pivo Herold Hefe-Weizen, 177
Plain Porter, 76
Plank Road brewery, US, 243
Plassey brewery, Wales, 80, 81
Platan brewery, Czech., 177, 179
Platman's, 219
Plzen (Pilsen), Czechoslovakia, 18, 179
Point Special, 237
Polar Brewing Company, Venezuela, 248, 249
Ponik, 177
Pony, 191
Poole brewery, England, 88
Poperings Hommelbier, 131
Port Dock Brewpub, Aus., 219
Port of Spain brewery, Trinidad, 251
Porter, 39, 187, 248
Porter House Brewpub, Ireland, 76, 77
Porteris, 170
Portland Ale, 237
Postin Oma, 121
Power Brewing Company, Aus., 214, 217, 218
  Stout, 200
Pragovar, 177
Prague Breweries Group, 178, 179
Premium Verum, 237
Primator, 177
Primus, 177
Primus Pils, 131

Prinzregent, 152
Prior, 177
Pripps brewery, Sweden, 68, 118, 119
Privat Pils, 163
Privatbräuerei Diebel, Germany, 148
Prize Old Ale, 96
Proberco brewery, Romania, 173
Progress, 96
Prohibition, 20–3
Prosit Pils, 134
Ptarmigan, 108
Publican's Special Bitter, 227
Pullman Pale Ale, 237
Pumphouse Brewpub, Aus., 219
Pumpkin Ale, 237
Puntigamer brewery, Austria, 165
Purkmistr, 177
Pyramid brewery, US, 243

Quintus, 141

Raaf brewery, Netherlands, 141, 143
Radeburger Pilsner, 152
Radegast brewery, Czech., 177, 179
Radius, 129
Raffo, 181
Raftman, 227
Ragutis brewery, Lithuania, 173
Rain Dance, 96
Raincross Cream Ale, 237
Rainier Ale, 237
Rakoczi, 171
Ram Rod, 96
Ramsbottom Strong, 96
Rapier Pale Ale, 96
Ratsherm, 152
  Trunk, 163, 164, 165
Ratskeller Edel-Pils, 152
Rauchenfels brewery, Germany, 66
Raven Ale, 108
  Stout, 200
Razor Back, 214
Rebellion brewery, England, 94, 96, 97
  Malt Liquor, 227
Red Ant, 214
  Baron, 227
  Bitter, 214
  Bull, 237
  Cap Ale, 227
  Dog, 227
  Erik, 113
  Hook brewery, US, 238
  House, 211
  Lion Brewpub, Wales, 84
  MacGregor, 108
  Sky Ale, 238
  Stripe, 250, 251
  Tail Ale, 238
Redback Brewpub, Aus., 214, 219
Redhook Ale brewery, US, 231, 232
Reepham brewery, England, 91, 95, 96
Régal, 145
Regent brewery, Czech., 175, 179
Reichelbräu Eisbock, 152
  of Kulmbach, 59
Reininghaus brewery, Austria, 165
Reschs brewery, Aus., 215, 218
Reserva Extra, 195
Reval, 170, 173
Reverend James, 82
Rex, 200, 202
Rezak, 177
Rheineck Lager, 221
Rheingold, 191
Rheinheitsgebot (German Purity Law), 23, 146, 155
Rhenania brewery, Germany, 160
Ridder brewery, Netherlands, 140, 141, 143
Ridleys brewery, England, 14, 26, 87, 89, 95, 96, 97, 104
Rifle Brigade Brewpub, Aus., 219
Riggwelter , 96
Ringnes brewery, Norway, 116, 117
Ringwood brewery, England, 91, 96, 104
Ritter brewery, Germany, 149, 160
Riva brewery, Belgium, 69. 127, 130, 136
Riverside brewery, USA., 238, 239
Riverwest Stein Beer, 238
Roaring Meg, 97
Robertus, 141
Robinson's brewery, England, 96, 97, 104
Rochefort brewery, Belgium, 68, 136
Rockies brewery, US, 232
Rocky Cellar Beer, 172
Rodenbach brewery, Belgium, 30, 131, 137
  of Roeselare, 66
Roggen Rye, 238
Rogue-n-Berry, 238

Rolling Rock, 238
Roman brewery, Belgium, 137
Romer Pilsner, 152
Rooster's, 97
Rose de Gambrinus, 131
Rose Street Brewpub, Scotland, 111
Rossa, 181
Royal Extra Stout, 251
  Oak, 97
  Pilsner, 119
Ruby Ale, 62
Ruddles brewery, England, 97, 104
Rudgate brewery, England, 87, 99
Ruedrich's Red Seal Ale, 238
Rumpus, 97
Russkoe (Russian), 170, 172
Ruutli Olu, 170, 173
Ryburn brewery, England, 97
Ryedale, 97

S-A, 82
SAS, 97
SBA, 97
SBB, 82
SOS, 97
SP Lager, 223
Saaz, 187
  hops, 178, 249
Saccharomyces Carlsbergensis, 41, 112, 115
Sachsische brewery, Germany, 157
Sagres Lager, 196
sahti, 120, 121, 122
Sail and Anchor Brewpub, Aus., 27, 213, 219
St-Ambroise beers, 227
St Amoldus, 187
St Andrews, 108
St Austell brewery, England, 92, 99, 100, 104
St Benoît, 131
St Bernardus brewery, Belgium, 137
St Feuillen brewery, Belgium, 135, 137
St Florian, 15
St Francis of Paula, 157
St Georgen brewery, Germany, 152
St Idesbald, 131
St Jakobus, 152
St Jozef brewery, Belgium, 137
St Landelin, 187
St Louis, 131
St Pauli Girl brewery, Germany, 25, 160
St Sebastiaan, 131
St Sixtus, 131
St Stan's brewery, US, 243
St Sylvestre brewery, France, 187, 189
St Vincent brewery Ltd, St Vincent, 251
Saison de Pipaix, 131
  de Silly, 131
  Régal, 66, 131
Saku brewery, Estonia, 170, 171, 173
Salem Porter, 97
Salisbury Best, 97

Salopian brewery, England, 61, 91, 93, 94, 97
Salvator, 152, 157
Salmbräu Brewpub, Austria, 164
Salzburg, 9
Samichlaus, 190, 192
Samson brewery, Czech., 179
Samson., 177
Samuel Adams Cream Stout, 67
    Boston Lager, 238
    Boston Stock Ale, 238
Samuel Smith's brewery, England, 95, 97, 98, 104
San Miguel brewery, Philippines, 210, 211
    brewery, Spain, 193, 194, 195
    Nostrum, 194
    Premium, 194, 195
Sandaya Brewpub, Japan, 209
Sandels, 121
Sando Stout, 211
Sandy Hunter's, 108
Sankt Gallen Brewpub, Japan, 209
Sans culottes, 187
Sans Souci, 181, 182
Sanwald, 152
Sapporo brewery, Japan, 51, 206, 208–9
    beers, 207, 209
Saranac, 242
Satan, 131
Scaldis, 126
Schaefer brewery, US, 238
Schaffbräu brewery, Germany, 149
Scharer's Brewpub, Aus., 219
Schele Os, 141
Schell brewery, US, 238, 244
Schielhallion Lager, 108
Schierlinger Roggen, 152
Schlägl, 165
Schlank & Rank, 163
Schlenkerla, 65 , 152
Schlitz brewery, US, 54, 238, 244
Schlosser, 58
Schlüssel Alt, 161
Schmaltz's Alt, 238
Schneider brewery, Germany, 69, 147, 152, 154, 157
Schöfferhofer, 154
Schooner, 228
Schultheiss brewery, Germany, 154
Schutz Deux Milles, 187, 189
Schutzenberger brewery, France, 185, 186, 187, 189
Schwechater brewery, Austria, 165
Scottish & Newcastle brewery, England, 12, 94
    Courage brewery, Scotland, 111
Scrimshaw Pilsner, 238
Seasonal Smoked Porter, 238
Seattle Pike brewery, US, 237
Sebourg, 187, 188
Sedlmayer, Gabriel, 18, 115, 154
Septante Cinq, 187, 189
Seven Seas Real Ale, 219
Sezuens, 131
Shakemantle Ginger, 97
Shakespeare brewery, N.Z., 223
Shakespeaare Stout, 98
Shanghai (Swan) Lager, 205
Sharp's, 242
Shea's Irish Amber, 238, 242
Sheaf Stout, 215
Shefford Bitter, 97
Shen Ho Sing brewery, China, 205
Shepherd Neame brewery, England, 87, 96, 97, 104
Shiner Bock, 23898
Shipyard brewery, Portland, USA., 232, 236, 237, 238, 239
Shirayuki, 207
Shokusai Bakushu, 207, 208
Shropshire, 97
Sierra Nevada brewery, US, 232, 233, 244
Sigl brewery, Austria, 164, 165
Signature Amber Lager, 227
    Cream Ale, 227
Silly brewery, Belgium, 66, 128, 129, 131, 137
    Brug-Ale, 132
Silver Fern, 223
    Pilsner, 113
Simba Lager, 200
Simon Noël, 145
Simond s, Farsons,Cisk, (Farsons) Brewers, Malta,182
Sinebrychoff brewery, Finland, 120, 121,122
Singha, 211
Single Malt, 97
Sir Henry's Stout, 164
Siraly (Seagull), 170
Sirvenos, 171, 173
Sjoes, 141

Skull Splitter, 109
Slaghmuylder brewery, Belgium, 132
Slaughter Porter, 97
Sleeman brewery, Canada, 227, 229
    Cream Ale, 227
    Original Dark, 227
Sloeber, 132
Smiles brewery, England, 91, 92, 97
Smith, John, brewery, England, 104
Smith, Samuel, brewery, England, 104
Smithwick's brewery, Ireland, 62, 76, 77
    smoked beer, 161
Smuggler, 97
Sneck Lifter, 97
Snow Goose, 238
Sociedad Central de Cervejas (Centralcer), Portugal, 196
Sol, 248
Solibra brewery, Africa, 199, 202
Son of a Bitch, 82, 83
Song Hay Double Happiness Beer, 205
sorghum beer, 203
Sort Guld, 113
South African Breweries, Africa, 169, 197, 198, 202
    Australian brewery, Aus., 213, 215, 218
    Pacific brewery, Port Moresby, 223
Southwark beers, 215
Spanish conquistadores, 246
Spaten brewery, (Spaten-Franziskaner-Bräu) Germany, 18, 19, 149, 151, 154, 158
Special Oudenaards, 128
Speciale, 198
Speight's brewery, N.Z., 222, 223
Spendrup's brewery, Sweden, 119
Spezial brewery, Germany, 160
Spiess Edelhell, 192
Spinnakers Brewpub, Canada, 227, 229
    Bitter, 97
Spitfire, 97
Splügen, 181
Spoetzle brewery, US, 238
Sprecher brewery, US, 244
Spring Valley, 207
Springhead brewery, England, 92, 97
Stag, 97, 109
Stakonice brewery, Czech., 176
Stan Smith's Oatmeal Stout, 67
Staples brewery, N.Z., 223
Star, 200, 202
Starbier, 154
Starobrno brewery, Czech., 175, 176, 177, 179
Staropramen brewery, Czech., 10, 177, 179
Stauder TAG, 154
Steenbrugge Dubbel, 132
    Tripel, 132
Steendonck, 130
Steeplejack, 98
Steerkens brewery, Belgium, 131
Steffl, 164
Stegmaier, 238
Steinlager, 222
    Blue, 222
Steirische Bräuindustrie brewery, Austria, 165
Stella Artois, 132
Stephansquell, 154
Sternbräu, 192
Stiegl brewery, Austria, 163, 164, 165
Stiftsbräu, 164
Stig Swig, 98
Stille Nacht, 132
Stillman's 80/–, 109
Stingo, 59
Stockan brewery, N.Z., 223
Stones brewery, England, 98, 104
Stoney's Lager, 238
Stoteczne, 168
Stoudt's Micro-brewery, US, 235, 239, 244
Straffe Hendrick brewery, Belgium, 132, 137
Straub brewery, US, 244
Stroh's brewery, US, 231, 236, 237, 238, 239, 244
Strong Suffolk, 98
Strongarm, 98
Strongcroft's Bitter, 223
Stronghart, 98
Struis, 141, 143
Sumida River Brewpub, Japan, 209
Summer Lightning, 98
Summerskill's brewery, England, 93, 100
    Best Bitter, 98
Summit brewery, US, 234, 244
Sun Lik, 205
Suntory brewery, Japan, 206, 207, 208, 209
Super Bock, 196
    Dortmunder, 141
    Dry, 208
    Ice, 62
Superior, 248

Superleeuw, 141, 143
Sussex Bitter, 98
Sussex Mild, 98
Swan brewery, Aus., 215, 218
Sweet China, 205
Sweetheart Stout, 109
Sydney Bitter, 215, 217
Sylvester, 141

Tabernash brewery, US, 239, 245
Taddy Porter, 98
Tafel Lager, 200
Tall Ships, 110
Talleros, 171, 172
Tally Ho, 98
Tambour, 192
Tanglefoot, 98
Taranaki Draught, 222
Tartu brewery, Estonia, 173
    Olu, 171, 173
Tarwebok, 141
Tas, 177
Tatran, 177
Taylor brewery, England, 91, 104
Tecate, 248, 249
Temperance Union, 21
Tennent's brewery, Scotland, 62, 109, 111
Terken brewery, France, 185, 187, 189
Tetley brewery, England, 24, 98, 104
Thai Amarit, Bangkok, 211
The Ghillie, 109
Theakston brewery, England, 95, 98, 104
Thomas Hardy's Ale, 98
Thomas Hardy brewery, England, 104
Thomas Kemper brewery, US, 231, 234, 238, 239, 245
Three Coins brewery, Colombo, Sri Lanka, 211
    Sieges, 99
Thurn und Taxis brewery, Germany, 160
Thwaites brewery, England, 90, 99, 104
Tientan Beer, 205
Tiger Best Bitter, 99
    Classic, 211
t'IJ brewery, Netherlands, 140, 141, 143
Timmermans brewery, Belgium, 125, 137
Timothy Taylor's brewery, England, 93
Tinners Ale, 99
Tipo Munich, 249
Titje, 132
Toby, 99
Tolly Cobbold brewery, England, 99, 105
Tolly's Strong Ale, 99
Tom Hoskins Porter, 99
    Kelley, 119
Tomintoul brewery, Scotland, 109, 111
Tomlinson brewery, England, 99
Tomos Watkin brewery, Wales, 80, 82, 84
Tongerlo, 132
Tooheys brewery, Aus., 214, 215, 218
Tooth's brewery, Aus., 214, 215, 218
Top Dog Stout, 99
    Hat, 99
Topazio, 196
Topsy-Turvy, 99
Tourtel, 187, 189
T'owd Tup, 99
Traditional Ale, 99
    Bitter, 99
    Brewing Company, Aus., 213, 214, 218
    English Ale, 36, 99
    Welsh Ale, 82
Trafalgar Pale Ale, 219
Trapper Lager, 227
Trapper's Red Beer, 222
Traquair House brewery, Scotland, 107, 108, 109, 111
Trelawny's Pride, 99
Triple Bock, 239
    Diamond, 109
Triumphator, 154
Trois Monts, 187
Troublette, 134
True Bock, 227
Trumer, 164, 165
Tsingtao brewery, China, 204, 205
Tuborg brewery, Denmark, 113, 114
Tui, 222
Tume, 171, 173
Turbo Dog, 239
Tusker, 200
Tutankamun Ale, 12
Twelve Horse Ale, 239, 242
Twenty Tank Brewpub, US, 245
Tynllidiart Arms Brewpub, Wales, 84

U Fleku brewery, Czech., 179
Uehara Micro-brewery, Japan, 209

Ueli Micro-brewery, Switz., 192
Uerige brewery, Germany, 160
Ukrainskoe (Ukrainian), 171, 172
Uley brewery, England, 95
Ulster brewery, Ireland, 75, 77
Umbel Ale, 99
Unertl brewery, Germany, 161
Uniao Cervejeira (Unicer), Portugal,196
Unibroue Micro-brewery, Canada, 225, 226, 227, 229
Unic Bier, 132
Unicorn brewery, England, 92, 95
Union brewery, Belgium, 127
    Cervecera, 195
Upper Canada Brewing Company, Canada, 227, 229
Upstaal, 187, 189
Ur-Krostitzer, 154
Ur-Weisse, 154
Uran Pils, 177
Urbock 23, 164
Ureich Pils, 154
Urfrankisch Dunkel, 154
Urpin brewery, Slovakia, 177
Urstoff, 154
Urtyp Pilsner, 141
Us Heit brewery, Netherlands, 139, 143
US, 230–45
Ushers brewery, England, 91, 94, 99, 105

Vaakuna, 121
Vaclav 12, 177
Vaita, 223
Valiant, 99
Valkenburgs Wits, 141
Van Ecke brewery, Belgium, 128, 131
Van Honsebrouck brewery, Belgium, 125, 129
Van Steenberge brewery, Belgium, 125, 130
Van Vollenhoven Stout, 141
Vander Linden brewery, Belgium, 128, 137
Vandervelden brewery, Belgium, 130
Vapeur brewery, Belgium, 126, 131
Varsity, 99
Vaux brewery, England, 90, 105
Vieille Cuvée, 129
    Provision, 132, 134, 135
Vieux Temps, 132
Vigneronne, 132
Viking, 99
Viking brewery, Iceland 123
    Bjor, 123
Village Bitter, 99
Vinedale Breweries, Hyderabad, India, 211
Viru brewery, Estonia, 173
Vita Stout, 222
Volkoren Kerst, 141
Voll-Damm, 194
Vollmond, 192
Vranik, 177

Wadworth brewery, England, 91, 94, 100, 105
Waggle Dance, 62, 99
Waikato Draught, 223
Wallace IPA, 109
Wallop, 99
Ward's brewery, England, 62, 99, 105
    brewery, N.Z., 223
Warstein brewery, Germany, 154
Warsteiner, 65, 154
Warszawski brewery, Poland, 167, 168
Wartek brewery, Switzerland, 192
Warthog Ale, 227
Wassaill, 99
    Winter Ale, 239
Waterloo Dark, 227
Watneys brewery, England, 105
Waverley 70/–, 109
Weihenstephan brewery, Germany, 150, 161
Weihnachtsbock, 164
Weiselburger, 164
Weitzen's Feast, 121
Weizen Gold, 164
Weizenberry, 239
Weizenhell, 154
Wel Scotch, 187
Wellington County brewery, Canada, 225, 227, 229
Wells brewery, England, 88, 90, 91, 105
Welsh Bitter, 80, 82

Brewers, Wales, 84
Werner Brau, 181, 182
West End, 215
    Flanders brewery, 30
    Lake Beer, 205
Western Samoa Breweries, 223
Westmalle brewery, Belgium, 68, 132, 137
Westvleteren brewery, Belgium, 68, 132, 137
Wetzlar brewery, Germany, 148
Wheat Berry Row, 239
Wherry Best Bitter, 100
Whistle Belly Vengeance, 100
Whitbread brewery, England, 17, 91, 100, 105
    brewery, Wales 84
    Mackeson, 67
Whitby brewery, England, 95, 99
White Dolphin, 100
Whitewater brewery, Ireland, 76, 77
Wickwar brewery, England, 88, 89, 96
Widmer brewery, US, 245
Wieckse Witte, 141, 143
Wieselburg brewery, Austria, 164
Wild Cat, 109
    Goose Micro-brewery, US, 238, 245
Willfort, 187
Willie Warmer, 100
Willpower Stout, 223
Wilmot's Premium, 100
Wiltshire Traditional Bitter, 100
Wiltz brewery, Lux., 145
Windhoek, 200
Winter Warmer, 100
    Royal, 100
Wisconsin, 243
Witkap, 132
Witte Raaf, 141
Witzgal Vollbier, 154
Wobbly Bob, 100
Wolverhampton & Dudley Breweries, England, 105
Wood brewery, England, 97, 105
Woodeforde's brewery, England, 94, 100, 105
Worthington brewery, England, 105
    beers, 82, 100
Wrasslers XXXX Stout, 76
Wrexham Lager Beer Company, Wales, 85
Wuhrer brewery, Italy, 181, 180
Wunster brewery, Italy, 182
Würzig, 154
Wuxing brewery, China, 205
Wychwood brewery, England, 92
Wye Valley brewery, England, 100

XL Old Ale, 100
XXX, 100
XXXB Ale, 100
XXXX Mild, 100
Xibeca, 194
Xingu, 248

Yakima brewery, US, 232, 234, 237, 245
Yates Bitter, 100
yeast, 29, 40–1
Yebisu, 208, 209
Yellow Mongrel, 215
Young's brewery, England, 95, 96, 100, 105
Younger's brewery, Scotland, 109, 111
Yperman, 132
Young Pretender, 109
Yucatan brewery, Mexico, 248
Yuengling brewery, US, 233, 245

Z, 208
Zagorka brewery, Bulgaria, 173
Zambesi, 200
Zamek, 177
Zaragozana brewery, Spain, 194, 195
Zatec brewery, Czech., 176, 177, 178
Zatecka Desitka, 177
Zatte, 141
Zhigulevskoe (Zhiguli), 171, 172
Zip City Brewpub, US, 245
Zipfer brewery, Austria, 164, 165
Zlaty Bazant brewery, Slovakia, 177, 179
Zum Schlüssel brewery, Germany, 149, 161
Zwettl Brewers, 178
Zywiec brewery, Poland, 167, 168

"33", 187
1066, 100
1857 Bitter, 215
1857 Pilsner, 215
2XS, 100
3B, 100
4X Stout, 75
4X, 100
6X, 100
7th Street Stout, 239